W9-DCC-385

HISTORY OF THE SOCIAL MOVEMENT IN FRANCE

Oesterreichiche Nationalbibliotek

LORENZ von STEIN

THE HISTORY OF
THE SOCIAL MOVEMENT
IN FRANCE, 1789-1850

Introduced, edited and translated by
Kaethe Mengelberg

THE BEDMINSTER PRESS

Readers of this book are invited to send their names and addresses to THE BEDMINSTER PRESS, *Vreeland Avenue, Totowa, New Jersey, U.S.A. to receive announcements and literature about other books in the Social Sciences published by* THE BEDMINSTER PRESS.

Contents

ACKNOWLEDGMENTS

I want to express my indebtedness to:

The American Council of Learned Societies for a generous grant which presented an essential contribution towards the expenses of research in European libraries and clerical costs of finishing the Introduction,

Upsala College, East Orange, N. J., for granting me a year's leave of absence to finish the translation and for offering its mimeographic services,

Dr. Terence K. Hopkins, Assistant Professor of Sociology at Columbia University, and Dr. Robert Wharton, Professor of Sociology at Upsala College, for continued interest in the project, encouragement and trust in its value for the history of social thought,

Mr. Jacob Goldstein for a thorough revision of the first draft,

Dr. Guenther Roth for critical analysis of the translation and the Introduction, valuable suggestions and assistance in the search for consistent English equivalents to Stein's basic concepts,

Mrs. Ruth Stoffer for her ever-ready willingness to cooperate in revising passages difficult to translate,

Dr. Benita Luckmann for giving the manuscript its final touches,

Margaret O. Ihra for intelligent and efficient secretarial work after the manuscript had reached its final stage, and

Dr. Manfred von Stein, grandson of Lorenz von Stein and custodian of his grandfather's literary bequest, now living in the United States, for giving me certain glimpses into the family history.

K. M.

Preface

When Lorenz von Stein's book "The History of the Social Movement in France from 1789 to the Present" came out in 1850, the Third French Revolution was still fresh in everybody's mind. In the preface of October 1849, the author states that "nobody dares to doubt that it really has been a social revolution," a fact which confirmed the correctness of his earlier prediction. The Revolution of 1848 verified the general consequences he had drawn from his analysis, that the state was now "thrown into the struggle of the two poles of society" (p. 5) and that "the social question is no longer a theoretical one" (p. 5) but "destined to become the substance of present and future developments" (p. 6).

Alexis de Tocqueville, who had been a member of the Constituent Assembly 1848, took the same point of view in his studies on the French Revolution and in his Memoirs. It is unlikely that the two authors ever met; but the similarity of their approach is striking. Both considered the French Revolution of 1789 an unprecedented and final break with the sociopolitical tradition of European history; both came to the conclusion that its "real object was less a new form of government than a new society" [144, p. 160]* and that "the age of social-democracy is inevitable" [144, p. 5]. Both interpreted the revolutionary drive of 1848 as the latest manifestation of the trend towards equality, the ideal of the original Revolution, which had failed in social relationships; and both considered it the task of the future age to come to grips with this ideal in practice. But while Tocqueville in essence confined himself to the role of an interpretative social historian, Stein embedded his analysis in a general concept of society and in a corresponding philosophy of history. He considered his book "an attempt to raise the as yet hazy notion [of the predominance of the social question] to distinct scientific perception" (p. 6).

There is no doubt that the "History of the Social Movement in France" —in spite of all its shortcomings—is a landmark in the history of social thought. Stein's reasoning in this book has become of lasting importance in several respects. In the first place, it is an early and important manifestation of historical materialism. While studying the changes in French society during the previous sixty years, he had come to the conclusion

---

* The numbers in brackets in the Preface and in the Introduction refer to the liography.

that the traditional approach in historical analysis was no longer satisfactory. Socialism and Communism in France had been the point of departure for his inquiry during his sojourn in Paris in the early 1840's. The growing response to these movements by the laboring class, disfranchised during early industrialism, convinced him of impending class warfare and of the necessity of social reform to avoid revolution. He began to conceive the structure of society as the basic factor determining the course of political developments. Before Marx, who was familiar with Stein's publications, developed his own approach to social history, Stein had expounded the concept of the proletariat and assigned a crucial role to class relationships in the historical process. Furthermore, his analysis led him to the conclusion that a constructive welfare policy was indispensable for the stability and progress of industrial society. Thus he became an early advocate of social reform as a result of scientific inquiry. Finally, in this endeavor to provide a stable basis for these explorations, his is "the first attempt to set up a concept of society as an independent term and to develop its content" (p. 6). It seems almost impossible to overlook his contribution during the growth of the social sciences in the 19th century, and yet this has been done fairly consistently in the international literature.

At first Stein's book aroused a great deal of interest in academic circles in Germany. A second edition appeared in 1855. In later decades, the original contributions of this work were almost forgotten. It was predominantly used as a standard source for studies of early French socialism and communism. When intellectual and practical awareness of the importance of political and social reform was newly awakened in Germany in consequence of the collapse after the First World War, a new edition was issued by Gottfried Salomon in 1921. It led to a revival of interest in Stein's early contribution to the growing science of society. This edition has recently been reprinted by the *Wissenschaftliche Buchgesellschaft, Darmstadt,* 1959. The fact that it had never been translated may partly account for the lack of appreciation of its stature.

My admiration for Stein, which goes back to my student days, finally motivated me to venture a translation. It seems to me that what he had to offer more than a hundred years ago remains of lasting historical interest as a document of analytical and constructive social thought during the 19th century and as a suggestive attempt to understand and come to grips with the past and present struggle for equality.

I herewith submit his opus to the English-speaking world in the hope of saving it from oblivion.

To the Memory of my Teachers
at the University of Heidelberg

S. P. ALTMANN

and

EMIL LEDERER

K. M.

Introduction

LORENZ VON STEIN

1815-1890

HIS LIFE AND WORK

by

Kaethe Mengelberg

LIFE AND CAREER

Lorenz von Stein was born on November 15th, 1815 in the village of Barby near Eckernförde, in the Duchy of Schleswig, which at the time was part of Denmark. His father, Baron von Wasner, Colonel of the Danish Army, came of noble stock; his morganatic marriage led to a complete break with his family, and he accepted the name of his wife, Stein. After the early death of his father, young Lorenz attended the Military Academy at Eckernförde for eleven years. A turning point in his life came on the occasion of a visit to the King of Denmark, to whom Lorenz revealed his true ancestry and his desire to study rather than pursue a military career. At the age of seventeen, he was sent, with the assistance of the Danish Government, to the High School [*Gymnasium*] in Flensburg and in 1835 to the University of Kiel. His academic training included two years of study at the Universities of Jena and Berlin. He was registered as a student of law, but he also got, according to the Continental tradition, a very broad training in the humanities and the social sciences [*Staatswissenschaft*]. He was particularly interested in philosophy, where, at that time, Hegel's and Fichte's metaphysics dominated the scene. The influence of these two great idealists shaped his thinking and the development of his scientific and philosophical concepts, and determined persistently in a number of ways his interpretation of history during all periods of his life. He received his doctorate in law with a dissertation on the history of legal procedures in Denmark (1841) at the University of Kiel in 1840.

He then went to Paris for further research in jurisprudence; the studies which he pursued in France gave him his first insight into the relationship between social conditions and the law. Several publications on judicial proceedings in France and on French municipal constitutions followed. But his qualifications were not only those of a scholar; he was continuously interested in current political events and endowed with a superior journalistic talent. During his stay in Paris he was a regular correspondent of the *Augsburger Allgemeine Zeitung*, an association which he kept throughout his life.

Stein's sojourn in Paris during his formative years, from the age of 26 to 30, was decisive for his intellectual development with regard to both the field and the method of his later scholarly work. His interest

in the socialist movement was aroused through contacts with such leading personalities as Considérant, Reybaud, Louis Blanc and Cabet, with
progressive workers' and artisans' associations, as well as through the
general political climate. He experienced France as a workshop where
history was being made. His impressions, and observations, in Paris gave
him a better clue to the understanding of social and political developments, past, present and future, than all the theoretical speculations of
his early youth. The years in France, finally, determined his unique position in the history of social thought, representing both French positivism
and Hegelian idealism.

In 1842 he published his first major work, *Der Sozialismus und Kommunismus des heutigen Frankreich, Ein Beitrag zur Zeitgeschichte*. It
was a spectacular success and was followed in 1848 by a second enlarged
and revised edition. The third and final version appeared in three volumes under the title *Geschichte der Sozialen Bewegung in Frankreich
von 1789 bis auf unsere Tage,* published in 1850; here Stein incorporated
the story of the lives and work of the representatives of socialism into
an account of historical events and of the social conditions of the working class. The newly conceived comprehensive introduction under the
title "The Concept of Society and its Dynamic Laws" placed his historical study into the framework of a general theory of society and of
the social movement.

His reputation as a scholar was therewith established. After his return
from Paris, he became *Privatdozent* at the University of Kiel and was
promoted to *Ausserordentlicher Professor* in 1846. But soon he was
caught up in the political controversies of his native country, and his
academic career became seriously threatened. He had always taken a
position in favor of Schleswig-Holstein's independence; in 1846 he had
signed a memorandum with eight other professors concerning the hereditary succession in the Duchy of Schleswig; it supported the position
taken by the German Confederation against any encroachment on the
rights of Schlewig by legal and historical arguments. During the short
period of independence of Schleswig-Holstein (1848-1850), Stein became
a Delegate of the Provisional Government in Paris; in 1949 he was
elected a member of the Representative Assembly. When, in 1850, Denmark reestablished its rule over Schleswig, Stein lost his professorship
and was forced to leave. His position was particularly difficult because—
although strongly opposed to Danish rule—he nevertheless was critical
about the position Prussia took during the struggle. The Prussian Government never forgave him; it not only denied him the opportunity,
offered to his colleagues, of finding a new academic position Prussia

but also used its influence to prevent his appointment in Würzburg, which the Bavarian Government was willing to offer him in 1854.

After his dismissal in Kiel, Stein seriously considered a career in journalism. He published a series of articles in the leading periodicals *Gegenwart, Deutsche Vierteljahrsschrift* and in the popular newspaper *Deutsche Allgemeine Zeitung.* These frequently appeared anonymously or under a pen-name, and dealt with the historical and political aspects of the Schleswig-Holstein controversy, as well as topics of more general economic, sociological and historical interest. Though written for the general public, they all carry the mark of scholarship, and could be of historical interest to sociologists even today. Among them are studies on the structure of society, *Das Wesen des arbeitslosen Einkommens und sein besonderes Verhältnis zu Amt und Adel* (1852), *Demokratie und Aristokratie* (1854), and a series of articles concerning the social movement in Germany, France and England published between 1849 and 1852 in *Gegenwart.* Others, like *Das Gemeindewesen der Neueren Zeit* (1853) and *Zur Preussischen Verfassungsfrage* (1852), dealt with public law in Germany, and still others with specific organizational questions of the German banking and monetary system.

Stein's broad and thorough training in the different branches of the social sciences, the ease and imagination with which he wrote, and his ability to combine a systematic approach with the analysis of practical details secured his success as a journalist during these transitional years. He was on the point of accepting an editorial position of the *Deutsche Allgemeine Zeitung* when the death of the political economist Nowak at the University of Vienna created an opening for a professorial appointment there. He had the powerful backing of his friend, Freiherr von Bruck, then Secretary of Finance, and that of the Minister for Cultural and Scientific Affairs, Baron Leo von Thun, who evaluated his abilities and promises for the future very highly. At this point, Stein's former antagonism against Prussia may have operated in his favor; the testimonial by von Thun elaborates on it at length and strongly stresses Stein's preference for the Austrian policy [39, p. 482]. Stein became professor of Political Economy at the University of Vienna in 1855. He held this position until his retirement in 1888.

For over thirty years he was active as a teacher and scholar at one of the oldest German universities; he had finally found an adequate setting for his abilities, which included comprehensive knowledge, a keen reasoning power, and a sometimes astounding intuition. He was a brilliant lecturer who attracted large audiences and exerted a strong influence on the younger generation. During a period of rapidly increasing specialization, he taught them to see the details within a general context and not to lose sight of the essential relationship between single facts and the basic trends in historical and social development. His approach was essentially a systematic one.

During the first decade in Vienna, he tried his hand in influencing the course of political events and economic development in Austria. Until 1866 he was convinced that Austria ought to play a leading part in the unification of Germany, and favored a customs union of Greater Germany. He was consultant to several ministries, and the minister of Finance directed him to write his expert opinion on *Die neue Gestaltung des Geld–und Kreditwesens in Oesterreich* (1856). He also participated in business, founded several corporations of which he was chairman or active member of the board of management; when in 1874 he wanted to be elected as a member of the Reichsrat, he introduced himself as "an industrialist as defined by Saint-Simon."

The high esteem in which he was held by his contemporaries manifested itself in the many honors conferred upon him: he was an active member of the Imperial Academy of the Sciences in Vienna, a member of the Academies of Rome, of Paris, Petersburg and Moscow; he was given an honorary Doctor's degree by the University of Bologna and high decorations of the Italian, Russian and Japanese Governments. In 1868 the Austrian Government made him a member of the hereditary Austrian aristocracy. He had always declined suggestions to adopt again the name of his father with the argument that he had no interest in belonging to the aristocracy of birth, but he apparently welcomed it to being ennobled on the basis of his merits; this—in an anecdotal way—tells the story of his social philosophy.

Practically all of Stein's writings reflect his original interpretation of history and social development and are permeated by his specific concepts of state and society; they will be considered later in detail. We shall list briefly his publications according to the traditional academic classification. He had started to work on a systematic presentation of the social sciences [*System der Staatswissenschaften*] already at Kiel, but his plan to cover the whole field never materialized; this opus has remained a torso presenting an over-all organization of the material, but the analysis is confined to statistics, population and economics in the first volume, published in 1852, and to the concept of society and the theory of social classes in the second volume, published in 1856. He never tackled the last volume, which was supposed to deal with political science, although his other publications show distinctly his line of thought concerning the proper place of constitutional and administrative problems in the social sciences. His aim was to draw a great canvas of cultural development and analyze European culture as a unit—the result of accumulated and steadily growing wealth and knowledge with a growing participation of the lower classes and the obligation of the state to facilitate this trend. Today this may appear commonplace, but the first one to formulate it was Stein. In his social philosophy and his scientific analysis of social development he elevated the ordinary working people from their subordinate role of sustaining the cultural edifice of the ruling strata, and integrated them as individuals into the functional system of state and society [5, p. 432]. His interpretative approach to social history had a lasting effect on the economic and social policy of the 19th century.

The predominating theme which Stein had pursued persistently since his Viennese appointment dealt with public finance and public administration. His contributions to both fields are of lasting scholarly importance and are the least controversial among his systematic works. He took the first important step towards a systematic theory of public finance [74] which had until then been treated only casually and unmethodically. He related problems of budgeting and financing to state constitution and public law. Problems of social philosophy did not enter here; emphasis was put on the causal explanation of facts and on a comparative study of international law. Towards the end of the century, his *Finanzwissenschaft* was considered one of the most significant German works in the field, equalled only by the publications of Adolf Wagner [29]. Looking back to the contributions of various scholars in this field during the 19th century, Popitz [43 pp. 404, 418] asserts in 1933 that there is . . . "common agreement that the most valuable accomplishments in the science of public finance in Germany are connected with the names of Lorenz von Stein, Adolf Wagner and Albert Schäffle." One has to admit that Stein had an admirable insight into the significance of administration and public finance within the field of the social sciences. He predicted the trend of developments which subsequently took place, though much later than he had anticipated.

The prominent part of his later publications is devoted to the theory of public administration (1865-1870, 1884, 1888). Up to that time, the empirical *"Polizeiwissenschaft"* of the cameralists had been the only academic subject concerning domestic politics. According to Stein, public administration comprises all areas of state activity, including public finance and international law, except those dealing with constitutional problems. He correctly assumed that these would be of growing practical importance in the future, because the state would have a leading part in the establishment of a stable society. He became the instigator of this new scientific discipline. By establishing the distinction between law and decree, he provided a legal basis for the executive power of the state, and took the first step towards an examination of administrative law which, however, he treats only as a subsection of the theory of public administration (*Verwaltungslehre*). To systematically organize all sectors subject to administrative action, he applied his trichotomy of personal, economic and social life; into this general framework he incorporated past and present legislation on population, health, education, natural resources, industry and commerce, as well as on labor, the poor and social assistance, frequently comparing it with the laws of France and Great Britain. His theory of public administration also presents the basis for his attempt to integrate the science of the state (*Staatswissenschaft*) with jurisprudence (*Rechtswissenschaft*).

His original and lasting contributions to this field are undeniable and emphatically acknowledged by all experts up to the present [13, 20, 42, 49, 61, 77]. In a recent article, Arthur Nussbaum evaluates Stein's contribution to the doctrine of international law, which in his opinion "contains elements of considerable significance" [40, p. 558]; Stein's "fundamental idea of international administrative law is unobjectionable and helpful" [40, p. 560]; it foreshadows the emergence of a law of international organization as a new academic discipline, a sufficient justification for reconsidering Stein's contribution to the theory of public administration.

In addition to these major works, there are many casual yet fascinating essays by Stein, some in the lighter vein on the role of women in the economy or the relationship between music and the social sciences; others of great erudition such as "*Der Wucher und sein Recht*" (1880), which Marchet [30] characterizes as "comprehensive and final," and "*Die drei Fragen des Grundbesitzes*" (1881) a comparative treatise on land ownership in Ireland, the Continent and America.

One experience in Stein's later life is a particularly colorful illustration of his versatility. It is his role as adviser of the Japanese Government in the 1880's. One of his most prominent students was Hirobumi Ito, a leading public figure during the Meiji Era (1867-1912). After the power of the Japanese feudal aristocracy had been broken in the early sixties, Japan needed a new constitution and administrative system. A commission for the study of Western European institutions was sent to Vienna to consult Stein. This was a challengig task, to which he devoted much of his time during the last decade of his life. Although the available sources of information on Japan were scarce and the difficulties of communication considerable, he nevertheless succeeded in meeting the needs of his visitors, strengthening their self-confidence and giving valuable advice as to the path to be followed in economic and political affairs. Stein showed appreciation of the traditional culture, religion and art, advised against indiscriminate Westernization, suggested gradual changes by first promoting foreign trade, and made specific propositions as to a new constitution. Stein's approach, which showed his understanding of cultural differences, proved to be most fruitful in practice. The lectures which he gave on this topic were later published in Japan. A Japanese translation of the *Theory of Public Administration* appeared in 1887. The fact that Stein was a convinced monarchist strengthened Ito's confidence in his guidance. The chapter on imperial power in the ensuing Japanese constitution comes very close to Stein's original draft. He remained a friend and advisor of Ito and other Japanese statesmen, as well as of Japanese students in Vienna for the rest of his life, and was held in high esteem by them.

Stein's contact with the Far East bore fruit also for the European public in the form of a series of publications on historical, legal and financial problems of Japan which, at that time, had not yet been systematically explored.

At the time of his death in 1890, Lorenz von Stein was considered to be a controversial figure by his colleagues, particularly with regard to his social philosophy and his methodology; both are, of course, inevitably intertwined, as are his merits and his deficiencies. He himself once stated, "I have aimed, in the first place, at devising a genuine system (*"wirkliches System"*) and then have tried to develop it as an organism of concepts and laws, which could ultimately be reduced to one simple principle . . . As a first step, it seemed necessary to me to devise a systematic order for the tremendous mass of political data in which every individual fact has its proper place. This proper place is in reality not so much a matter of adequate organization but of the organic role of each individual fact."[1] In later years he defined science as "the comprehension of the basic unity of all specific activities and facts as the manifestation of the divine destiny of existence."[2] His opponents considered his teleological approach to history untenable and frequently felt entitled to criticize him and disregard his specific contributions, many of which bear the mark of careful causal analysis. Schmoller, [52, p. 141] however, tipped the scales in his favor; he argued that teleology as a

---

[1] *System der Staatswissenschaften* 1852, Vol. I., pp IX, X.
[2] *Lehrbuch der Nationalökonomie* 1887, p. 32.

heuristic principle may be a useful tool in all the sciences, and that a causal and a teleological approach are not necessarily contradictory but may supplement each other. Schmoller saw the significance of Stein precisely in the fact that he, just like Montesquieu to whom Stein frequently referred, was not a specialist. On the other hand, he was well aware that Stein's universality had its disadvantages; he was often not interested primarily in facts but in their place within his willfully conceived system. Such an attitude may easily lead to an arbitrary selection of material which is irreconcilable with scientific investigation. However, Stein's faults on this score are minor compared to his truly scholarly contributions.

Carl Menger, the leading Austrian economist of the late 19th century and one of the founders of the marginal utility theory, questioned Stein's claim of competency in the field of economic theory; at the time the theory of marginal utility was in its infancy, struggling for recognition and attempting to provide the basis for economics as an exact science, Menger felt that Stein's approach counteracted these intentions and was a factor in delaying their success. But, in spite of these misgivings from the viewpoint of a theoretical economist, and regardless of the general criticism that Stein's philosophy and his continuous resistance to concentration on specifics led to arbitrary interpretations, he did not deny that Stein's intuition had frequently led to fruitful results. Menger particularly acknowledged Stein's role as an originator of the concept of society; he appraised the "Social Movement in France" as an epochmaking study which for the first time had brought socialism and communism as serious issues to the attention of educated Germans; he considered it to be a classical source book for all later German publications in this field [34].

One characteristic limitation of Stein repeatedly pointed out by his contemporaries was his inability to train his students in the method of scientific investigation. Blaschke, in his obituary on Stein, states: "He lectured about what he knew and what he thought without ever teaching his students how he arrived at his knowledge," and adds the explanatory comment that "his individuality was too distinctive to be transfered to students by methodological directives" [5, p. 433].

Stein's attraction as a teacher and the stimulation which his students always gratefully affirmed was mainly the result of his efforts to come to a synthetic view and to enrich the specialized disciplines by analyzing their relationship. At a time when specialization began to break down the comprehensive approach, it may explain his popular success as well as the antagonism which he encountered among expert scientists.

STEIN'S VIEW OF THE SOCIAL PROCESS

Stein reflects in a peculiar way the confluence of a variety of trends in socio-historical studies prevalent at the middle of the 19th century. His position in the history of social thought is to a great extent determined by the influence of German idealism, which dominated the first half of the 19th century. There are many features which bear the mark of Hegel's thought; but there are others, especially in the analysis of contemporary society, in which he goes beyond Hegel by setting the conflict of interest between social classes in the center of his interpretation of history. His methodological approach is also akin to that of German idealism, which starts out by giving a specific goal of history and defining man's role in accomplishing it. But once he became absorbed with a particular problem, he explored facts and events in their mutual relationship, and his method of investigation was strictly empirical. Stein's scientific and philosophical position provided the link between Hegel and Marx as well as between Hegel and sociological positivism.

The main substance of Stein's social concepts was originally formulated in the first section of the present book under the title "The Concept of Society and the Law of Social Dynamics." He later enlarged and elaborated them in his theory of society (1856). He subsequently used them in all his books and articles, although the emphasis of his interpretation of the various factors changed considerably.

Society as an independent area of study in the social sciences had not yet been established in Germany. Civil society in Hegel's philosophy is only a historical concept and represents a subordinate phase in the development towards a state of freedom and reason. Stein effected the final separation of state and society. He proceeded on the assumption that society was a permanent aspect of human life. The origin of society lies in the contradiction inherent in the individual—the contradiction between his infinite striving and the narrow limits of his power. Only as a member of the human community can man hope to raise his life beyond the confining bounds of mere physical existence, to control nature, to develop a culture and to fulfill his destiny of striving towards perfection. Society, in which human existence as we know it is unalterably embedded, is an interdependent system of individuals based on the division of labor; "it is the spiritual order (*geistige Ordnung*) of men in contradistinction to the material order of goods, the economy, and the unifying (*rein ein-*

heitliche) order of the state;"[3] "the existence of society can be recognized by the disturbances which can be neither explained nor eliminated by economic or political measures."[4]

The differentiation of wealth and status establishes a class pattern in any society. Acquisition of property originates from conquest and power, and is constantly modified by the natural inequalities of people striving for self-realization. Property and education[5] are the two pillars that sustain the social structure; they determine the position of the individual within society, differences in property and education coincide with functional differences. Stein's concept of class is based mainly on the distribution of property; his emphasis is on the source of income; he often speaks of the "property-owning vs. the propertyless class" and therewith follows the classical approach that classes are determined by the position of people as capital owners or laborers in the productive process. He thus anticipates Marx's approach in the analysis of the class struggle. Stein acknowledges, however, that education and occupation also play a role in determining the class position; nevertheless he considers property as the essential factor inasmuch as higher education, status and a cultured life can only be attained, as a rule, by those who own property. In his study on France, he regards property as the decisive factor in modern society, which perpetuates the class pattern based on inheritance and reflects the contradiction of industrial society between reality and ideology calling for resolution. Later, in his theory of society, he shifted his position by accentuating the role of innate personal differences rather than property in the process of selection, and thus justified inequality of income and status as the result of superior contributions. He changed from a severe critic to a defender of capitalism. This does not imply, by any means, that Stein, even in his later years, regarded the status quo of society as satisfactory; his later writings, particularly his theory of public administration, contain many suggestions and requests for changes which to him appeared not only consistent with the system, but rather indispensable in order to preserve it. Stein frequently states that a proper balance between equality and inequality has to be found, since the unfair preponderance of the levelling effects of equalitarianism and the exploiting and antagonizing effects of privileges lie at the core of friction within society.

---

[3] *Gesellschaftslehre* (1856) p. 16 and *Demokratie und Aristokratie* (1854) p. 311.

[4] *Gesellschaftslehre*, p. 23.

[5] Stein uses the term *"Bildung"* defined in *Handbuch der Varwaltungslehre und des Verwaltungsrechts* 1870, p. 107, as "The state of intellectual development of the individual, the sum total of acquired intellectual capacities." In other contexts he interprets it as "possession of intellectual goods" (*"Besitz geistiger Güter"*).

In his concept of the state, Stein distinguishes between the ideal and the real state. The ideal state stands outside the class struggle. It is the personification or "organism of the general will;" its well-being is dependent upon the well-being of all its citizens, and it can further its own interest only by furthering the development of all individuals. Therefore, the state has to prevent any part of society from imposing its will on the whole of society. The state's predominant purpose consists in providing those conditions for the development of the self which the individual is unable to create by himself. But this definition of the state is merely an abstraction, an ethical ideal. In reality, this ideal becomes constantly distorted, because government posts are usually occupied by persons of a higher status and are used to make their superior social position secure. The class struggle therewith invades the domain of the state, and state power becomes misused in the interest of the upper class.

Since the ideal state represents the general interest, its highest organ should stand above and beyond all special interest groups and be altogether independent. Stein therefore considers monarchy the most appropriate form of state organization. This position does not, in itself, reflect a conservative point of view. The battle between conservative and progressive forces is carried out in society and between the classes. The form of the state does not by necessity determine the nature of its policy; there were republics which were solidly conservative and enlightened monarchies which did not identify themselves with the ruling class.[6] Stein looks with critical skepticism on "popular sovereignty," which to him is an illusion hiding the complete subjugation of the state to society. Modern nations would be served best by a constitutional monarchy favoring and promoting the interests of the lower classes, making individual self-fulfillment possible (*Soziales Königtum*).

Hegel's influence on Stein's analysis of the function of the state is clearly discernable. To Hegel, however, the state was the supreme authority, an altogether independent domain where reason unfolds itself; it ruled exclusively in the true interest of the individual. Stein retained Hegel's ideal of the state. In contradistinction to Hegel, however, he maintained that according to sociological analysis the actual state is necessarily controlled by the ruling class. He saw both state and society as the arena in which individuals contested for power. He therewith divested the historical state of its metaphysical quality. It required only one further step for Marx to deprive the concept of the state altogether of its glamor by simply discarding the concept of the ideal state [60, pp. 199, 206].

---

[6] *Demokratie und Aristokratie* (1854) p. 309 ff.

Stein's interpretation of constitutional as well as civil law also marks
him as forerunner of economic materialism. He considered changes in
constitutional and civil law to be the result of economic factors rather
than of ideas. Constitutions reflect the power of the various groups of
society; they cannot be conceived and construed merely on the basis of
an ideology. In order to be workable, they have to correspond to the
social structure, and are therewith the result and not the moving force
in the power and property distribution within society. "A constitution is
never the result of chance or of mere doctrinal opinion; any appropriate
constitution is the definite manifestation of the social order of the nation,
and only as such it is justified, stable and valid."[7] Nor is the history of
law an autonomous development; changes in law can only be explained
by considering state and society as two different entities.[8] All positive law
is conditioned by the basic form of society; the prevailing forms of property, whether landed or moneyed, determine the law; changes in property
distribution affect the law. The various social strata and groups of society,
which are in constant flux, try to manipulate and control the law and
succeed in securing legal protection for their interests. New codifications
of the law are the result of transformations of the social order. Jurisdiction
and legal institutions are therefore part and parcel of the social structure.
Stein circumscribes this condition with the term *"Gesellschaftsrecht;"*[9]
law, as such, reflects the distribution of interests and power in the different social orders and is conditioned by the class structure of society
[60, p. 171 ff.]. Stein gives a detailed description of how changes in the
distribution of property affect the social order and the law: the origin of
manufacturing and trade, and the growth of towns and cities is traced
to the growing scarcity of land due to population increases, and equality
as a social ideal appears as a result of the accumulation of wealth of the
townspeople. Stein summarizes his position by stating: "Half of history
is the history of property" (*Besitz*).[10] Another example of Stein's inclination to favor economic factors in the interpretation of history may be
found in *Die Entwicklung der Staatswissenschaft bei den Griechen*

---

[7] "Der Sozialismus in Deutschland" (1852). The failure of Germany to accomplish unification in 1848 is explained by the fact that a constitution presupposes
a civil society which at that time was not yet fully developed in Germany. *ibidem*
p. 558.

[8] *Die Gesellschaftslehre* (1856) p. 71.

[9] This interpretation led Stein to make demands for far-reaching changes in the
study of law; he insisted that students of law should be fully trained in political
economy. *Gegenwart und Zukunft der Rechts- und Staatwissenschaften* (1876).

L. Goldschmidt's review of this book [12] subjects Stein's position to incisive
criticism, specifically with reference to the training in jurisprudence, generally with
reference to his methods of investigation.

[10] *Gegenwart und Zukunft der Rechts-und Staatswissenschaften* (1876) p. 151.

(1879). He states that the legislation of Lykurgus, Pythagoras and Solon are not understandable "without taking the power of property and its influence"[11] into consideration; in his essay *"Die Staatswissenschaftliche Theorie der Griechen vor Aristoteles und Plato"* (1853) he makes the interesting comment that even the theories of state and society are the reflections of actual conditions and that science cannot predict the social order of the future, but only determines our consciousness of the existing social order. He verifies this thesis with the help of several examples[12] and thereby makes an early contribution to the sociology of knowledge.

Stein's demand that the state take a leading role in the welfare of the people became the basis for his interest in state administration. He considered the administrative function of the state of highest importance, particularly with regard to the enforcement of public versus private interests. Through a system of administration, the state embraces the whole sphere of the economy and of society. The task of administration is to provide favorable conditions for the development of the individual to the extent that he is unable to pursue this goal on his own.[13]

Stein's later shift from the analysis of the social movement to the exploration of the various fields of public administation was neither a matter of whim nor of indifference to labor problems under capitalism. Once one accepts his premises one sees its inner consistency. This interest in state administration can already be detected by his frequent references to administrative measures in his book on the social movement in France. In it he attributed an important role to state action in the improvement of the condition of labor.

Stein's analysis of social processes is characterized by the juxtaposition of state, society and the individual. The moving force in history is the individual and his destiny. Any deviation from this purpose within society, or by state interference, leads to contradictions and conflicts. Every individual wants to acquire and to strengthen his independence. But since dependency between individuals and between classes is an inherent feature of society, constant friction ensues. The state is powerless to prevent the ruling class of society from interfering with its mediating function. The triangular struggle between individual, state and society, all of which are highly intertwined, presents the neverending process of the realization of freedom. It shapes the course of history by dialectical resolutions of contradictions; temporary solutions can be found either through revolution or reform, but as time goes on,

---

[11] *ibidem,* p. 266.
[12] *ibidem,* p. 123.
[13] See particularly *Handbuch der Verwaltungslehre* (1876) p. 328.

with each new stage of development, new contradictions will arise, since they are inherent in any human community.

Stein distinguishes three stages of historical development, which are characterized and distinguished on the basis of their respective social structure: patriarchial society, estate society and civil society; they repeat themselves in the historical process of different cultures. They are not even clearly separated during the growth of any one culture, but may coexist in various social contexts or geographical areas. Stein presents the three historical stages in terms of ideal-type constructions.[14] The status symbol of the patriarchal order is landed property; differences in land holdings convey inequalities of rights and obligations. Acquisitions through commercial or manufactural pursuits and labor are not recognized socially. A strong antagonism prevails between the patriarchs and the industrial class. In guild society or estate society (*Ständestaat*), occupation is the decisive factor in determining status and privileges; the social order is structured on the basis of socio-economic functions performed: the main estates are the nobility, the clergy and the third estate, with a variety of subdivisions. This type of society is frequently shot through with patriarchal principles, particularly where hereditary rights are concerned. Members of the upper classes may attempt to perpetuate their position through legislation which resists changes. Stein calls such a society a caste society, which he considers to be a symptom of petrification and decay. Nevertheless, channels for self-realization and social mobility also exist in an estate society, particularly within the clergy. The third type—civil society—is essentially an open society, in which inequality by birth and preferential rights to specific occupation do not exist.

The emergence of modern European society is, according to Stein, the most advanced stage of universal history proceeding towards the realization of freedom. Other cultures declined or stagnated; Christian- Germanic culture (this is the term Stein uses in talking about the Western World) is the only one which overcame the throttling effects of a caste system developing in the later stages of Oriental, Greek and Roman societies. In European society, for the first time in world history, the dignity of labor was recognized, work was considered a moral obligation and a source of strength; this provided a fertile soil for the rise of the idea of equality.[15]

Nevertheless, the realization of equality and freedom in our society

---

[14] See *Gegenwart und Zukunft der Rechts-und Staatswissenschaften,* (1876); also *Verwaltungsrecht,* (1876), p. 11, 394 and *passim.*
[15] *"Ideen zur Geschichte der Arbeit"* (1849).

is threatened by inherited property rights, favoring inequality of education and opportunity. His early prediction of the alternative of "social reform or social revolution" is based on this contradiction in civil society; only in later years does he voice confidence in the creative power of industrialism to provide a social order in which the recognition of equality and the necessity of a class society—the basic contradiction of modern times—will have reached a compromise solution.

Stein elaborated his concepts first and foremost to interpret the sixty year period after the French Revolution. In the context for which they were devised, they are—in spite of their shortcomings—useful and enlightening. They enrich our understanding of the past and the present. His historial studies, with the emphasis on social dynamics, opened new avenues for the analysis of historical developments. His attempt to subtantiate his concepts as living forces in the unfolding of world history seems less fortunate;[16] it drove him to unjustified generalizations and made him neglect empirical sources of evidence in order to give his intuitive insight the proper scientific weight. In other words, he did not succeed in developing a consistent social philosophy. He was much more successful in providing a conceptual framework for the analysis of a specific historical period. It can only be regretted that he never used his original approach again for another historical study.[17] Stein's main contribution to social history consists in providing a new approach to his historical analysis rather than in his venture to systematize his concepts for an interpretation of the history of mankind as a continuous process. His basic contribution to the development of a science of society has been only seldom acknowledged. Only a few scholars admit that his concept of society, his theory of social dynamics, his claim that social factors determine the course of history, and his demonstration of the relationship between ideology and the class structure marked the beginning of the new social science of sociology.[18] That he is almost forgotten today

---

[16] Nitzschke [38, p. 108] has summarized Stein's account of universal history on the basis of the expositions spread among his various publications.

[17] Carl Schmitt [51] e.g. voices his surprise that Stein never subjected the Austrian Monarchy to such an analysis, although he lived in Vienna for over thirty-five years.

[18] Ernest Grünfeld [13] of course, in his book *Lorenz von Stein und die Gesellschaftslehre* does justice to him in this respect. His role as a pioneer of the science of society in Germany is appreciated by Waentig, Gumplowicz, Gothein and Spann. The Marxist Max Adler [68] pays tribute to him and states that Stein as a social philosopher leading from Hegel to Marx is not at all properly valued. "His *Gesellschaftswissenschaft* is so excellent that even today it can be of valuable service for the acquisition of sociological insight." (p. 48).

Franz Oppenheimer [41] considers Stein's book on the Social Movement the first most valuable manifestation of German sociology, vastly superior to Spencer, and in

may be partly due to the fact that academic sociology took an altogether different path than did Stein in his *Gesellschaftswissenschaft*, which is only a small section of modern sociology. Stein's *Gesellschaftslehre* is predominantly an analysis of the various social orders which are determined by the interplay of social classes, their interests and their power; it is based on his particular concept of society which, although seen as an independent entity, presented only one aspect of the human community. The state retained the superior function of representing the general interest. Stein's science of society thus remained a subsection of the science of the state (*Staatswissenschaft*).

Stein's own attitude toward sociology as a new independent discipline was very skeptical. In a letter (1885) to Gumplowicz he states: "I am eager to know about sociology, since it has always been impossible for me to formulate what it really is; according to the Franco-British confusion of terms and concepts there is nothing left that could not be considered as sociology, one way or another, including electricity and bacteria." Gumplowicz adds: "How distrustful the founder of the science of society was towards sociology, and how he was at a loss to classify sociology among other sciences is indicated in another passage of his letter in which he expresses the hope 'to find out of which branch of knowledge this sociology is a definable part'" [89, p. 132].

"THE HISTORY OF THE SOCIAL MOVEMENT IN FRANCE 1789-1850."

The main body of this book presents a history of the socio-political struggle in France during the sixty year period from the great French Revolution to the establishment of the Republic in 1848. It leads us through the various stages of the first Revolution, the history of the Constitutions of 1791, 1793 and 1795, the rise and fall of Napoleon, the Restoration, the July Revolution, the period of the Bourgeois Monarchy, and finally the struggle for supremacy between the bourgeoisie and the

---

some respects even to Comte. (pp. 893, 901)

E. H. Huber [19] in his comprehensive review of *Die deutsche Staatswissenschaft* (1934) recognizes his important position, together with Mohl's, as an originator of the science of society, who, "by observation and interpretation of the living reality were led—almost against their own will—to acknowledge the autonomy of society as different from the state" (p. 12).

proletariat after its downfall. The events are interpreted in terms of the changing power position of the surviving elements of feudalism and the third estate on the one hand, and the struggle of monarchy to reestablish itself as a representative of the "independent" state on the other hand.

Interwoven with this sociological· interpretation of French history—which for that time is a highly original approach—is an analysis of the social forces which led to a new class antagonism. These movements are seen as the result of the failure of the French Revolution to realize the professed ideal of equality.

The abolition of feudal privileges, the recognition of civil liberties and of political equality provided the framework for the newly emerging acquisitive society; but its advent also brought forth the industrial working class. The feudal system of mutual obligations had been dissolved; poverty, rootlessness and insecurity of income spread among the growing number of people who provided the labor for manufacturing enterprises. Without any protection by the law and without any organization of their own, the workers were at the mercy of the highly competitive market and ruthlessly exploited; they spent their life in misery which neither hard work nor thrift could overcome. The promise of liberty had led them into an apparently hopeless condition of socio-economic dependence.

People discovered the fact that even the most equalitarian constitution, based on human rights and guaranteeing freedom and equality in the pursuit of their interests, was not a satisfactory basis for personal independence; the perpetuation of dependence is the result of socio-economic conditions. Political equality can provide equal rights before the law, but not economic equality, which is of more vital importance in every-day life.

The masses, under the impact of their experiences in the developing industrial society, were determined to change conditions according to the ideal of "liberty and equality for all;" they became a new force in the political arena, a militant socio-political power, the proletariat. Their initial struggle for political rights turned into a struggle for social reform and institutional changes. Private property and—to a more limited extent—the family became the main targets of attack in the struggle for equalization of opportunities; for inequality of property and inequality of education resulting from property rights had remained an obstacle in the path of equalization.

Stein considered this new antagonism between labor and capital to be sharper and broader than the foregoing one between the nobility and the third estate.[19] In a society which proclaimed liberty as the highest ideal, it deprived the worker of the possibility of striving successfully for independence. It had created a new class pattern which tended to perpetuate inequality by making it hereditary and to reestablish estate society. While Hegel saw civil liberty as achieved within the framework of monarchy as the final stage in which freedom might be realized, Stein, a half-century later, called attention to the new type of dependency and the new contradictions inherent in modern industrialism. He once raised the question: "How shall this problem [the contradiction in the condition of the proletariat] be solved? We are not so presumptuous as to assume that we can suggest any solution. One person has never solved a problem which is addressed to humanity as a whole. All we can do is to state the problem clearly."[20]

The attack on private property by the worker is the logical result of his social conditions in early industrialism. It appears in the form of communism—which is merely a negation of property and the individual —and socialism which goes beyond this negation and defines the future form of social existence.[21] Only communists and socialists seemed to be aware of the fact that a society based on private property will frame a constitution which will protect the interests of the property-owning class and maintain the existing system of inequality and dependence. This trend is also reflected in the endeavors of the owning class to make political rights dependent on property ownership by making the right to vote dependent on tax-paying ability. Only a socialist society will finally succeed in establishing the realm of liberty and equality, the ideals of the French Revolution.

It was Stein who gave the socialist viewpoint—by that time mainly developed by Saint-Simon—of the relationship between state and society a concise formulation. He developed the concept of the proletariat, which he considered to be the working class in industrial society, united by the awareness of their revolutionary role. He thereby gave a specific meaning to the term "proletariat" and carefully circumscribed its role in the history of the 19th century. He considered the ensuing struggle unavoidable and did not hesitate to acknowledge that the approach of the socialists, with their emphasis on socio-economic rather than political conditions as crucial issues of world history, gave rise to a new science of society. "Socialism and communism gain the significance they have first of all due to the idea of society and the assumption that society has

---

19 *"Die sozialen Bewegungen der Gegenwart."* (1848).
20 *Der Sozialismus und Kommunismus in Frankreich* (1848) p. 325.
21 *"Blicke auf den Sozialismus und Kommunismus in Deutschland"* (1844) p. 13.

a history of its own."[22] Stein fears that the victory of the proletariat would establish the absolute rule of the laboring class, subjugate the state to the interest of labor and result in the victory of despotism. He touches here upon the problem of the dictatorship of the proletariat, which became acute only seventy years later; he sensed the indissoluble conflict between liberty and the enforcement of permanent equality.

But even if communism and socialism are a danger to the social order, censorship of the press and attempts to control free discussion are the most inappropriate methods to forestall their advent.[23] Communism and socialism are ideas which can only be conquered by the mind. The attempts to suppress doubts about the present state of affairs, to prohibit opposition, will only give moral support to those who oppose these new movements without ever allowing for constructive criticism. The threat of a communist revolution can never be mastered by thought control but only by basic social reform.

The social movement of the proletariat played an important role in the strife for political power after the July Revolution which terminated the struggle of the acquisitive society against the reinstitution of feudalism. The enthronement of Louis Philippe marked the beginning of industrial society with capital as the ruling power. Constitutionalism, with voting rights restricted to the higher income group, safeguarded the interest of the upper bourgeoisie.

The period of 1830-1848 is characterized by a complex triangular struggle between the monarchy, the ruling class and the growing political influence of the proletariat. The monarchy, instituted by the property-owning class to control the antagonism of the working class, attempted to assert its independence from the bourgeoisie and establish a system of personal government by devious means, disregarding the interests of the class which sponsored it. The growing tension between these two powers led to the demand for electoral reform and thereby to a strengthening of the republican movement. Republicanism was originally the political goal of the left-minded democrats who stood for liberty and equality. However, the more it became evident that the lack of social rather than political rights was the essential impediment in the way of the realization of these ideals, republicanism became predominantly the idea of the social movement and a reflection of the antagonism of the laboring class against monarchy as a representative of the bourgeoi-

---

[22] See Preface to *Sozialismus und Kommunismus in Frankreich* 2nd Edition, (1848), p. VIII.

[23] See *"Der Sozialismus in Deutschland"* (1852) p. 537, and *"Blicke auf den Sozialismus und Kommunismus in Deutschland"* (1844) p. 47 ff. with reference to the suppression of the *Rheinische Zeitung*.

sie. Its main practical aim was universal suffrage. Here we encounter the first indications that the working class movement hoped to get control of the state by parliamentary means, a trend which in later decades— through the social democratic wing—became so powerful within the socialist labor movement.

During the reign of Louis Philippe, the struggle for electoral reform became the temporary meeting ground of left-wing bourgeois liberals and the adherents of social reform. But these tendencies were repeatedly defeated in the 1830's. Republicanism as a political party movement broke down; but behind the screen of political events during the July Monarchy, the labor class developed slowly but consistently into a political power of its own. It remained in the background of the political struggle until finally the regime of Louis Philippe was overthrown by the opposition of the united bourgeoisie, "because neither monarchy nor the danger of social revolution will prevent the owning class of industrial society from destroying personal government which does not respect the principle of popular representation." By 1848, industrial society brought the state under its control and found an appropriate political order in constitutional republicanism.

It is Stein's contention that only a monarchy committed to social reform can survive in industrial society by exercising its functions as a constructive mediator between the opposing classes, and it is his hope that the surviving monarchies of Europe will take this path. In the French Republic, the state as an independent entity no longer has an acting representative. What is considered popular sovereignty is, in fact ,the sovereignty of society, in which two antagonistic classes confront each other and are ready to engage in a life-and-death struggle unless they discover a common interest. Stein considers the republic of mutual interests a possibility and the only alternative to a monarchy of social reform for a peaceful growth of modern industrialism. It would be necessary that, on the one hand, the property-owning class be willing to accept the justified demands of the working class, which would enable the laborer to gain capital through work; the ruling class would have to refrain from such prerogatives as prohibition of labor associations and strikes, the enforcement of factory regulations and factory courts, etc. On the other hand, labor would have to give up its struggle against the bourgeoisie and capitalism, the existing order of society and constitutionalism. Such a development would take decades; and there was not the slightest prospect in evidence for a change in attitude on either side.

The demands of labor crystallize during the period under consideration in demands for a special *Ministère du Progrès* and for the "right to work";

the former was unsuccessful and led into the dead-end alley of the conferences at the Luxembourg, and the latter resulted in the establishment of the *Ateliers Nationaux*. The latter were a complete failure, because, in a society of private enterprise, the attempt to make the state responsible for providing work for the unemployed is a glaring contradiction. The bitter mood of the proletariat and the disappointment of not coming to grips with the social question within the framework of the newly established Republic led to the June revolt and the total defeat of the proletariat for the time being. The revised Constitution of November 1848 discarded the concept of the right to work and restricted administrative social measures to assistance to the needy. The principal demand of labor to transform the state into a responsible authority for social welfare had been rejected. The ruling position of the capital-owning class in industrial society was secured.

Yet Stein concludes his socio-political analysis on a note of cautious optimism. The obligation to remedy the ill effects of competition on the labor market by public assistance had been approved; the acceptance of universal suffrage—the first acknowledged social right of the non-propertied class—opened the possibility of a successful struggle of the dependent class for further social reforms through administrative measures, provided the socialist and the democratic parties joined forces to cooperate towards that goal.

The analysis of the French Social Movement brought to a head two major new conclusions: the first was that "labor without capital stands now besides property as an independent and autonomous factor in human society," . . . the second was that "this element is of great importance as regards the transformation of the state and its public laws and is an element one would have to reckon with one way or the other with respect to all major constitutional problems" . . .[24] "The foundation and point of view of French socialism was therewith completely abandoned. Socialism and communism in the hitherto existing meaning of the word have become mere individual symptoms of an infinitely more comprehensive problem."[25]

The events of 1848 have shown that Stein's anticipation in 1842 of a showdown between the classes was correct. He did not accept this as the final answer to the problems he had posed. In another essay[26] he states: "The great question of a better relationship between capital and

---

[24] *"Der Sozialismus in Deutschland"* (1852) p. 560.

[25] *Ibidem*, p. 562.

[26] *Der Sozialismus und Kommunismus in Frankreich*, (1848). See particularly the footnote p. 326ff., signed by the editor, but obviously written by Stein.

labor, of a labor organization, of social equality is not solved . . . it burns like a deep and deadly wound . . . in the conscience of European society after the disgraceful events of June 1848. . . . We cannot predict what will be the shape and the development of this question in the near future." He hopes that not only France, but also the German states, will give the lower classes the right to participate in the affairs of the state. "When the proletariat becomes involved in public affairs, the social question, e.g., the problem of capital and labor relationship will no longer be subject to one-sided theoretical interpretations, to utopian schemes and to the prejudices of party politics. It will be transferred to the realm of legislation where all interests and all moral elements representing the nation (*Volksgeist*) contribute to the organic growth of actual social conditions."

The socio-political struggle during the period in question is determined by the attempt to realize the ideal of human equality. The contradiction inherent in the concept of a "society of equals" is the source of major political conflicts which follow the French Revolution. Since society is an order based on the different capabilities of men and the different social functions are endowed with different degrees of prestige, the inequality of income is indispensable. A truly open society, providing chances for everybody according to his ability and regardless of his social background, would come as close to the realization of liberty and equality as is at all possible. Such a society can grow out of the established industrial society through social reform. The belligerent attitude of the proletariat towards industrial society and its corresponding political order is mainly due to the hopeless situation of labor. This antagonism could be eliminated if the worker would have a chance to acquire capital either by state or cooperative bank institutions, lending at cost, or by raising the income level so that he might accumulate it through savings. Other specific measures which Stein considered desirable are elaborated in his work on public administration; they include practically all the measures of modern labor law and social legislation, including public education, public housing, and public health.

Stein's suggestion to further capital acquisition by the worker as a means of alleviating the condition of his dependency is, of course, outdated today. To the extent that it is at all possible, it can hardly enable the laborer, in an era of large corporations, to establish his own enterprise and to thereby gain independence. Today, the struggle for an elimination of proletarian living conditions has shifted to the security of a well-paid job.

If we reconsider Stein's conclusions from the vantage point of the present, it becomes clear that, in his study on the social movement in France, he foresaw the development of a welfare state—towards which industrial societies in Europe and, to a lesser extent, also in the United States have been striving—possible and necessary for a flourishing future of Western civilization. The fact that this development took place, not as he expected, through the superior insight of the ruling class, nor by authority of the monarchy of social reform, but under the pressure of unionization and the class struggle which he considered dangerous and destructive, should not prejudice us against valuing his vision.

STEIN'S POSITION IN THE HISTORY OF SOCIAL THOUGHT IN GERMANY

Stein's contribution to the growth of the social sciences extends over many areas and has exerted a significant influence in different directions. To give a comprehensive analysis of the abundance of material which he expounded and of the wealth of ideas he had to offer is not the subject of this introductory essay. But it seems appropriate to explore the influence of the present book on social thought in Germany at the time of its publication and during the following decades. It was, first, a powerful factor in calling attention to the social forces which influence the course of history and, secondly, contributed greatly to the growth of interest in welfare policy among German social scientists. These two major areas of Stein's influence correspond to the two different preoccupations of Stein before and after 1850. Both these trends of thought had already emerged at the time when Stein wrote this book.

Stein and the Socialists

Lorenz von Stein has frequently been classified as a forerunner of economic materialism; he was the first in German literature who proclaimed the preponderance of societal factors in determining the course of history, as against the influence both of ideas and of mere factors of political power. His relationship to Marx and Engels is, therefore, of particular interest.

The first edition of Stein's book was published in 1842, at a time when Marx had just come to Paris to study economics and the socialist movement. It was obvious, and has meanwhile been documented, that Stein's book did not escape Marx's attention. Marx's essays on "The Class Struggle in France" (1850) and "The 18th Brumaire of Louis Buonaparte" (1852) are based on the same concepts and the same interpretations of the course of French history; the role of the proletariat which Stein formulated already in the first edition of his opus in 1842 is actually the central theme of the "Communist Manifesto" of 1848.[27] Yet the question whether Marx was essentially stimulated by Stein's book, and to what extent Marx's theory was influenced by Stein's analysis, has never been answered definitely, although it has been a matter of controversy for many years. In a recent publication [125b] Robert Tucker disregards all uncertainties by quoting a passage of Marx concerning the role of the proletariat in the coming revolution and claiming "all this is straight out of Stein" [p. 116]. There is certainly a striking similarity of the two authors' approaches to the political events of the forties and their interpretation. One has to keep in mind, however, that both Marx and Stein were under the same influences, not only as expounders of Hegelian thought, but also as students of French socialist theories; they became acquainted with the same sources and the same group of people [119, p. 174], the same economic conditions and the same intellectual atmosphere in Paris which abounded in new ideas and concepts concerning industrial society challenging social reformers. It was a period of great tension and productivity. The effort to come to grips with the acute problems of the time was a collective one, and it seems not only impossible but also unimportant to determine to whom credit is due in each single case. Thus Masaryk [103] emphasizes the fact that the rise of historical materialism was due to the intellectual climate of France in the 1840's, that it manifested itself in the writings of many authors, and cannot possibly be traced to any one writer of that time. He states: "I believe the influence of Stein on Marx was less marked than Sombart and Struve assume. Stein's interpretation is derived from the study of French socialists. Marx explored their writings also, although somewhat later. In addition, Stein was—just like Marx—a Hegelian; their development runs along parallel lines. I admit that Stein has contributed to the clarification of Marx's thoughts because his book is—considering the time of its appearance—certainly excellent; but it seems to me that Saint-Simon and Louis Blanc exercised a more direct and a deeper influence than the textbook-like exposition of Stein" [p. 39]. Georg Adler, on the other hand, assumed that "Marx must have been greatly stimulated by

---

[27] Heberle, Rudolf [94 p. 63] states "The first to point out the essential relationship between these thought systems [socialism and communism] and the rising movement of the industrial proletariat was probably Stein."

Stein's book." "Marx was acquainted with it before he studied the writings of the French authors." "Stein had found the material for his profound insight into the modern social movement in the writings of the great French socialists from Saint-Simon to Louis Blanc, but none of these authors stated all this as concisely and clearly" [1, p. 16].

Stein was certainly highly indebted to Saint-Simon, whose writings contain the earliest notions of historical materialism. While Vico, Montesquieu, Rousseau and Ferguson occasionally state the influence of socio-economic factors on political events, Saint-Simon, in attempting to discover the basic principle of historical development, conceived of social classes and their interrelationship as the propulsive force in history; the state is the institution used by the ruling class to suppress the lower classes and the antagonism between the propertied and non-propertied classes (*propriétaire and non-propriétaire*) is a decisive factor in any socio-political change.[28] But Saint-Simon did not yet envisage any active and autonomous partaking of the proletariat in industrial society. Stein leans heavily upon Saint-Simon in his theory of class formation and class struggle, and in his attempt to explain the history of his time in terms of changes in the social structure. He also elaborated Saint-Simon's interpretation of socialism as the first manifestation of a "science of society."

The original contribution of Stein was the sociological interpretation of the proletariat as the labor force in modern society and as a class-conscious unit struggling for power in pursuit of their interests. Practically all authors who explored the Stein-Marx relationship objectively have acknowledged this fact. Koigen [25, pp. 240, 251] states: "The great merit of Stein is his sociological characterization of the proletariat" and ". . . to have made it the central point of his analysis." Friedrich Muckle concurs by stating: "Historical priority of a sociological interpretation of the proletariat goes to Stein" [108 p. 34], and "Lorenz Stein has been the first author who delineated the proletarian class from other social phenomena by a strong emphasis on its typical characteristics, he recognized it as an eminent factor of future historical developments" [107, p. 329].

Földes [8, p. 295) comes to the conclusion that the concept of the proletariat is the most original contribution of Stein which had not yet been conceived by Saint-Simon or Louis Blanc; and Simkovitch [119, p. 175] points out that "Stein was the first historian of the fourth estate, the philosopher of its coming revolution and the only one who dealt with

---

[28] Stein acknowledges this, stating: "It was Saint-Simon who first called attention to the opposing forces of owners and non-owners. For this reason and not so much for other partly bizarre ideas, he became the first socialist of France." *"Die Sozialen Bewegungen der Gegenwart,"* (1848), p. 303.

this subject without partiality or bias." The opinion of Peter von Struve, [59,] a Russian Marxist, may be of particular interest. He states: "Stein was a bourgeois, a definite defender of private property and an equally definite opponent of communism, but his book was nevertheless a brilliant and epoch-making performance when it appeared." [p. 229].

What was new in the Marxian interpretation of the history of capitalism was the theory of the inevitable destruction of capitalism due to its inherent contradictions, and the positive accent given to the course of future events. Stein considered the situation as dangerous and the threat of the proletarian movement as disastrous for the future of society; he believed in the possibility of avoiding the "rule of labor" by appropriate social reform. But his social analysis provided Marx with an essential element for the construction of his own system of scientific socialism by assigning to the proletariat the role of the antagonist in industrial society in accordance with Hegelian dialectics. Marx [140] himself stated in a letter in 1852 that it was not he who had discovered the existence of classes in modern society or the class struggle; this had already been done before him by bourgeois historians; "What was new on my part was to show 1) that the existence of classes is tied to definite historical struggles of evolution (*Entwicklungskaempfe*) within the area of production, 2) that the class struggle necessarily leads to the dictatorship of the proletariat and 3) that this dictatorship is the transition to the abolition of classes and to a classless society." This marks off quite correctly Marx's own contribution from those of his forerunners.

Marx was doubtlessly indebted to Stein, with whom he became acquainted at a decisive turning point of his life. Plenge [113, p. 66] summarizes it very distinctly: "Stein had already formulated what was as yet a dim notion of sentiment to Marx, the class struggle, the proletariat, and communism as its inevitable goal . . . Yet it would be altogether wrong to consider Marx a plagiarist . . . In contrast to Stein quiescently abiding by his state philosophy, Marx could well consider himself as the greater scholar for whom Stein had prepared the way . . . It is clearly noticeable that Marx from then on acquired a new center of intellectual interest . . . The relationship of state and society became completely reversed." The assertion that the state was nothing but the instrument of the ruling class, that none of its activities was ever independent of it or even geared towards the welfare of the lower classes, is a point which clearly distinguishes him from Stein, who never abandoned the position that the state—despite its dependency on class domination—could and should play the role of a mediator in society. Marx came to different and less ambiguous conclusions, going far beyond Stein's deductions as to the future class struggle and policy. Max Adler [68, p. 45] points out that "the opinion prevalent in bourgeois criticism of Marx which considers Marx's basic concepts as nothing but a variation of Stein's precepts is completely thoughtless." While to Stein the future was a matter of freedom, of choice and of idealism, Marx's analysis of capitalism is predominantly geared towards his theory of the inevitability of historical processes; his analytical interest is centered on resulting political developments rather than on a dissection of the past and the present.

In his analysis of the events of 1848, Stein never identifies himself with any class position; he takes a rather detached point of view, fully realizing that the capitalists were superior in power and that socialist and communist groups had no workable alternative to offer, as the failure of the public workshops illustrated. Marx and Engels, on the other hand, took a predominantly political and partisan position, based on their own theory, that a classless society would grow out of industrialism through the dictatorship of the proletariat and the destruction of the traditional power of the state.

The evaluation of Stein's work and its possible influence on the theories of Marx and Engels has been subject to frequent changes. It repeatedly reflects an emotional attitude, concerned with stressing Marx's originality and his independence from "bourgeois" historians. In 1848 there appeared a lengthy review of Stein's book by Moses Hess [16]; he was a friend of Marx during his formative years, before economic materialism had become a cornerstone of Marx's social philosophy. Hess was an utopian socialist [see also 65] whose approach to history Marx later denounced as "German or True Socialism" in the "Communist Manifesto." Hess criticizes Stein's preoccupation with the role of the proletariat in the revolutionary movement "which is repeated ad nauseam;" he belittles Stein's notion that socialism is the result of poverty and destitution, while Hess considers it to be the result of sympathy and compassion; his negative criticism of Stein's book, despite the fact that Hess was a socialist and intended to attack "the Hegelian of the center, unable to comprehend the theoretical truth of communism" (page 78), is nevertheless based on an idealism equally alien to Marx and to Stein.[29]

That Marx was thoroughly familiar with Stein's book is clearly proven by his article against Karl Grün [32, 58]; it is a biting criticism of Grün, who is denounced as parroting Moses Hess and plagiarizing Stein. A few

---

[29] Struve [59, pp. 231 and 275], takes an even more critical position towards Hess by stating: "Hess is still more abstract, more idealistic and philosophical than Stein, he shares Stein's weaknesses without having his realistic force." "Stein's interpretation was much closer to Marx's thesis than the 'humaneness' of Hess."

interspersed remarks give us at least some indication of Marx's opinion on Stein at that time. He writes [58, p. 49]: "From all this one is able to see that Grün's concoction stands far below Stein's book, who at least attempted to trace the relationship of socialist literature to the factual development of French society." "Stein himself is extremely vague when he speaks of 'political factors' in industry. However, he shows that he is on the right track by adding that the history of the state is intimately connected with economic history." Until the republication of these articles in 1896 [58], it had remained uncertain and a matter of conjecture and subjective interpretation whether Marx had read Stein's book.

The only author who completely denied the influence of Stein on Marx in later years was Franz Mehring, a Marxist and a well-known authority on the history of the German social-democratic party; as such, and in view of Stein's growing conservatism and antagonism against party politics in later decades, Mehring takes a biased position regarding Stein's book. He attacked Struve and also Sombart's [120] favorable assessment of Stein by stating that "the historical significance of Stein's book is limited to its influence on bourgeois classes" [33, p. 453]. "Stein was a compiler; when he used his own mind, he wailed about 'subversive tendencies' or glorified 'social monarchy'; for those who had studied French socialism at its own sources, Stein's book meant nothing new" [33a, p. 380]. Mehring never accepted the fact that Marx showed a detailed knowledge of Stein in his Anti-Grün, but only admitted that it was "possible that Marx had read Stein, but that he certainly knew about French socialism and communism long before the appearance of Stein's book. . . There is not a word of truth in the whole tissue of falsehood of Stein's influence on Marx" [105, p. 187]. However, in another context he admits that Stein "uncovered the socio-economic basis of French socialism and communism and the class struggle between the bourgeoisie and the proletariat. It was a sour and unripe apple, but it was an apple of the tree of knowledge all the same" [104].

The most interesting question of what Marx, Engels and Stein thought about each other can only be deduced from occasional scanty references. Marx certainly never acknowledged having received any stimulation from Stein. The comments in his Anti-Grün, though not unfavorable—due to the fact that he wanted to illustrate Grün's plagiarism—indicate that Marx looked down upon Stein as having merely presented a rehash of Saint-Simon's theory. He did not consider him as an original thinker. There is one other reference to Stein in his correspondence with Engels [141]; in a letter of January 8, 1868, referring to Dühring's review of Das Kapital, Marx writes: "The funniest thing is that he (Dühring) puts me together with Stein because I use a dialectical approach while Stein ties up the greatest trivialities in clumsy trichotomies coated by Hegelian categories." Engels' remarks are equally polemical when he speaks of the wilted misery (*matte Elendigkeit*) of Stein's book, or states that "among the professors and bureaucrats in Germany there were some clever speculators who translated foreign sentences into undigested Hegelianism—like Mr. Stein" [78].

Stein's opinion on Marx remains a matter of conjecture; we know for certain only that he was familiar with his early writings. The second edition of *Der Sozialismus und Kommunismus in Frankreich,* which appeared in 1847, contains a comprehensive bibliography organized by countries; under the subdivision "Papers which go beyond the French movement" Stein cites: "Karl Marx. *Misère de la philosophie. Réponse à la philosophie de misère de M. Proudhon 1847.* A comprehensive criticism of the latter work by Proudhon in two sections" (p. 588). He also mentions periodicals to which Marx contributed, such as the *Deutsch-französische Jahrbücher* and the *Rheinische Jahrbücher* and adds that the "first edition of 1845 was politically radical, the second of 1846, radical communist" (p. 590). There are several testimonies, however, as to his assessment of Engels' historical studies. Referring to *Die Lage der arbeitenden Klassen in England,* he states: "This altogether competent treatise has to its credit to have drawn public attention to the center of the organized proletariat, the English working class" (p. 587). In his article on *Die Soziale Bewegung und der Sozialismus in England* (1849), Stein discusses Engels' book at length, stating that "It is grandiose in its one-sidedness; it is based on the thought that the basest part of society makes up its major part, that society itself is at fault when the individual has to suffer and even in whatever misfortune the individual may bring about. This interpretation approaches the ridiculous, if, for instance, the bourgeoisie is held responsible for the fact that the dirty Irish are unwilling to mend their clothes and live on potatoes in order to get drunk on Sundays. We are definitely opposed to such an analysis of social conditions. Whatever may be true in this presentation becomes implausible and ineffective through the falsehoods it contains which are obvious to those who are familiar with the facts. Those, however, who do not know the conditions, are nothing but pamphleteers who stir up trouble in society without being able or wanting to suggest a cure or improvement. Nevertheless, it is owing to Engels that we have a picture of the extremes to which the reckless use of peoples in industry can go" (p. 469).

Some years later, in his article *"Der Sozialismus in Deutschland"*

(1852, Stein devoted a considerable section to the literature on socialism and communism in Germany. He separates scientific literature, under which he mentions his own works and those of Mohl, Bensen and Stirner, from propaganda publications. He does not mention Marx or the Communist Manifesto, but deals with Weitling, Grün, Hess, as well as Engels' book again, of which he states: "The treatise had a considerable after-effect in Germany. It presented a picture of the deepest misery in the dirtiest part of a dirty factory town in England; full of undeniable facts about this wretched sphere of industrialism, written with warmth and elegance, without any question the best invective written in Germany against industrial society; a partisan book as no other" (p. 538).

This all goes to show that Stein was familiar with socialist and communist literature and that he weighed their importance in the over-all picture. The fact that he never mentioned Marx again may have been due to the conflict in which he found himself: that his earlier writings prefigure Marx's approach, of which he disapproved. In his criticism of Engels and in his articles on the social movement in Germany, France and England, (1848-1852), his stern opposition to the ensuing class struggle, to communism and to the possibility that labor might take the change of social conditions into its own hands, is already fully discernable. He never explored Marxism or the ideology and political practice of the various socialist parties, although this would have been the logical sequel to his study of France in the 1840's. Perhaps in order to escape the necessity of dissecting later developments, he even refrained from publishing another edition of his book on France after the second edition of 1855 had sold out. His last edition of the *Handbuch der Verwaltungslehre* (1888) contains a survey on the international literature on socialism and the labor problem (pp. 77-82, 206ff). At the end of the chapter "Classes and class movement" he mentions Robert Meyer with reference to his *Emanzipationskampf des vierten Standes* as "the first author who has conceived and elaborated the idea of an independent class and its movement." He also recommends Meyer as a source of information on "how Lassalle and Marx have provided the theoretical foundation, especially with reference to the question of finance capital; and how the struggle against finance capital resulted in a general principle of the negation of property and led to a break with the Lassallians" (p. 81).

Stein may have felt that the socialist movement, drawing its strength from the relentless antagonism against bourgeois society, moved in the opposite direction from what he considered the most promising road towards freedom. Consequently he chose to ignore its ideologists and politicians. Intellectually he withdrew from this sphere of world affairs and persisted only in advocating his own modest remedies, rather than analyzing the forces at work in modern society, the origins of which he had demonstrated so successfully.

Stein and the Social Reformers

While the traces which Stein left on the development of economic materialism remain obscured due to lack of information and the partisan attitude of the socialists, his influence on welfare policy in Germany is clearly discernable. The publication of Stein's book on socialism and communism in France made an enormous impression in Germany. "It opened the cover of Pandora's box . . . for the educated it pushed the door open to the subterranean channels which long ago had been hollowed out beneath the surface of society. What the regime of Louis Philippe had done in practice, was now also accomplished in theory: the bourgeoisie became aware of itself" [128 p. 584].

Stein's analysis of the coming class struggle had a lasting influence on the direction which political economy took in the following decades. This discipline, at that time in its infancy in Germany, centered around the analysis of the competitive market and on the quantitative aspect of production, without any concern about its negative impact on human welfare. The Manchester school had based its arguments on the assumption that free and equal individuals competed on the labor market and that "free competition" was the soundest way to select the able, that it promoted the well-being of all by enforcing maximum effort and maximum production. But it slowly became evident that, even though liberty prevailed, the market did not seem to provide a fair competition because of the inequality of the initial status of the competitors which made it impossible. Free competition, in theory the best method of giving a fair chance of success to everybody according to his ability, had in practice resulted in exploitation and pauperism of the larger part of the workers. Mohl [142, pp. 490, 501] had already raised his warning voice in 1840: "Fifty to sixty years have sufficed to produce millions of factory workers and to corrupt them at the core; a shorter period may be sufficient to have them confront in closed battle formations (*geschlossenen Schlachthaufen*) the other elements of society." "Every voice raised against these deeply immoral and extremely dangerous consquences of the economy of competition should be received as a blessing."[30] Classical

---

[30] Robert Mohl's line of thought shows a close kinship to Stein's. Whether priority in formulating the need for a new "science of society" goes to Mohl or Stein seems controversial. Gothein considers Mohl a forerunner of Stein, but Grünfeld denies this. See Grünfeld [13, p. 211]. Mohl and Stein have frequently acknowledged their mutual indebtedness. See also Nitzschke [38, p. 134].

economics could not possibly grasp this fact, because it lacked the necessary frame of reference. In order to understand and explain these unhappy results, it was necessary to analyze society in its historical context as a composite of different groups whose power and interests vary. Stein's general approach to the social sciences, his assertion that state, society and the economy are just different aspects of the same entity, and his specific thesis of conflicting class interests in modern industrialism appeared to be much more realistic and convincing. He claimed that "economics so far has subordinated the individual life to the operation of the whole and has never strayed from this position to consider the individual which makes up the whole."[30a] He formulated the task of responsible citizens as one "to find a form of social life in which private property is preserved and yet does not present an insurmountable obstacle for the full development of the personality."[31]

The position which Stein took in calling for social reform within the framework of industrial capitalism was certainly not exclusively his own. It reflected, at mid-century, the temper of the social scientists, as well as other figures of public life in Germany, and corresponded to the general dissatisfaction with the social consequences of early industrialization. It was Stein's merit, however, to have given the new approach in the discipline considerable impetus by providing a foundation in his general theory of society. Industrialism and capitalism, which had been accepted and interpreted as being the final and superior answers to providing an adequate living for the people, came under scrutiny now: they were increasingly seen and evaluated as a stage of development carrying the seeds of their own disruption. Warnings against the negligence with regard to human values resulting from unmitigated liberty in the pursuit of business gained momentum and became crystallized in a variety of social reform movements.

The opposition against *laissez faire* and the call for constructive support of the laboring class sprang up in different circles and was not restricted to any specific doctrine. It came from different social groups and was tied up with different ideologies—socialist, conservative and liberal—all of which, oddly enough, showed traces of Stein's reasoning. Lassalle's analysis of the role of labor in modern society and the suggestions he proposed for further action have an unmistakable similarity to Stein's analytical arguments; the demand for universal suffrage as a constitutional right of the fourth estate, the need to provide capital for laborers in order to establish their independence, and the idea that the

---

[30a] *Der Sozialismus und Kommunismus in Frankreich.* 2nd edition, (1848), p. 212.
[31] *Ibidem.* 1st edition, (1842), p. 26.

state was the proper institution to carry out the demands of the laboring class—all this had already been formulated by Stein, although Lassalle, as a political leader of the working class, made an altogether different use of these arguments [13, 73, 109, 117]. Leading figures of the church— both catholic and protestant—raised their voices in concern about the worker's plight; their presentation goes far beyond a call for charitable assistance to the poor; it shows anxiety about the general state of society to which Stein had called attention. Bishop von Ketteler, the first Catholic priest to approach the problem of pauperism as a result of the laborer's class position, goes so far as to proclaim: "The statement 'property is theft' contains—side by side with a great lie—also a terrible truth" [138, p. 15]. What he demands is not charity, but labor association to right a wrong. Victor Aimée Huber, representing the Protestant view, followed a similar line of thought as political pamphleteer and advocate of cooperatives.

Stein's position has also been used to bolster the conservative view of the church. The catholic periodical *Oesterreichische Monatsschrift für Gesellschaftswissenschaft und Volkswirtschaft*, founded by C. V. Vogelsang, clearly reveals this influence. In an article *"Staatssozialismus und soziales Königtum"* Vogelsang [126] refers to Stein repeatedly and quotes him in his argument for the reestablishment of enlightened monarchy in order to cope with the misuse of liberty in a commercial bourgeois society. Schmoller [118] confirms that "the doctrine of the monarchy of social reform as conceived by Gneist and Stein had taken roots in spite of all derisions of the socialists."

The most meaningful and appropriate use of Stein's contribution, however, was made by the economists at German universities who, liberal in outlook, yet came to the conclusion that state intervention and labor organizations were necessary to prevent the disregard of human welfare in industrial society [111]. Stein left his mark on Roscher [115], Knies and Hildebrand and their approach to economics representing the Historical School; Carl Dietzel's [76] theory of society is direct offshoot of Stein's; Schmoller [52] appraised him at length and considered him "one of the most meritorious German social scientists;" (p. 114) he adds in refutation of adverse criticism that Stein is an author "whom nobody reads except scholars and from whom one can steal and plagiarize without scruples about ignoring his name or running him down." (p. 115)

During the year which had gone by since the first appearance of Lorenz von Stein's analysis of modern industrialism, his position had finally become common property of a leading group of economists. However, when Adolf Wagner, as the leading figure of so-called *"Kathederso-zialismus"* advocated a basic change in the distribution of income by radical tax reform, Stein, towards the end of his life, took a vigorous stand against such measures.[32] His main argument was that progressive taxation would endanger not only capital formation, which he considered to be the prerequisite of the expansion of the productive capacity, but social independence as well, because the power of taxation would thus be misused in the struggle between the classes instead of being confined to its proper limits of the "reproduction" of given conditions. Adolf Wagner devoted two comprehensive and most interesting articles [63] to a critical analysis of Stein's contention. He showed that Stein's arguments led him into blatant contradiction with his earlier interpretation of capitalism and social development, by lumping together state-socialism with socialism and communism. Adolf Wagner suggests that civil society will slowly be replaced "by a new period which one might call the social period [63, p. 67] in which "under the leadership of a monarchy of social reform [63, p. 119] and with the preservation of private property extreme differences of inequality will be eliminated by public measures." He thus became an advocate of a policy which Stein once considered as the justified and cogent conclusions of his own analysis.

Stein's Changing Perspective

Stein's ideas and concepts have to be evaluated with reference to the different stages of his life. Since he took—at various periods—diverging positions in explaining events and predicting the course of the future, he was bound to become a controversial figure among contemporaries. It may also account for the growing antagonism of Marx and Engels and other socialists in their polemics against Stein over the decades. Felix Gilbert [11, p. 24] comments upon the fact that "scholars have only to a very limited degree been aware of what they owe to Stein," in pointing out that Stein's position was not only marginal in relation to history, sociology, law and economics, but that he also stood on the borderline between idealism and positivism. But even this seems a simplification because it does not take into consideration his later development, when he tried to act as mediator between both, according to Nitzschke [38, p. 135]: "His theory of society of 1856 is an attempt to unify the . . . empiricist concept of Western Europe with the idealistic one of the German social scientists. However, he did not really succeed."

---

[32] "Finanzwissenschaft und Staatssozialismus" *Lehrbuch der Finanzwissenschaft.* (1885). Vol. I, pp. 148-160.

Nitzschke distinguishes three major periods in Stein's intellectual development. During his student years, until 1841, he was under the influence of Hegel and Fichte, with a bent towards realism already apparent at that time. Stein's second phase, according to Nitzschke, runs from 1841 to 1851 under the influence of French thought; his interest is now focused on society instead of law, and changes from idealistic philosophy to an investigation of the reality of life. By that time, economic interests are to him the moving power of society and of history. Up to this point, when he was in his early thirties, his growth seems to have been consistent.

The break which took place in the early fifties and resulted in a turn towards conservatism flavored by romanticism is much harder to explain and therefore mostly a matter of conjecture. Nitzschke illustrates this change in an extensive analysis of his articles written in the fifties, without, however, explaining the matter. Herbert Marcuse [31] believes that the roots of Stein's conservatism can already be detected in the "Social Movement"; he interprets Stein's criticism of communism as "the veering away from the dialectical direction and following the ideas of positive sociology" [p. 387] in which the concept of contradiction is out of place and "social antagonisms are just a means for establishing social harmony" [p. 329]. Stein himself confesses to have contributed to "dangerous consequences" by assuming that the social order is merely a reflection of economic conditions; nevertheless, he also gives a warning "not to forget the practical basis of material life while aspiring to explore the superior essence of society."[33]

The inconclusiveness of Stein's social philosophy emanates from his attempt to bring economic materialism and idealism into one system [2, p. 189]. It has its origin in his interpretation of the role of the state which is contradictory in itself. The state cannot be both an instrument of the ruling class and the impartial authority concerned about the welfare of all. Due to this basic inconsistency, Stein frequently contradicts himself, moves in circles, and feels justified to come to altogether different conclusions at different periods of his life.

If we compare the main theses of his book on France with later utterances regarding the labor problem, the change of Stein's position seems quite drastic. The social reform which he proposed to forestall social revolution had to be radical in order to accomplish what he considered the justified expectations of the proletariat. He envisaged a society in which the pattern of selection and promotion was exclusively

---

[33] "*Das Wesen des arbeitslosen Einkommens und sein besonderes Verhältnis zu Amt und Adel.*" (1852). pp. 145, 146.

based on qualifications and merit and in which inherited privileges due to property were completely abandoned. It seems impossible to have expected such changes during the early period of European industrial capitalism. To have asked for them indicates Stein's basic criticism of the status quo.

The changes in his point of view after 1850 became more and more prevalent in his later years and led to growing conservatism; he insisted that spiritual rather than material forces determined the course of history. Society, instead of being mainly a reflection of economic relationships, is now seen as an intricate organism in which every social group has its proper function. He shifts emphasis from the call for equality to the necessity of inequality, which he now explains as a result of innate differences between individuals and in terms of differences in education. The existing class pattern therewith becomes the proper framework of selection, and industrial society the most adequate social order to provide necessary opportunities to all individuals for the fulfillment of their destiny. Furthermore, the plight of the proletariat and the labor movement, which he once described with compassion and sympathy, is viewed with growing criticism as "mob-rule" and "demagogy," a process of cultural degeneration; universal suffrage is seen as a constant threat of the victory of the dependent masses over the state. He even undermined his own concept of the proletariat by the qualification that a considerable minority among the non-propertied class is able to acquire capital and that its interests therefore run counter to the majority.[34] This distinction between the class movement and the labor problem, which "the first half of the century did not yet know"[35] now enabled him to approach these two problems—the identity of which he had first established—separately, by condemning the class movement on the one hand, and on the other by suggesting solutions to the labor problem by way of administrative policy. Good will of the ruling class, the authority of an enlightened monarch, and christian charity were now considered to be the essential factors for the solution of the social question within the framework of industrial society. It signifies a strange metamorphosis of his original approach.

Two features characterize the change of position by Stein after 1850. He abandoned the idea and concept of "contradiction" in the capitalistic system which might lead to a new stage of social development, and refused to appraise labor's own effort to solve its problems through

---

[34] *Handbuch der Verwaltungslehre* (1888). 3. Part. *Die Verwaltung und das gesellschaftliche Leben,* p. 70ff.
[35] *Ibidem* p. 197.

unionization and the organization of the social-democratic party. His antagonism against all manifestations of the class struggle is all the more surprising because much of what happened between 1850 and 1890 he had clearly predicted earlier. It also seems inconceivable that he would not have realized that without the fervor and pressure of the socialist movement, social legislation would never have been enacted.

To explain the story of Stein's life and his intellectual development as opportunism is untenable, and has also been disproved by the fact that the roots and the beginning of his change are apparent before, and are independent of, the offer of his Viennese appointment [39]. It seems that Carl Schmitt [51] comes closest to a genuine explanation by tracing the final turn towards conservatism to the shocking and almost traumatic experience of the events of 1848, which destroyed the bridge between the socialist movement and the bourgeoisie. "The end of the European revolutionary movement of state and society meant for him also the end of the brilliant philosophical impulse by which he had comprehended the social movement in France before 1848" [51, p. 644]. What followed was a process of accommodation and adjustment. By the middle of the 19th century, industrial society had asserted itself, and the threatening forces which had led to a showdown in 1848 were under control all over Europe. Stein interpreted this as the stage of a new equilibrium between the social order and state organization which might endure, provided the ruling class lived up to its obligations. For those who lived the lives of the upper bourgeoise, the deeper conflicts were now hidden under the flourishing of industry and commerce, and could be easily ignored. Stein never touched upon these problems again. He never regained his critical verve; not only had his viewpoint changed, but also his temper and his intellectual intensity. Originally a secessionist, he later viewed society like an academician.

The *History of the Social Movement in France,* the intellectual harvest of his early years in Paris, remains his masterpiece and deserves, as a work of great originality, a lasting place in the history of social thought.

KAETHE MENGELBERG

New York

April 1964

Lorenz von Stein: The History of the Social

Movement in France, 1789 - 1850

Part One

The Concept of Society and the Social History of the French Revolution Until 1830

PRELIMINARY DISCOURSE

THE CONCEPT OF SOCIETY AND
ITS DYNAMIC LAWS

Introduction

The present generation has begun to observe certain phenomena which had formerly remained unrecorded in everyday life as well as in science. . . . Powerful events have taught us that these phenomena are consequences of a force permeating the life of nations and of individuals; that they are by necessity interrelated, and that human knowledge has made one of those discoveries which suggests that behind the known world and its order there seem to be still greater powers and elements, which were, originally, viewed with skepticism and a certain awe, but for which there existed neither a name nor a law.

Our time is distinguished through the discovery of such fundamental forces in all areas. We have made unsurpassed progress in every field of knowledge. Knowledge about human life has also found a new field of inquiry, which it designates with a familiar term—i.e. the concept of society, the elements of society and the dynamics of society . . .

Society is one of the most difficult concepts in political theory, not only because this concept is so general that it is hard to give it a specific meaning, but especially because one has got used to associating with this term a more or less precise meaning. This meaning was completely arbitrary, since there had hardly arisen an occasion which would have made us aware of the substance of this concept. Whoever speaks of a science of society—as one talks of political science or economic science— is not only obliged to define the term, but also to oppose the mass of vague conceptions about it and the general belief that anybody might be right and should be allowed to assume whatever he pleases. If society is just as real, just as universal and just as necessary as is the state, then it must be possible to accomplish for the former what is considered necessary for any more thorough analysis of the latter: a conceptualized knowledge about its essence and a clarification of the inner contradictions of the term. If social life is not an inorganic and accidental accumulation of experiences but an independent and unique form of human life, there must be a vantage point from which it may be understood so that the variety of its appearances may be grasped. This vantage point is given in the concept of society . . .

THE CONCEPT OF SOCIETY

The Community of Men and its Unity

The greatest contradiction in human affairs is that between the individual and his potential fulfillment. In every individual there is an invincible striving for complete control of the external circumstances of existence, and for maximum possession of knowledge and of material goods . . . But at the same time every individual is an infinitely limited being; his strength, his knowledge, even his time, barely suffice for the procurement of the basic necessities. He cannot even enjoy the pleasures his short life has to offer, still less do all the work that is required to gain them. His innermost nature aspires towards the best and the most beautiful, but what he alone can consider attainable during his own limited life is the measure of his poverty.

However, there is no such thing as an absolute contradiction, and the above sentences do not contain one. But the solution cannot be found in the sphere of the individual life. The limits of individual strength and individual life are transcended in the unlimited multitude of people, which possesses unbounded strength and unlimited time for the achievement of human goals. The increase in the number of people is the first requirement for the fulfillment of human aspirations. This multitude is in itself nothing but the simple aggregation of indivduals. Since every person is independent, the mere number of individuals is only an infinite multiplication of the contradiction between inner yearnings and physical strength, the endless repetition of individual poverty. If this multiplicity is to bring the individual closer to his fulfillment, another element must be added. The multiplicity has to be made useful to the individual . . . The solution for the limited individual lies in mutual interdependence, in the community of men . . .

The community, which exists for the sake of the individual personality,—which encompasses these personalities,—can only be understood in terms of the individual personality. The community can hardly be of a different nature than personality. On the contrary, in order to identify and fulfill its task, the community must itself be a living entity. Personal life is distinguished from impersonal and natural life by being self-determined; it bears within itself the need and the strength to set its goals and activities. The agent which carries out the goals set by self-determination is volition. The accomplished self-determination is action. Every personal life is a unity by virtue of its will-power. Whatever lacks will is without self-determination,—it is the natural, the thing. Only as a result of action does life appear to be a self-determined unity; things cannot act. If the community is independent of the existence of any one individual, and if the community possesses the essential attributes of personality, it must have an independent will which enables it to regard itself as an independent unity and to fulfill its self-set goal . . . Such a community, with an independent will, is what we call the state . . . The state is the personification of the community of men in terms of its will and action . . .

Any object controlled by a person's will has a twofold life. It serves and obeys the unity of the whole, yet it also exists according to its own laws. It is subordinate to the will of a person. Whenever this will relaxes, the object tends to reassert its own independent dynamics . . . Now, what is that object that is subordinate to the state but nevertheless retains its own motions? Clearly, since the state represents the personal community of men, this object is nothing but the independent life of all individuals. They are subjected to the will of the state whenever it becomes manifest; but the state cannot dissolve this independent life altogether, which, therefore, continues to develop and progress according to its own laws.

At this point, the concept of the community of men has to be revised. It is no longer identical with the concept of the state. The independent life of all individuals—the atoms and objects of the state's will, as it were,—is neither completely comprehended nor explained by the concept of the state. What, then, is the content of this second element of the community, and what are the rules and laws of its independent life?

The Organism of Economic Life

The life of each individual, built on the contradiction between his inner infinite strivings and the limitations of the external world, is a permanent struggle with this world . . . Labor is the regulated and purposeful activity of the person struggling with the material world and reshaping it for the satisfaction of his needs. Goods are the result of labor capable of satisfying our needs and serving our pleasures. In this sense, the life of all individuals consists of creating goods. Here the limitation of the person shows up most clearly. Nobody is able to produce all the necessary and desired goods by his own labor . . . Only the community of work and production can provide this wealth of goods. The aspirations of man therefore lead to the organization of work for the production of goods. At first glance, this organization may appear accidental and arbitrary from the viewpoint of the individual. But actually it is a phenomenon just as powerful as is the will of the state . . .

Every object transformed into a product by labor is *property,* and the essence of property is the exclusion of every individual from the possessions of other individuals . . . However, there is an element of transcendence in the concept of property: the demand of the individual for the product and for the work of other individuals. We need not prove here that property can never be fully utilized by its owner alone . . . The interaction of those who own and those who work is not mere co-existence, but rather a dependence of the activity of one group upon the possessions, the will, and the activity of the other. This mutual dependence, which is inherent in the nature of labor, is neither accidental nor arbitrary; it is independent of individual whims and is enforced by the nature of production. It is the organization of co-operative production, part of which has been termed the division of labor . . . This whole area of production and distribution of goods is most appropriately called the *economy.*

The economy has its basis in the fact that the realization of personal fulfillment in the outer world is only possible through the community of men. Political economy looks at the economy only from one point of view; it shows how the unity of men succeeds in controlling resources and in acquiring wealth . . .

The economy, however, is not restricted to the phenomena of wealth and poverty, nor to the laws according to which they change, nor to the organization of labor and possessions, which it presupposes as well as determines. The impact of the economy goes beyond that. Through the intimate relationship between property and personality, the economy affects the very core of individual life. Here a new series of phenomena can be observed.

The Order of the Human Community

. . . It is one of the most remarkable facts that natural objects which man puts to his service have almost as much influence on him as he has on them . . . How very much does the total outlook on life vary depending on differences in occupation! The farmer, the city dweller, the nomad, the laborer, the supervisor, the scholar, the artist—how very differently do they view the world. How very much do they differ in physical strength, in knowledge, and in the work which is done by each of them. And still—the individual behavior of each of these does not spring from his individuality but rather from the peculiarity of the goods to the production of which his life is dedicated. Here is a large and promising area of investigation. It is, no doubt, true that in general the specific function of a person in the economic system creates and conditions his particular personality.

. . . Also, the extent to which man owns property has a conditioning effect on the development of his personality. Greater wealth makes possible a higher degree of devolopment. It is true that powerful personalities will always offset this principle; but as a rule, the difference in possessions produces a difference in individual development . . .

The occupational role of the individual requires him to adjust his individuality to his work This makes him more suitable for his specific function but also less suitable for any other. He is, therefore, bound to his specific task; it is difficult, or even impossible, to change to another one, even though it may rank higher and be more rewarding. . . . The individual seems to be completely free to decide originally which way he wants to take; but the decision keeps him on the path on which he has started . . . He is no longer the master of his career; the career becomes his master. According to this law, thorough training subjugates the individual and determines his earning power; it eliminates his arbitrary freedom; it ties the free individual inescapably to the sphere determined by his work.

According to the laws of the economy, the various occupations are organic parts of a whole . . . Through his occupation the individual enters irrevocably into the economic order at a specific point; he cannot leave it at will. Thus the organization of economic life becomes the order of human community.

. . . As we have shown, everybody is dependent on the acquisition of goods for his personal development . . . Labor presupposses material . . . Everybody possesses his labor power, but the resources are limited. Those who own the material also control the economic opportunities for all those who do not have property. The latter—if they are to utilize their labor power—are dependent on material which is the property of somebody else, material which they cannot use without the consent of the owner. Therefore, all those who own nothing but their labor power are dependent on those who own property.

The order of the human community resulting from the laws of the economy is forever and unalterably also the order of the dependence of those who do not own upon those who do. These are the two large classes which necessarily evolve in the community. No historical movement or theory has been able to eliminate their existence . . .

The Concept of Society

. . . Property appears in a variety of forms. We distinguish three major classes: landed property, moneyed property and industrial property of fixed capital. Each of these classes is subdivided into different groups. Landed property can take the form of land proper, of the right to let on lease under various conditions, of house ownership which yields rent; moneyed property can take the form of unredeemable capital which merely yields rent, or be used as productive capital; industrial property consists of factories, machines, ships, warehouses, etc. . . . Since all these possessions have their common denominator in the value of money, the ranking of the possessions as well as of the owners is determined by the amount of value which the possessions have. The kind of property determines the individual life sphere, the amount determines the rank order of the owners.

In a similar fashion, there are many different types of work; and work has, to a greater extent than ownership, the power to shape the free individual according to its peculiarities. The concept of work contains two elments: the mental and the physical activity of man. Depending on which of these two elements prevails, we distinguish between free and mechanical work, the former being superior and more remunerative. Again, management of labor is an independent task, subordinating labor of all kinds. Thus, a rank order develops within the class which is dependent on work . . .

The mutual relationships of the classes and the various groups within the classes are in a constant flux, producing ever-changing conditions. The most important factor in these relationships is the relation of specific types of work to specific types of ownership. Work determines the life of the workers in the same way that the type and amount of ownership determines the life of the property owners. Therefore, the relationship of individuals of the unpropertied class to a specific kind of property also establishes a close relationship with its owner. The dependence of labor upon materials develops into a dependence of the worker upon the owner. Although the latter plays the dominant role, he is nevertheless also bound to the dependent worker, due to his needs. From an originally circumstantial relationship there eventually develops a basic relationship; new terms, new facts in the life of the community, and new concepts emerge. In the realm of landed property, this relationship is originally and externally that of master and servant—

the system of domestics and manorial dependents—a relationship which, because of the nature of the property, can only evolve on a landed estate and in domestic life. The intrinsic relationship which develops out of mutual dependence and service is one of loyalty and devotion; this lends a noble quality to the dependence. In the factory there is nothing of this kind, because here, instead of the personal lord who rules the servant, the general rigid organization of labor, which transcends individual arbitrariness, controls the worker. The situation is different again in business life, where the employed person is more of an assistant with limited authority than a servant. These distinct forms of social organization reflect the general principle of dependence of the non-owners on the owners . . .

The description and analysis of these forms of dependence open up a large field of study which is all the richer the less it has already been subject to investigation, and all the more important the deeper it reaches into personal life and the more irresistably it affects what is truly free, i.e. the human personality. There will be a time when this area of social reality will be considered worthy of the greatest scholarly effort. This time is approaching; its basis is the realization that the perfection of personality is the highest goal of man's life in this world.

If this order is stable and beyond arbitrary change because it grows out of the element of property and work reaching far beyond the individual, can one then assume that the individual is at least able to define his own position in this order in accordance with his desires and his individual tastes?

The answer is no. Closely interwoven with the order of society is another power whose source until now has been almost exclusively sought in the sphere of ethics and law . . . This power is the family. The family raises the children, and since the position of the family is determined by the husband's position, the children get the education which is made possible and, as it were, naturally determined by the position of the head of the family.

The family determines the position of the individual in the community. It is quite natural that a family is able to convey to its children only the kind of expectations which it holds itself. The condition of the family thus extends far beyond the life of its head; it controls the future of his descendants. Although some break through these limitations, the position and fate of a family are as a rule decisive for the families of its descendants. With few exceptions, the children of farmers become farmers again; the children of laborers become laborers; indeed, they even work in the same trade as their fathers. Only the exceptional and the lucky move from one class to another. However, the exceptional gifts are not less rare than the exceptional chance.

In this fashion the economic order becomes the order of men and of their activities: through the family it becomes the permanent order of subsequent generations. The community of men whose organic unity of will is expressed through the personality of the state achieves in that social order an equally stable, equally great, and equally powerful organic unity of its life; this organic unity, conditioned by the distribution of possessions, regulated by the organization of labor, set in motion through human needs, and bound to the family, is *human society*. All these elements originate in the concept of society. None of them separately can offer an explanation of human life, because none of them encompasses the whole individual and the whole of his life . . . It is only through the concept of society that the concepts and sciences of economics, of labor, of householding economy and of national economy, of the family and of law, gain their highest common perspective. Only here do they attain the highest point of this worldly life, i.e. the individual and the fulfillment of his destiny.

THE PRINCIPLES OF THE STATE AND OF SOCIETY

The Concept of the Life of the Community

After having defined the abstract concept of society, we may now look at the more general entity of which society is only a part . . .

The potentialities of the individual were our point of departure. They cannot be realized as long as the individual lives by himself. These potentialities, therefore, represent both the necessity and the essence of human community, which, in turn, has an existence independent of the individual .

As a precondition for the individual, containing and encompassing the individual, the community is itself a living personality. Unquestionably the community has a life of its own; unquestionably, its life affects the individual life with great and irresistible power. Everybody feels himself not only surrounded and steadied by this community, but also swept away by it when there is agitation, or restrained when the community is inactive. Nobody, no matter how powerful or indifferent, has been able to resist completely the vibrations of community life; in fact, community life is the light, air and soil for individual life. Like every great and general power, it is tacitly present at any point; it is irresistible because it presents the conditions for the attainment of almost any purpose . . .

Life is motion which in any given unit is brought about through the movement and countermovement of the personal and the non-personal. The former tries to subdue the latter, which in turn constantly tries to detach itself. The absolute victory of the personal, the complete destruction of the non-personal in the personality, is the one frontier of life; for this absolute domination of the purely personal, which is contradictory to the concept of mortal man, represents the existence of the Transcendent, the Deity. The victory of the natural means death. But life is movement between opposing poles. Therefore, life is a struggle, just as thought, which is the life of the mind, is for the same reason able to express itself only in terms of contrasts. The whole is the human community. What is the personal and the non-personal in this human community?

The personal, self-determining element in it is the state, the personal organism of the general will. The non-personal, which does not derive its organism and its movement from the general will, and which there-fore establishes a general and stable order on the basis of the natural components of life, is nothing else but society. State and society are essentially not only two different forms of human existence, but they are *the* two different life components of every human community.

Since life represents a constant struggle of the personal self-determin-ing element with the non-personal and the natural elements, the life of the human community is a permanent struggle between the state and society. If this is correct, a perfect and undisturbed harmony between state and society, a condition in which society is completely merged with the state, is as unattainable as the Divine. An absolute peace be-tween both is precluded by the very essence of life. And it is also certain that the complete dissolution of the personal in the unpersonal, the extinction of the idea of the state within the order of society, means the death of the community. The world does know death. There are no perfect nations, but there are dead nations. They are the ones which no longer have a state, i.e. those where the power of the state is com-pletely concentrated in the hands of society. The character of a nation's life emerges in the constant struggle between state and society . . . The past as well as the present is nothing else but this struggle. The near as well as the distant future will be nothing else but the constant struggle betwen the idea of the state and that of the social order . . .

But it is not sufficient to say that the state represents the personal element and society the non-personal element of the human community. Both are equally alive, both aim at something definite; does therefore each of them have a principle of its own which is opposed to the other? . . .

The Principle of the State

. . . The state is the common will, the personal unity of all individuals. . . . Since all individuals contribute towards the formation of the state's personality, their stage of development determines the stage of development of the state itself. The conclusion is obvious: the more intelligent the citizens who live in a state, the more intelligent is the state; the more wealthy they are, the wealthier is the state; the more vigorous the citizens, the more vigorous the state. If, however, the sum total of the citizens' intellectual, physical and material possessions declines, then the state will regress. Therefore the following highly important statement can be made, namely: that the degree of accomplishment of all individuals determines the developmental stage of the state . . .

In order to attain its own highest goals, the state, through its supreme power, must further the progress, wealth, vigor and intelligence of all its citizens. The state can only further itself by furthering the interests of its citizens . . . The basic principle of the state . . . is contained in the achievement of this task . . .

The state as an independent personality is above all an organism . . . The will of the state, like that of any personality, turns into a decision through deliberation; to execute its will the state possesses means of coercion which compel obedience . . . The active participation of the citizens in shaping the will of the state raises, more than anything else, the individual above the narrow limitations of his life. In fact, the full growth of the individual's strength and dignity depends upon it. If the state wants to achieve the highest development of all individuals in accordance with its set goals, it has to assure first of all the organic participation of its citizens in the affairs of the state.

This organization of individual participation in the organic life of the state, particularly in the formation and determination of the personal will of the state, is called the constitution of the state. The right of the individual to participate in the affairs of the state is his *civil liberty*. The principle which governs the state, therefore, presupposes for the realization of this principle first of all a constitution which addresses itself to every citizen and guarantees liberty to the individual. This is only one part of that principle . . .

The activity of the state, carried out by its organs and constituting the external life of the state, is called the administration of the state. Any state, no matter at which stage of development, has an administration . . . It must aim to promote by legitimate means the highest development of all citizens. The state administration exists in its purest, most ideal form if the life of *all* citizens is its exclusive concern. It will be less effective to the extent that the number and need of those who are neglected by the state rises; it will be more perfect the more it proves able to offer everybody the possibility of highest personal development. This is the other part of the principle of the state.

If it is correct that this principle of the state with its two contents, constitution and administration, is not arbitrarily adopted but inherent in the nature of the state, i.e., *a conditio sine qua non* for it, it follows that the state must strive for the realization of this principle. The state often acts contrary to this goal, apparently without intention, and often without knowing it .The individual state, however, can die. Death occurs when constitution and administration exist without regard to individual well-being, i.e., when the state exists only for its own sake. All absolute states succumb to this kind of death, quicker and more violently the more they disregard their task. As long as the higher goal of the state is manifest in any constitutional or administrative sphere, there is life and hope for its improvement. It is possible that, having disappeared altogether from the constitution, the purpose of the state continues to exist only in the administration. History knows many examples of this so-called enlightened despotism. But since constitution and administration are necessarily interconnected, there will either emerge from the administration a free constitution, as in the Germanic states, or the administration will also cease to exist. The idea of the state is alive whenever we can observe in the human community the unified striving of all, in constitution and administration, being directed towards this goal. And again, wherever the community, as a whole or in part, is looking for help, it turns necessarily to the state; it knows unconsciously that the commitment to its goal will cause the state to render help to those who are in need. For the state is adversely affected by the unsatisfied needs of its citizens and, any help given to them will benefit the state as well.

This may explain a phenomenon characteristic of the origin of the modern European states. Among the great variety of state forms, monarchy is the purest manifestation of the independent personal state. It has risen out of the need of the suppressed groups of various peoples; it has gained power everywhere by natural support of the people; and it has been most stable wherever it has used its power in accordance with the above idea of the state. It is jeopardized if it deviates from it; its past has rested on this principle, and its future will do so also . . .

On the basis of this principle, we may develop a complete, harmonious idea of the state. It is not difficult to devise the ideal of a perfect constitution and the design for a truly good administration. But why then does any state rarely succeed in realizing these ideals? What is it that makes a state use power for the opposite ends; what arrests it when it should progress? Clearly if this happens, it cannot be caused by the state. If the state operated exclusively in accordance with its nature, it could not possibly act against it. There is something within the state operating against it. This something is *society*. Does society adhere to a different principle of existence than the state? If so, what is this principle?

The Principle of Society

For centuries, many great men have tried to formulate the principle of the state, but nobody thought of the possibility that there might also exist a principle of society. And yet it does . . .

The organism of society, too, like that of the state, grows out of the need of the individual personality; it too serves the individual's full and harmonious personal development. However, while the state integrates, for this purpose, individuals into a personal unit, society subordinates individuals to other individuals . . . Therefore, in society the *relationship of individuals* is the basis of all development.

Since a single person can accomplish very little to attain his goals, he has to use other persons for his own purposes. The more others obey and carry out the will of an individual, the more wealthy, powerful and happy that individual is . . . There is, therefore, a general human tendency to attempt to subject others to one's service. The dependence which this service presupposes, the subjugation of one personal life to another one, is based on the *possession of the means* by which one person can force another into subordination . . . Acquisition of means which results in dependence of others, becomes, therefore, the necessary and unavoidable life task of each individual; this is not an accidental and arbitrary occurrence, for the highest ideal of individuality is realized by these means and the resultant dependence of others.

In this fashion, acquisition, possession and dependence, which turn a community into a society, gain their real significance. They are no longer mere facts but elements of personal development; society is not merely an order of persons, but it is an order which also represents the various stages of social development among men. Thus it becomes apparent why society and the organization of society is necessary and why the individual untiringly seeks to achieve a higher position in society. This apparently external position determines the *degree of individual perfection.*

The efforts by which the means of one's own independence and those of the dependence of others are acquired, directs the life of everybody in all societies. It is the moving force in society. It is, of course, of infinite variety for different people under different conditions. . . . It is essentially identical in all societies because everywhere it serves to procure, for the individual, the means for personal perfection through the dependence of others. The awareness of this which regulates all outward activity, which is always present and alive in every individual, determining his social position, is called *interest.* Interest, which is the center of all human interaction and therefore of all social motion, is *the principle of society.*

Dependence based on the distribution of wealth determines the concrete form of a society; interest is society's dynamic principle . . . The interests of those on whom, because of their property, others are dependent are directly opposed to the interests of the dependent. This first class of society wants to enlarge and strengthen the system of dependence; the others want to abolish it. This is the general character of any society; its specific features are determined by the conditions which regulate the distribution of property and the relationship of dependency. If the property is real estate, the interest of the owner is to leave the property intact and undivided, while the non-owner wants to parcel it out and acquire it for himself. If property is in the form of capital, the interest of the owner aims at appropriating the whole investment value and therewith the whole return of capital, while the non-capitalist demands freedom from the domination of capital in earning his wages. If property is industrial, the owner wishes the profit to go only to the management, while the laborer strives at gaining a profit share beyond his mere wage. If all three kinds of property are present, one type is opposed to the other; the landowner does not want to be dependent upon the capital owner and vice versa; the same is true of the relation between capitalist and entrepreneur. Within the same class, the interest of large property is adverse to the small property holder, because the former always wants to force the latter into dependency. The more intimately the types of property and acquisition permeate each other, the more diversified and involved become the various interests, and the more difficult it becomes to describe them in simple terms . . . This interrelationship of interests, however, can be subjected to a clear, comprehensive and systematic analysis; it is the primary subject matter of the science of society. This is the much-sought basis of the science designated to absorb, in the near future, all areas of the so-called "sciences of the state" (*Staatswissenschaften*) . . .

We have stated that the principle of the state consists of elevating all individuals to complete freedom and to their fullest personal development. Furthermore, we have shown that the principle of society consists of the subjugation of some individuals by others, the perfection of some through the dependence of others. What follows?

Decidedly this: that the principle of the state is in direct contradiction to the principle of society. It is true, as we stated earlier in general terms, that two opposite poles, repelling each other and fighting against each other, are present in any human community; it is true that these two poles—state and society—determine the life of the human community precisely because they are opposed to each other. It follows that social life can only be understood by comprehending the nature and the strength of these two elements . . . Both elements are rooted in the principle of the individual; therefore, they determine each other and belong together; their actions, though contradictory, are yet regulated by a common higher principle. This struggle between them produces a movement regulated by definite and intelligible laws.

Since the contrast between state and society determines the life of the human community, these laws are the general laws of the life of the human community. They will determine the future as they have ruled the past. They represent the realm of necessity within the freedom of social life; they are the eternal matrix according to which mankind has to move . . .

ORIGIN AND CONCEPT OF SOCIAL DEPENDENCE

The Initial Source of Dependence

. . . We speak here of the pure concept of the state in the sense in which it is a realization of the ethical idea . . .

The ideal concept of the state encompasses the multitude of individual personalities, without making any distinction between them. Within the conceptual framework of the state all individuals are equal and free. But the totality of members of a state for whom this principle of liberty is valid are the very same persons who constitute the social order of the community. The development of this concept, and the description of the actual society, show that the members of a multitude can neither be conceived of as being equal nor are they equal in fact. The existence of a ruling and a dependent class is the most general and unalterable fact in any society. Since every state contains a society, the contradiction between state and society is ever present. Every state reflects this contradiction. Every state is affected by it and has to combat it. The state is confronted with the question of the interdependent relationship between itself and the elements of society.

Since wealth, power and fortune of the state depend on the well-being of its citizens, the position of the ruling class, considered inde-pendently, is in complete harmony with the idea of the state. The state necessarily wishes that this class should exist; it must protect and preserve its members, since through them the ideal environmental conditions for the development of the individual are provided. But the position of the dependent class definitely contradicts the idea of the state for exactly the same reasons . . . The full development of the state is impossible if thousands of people will never be able to develop their individual gifts. The state, therefore, has to eliminate the existence of the dependent class; the existence of that class, not the existence of society as such, is contradictory to the aims implied in the concept of the state.

The state as a living entity conscious of its task has the will and the strength to work towards an elimination of this contradiction. In principle, the road to be pursued is simple. We have seen that realization of the principle of the state is accomplished by the constitution and by the administration. To alleviate the dependence of the lower classes, the state will, in the first place, guarantee by the constitution the equality of all citizens under the public laws. This will become the supreme principle of the law; in the sphere of administration its first concern will be to raise the status of the lower classes . . .

However, since the existence of the social order depends on the preservation of dependency, any step in this direction is contrary to the established social order, in particular to the social position of the ruling class. The state moves into a direction opposite to that of the ruling class; such a conflict reflects the contradiction between the principle of the state and the principle of society. For the ruling class stands to lose its power position and the many enjoyments resulting from it if the endeavors of the state succeed. The ruling class, being the more wealthy class, even has to provide the material means to improve the lot of the lower classes, thereby curtailing its own advantages. The ruling class, therefore, is by its very nature the true adversary of the ideal state, which threatens its existence . . .

The consequence of this peculiar conflict can be clearly stated in one sentence: Since the higher class of society is unable to change the state, or to eliminate the state altogether, or to resist its power, it aims if possible at taking exclusive control of governmental power. This is the first natural law of all relationships between state and society.

How the Ruling Class Gains Control of the State

. . . If it is true that it is in the interest of the ruling class of society to take possession of the state, the question arises whether the state has the means to defend itself against the power of this class, and, if not, in which manner state power is seized by the upper class . . .

To begin with, the state is . . . merely a fictional concept; its existence is only abstract . . . It does not possess a concrete form; there is nothing that would represent it exclusively . . . To the individual, it only appears necessary to have a state . . . To become real, the state needs the individuals; it depends on the individuals to develop its organs. These individuals, however, are all members of society; and it is society which determines their individual positions. Since the state has to transfer decision-making and executive power to the individuals, social life is inextricably interwoven with the life of the state. The individuals, by participating in the life of the state, project their social claims, hopes and opinions into the constitution and the administration. Therefore, the true concept of the state never fully evolves, because the spirit and the mode of operation of the actual state is thoroughly permeated by social elements . . . The state is unable to exist apart from society; it cannot escape the elements which determine the social order, because it is represented by persons who occupy, independently of the state, different positions in the class structure of society. The state loses all independent power to act in opposition to the ruling class, due to the unavoidable fusion of state and society. Although in theory the state is the governing power, in reality it is subordinate to society. If this general statement is correct, the frequently proclaimed demand that the state alone ought to resolve the conflict and remodel society is therefore pointless. The struggle between liberty and dependence is rooted in society, and society becomes the true fountainhead of liberty and dependence. . . .

The ruling class captures the state by organizing and securing a dominant position in the constitution and the administration . . . If the will of the state is to be subjected to society, the constitution has to be set up in such a fashion that the dependent class does not participate in the formulation of state policy, or in such a way that the wishes of the upper class prevail . . . This can be accomplished by establishing prerequisites for participation which only the upper class is able to fulfill . . . The first and most logical qualification is one of property. This is most clearly seen in the so-called property qualifications. All constitutions therefore start out and end up with property qualifications, the more so the more the constitution is socially conditioned . . . It may be a specific kind of property; it may be a specifically privileged property; it may be a specific level of education which is made a prerequisite for participation in state activities . . . The differentiation of property constitutes the essential difference among various constitutions . . . If a specific kind or a specific amount of property distinguishes the ruling from the dependent class, then only those who own this type or amount of property will be entitled to political participation. To illustrate this principle, we may mention the feudal system, where only a privileged type of landowner-ship entitled the aristocracy to representation . . .

The second sphere of state life is the administration, which comprises more than the constitution . . . Administrative functions are performed by permanent organs of the state; they act in the name of the state, and command the whole power and authority of the state for all their actions . . . Within circumscribed limits, they possess complete freedom and the entire right of the state to decide upon the application of the general rule to specific cases. Therefore, their power is great; in fact, as a whole, administrative power is the greatest power in the human community. These state organs are designated by the term of public office . . . If the ruling class wants to control state administration, it has to control public offices.

In general, this is accomplished by making the conferring of office dependent on personal qualifications which only the members of the ruling class possess and on which the ruling classes decide. However, the ruling class seldom stops at that. The rules for holding office grow out of the interest of the class as a whole, but at the same time this interest is the individual interest of each member of that class. Once class rule is secured, the individual interest predominates; and the filling of offices is subject to distinctly personal conditions, such as kinship, wealth, influence or connections. In this manner the ruling class obtains control of the organs of state administration . . .

The administration therewith loses the power to represent the true conception of the state independent of the influence of the social order. By obeying the legislation which is under the control of the ruling class, the state administration, dominated by members of this same class and surrounded by its elements, serves generally and specifically their interest. This completes the explanation of our original assertion that the whole power of the state in all its parts and relationships does not fall to society in general, nor to the people as such, but to the ruling class of society . . .

The Actual Development of Social Domination, Class, Social Privilege, Estate and Caste

. . . Since both the constitution and administration of the state are controlled by the ruling class, legislation and law enforcement are carried out in the interest of the ruling class, which, through its dominating social position, also becomes the repository of political power. This means that in the constitution and administration, state authority is always applied to preserve and promote those social conditions on which rest the dominating position of the ruling class and the dependence of the dependent class . . . The dependence of one class on another rests on property, and all property is acquired. Acquisition of property, inasmuch as it is open to members of the dependent class, will endanger the stability of the ruling class and its control over the state. In order to maintain the status quo of the social order, those who do not own property have to be excluded from acquiring it. This is accomplished by the law which sets up the principle of inalienability and indivisibility of landed property, or by limiting the sale and inheritance of land to members of the ruling class. Thus, the property-holding class always becomes dominant, although domination takes a variety of forms: primogeniture, entailed estate (*Fideikommiss*) and other such institutions.

However, one kind of property can still be acquired, e.g. the accumulation of capital invested in all kinds of enterprises. All labor is directed towards the acquisition of capital. The simplest preventive measure is to restrict acquisition and to legally exclude the members of the dependent class, as is the practice of the craft guilds, corporations, the holders of franchises, of monopolies, etc. However, if free enterprise prevails, other safeguards develop. It is a well-known economic principle that capital can be gained from work only through profit. It is profit which capital-owners need in order to perpetuate their rule over labor, and it is this same profit that labor wants to acquire in order to break down the barriers between labor and ownership. This is the point at which state administration regulates economic life in order to preserve the existing social order by state authority. It subjects the laborer to the control of the employer, and declares the attempts of the laborers to gain a share of the profit by withholding their labor as unlawful. This results in the policing of labor, which is as powerful and important a weapon against labor as are the laws of guilds and monopolies.

These two factors are the first to reveal the character of the domination of the more powerful social class over the state. We can express them in the concept of social right (*Gesellschaftliches Recht.*) Grown out of the nature and the needs of society, social rights (or socially conditioned privileges) provide a stable system of stratification and prevent social mobility. The study of social rights, which play such an important role in the life of all people, has not yet found its place in science. If we learn to understand the character of society, social rights will eventually be assigned their proper place.

Since social privileges develop as a result of the control which the ruling class exercises over state administration, the extent of these privileges is an indicator of the amount of power which that class holds. The more powerful the ruling class and the more pronounced its privileges, the more rigidly they will be used, since they are the ones which protect the dominant position of the ruling class. The longer this domination lasts the more elaborate the privileges will be . . . The social system of legal privileges is the measure of the power a single class possesses over the state. It is therefore an important concern of our times to analyze this social system of legal privileges as a separate entity.

After the autonomy and domination of the ruling class are secured, a new concept of the family and the right of the family evolves. Families transfer their social position to their descendants; in all societies birth is the fact which ties family members to a class. The resolute domination of the upper class aims at deriving a right from this fact by tying the individual, independent of the material circumstances, and solely on the basis of family and birth, to his class. This is what happens long before it becomes a law. But only through the law does birth cease to be accidental. Thus the principle develops that birth separates the classes and that acquisition and property only determine the subdivisions within the classes. If this is legitimized by the state, the class changes into an *estate*. Through the law, the estate bestows certain privileges or disadvantages on the person, without regard to other social conditions, exclusively on the basis of birth. Social rights and privileges culminate in the rights and privileges of the estate (*Ständerecht*), which sets absolute boundaries to the activities of the individual. . . . The state now interposes itself between the individual and his attempt to achieve a higher social position. The order of society, guaranteed by estate right, becomes fixed; the rule of the upper estate is absolutely secure. In this way its natural inclination to control the state, in order to prevent it from exercising its function of raising the lower classes, has succeeded.

. . . Even though the rule of the higher classes is thus securely established, a change in the situation and a consequent suspension of their rights are still conceivable. If the rule of the upper class is to be invulnerable, it has to be attributed to a factor beyond human control. Here arises a conception by means of which the domination of the higher class reaches its summit. The state, as the highest manifestation of personality, the supreme power, absolutely independent of the individual, necessarily self-creating and a compelling force, develops the quality of the sacred and the inviolable. Society accepts the state as its superior and submits itself to it. Since the ruling class identifies itself with the state, it soon claims the idea of holiness, inviolability, and divine authority for itself and for its privileges. The position of the ruling class is such that an attack on it necessarily entails an attack on the constitution and administration of the state. It attaches to its politically entrenched position the reverence which is due to the state as such. The specific social form of the state becomes identified with the idea of the state itself; and since this form of the state represents the social position of the classes, the class pattern itself also comes to be interpreted as the divine order of human affairs. In this way, the domination of the class comes to transcend mere estate rights; it becomes a sacred privilege, and any attempt to destroy the social differences within society becomes a crime against the deity. At this point, the estate system based on legal rights ceases to exist; the social differences decreed in the name of the deity and divine laws become sacred, and the thus-sanctified classes become *castes*. Castes, and the institution of caste in general, signify the final and absolute victory of society over the state. The caste state entails absolute identification, not only of state power and state laws, but also of the idea of the state, with the status system of society. Such a society can be described as the absolute society . . .

It is not by chance that a dominant class develops suitable privileges, that the class thus privileged becomes an estate, and that the estate tends to become a caste, because this development is inherent in the nature of class relations . . . This is a general law of social development within the state; . . . it gains practical interest if one observes its operation under the specific conditions of any one society . . . Because it encompasses the whole of history, it never exhausts itself suddenly in a single generation. Just as the life of nature needs centuries to proceed from one state to another in slight transitions, . . . so the life of society moves towards its irrevocable goal in a grandiose, quiet pace of thousands of small, untiringly repeated attempts, formations, repetitions, deviations—but always with unshakable consistency. The infinite wisdom of divine guidance has ordered conditions in such a way that only a few of the great movements which make up history affect the sphere of the individual. A change in the social order is never so sudden that it is accomplished in one generation. Its preparation goes back to other generations, and its completion requires new generations. Therefore, the individual experiences only a small part of the processes taking place . . . And for this very reason the thought, the will and the action of the individual are powerless against this movement. How negligible compared to this law appears the power of those who want to accelerate the life of their times by sheer intellectual endeavors or of those who want to stop or guide it by the power of arms . . . But what can be done, if this law is known, is to detect its traces in individual events . . . As in every practical science, so here also it is of great importance to perceive the various manifestations of that law of human dependence. A new field of investigation opens up here for the science of society, which includes the history of society. The first principle which determines this history is the following: there is a tendency that class systems create social rights and privileges, that these rights and privileges foster the development of estates which eventually harden into castes. It may happen that all the four elements—class, social rights and privileges, estates and castes— fully or only partially developed, exist simultaneously within a social order, as in contemporary European society . . . There are still mere classes, such as owners and non-owners; and there are social rights such as guilds rights, prerogatives and special rights of land ownership; there are estates, based on the distinction between the aristocracy and the commoners; there are traces of the caste system in the priesthood of the Catholic Church. All these parts of society strive towards the same goal, but each attempts only to reach the level directly above it. Those who merely own property want specific social rights; those who have some of them want more, wish to stabilize them, and to make them more profitable. If they are satisfied with what they have, they attempt to secure the same for their children; and they want to display their safe position by some kind of distinction, so that an estate comes into being. Those who are members of an estate aspire to raise the rights of the estate over and above the will of the legislating state, to establish status differences as an eternal law of nature, as the true basis of any social order and as the divine rule of human affairs, so that they are elevated to a caste. Those who have reached a caste-like position want, as the medieval Catholic Church, to subordinate the state to the church; or, as the new Catholic Church, they want the complete separation of church and state in order to establish a clerical order beyond all other powers and elements of state and society. All these developments are taking place in Europe today; therefore the life of European society today is so infinitely varied, so restlessly fluctuating . . . The immaturity of our science still conceals how much there is to learn, to describe, and to analyze . . . In spite of their endless variety, the lives of the people can be comprehended on the basis of the law that we have established: the movement of every social order is a development towards social dependence in different stages as indicated above . . .

The Concept of Social Dependence

. . . Until now it was not possible to search for the reasons of this dependence, because the concept of society itself had not yet been developed.

If the state is the supreme manifestation of the idea of personality, and if the state is willing to perform its vital function, (i.e. those of furthering the highest possible development of the individual,) then the state by its very nature is free. Freedom, which is the highest level of individual self-determination, is also the first principle of the state; the state by definition cannot be dependent. The concept of the ideal state precludes dependence . . . In reality, however, an essentially different situation develops, because society is the state's "body" and attempts to use the state's power for its own purposes. The dynamic principle of society, and of all social classes, is interest, which aims at preserving or improving one's established social position. Every superior social position is based on the dependency of others. Interest always expresses itself by establishing, securing and increasing the extent to which others become dependent on oneself. Whoever is dependent has to serve through his work and to hand over what he earns to whomever he serves. Dependency deprives the dependent person of personal independence and of freedom. This functioning principle of society, by rendering one class free and independent, subjugates the other. The ruling class deforms the state by taking possession of it, by developing privileges, estates and castes, and by using the constitution and administration of the state for its own ends. Through this process, the state develops traits which contradict its own higher idea. The state justifies and protects subjugation of one class by another, while its true nature requires the opposite. The state thus becomes the servant of a power which is basically opposed to the state's own ends . . . The state thus sanctifies by law what, according to the original idea of the state, it should condemn: the rule of one part of society over another, the rule of interests over the unlimited potentialities of the development of the free personality. As a consequence, the state itself becomes dependent.

This now is the concept of dependency. Dependency develops if the state is forced to serve a special social interest. Legal dependency prevails if the state changes a specific privilege which, without state authorization, is a mere social fact and subject to free attack, into an irrevocable right. Political dependency develops when one class of society has the exclusive power within the state . . . It is now clear where this dependence lies and how it comes into being. It has its roots in the system of social dependency. This originally natural dependence develops into *Unfreiheit* as soon as the state accepts it as a constitutional principle. All confusion about independence and dependence does not originate with the state, but with society and its relation to the state. A clear conception of true independence and dependence, and of the means to combat the latter, begins to evolve with the acceptance of the principle . . . that the actual constitution is a consequence of the social order within the organism of the state.

If this is so, then it is true that *Unfreiheit* is a necessary and inevitable feature in the community of men. Society is based on it, and the constitution is based on society . . . In reality there is no constitution without some elements and some degree of dependence which is recognized by the state. This is the true meaning of Rousseau's statement that the Republic is only fit for the Gods. The ideal republic is impossible; the constitution guaranteeing absolute freedom can never be actualized in real life, because it is always based on a society; in turn, society is based on dependence and the struggle of the ruling class for the exclusive control of the state. The life of the human community consists of a continuous movement and perennial struggle for dominance and for liberation . . .

The dominance of the ruling class is not in contradiction with the right of personal development . . . The position, the power and enjoyment which it entails is the goal of all men. By striving for it and by holding his own, the individual obviously acts in harmony with his own life task and with the basic laws of human nature. He is, therefore, morally justified in making the pursuit of his ambitions and the defense of his possessions the major endeavor of his social life. This is the element of freedom in the midst of dependency . . .

It is worthwhile to realize this clearly, most of all for those who suffer through it. Usually there is an inclination to reproach the powerful and the privileged for being callous, to interpret the frequently extreme defensive measures they employ to defend their status and property, by virtue of the given social order, as a crime against humanity, . . . a defiance of what is noble and lofty, a declaration of war upon freedom. But how is it possible to accuse—on behalf of an ideal—somebody who has succeeded in realizing it for himself? . . . The upper class defends for itself the accomplishments which are everybody's goal but which only the few have attained . . . As long as their superior position is a result of personal merit, a consequence of personal labor, it is also in harmony with human fulfillment and human rights. The submission and the dependence of the lower classes is a default in the development of humanity, . . . but it is not a contradiction to the superior position of the privileged. The contradiction develops only when the upper class uses its power to exclude the lower from the acquisition of possessions through which individuals might be able to join the upper class as equals. Only the imposition of such restrictions and legal privileges of all kinds gives rise to that discord in the community . . . The mere existence of classes in society is an inevitable fact, determined by the limitations of the individual and the character of property; this fact contradicts the idea of personal fulfillment, but it can be resolved through labor. The true and absolute contradiction to the idea of personal fulfillment arises when the relationship between the classes becomes legally fixed in the form of special privileges, estate, and caste, by the state which is controlled by the ruling class, and when the work of the striving individual cannot change this relationship because it has been made inviolable by the state. This is where true dependence begins . . .

If this really does happen, if the ruling class is able to usurp the supreme power of the state, to prohibit the upward mobility of the lower class by legal restrictions, how is it nevertheless possible that there exists a movement toward freedom? . . .

THE PRINCIPLE AND THE DEVELOPMENT
OF SOCIAL INDEPENDENCE

The Point of Departure

. . . Most people feel . . . that the state, in accordance with the idea of the state, is the representative of independence and that its constitution, precisely because it is dependent on society, is the expression of liberty. They usually demand that the state as such gains independence entirely by its own power and guarantees it by the constitution. This expectation is the result of a grave error which presumes that the state as such is able to resist the impact and the demands of society.

We have already described the true relationship between state and society. It is positively certain that the state as such lacks this ability . . . because it has no existence apart from society. Each of its citizens, as well as each of its servants, belongs by birth, education and the social opportunities open to him to a definite stratum of society . . . The will of the state is personified by people whose lives are anchored outside the state, i.e. in society. The actions of the state are directed by the same persons who have a personal interest in using the state for the benefit of their class; the state does not have one single organ which it can call exlusively its own . . . The state is powerless to escape the domination of society; once subjected to it, it is even less capable of preserving the principle of liberty over that of social dependence. This has to be stated particularly for the benefit of a well known party . . . which still perserves the hope that the victory of freedom could be gained and secured solely through a constitution reflecting the pure idea of the state. This is not much else but the belief that the state has the power to overcome social dependence by an act of will. The party which holds this opinion is the democratic party . . . It is right in the abstractly correct interpretation of the idea of the state; it is wrong in its complete misinterpretation of the nature and the power of society . . . However, this party will change as soon as it preceives the weakness of the idea of the state in relation to the order of society . . . If the state can not help itself, and if society can not be free according to its own principles, the possibility of true progress has to rest in a force which transcends both and is more powerful than both.

There can be no doubt that this higher element comprises both phenomena; they are both conceptually implicit in the nature of the personality . . . The pursuit of the true goals of the personality resulted in multiplicity which became unified in the state and ordered in society. It is possible to look at the state and society in a variety of ways, but they can be envisioned only as a condition of individual development. As long as they serve this goal they fulfill the true purpose of their existence; otherwise they are in contradiction to the higher purposes for whose sake they, as it were, existed. In this case, it is only this higher force which can compel them to serve again their proper purpose. The personality and its fulfillment, therefore, is the factor which—more powerful than state and society—renders them both serviceable to social independence. We have now reached the second major problem of the theory of the movement of society and state: that of the progress of liberty as it asserts itself against the perpetuation of social dependence . . .

The following will be more comprehensible if we first discuss the three principles of the movement towards liberty. Since social dependence is due to the very nature of the social order, and since the social order is more powerful than the state, it follows that the movement towards independence has to begin and has to run its course not in the area of public life but *in the area of the social order*. This is the first principle of the history of social independence within society. Second, since the social order determines and governs the order of the state, it follows that a *change of the constitution and of all social rights* has to take place, once the social order has been transformed by the effort of the individuals in the direction of securing more social independence. This can happen in two ways: either through *reform* or through *revolution*; each has its specific features and each takes its specific course . . . Third, since the state, according to the idea of the state, represents the principle of freedom, the change always begins with the growing interest of the more liberal elements of society in the idea of the state and in a *development of new theories of the state*. For the same reason, the change is accomplished only after these more liberal elements of society have succeeded in producing a new constitution.

These are the three principles in terms of which the movement towards liberty struggles against the trend towards social dependence. The following chapters will give a detailed analysis of each of these principles.

The Basis of All Movements Toward Social Independence

The inevitable fact that the ruling class takes possession of the state is the basis of all social dependence. Obviously, if this social domination were nothing but a force external to the personality, it could accomplish very little against the physical power of dependent individuals, still less against its own inner contradiction. The permanence of this domination in a variety of forms, its recurrence after it has been broken temporarily, and its tacit acceptance by the masses of the people indicate that it is not merely an external force but is inherently justified. The true nature of the state constitution, as determined by the social order and the social movement, cannot possibly be understood as long as the dependent class does not have the courage to acknowledge the inherent truth of this domination and the ruling class does not have the strength to recognize the extent of this domination . . .

To develop its plans, to deliberate upon decisions and to realize its will, the state requires the best, the most intelligent, and the strongest personalities for its service. The excellence of all state action depends to a much greater extent upon the person who is appointed to carry out decisions than upon the decisions and rules as such. Able men have always remedied inadequate conditions, and incompetent men often spoiled good ones . . . The state always tends to choose its representatives and officials from the ranks of the socially superior class. Membership in this class thus becomes the prerequisite for the participation of its members in state activities . . . This fact in itself does not create the dependence of the state. The lower class would never complain that the superior members of the higher strata are invested with authority in public affairs; and, even if it did complain, it would remain powerless against this fact.

Many people believe that the rule of the haves over the have-nots is based on the material power of the former. It is assumed that the dependence of the latter would cease as soon as the former lose their power—as if the social order would depend exclusively on the external position of those who profit by it. This interpretation is altogether false. The material superiority of the property-owners is not the *cause* but only the *consequence* of the power inherent in ownership. It is property in the first place which endows the individual with superior firmness, a keener perception and personal excellence that places the members of the property-owning class above the individuals who have no property . . . Second, property makes the non-owners serviceable to the owners, who pay them wages, hold out prospects for a rising income, and generally multiply the number of the members of this class. Since both these phenomena are consequences of property relations, it is clear that property is not so much dependent on power as that power is the outgrowth of property rights . . . If it is true that not only social domination but also participation in affairs of state is unalterably dependent on the nature and the distribution of wealth, it follows that any change in the social order, any abolition of the political dependence of the ruled, is impossible unless it is based on acquisition of property which alone is the true foundation of freedom.

Since the abstract concept of the personality presupposes such liberty, it is natural to derive from this concept the demand to abolish any form of social dependence . . . However, all ideas of liberty and equality which rest on nothing but this concept have proven to be of temporary importance only . . . The reality of a social order—and also any change in this order—cannot be influenced by a mere concept, . . . but it is also true that social conditions cannot be changed by external power alone; the most that the greatest power can accomplish is a forceful change in the membership of one or the other class. It is conceivable that the physical power of the lower class is momentarily great enough to seize all property by sheer force. But it is impossible for the lower class to eliminate the domination and dependence which are inevitably tied to property . . . If a genuine elevation of the hitherto dependent class to social independence and political liberty is to take place, it has to be preceded by the acquisition of that property which alone provides the necessary conditions for this rise. As long as this has not happened, any endeavor to change the existing order, no matter how contradictory to the idea of personality, is either a social or political utopia or a crime. Neither law nor force will make the dependent class free unless the dependent class has already created the preconditions of its independence for itself . . .

The only method, therefore, of accomplishing this change peacefully and permanently is to create opportunities for the lower class to acquire possessions. This statement—as simple and incontestable as it is—has been very frequently rejected. It has been more common to help the lower class by giving it political rights without securing its social independence . . . To do so, however, is to try the impossible and the untenable . . . Another fact has often not been explained because it would have revealed the fallacy of this approach. The propertied classes always know, if not by reflection, then by intuition, that their independence truly rests on their tangible and intangible possessions. The demand of abstract theorists who want to give liberty to all people without concern for this prerequisite, therefore, comes into conflict with the more enlightened members of the ruling class. The latter are practically compelled to take a stand against liberal movements which fail to hold any promise for the future. This awareness of the inherent impossibility of directly granting freedom to the masses, who do not possess the prerequisites, easily develops into an aversion against liberty in general . . . This attitude is called moderation and prudence; in a political context it is identical with careful consideration of the material and spiritual conditions of liberty . . .

Since the social order is the precondition of freedom, and since all development toward political liberty presupposes certain social development, the true history of society, as well as of liberty and of the state, is essentially the history of the distribution and the growth of the products of society among the lower class. This is an area of investigation not yet touched by historical research . . .

The Preconditions for the Development of Social Independence

Freedom is the self-determination of the personality in the intellectual realm as well as in that of the material world. It posits the individual's domination over the sphere of intellectual as well as material goods.

We call the possession of intellectual goods education (*Bildung*). Just as the spiritual determines the material, education is the first absolute presupposition of the rule of a social class. Therefore, the first condition for the elevation of the dependent class is the acquisition of education. On the other hand, a genuine education represents the first precondition for the granting of social independence to the subjects. To these general and incontestable statements either too much or too little attention has been paid. On the one hand, it was believed that education could solve the whole problem of social dependence; on the other hand, the inner relationship between education and the unfolding of the principles of society and its growing wealth was not sufficiently understood. . . . Every education, as the possession of intellectual goods, of knowledge and capabilities, is, to begin with, of importance primarily to the individual. But the individual has his place in the established order of society. This order is imposed from the outside in that it determines and dominates the individual. Acquiring an education is, as an internal process, to a certain extent independent of the social order. Intellectual goods are unlimited; everybody may acquire them without thereby restricting his fellowmen. In the realm of education, there exists the possibility of improving the condition of the dependent class without giving rise to contradictions in the social order, which, therefore, does not resist it. The spread of education necessarily constitutes a beginning of the development of freedom. When the lower class strives for education, the first element of the movement towards freedom is already present. Wherever this striving for education becomes articulate, the first stage of the struggle of the dependent against the ruling class has already begun. Where state or society promote the education of the population at large, it is safe to assert that state and society— whether or not liberty prevails—envisage liberty as the final goal. The promotion of education, therefore, is the invariable characteristic of free people . . .

The assumption of an equal ability for acquiring an education reflects the doctrine of human equality. Popular education inevitably reaches a point where, reflecting on the person's ability to be educated, it articulates the theoretical equality of men as the principle from which the movement of the lower classes arises. The principle of human equality, criticized as often as it is praised, is a natural phase in the development of popular education in opposition to the social order . . . By establishing the principle of intellectual equality for all individuals, a direct contradiction arises to the established order of society, which embodies domination, dependence, and therefore also inequality. The moment at which the principle of equality appears is the historical moment at which the idea of liberty emerges as an antithesis to the social order. "Equality" becomes the slogan of the dependent classes striving for liberty. What type of social order is affected is irrelevant; but the establishment of the principle marks the beginning of the movement toward liberation. In this fashion the dependent class acquires and becomes aware of non-material possessions. This effort is not transitory; it is permanent and repeats itself continuously. But, alone, it is as powerless over the positive order of society and social laws as is mere thought over nature. To bring about change in the external world, this effort has to lead to a struggle for the tangible goods.

External material possessions are the products of raw material and labor. Labor is the mechanical activity of the individual in the process of applying knowledge and ability. Labor, therefore, will be better and more valuable, the greater the knowledge and the capabilities of the individual are. These, in turn, are the content of education. Thus, education is not merely the possession of knowledge but is also indispensible for the acquisition of material goods. To control nature by the power of reason is the goal of men; the function of popular education, therefore, is to facilitate the acquisition of material goods. The higher the level of education of the whole population or of parts of the population, the more determined will the population be to either acquire or demand the rights for the acquisition of material goods. Any nation whose populace is well educated will always and of necessity display an irresistible drive toward material well-being. . . . This is the point at which, as it were, the living mind enters the material world. . . . Without this turning of the mind towards acquisition, all science remains powerless and—like anything which is one-sided—does more harm than good. An education without practical application does not serve its proper purpose. . . . Where, however, education permeates the productive activity of man and raises its intellectual qualities, the third stage of the movement toward liberation begins. We will call it the material stage.

Wherever education leads to a growing interest in the acquisition of goods, two possibilities of social development are open. One of these possibilities is that the total amount of resources available is large enough to give everybody his share in accordance with his personal intellectual development, while the economic institutions and conditions would, at the same time, allow for a fair amount of acquisitions to be made by the individual. The other possibility is that the total amount of resources is already distributed, and that the conditions, although allowing for and even favoring education, render the acquisition of possessions or a surplus of acquisitions beyond the level of mere subsistence impossible. Social development . . . must inevitably arrive at one of these two points. . . . What are the consequences of these observations for society and the state? Or what is the course of the movement of liberty in the realm of material goods, as opposed to the movement of dependence? Here we touch upon the contemporary scene, although we deal with very general principles.

Basis and Origin of the Political Movement

It it is true that education leads to the desire of acquiring corresponding material goods, and if the latter is impaired by social privileges, how then does the lower class gain possessions by virtue of its education despite this handicap? . . .

By way of owning property, people want to satisfy their unalterable needs for the control of their natural environment and for enjoyment of this domination. Labor is the means of accomplishing this. It has been said that work itself provides satisfaction; but that is only true if its results—the possessions and their enjoyments—are not dependent on the effort of working. All labor which is conditioned by actual needs requires more effort than it gives satisfaction. Human beings naturally strive to satisfy their needs . . . without having to work; the satisfaction of needs without work we may simply call *unearned income*. Such an income is therefore a universal goal of human endeavor. . . . Those who own property . . . are able to satisfy their own needs and desires by the labor of others, without having to work themselves. Therefore, the ruling class has the opportunity of satisfying this natural desire for an unearned income. . . . It attempts to secure this income by instituting social rights. The economic independence of the ruling estate rests on this legal protection of property . . .

Thus the establishment of social rights makes work superfluous for those who own property. As a natural consequence, the ruling stratum

of society soon stops working and forces the propertyless estate to labor
for it. The contrast between the haves and the have-nots thus gains
another positive characteristic; the upper class is no longer merely the
propertied and privileged class but the class which does not work,
receiving its income from the work of others. Property is therefore no
longer set off from mere lack of property, but property and labor
become opposites. In an estate society, this represents the true character
of its social order . . .

Since property attains its value only through labor, it becomes possible for the third estate to get hold of the value of the possessions of
the propertied estate. The more advanced the education of the third estate, the quicker will this process be; the more the ruling stratum has
withdrawn from work, the more pervasive this change will be. Since the
ruling stratum has nothing to oppose to living and acquisitive labor
but lifeless and limited material property, it does not have any means
at its disposal for struggling successfully against the continuously
growing effort of the working population to establish itself as the master
of economic value. . . . The working population, using its education to
promote acquisition, watching its education grow with increasing wealth,
reaches a point at which, for the majority of its members, the intellectual
and material conditions have been realized which are conducive to social
and civil liberty. Through persistent work it has gained property; and
in addition to education, it has acquired the value of property in the
form of *capital*. From now on, there is no essential difference between
the working estate and the ruling class.

However, . . . the difference continues to exist in public law, social
rights and constitutional law. The working and dependent class, excluded
from public power, cannot enforce any change in its legal position
which would reflect the actual change of its conditions. The existing
legal order is no longer reasonable; . . . its appropriateness to the social
order and to the distribution of wealth is destroyed through that growth
of property, and a decisive contradiction emerges. The legal framework
of society, and with it the constitution of the state, continue to exist
along traditional lines, although these no longer correspond to the
reality of the social order. . . . This contract between the real and the
merely legal society becomes the point of departure of the social
movement toward liberty. . . . The old law and the old constitution
are threatened from the moment when the labor of the dependent class
succeeds in producing property for itself. The time is ripe for legal
changes . . .

Concept of Political Reform

The natural and reasonable solution of this contradiction is *political reform*. . . . Political reform occurs whenever the government, overwhelmed by internal or external pressures, yields to the demands of the hitherto dependent class and introduces the necessary changes in the constitution and the administration. . . . These reforms result from the structural changes in society; their purpose is to bring about changes in public and constitutional law which establish legal equality for those who have already gained social equality. These reforms may be introduced in various ways and in various degrees; but they always have to be carried out by the constituted authorities in order to forestall a revolution. Even a complete change in constitutional law, if carried out by the established organs, is not a revolution but a *reform*. . . . It is an act of *free decision* by the human community, an act which reflects the rule of the spirit over external circumstances, an act of subordination of privileges and special interests to the superior life of the whole. Since true progress in all spheres of life rests on this organic unity, only reform provides unhampered development and avoids unnecessary sacrifices by any one section of society.

. . . Even before nations come to understand through science and experience the disadvantages of a revolution, a correct instinct restrains them from attempting revolutions. Wherever social conditions have been changed by the dynamics of work and acquisition, . . . the need and demand for a corresponding political reform will emerge. The emergence of these demands always deserves the most careful attention, for they always reflect a contradiction which has developed between the new and the old order of things, and point to means for a cure offered by the higher nature of things. Blessed be the country which follows this course. If it disregards the unmistakable symptoms and tries to preserve the old order of state and society with unbending egotistic persistence, there will take place, instead of a peaceful and healthy progress, the violence of a revolution; and it is always uncertain whether its benefits will outweigh the damage done.

Concept and Law of the Political Revolution

. . . If the idea of the state, as well as the interest of its citizens, necessitates a reform, how is it possible that reform is not forthcoming through the state in accordance with the basic changes in society?

We have shown above that, in all forms of the state, the class which rules society also comes to control the state. The social movement aiming to change the state originates within the class which is subjugated to the rule of the powerful. It aims at the elimination of this rule as well as of the corresponding privileges. This class, in fact, demands of the ruling class that it shall use its own power to divest itself of this very power; that it therewith sacrifice its own interests to those of its opponents . . . Therefore, it can be easily understood that members of the ruling class are stubbornly opposed to these demands, which would undermine their own elevated position. . . .

The upper class does not do what the lower class is asking for: it does not permit the enactment of a new legal code corresponding to the new pattern of the distribution of goods; on the contrary, it is opposed to these demands, and consequently conditions favoring a revolution develop.

A valid legal system contains two elements: it is the pronounced will of the state, and it is a result of circumstances. Every true law contains both elements. Wherever a law contains only one of these elements, it has become contradictory to its own nature; therefore, of necessity, it must try to encompass both elements or else perish.

Under the social conditions just described, the ruling class retains its old rights only formally, i.e. it still controls the will of the state, while the substance of these rights, i.e. the inner consistency of its domination with the social distribution of material goods, has been destroyed. The formerly dependent class, on the other hand, has become equal to the ruling class with regard to the acquisition of goods, but the element of formal validity, the recognition of its rights by the will of the state, is still lacking.

It is clear that these conditions are contrary to the idea of justice. Once these conditions have developed, it is inevitable that the above two imperfect manifestations of rights will strive to achieve inner consistency. The upper class demands legal control over the possessions of the lower class; the lower class demands legal recognition of its rights by the state. These mutually exclusive demands lead to conflict. Since they reflect the conditions of the two major classes of society, the struggle is always a struggle between these two; it is the result of the original opposition of the dependent and the ruling class in any community. . . . The objective of this struggle is, of necessity, the change of the constitution in favor of the hitherto dependent class. Since social rights determine social power and the distribution of property, the result of this struggle is a more rigorous limitation of the rights of the dependent class, if the ruling class is victorious; if the dependent class is victorious, the traditional social rights are abrogated by way of a constitutional change.

This struggle between the two major social classes is the *revolution;* the prerequisite for it is the acquisition of property through labor by members of the dependent class; its goal is the realization of the idea of justice, its objective a corresponding new constitution. . . .

As soon as the propertied class in a' society stops working and only those who do not own property engage in productive work, the material beginnings for a transformation of the state emerge to the extent that intellectual independence grows through education; and if the owning and no longer acquisitive class does not yield to the demands of the advancing lower class, the first, material, basis for a revolution is established.

Since the revolution wants to establish a new form of government, investigations and opinions concerning the new constitution usually precede it. . . . Since the principle of social reform is the idea of equality, all such theories about a new constitution have in common the idea of equality. Wherever constitutional theories and drafts of new constitutions based on the idea of equality emerge, popular education has reached a stage of self-awareness and the second, the intellectual, basis of the revolution has been established.

The revolution is therefore a necessary, quite natural event, as soon as the dependent class has acquired the material and intellectual social prerequisites for its equality with the ruling class and the latter refuses to acknowledge this equality by changing the constitutional law and extending social rights. Any revolution in which the dependent class comes forward with these demands without being readily prepared materially as well as intellectually, is contradictory to the principle of justice, and will be unsuccessful because it does not reflect the truth. The result of every false revolution is a more severe subjugation of the dependent class.

Since the revolutionary movement rests on the social foundation of property, the demands on state and society can never go beyond the corresponding actual order of property. Every revolutionary movement contains an element of profound contradiction. It demands equality, but is based upon the unequally distributed property of the members of the dependent class. In principle, it is concerned about equal rights for all members of the dependent class; in fact, however, it is only concerned with the success of the revolution for the benefit of those who have already acquired these social possessions. No revolutionary movement can possibly avoid this contradiction. Since a revolutionary movement cannot do without educated men, and since the doctrine of equality is merely the expression of the awareness of this intellectual possession, it has to begin by admitting all people who approve of its principles without consideration of their social qualifications for participation in the benefits of the revolutionary movement. Every revolution, therefore, makes use of a class of society to which it neither wants to be nor can be beneficial. Every revolution, as soon as it has ended successfully, will find antagonists among the masses which have carried out the revolution. This fact explains why, after a revolution in contemporary states, the structure of the society becomes heterogenous, as is the case in present-day Europe. . . . This is the root of the frequently gross injustice which inevitably occurs in any revolution. Since sections of the dependent class who do not own property but participate in the revolution are not qualified for equal status but do raise the claim for it, many things will be done in the name of a principle which cannot be justified. The revolution, therefore, is always, not only the beginning of a new order of society, but also the beginning of a new contradiction within this order. This becomes immediately apparent in the new constitution after the victorious revolution.

Most people assume that new revolutionary constitutions are essentially derived from philosophical theories inherent in the theoretically conceived, ideal constitutions which reflect the general principles of equality. . . . But the first look at the course of all revolutionary movements reveals immediately that an actual revolution has never accepted the previously drafted theoretical constitution but has always produced an independent constitution. Contemporary developments illustrate this phenomenon in the most striking manner. It can be explained by the fact that the original moving force in the revolution is not the idea of equality, but the unevenly distributed social wealth; and that not philosophical theories but social classes make the revolution. . . . It is very important to bear this principle in mind, if one wants to evaluate a revolution soberly. According to its nature, the acquired property of the dependent class provides the title and the power for reorganization of the legal basis of the state and of society. Therefore, the new constitution, in order to become the true basic law instead of remaining only an abstract postulate, must inevitably be based on property qualification for the participation in government. The principle of a social movement necessarily implies that property which has made one part of the dependent class powerful shall become the dominant factor in the society by determining the difference between the ruling and the dependent class. Since the social order determines the state constitution, it necessarily follows as the principle of all revolutionary constitutions that the property which is acquired becomes the qualification for participating in constitutional life, excluding those who do not own anything.[1]

. . . The acquisition of property and the increase of the awareness of its prerogatives in the social and political order is the *first stage* in the development of the idea of freedom; . . . political reform or political revolution is the *second* stage thereof. Is the movement toward freedom concluded with the revolution? Or does that contradiction inherent in any political revolution indicate that there is a *third stage* toward which the development of the individual's self-realization tends?

Indeed, . . . this leads us to the contemplation of the contemporary scene and our own future.

THE SOCIAL MOVEMENT

The Foundation, the Concept and the Principle of the Social Movement

Every political revolution does away with the rule of property derived from high social position or unearned income and replaces it by property gained through labor which then becomes the new basis for the class order. Property acquired through labor can be preserved, in relation to the acquisition of others, only by one's own continued labor . . . Therefore, acquired property remains necessarily acquisitive. It is composed of two parts: resources which have a certain value and utility, and the owner's labor-power. Resources which are

---

[1] To avoid misunderstanding, we distinguish revolutionary movement from similar phenomena: . . .

   a) *Sedition* is the rebellion of people against specific administrative acts or a single agency; usually it is without any social overtone and therefore easily controlled.

   b) We speak of *insurrection* if a part of the country rises against the whole. Here it is possible that the social order of the part is threatened by the constitution of the whole, but just as often minority groups or economic discrimination are the cause.

   c) The *revolt* is the rise of the population against its ruler, whether monarch, dictator, aristocracy, or conqueror.

   d) The *political revolution,* however, is the uprising of the dependent, or already property-owning class, against the constitution of the state which excludes it from its natural political and social rights.

subject to acquisitive labor are called capital; it becomes productive through the labor of its owner . . . Next to acquisitive capital we find the purely personal capacity for acquisition, i.e. labor-power, which is inherent in every person. It is the prerequisite of acquisition; it does not necessarily produce property, but it continuously strives for it. In order to gain property, labor-power must be applied to resources. Labor-power must therefore be linked to acquisitive capital, in order to acquire property by the productive process of capital in operation.

Acquisitive capital, on the other hand, transcending the individual labor-power of the owner, is dependent on the labor-power of those who do not own any capital. In this fashion, a natural and organic relationship develops between capital and labor which rests on their mutual needs.

In this way, the differences between the two major classes in all societies, the owners and the non-owners, are established after any political revolution. The class of owners is the one which owns the acquisitive capital; the class of non-owners is the one which has labor at its disposal without owning capital . . . This state of affairs precedes any social movement; it dominates the whole contemporary scene; it reflects the truth as well as the contradiction, and, in the last analysis, the great question of our time.

At first, this state of affairs is completely harmonious, compatible with the concept of the personality. Acquisitive capital represents the material development of man attained by personal work; labor without capital constitutes the capacity for and the challenge of future attainment. Capital is available for acquisition; . . . therefore, the freedom of acquisition implies the recognition of the individual's freedom to work his way up to the acquisition of property. It is true that labor as such is dependent on capital because labor needs capital; but it is not less true that capital also depends on labor because it is acquisitive. The social order which develops on this basis, therefore, appears to be completely natural and even free. Through mutual needs, the dependence between classes becomes mutual; and through the possibility of capital acquisition which is granted in principle, the growth potential of each individual is acknowledged.

This type of social organization also reaches the point where it produces social dependence, as does any other social order. The actual acquisition of capital, the possession of tangible personal goods, is the goal of acquisitive action. Hence the exclusion from the acquisitive process contradicts the idea of liberty. If, therefore, it becomes evident in the social order based on acquisition that labor without capital is excluded from capital acquisition, we have reached the stage at which social dependence and social contradictions also develop in this social order . . .

The amount of capital determines the social position among capitalists. Hence acquisitive capital immediately adopts the dynamic characteristics of personality and endeavors to expand continuously. Acquisitive capital differs from pure ownership, which is usually self-sufficient. The growth of capital, just as its origin, results from labor, because the surplus value and price of the product exceeding costs is allocated to capital as *profit*. Wages are the main cost factor, so that the higher the wages, the smaller the profit and the growth of the capital. Capital units competing for growth tend to keep wages as low as possible. It is quite unreasonable to blame the acquisitive capital for this, for it is its nature to act in this and in no other way.

The needs of the laborers determine the limit of wages, but any surplus made by the cooperation of capital and labor is transferred to capital . . . If the laborer would receive it, the capitalist would go without. In this way, the harmony between capital and labor is disrupted, and the contradiction between the two main classes in the acquisitive society emerges.

This contradiction has a definite character. Gain is the interest of capital and also the final goal of the worker who is yet without capital. The interest of capital is therefore in conflict with the purpose of labor. This is the contradiction which dispels the original harmony.

Since labor without capital is necessarily dependent on capital, capital . . . is able to dictate the conditions under which labor is hired. These conditions are not arbitrary, as the blind opponents of this social order assume; because the interest of capital requires it, they have to affect wages in such a way that acquisition of capital by the worker is precluded. In pursuing its own interest, capital becomes the power which enforces the permanent inability of the laborer to own capital. Whosoever has no capital is unable to acquire it. Therewith the property-owning class and the class without property develop into an owning and non-owning estate; property and the lack of property becomes fixed for generations, and the social order becomes rigid and closed.

The social position of each individual is now definite and unchangeable. It reflects a contradiction to the concept of labor by suspending the use of labor for acquisition and the gaining of property. It is a contradiction to the concept of the free personality in that it restrains the individual in the fulfillment of his aspirations. And it is contrary to the idea of liberty in that it fetters the development of human community . . . and in that it changes a society which in principle is committed to social freedom into one in which dependence prevails. It not only excludes the non-owners from the acquisition of capital, but it also renders labor without capital dependent on productive capital and non-owners on owners. This dependence, if rendered permanent, is a dependence of the working class on the property-owning class . . .

It is plain what the difference is between a society based on acquisition and a society based on property-rights which preceded it and led to the political revolution. During the former stage, the property-owning class did not work, thus making it possible for those excluded from it to acquire property. But now the ruling class works; and it is precisely the labor of the property-owning class which, as competition, makes it impossible for the non-owners to acquire property.

Furthermore, it is clear that the gradual escape from social dependence is much simpler at an earlier stage than at a later stage of development; because in the earlier stage only material wealth and labor are opposed to each other, while, in the latter, the opponents are working capital and labor without capital. Nevertheless, the idea of social independence also evolves from the latter.

There is one area of wealth where neither profit nor restrictions exist; it is the realm of "intellectual goods". Education, even though difficult to obtain, is yet potentially available for the non-owner. Just as education marks the beginning of the struggle for social independence against the society built on property, it plays the same role against social dependence in the acquisitive society. There are a great many people who let themselves be deceived with regard to the tremendous importance of intellectual goods in any society, because it appears as though only material wealth counts. Nevertheless, these goods have always fertilized, bred and cultivated the seed of human liberty; for they are heirs as well as progenitors of liberty. As long as a nation possesses intellectual goods, it cannot remain in bondage; as long as education advances, restraints on liberty cannot remain permanent; as long as a society cares for the education of all, it wants true liberty.

As the opportunities for the education of the working class improve, a point will be reached at which the idea of *equality* emerges . . . The origin of this idea . . . signifies the moment when the principle of liberty becomes opposed to the foundation of the social order . . . The growth of education among the laboring class which is unable to accumulate property makes this contrast evident without being able to dissolve it. Equality of education leads to demands for equality of acquisitive opportunities, without providing the means by which these could be created.

In this fashion . . . society offers equal opportunities for acquiring an education but not for acquiring goods, which means, in effect, that it fosters the demand and the desire for social independence but does not make it possible to fulfill this demand. This is a profoundly contradictory condition, . . . one which is no longer a theoretical but an objective condition of European society, and of crucial importance for the future. All other problems are by comparison of secondary importance. There is no doubt that in the leading countries of Europe political reform and political revolution have come to an end. Social issues have taken their place; their tremendous impact and the serious doubts they raise surpass those of any other movement. These issues, which are now acute, seemed to be merely a remote shadow only a few years ago; now they present a challenge to all privileges, and any attempts to relegate them to their former insignificance are in vain . . .

Communism, Socialism and the Idea of Social Democracy

The precise moment at which the idea of personal equality emerges is the moment at which the dependent class becomes conscious of the contradiction inherent in the acquisitive society . . . As soon as the principle of equality is confronted with the social inequality based on acquisition, the inquisitive minds begins to search for a logical solution. This intellectual effort precedes the factual struggle; inconspicuously, it forces its way, as it were, under the surface of the social order. The more stable the society, the firmer will the oppressed, under the external pressure, cling to the result of their thinking. This advance of the idea of equality has its own highly important history, and neither the idea of equality nor its development in history is accidental. The main phases are clearly discernible: constitutional theories prevail at the beginning of the political revolution; then, with the emergence of the social movement, *social theories* are developed. Although such theories are the work of individuals, they are based on the common demand to promote the personal development of each individual by creating opportunities for the acquisition of material goods. All ideas, suggestions, and investigations touching upon this problem are part of the social movement. The processes of thought of the dependent class always manifest themselves in three great phases which, however, are closely interrelated . . .

The first and most natural notions about the differences between the haves and the have-nots in terms of the principle of equality are the ones which simply regard property as such as the reason for all social dependence. Since wealth is limited, only a part of the community will be able to own it; but since possessions are the absolute condition of acquisition, the owner will necessarily and always keep the non-owner dependent. If dependence is to be abolished, its basis, private property, has to be destroyed. There should not be any personal property at all. The first application or the first social content of the idea of equality is the negation of personal property.

But man needs products, and production requires raw materials. These raw materials, in order not to belong to any individual but to remain available to all, have to become the property of the entire community. In order to produce the necessary supply of goods from the commonly owned materials, labor has to be available. Such labor, if done for the individual, would immediately produce new property. To avoid this, and also to avoid the reappearance of dependence, labor has to be performed, not for the individual, but exclusively for the community. Society receives the total produce, and society distributes it according to the principle of absolute equality. In this way equality is maintained in spite of labor and material.

These basic ideas are the solid core from which a variety of systems of communal life may be built, all based on the simple principles of the abolishment of private property and the institution of collective ownership. All systems and ideas which acknowledge these principles are called *communistic*. Therefore, communism in all its variations is the first and still very crude system of the social idea of equality, and represents its first application to the social order and its foundation, which is private property, whether in the form of mere possessions or of capital.

However, all forms of communism, aside from the fact that it cannot be realized, contain a contradiction with its own principle, which appears all the more powerful the more closely it is examined. Under communism, just as under any other social order, the community must work through individuals, and therefore the distribution and control of labor also has to be carried out by individuals. If the individual worker were entitled to choose his job, then anybody needing his work would soon become dependent upon him—the very condition which commnuism desires to abolish. Only the community, therefore, can demand and direct labor. But since this community is represented by individuals acting and exercising authority in its name, these individuals become the rulers of labor, and all workers—that is, the whole community—becomes dependent on them. Thus communism would create not only poverty, which might still be acceptable for the sake of liberty, but also real slavery, which is in total contradiction to the idea of equality. Communism is unable to solve this contradiction. It becomes clear that communism would of necessity replace social dependence by a new and less bearable dependence. The idea of equality turns away from communism in order to follow a different path . . .

. . . What remains? Communism is no solution because, under communism, work, the manifestation of individual self-determination, supposed to reflect freedom and individual development, loses its essential characteristic and is no longer free. The acquisitive society ceased to be free because work was unable to provide material independence. The features of communism are the same, with the difference that, instead of individual capital, collective capital wields a despotic control over labor. The only other solution envisioned consisted in a reversal of the relationship; capital ought to be controlled by labor . . .

Such an order of human affairs can be conceived in a variety of ways . . . All those systems, and all ideas and investigations aiming at establishing labor's control over capital in this way (present labor controlling past labor) and making labor the guiding principle of society, may be called *socialist*. Socialism is the second blueprint for a social system based on the social idea of equality. Socialism in all its variations is infinitely superior to communism. Its basis is labor, and thereby individuality, this fountainhead of all true wealth and of all diversification. Socialism does not desire to realize the abstract equality of men, any more than it desires to eliminate a person's individuality . . . Socialism does not desire, as communism does, to abolish differentiations among individuals and therewith society and the order of the whole; it aims to build society on the principle of labor independent of property. However, socialism also contains a contradiction . . . It aims at the control of labor over capital. Capital is different from mere property, inasmuch as it represents an accumulated surplus of former labor. The product of labor is supposed to be controlled by labor, . . . past labor to be subordinated to present labor. However, present work is only valuable because it is also the result of a continuous process of work, and no work will be very valuable unless it is based on an accumulated mass of work. Therefore, the nature of acquisition contradicts the principle of socialism. Mere possessions could be subordinated to acquisitive labor because they were idle and did not originate from work; however, capital will resist this subjugation because it is itself the product of work. Socialism, therefore, is forced to a number of alternatives, all of which aim more or less at the abolition of private property. This feature of socialism, which has a similarity to communism, most clearly displays its basic fault. It is at this point that the whole class of property owners turns against it and that it becomes subject to attack, not only by this powerful class of society, but by its own principles as well . . . Socialism in all its various forms is, therefore, not the last stage of the social movement.

Socialism as well as communism are in essence only the systematized demands of *one* class in the acquisitive society. This class is weak compared to the other; if it wants to be strong enough to strive for the realization of its hopes against the resistance of the ruling class, it must join forces with the power which, according to its very nature, has the task of raising the status of the lower class. This power is the state.

The Idea of Social Democracy

There is no doubt that the state, as a concept as well as in reality, suffer through the dependence of the lower, the merely working, class. The larger this class, the greater the size of the dependent elements, the poorer the whole community, the less powerful the state, and the more easy does it become to disturb the peace through the growing antagonism of these two elements of society. It is in the interest of the state, therefore, to assist the poorer class; and the lower class of mere workers turns to the state to seek support for the realization of its idea of social equality as soon as they realize the impracticability of communist and socialist theories . . . The laboring class is in need of capital. Capital cannot be given away by the individual capitalists without destroying their social and economic position. Only the state owns no property just for itself; whatever it has and whatever it is able to acquire belongs to the people. Labor, therefore, first turns towards the state as capital owner and desires to form a coalition between state capital and the labor power of the working class. The state shall become an entrepreneur and give the profit . . . to the workers . . .

We call this proposition the idea of an *organization of work;* all projects which make the state act as an entrepreneur, to distribute the profit to the laborer so that he may acquire capital, are part of this idea . . .

A further possibility suggests itself. If individual independence in the acquisitive society can only be gained by individual acquisition, the only solution is to give capital to the individual. One has to capitalize the ability to work and to endow the beginning process of acquisition with the capital which is supposed to materialize only through acquisition. This would mean extension of credit to the capital inherently present in the earning potential of the individual. The state has to establish institutions so that every individual can receive credit, i.e. material to be utilized by labor, according to working ability . . .

This is the idea of the *organization of credit,* which is superior to the idea of the organization of labor. The idea of the organization of credit also allows for the existence of more than just one system. By leaving the realm of economic development to the individual, it guarantees the highest degree of freedom; the great significance of this idea cannot be erased by fallacious proposals.

In order to extend credit, . . . the state has to be able to dispose of it . . . But the state is controlled by the ruling class of society. The demand that one of these ideas be realized implies that the rulers use their authority to strip themselves of their power and transfer it to the ruled. The obvious contradiction which this entails forces the members of the non-owning class to conceive of a constitution which would empower them to use the state for the improvement of their conditions through the acquisition of capital . . . They have come to realize the inevitable necessity for a state constitution based on the rule of the non-owning class . . .

This democratic trend originates in republicanism. The republican or democratic movement conceives of the individual as being independent of his property, i.e. as a purely conceptualized personality. Since all people are basically free and equal and entitled to the right of self-determination, it follows that a free constitution should provide an equal share to all in determining the will of the state or the legislation . . . The movement of political democracy does not go further, . . . but with regard to the form of the public will it is in accord with the social movement. A natural and inevitable alliance of these two elements develops: The republican or democratic element considers it its main task to provide a clear formula for a constitution and to define the legal framework of a democratic government, while the social movement is concerned with the administration and administrative tasks, i.e. the social use of the means available to a democratic government. This is the theoretical concept and the meaning-content of the phenomenon of social democracy which constitutes the last stage of the purely intellectual movement of social ideas.

Thus the principle of social democracy encompasses universal suffrage in the constitutional realm and the abolition of the social dependence of the working class in the realm of administration. In a social democracy the constitution is the democratic and the administration the social element. The natural and necessary development of the movement towards liberty leads to this alliance; it is the last stage in the movement of the lower class fighting against its social dependence . . . The form which the social movement may take at this stage may be either that of social reform or that of social revolution . . .

. . . Dependence of labor upon capital is a contradiction to the idea of freedom and therefore cannot last. Either the idea of liberty has to be destroyed in the mind of the working class, or the idea somehow has to strive for its realization; no power in the world is strong enough to restrain it from doing so. The ever fertile soil for the idea of liberty is provided by the opportunities of acquiring knowledge, i.e., an education. Wherever there are educated people, social ideas are present; wherever educational facilities grow, they will advance towards the principle of equality; and wherever the working class becomes aware of this principle, it must eventually be elevated to the heights of the idea of social democracy, no matter by what devious ways. This idea is neither a theory nor a sudden fancy; it inevitably emerges within the social context as soon as conditions are ready and preparations accomplished. It is blindness not to see this necessity; it is folly to oppose it directly. For it is the expression and the awareness of the inner contradiction between the idea of freedom and the order of the acquisitive society.

Social Revolution

. . . The contradiction between the existing social order and the higher concept of liberty becomes clear in the mind of the lower class . . . The belief in the rightness of freedom and in the possibility of its realization becomes stronger the less the ruling class cares about freedom and the more definitely the lower class believes that this truth . . . is being denied only for reasons of self-interest . . . The principle of social equality, then, begins to take definite shape in this part of society and brings all the thoughts of its members into a strong focus.

Whenever this happens, an event of supreme importance has taken place. Until then, the lower class of society has been held together only by the force of the economy, by an external factor, by work. It is not yet a unit, but rather an amorphous mass; the workers live under similar social conditions and have similar social functions, but they do not yet form a community aware of its own will. This newly developed community based on a common understanding of their conditions and needs transforms itself into an independent power, consciously and purposely opposed to the present order of society. As such, that class is called by a new, but appropriate name: the proletariat.

The proletariat asks the ruling class, in the name of equality, for something which this class neither desires to offer nor possibly can offer. It asks the state to do what is contrary to the very concept of the state and its laws. It soon discovers that it cannot hope to gain satisfaction from either the state or society. In recognizing that the ruling class, on which the proletariat is socially dependent, also controls the state, the proletariat takes the view that the exclusive reason for the state's refusal to support its claims is the desire to avoid interfering with the social and personal interests of those who control the state . . . Thus, the belief emerges that the proletarians are called upon, and are able, to help themselves by acquiring the power of the state. Consequently, the consider themselves entitled to seize governmental power in order to realize their social ideas.

However, it is very difficult for this to happen in reality. The proletariat is actually the weaker part in society. To begin with, it is not correct to say that the proletariat outnumbers the property-owning class; it is even less correct to maintain that it is stronger or more courageous or more determined than its opponents. It can, however, happen in individual cases that the proletariat seizes power through a coincidence of events. When this happens, it is always a result of an alliance with the democratic party, and this revolution by which the proletariat and the democratic party subject the state to their control is called a social revolution . . .

By gaining control of the state for the proletariat or labor without capital, political power accrues in the hands of a single social class, which is contrary to the inherent nature of the state . . . It will use the state for the special interests of its own social position. By virtue of this power, it will then subjugate all other interests and endeavors; it will deprive the vanquished of the right of self-determination and for this reason will deny them political rights. Through the exclusion of one-half of the community from what ought to be the common will, state and society cease to be free. Lack of liberty is not less of a reality if labor controls capital than if capital controls labor. The victory of the proletariat is the victory of social dependence, whereas it was supposed to be the victory of freedom . . .

The lower class, as the ruling element under such conditions, does not have the prerequisites of true authority; it has neither the material goods on which authority rests, nor is it superior in knowledge to the property-owning class . . . The proletariat lacks the true inner justification for seizing control of the state . . . Therefore it must—almost un-intentionally—seek extraneous support to uphold its power . . .

Its first external prop is the state constitution. The principle of all social democratic constitutions is the election of representatives and officials by universal suffrage . . . Many people believe that the proletariat is the greater numerical power in society, so that universal suffrage would put the social party or the proletariat at the head of the state. But we confidently claim that such is not the case . . . Only if the social-democratic movement retains its alliance with the movement for political liberation can a majority be attained. As soon as the social-democratic party stands by itself it is by far weaker. Nevertheless, it will insist on universal suffrage, . . . because it knows that it is stronger with the general vote than without it. However, universal suffrage alone can neither put it into power nor keep it there.

If this is impossible, there is only one other way open for the proletariat, namely sheer force. It is therefore inevitable that, with the emergence of the rule of the proletariat, despotism develops, a despotism of a specific and terrible kind. Like all domination, this despotism is directed against whatever threatens its rule . . . The proletariat must use its power to destroy not only the opposing class, but also the social foundation of this class. Here a struggle starts which we call *terrorism,* a bloody and essentially endless struggle. Terrorism is the most dreadful phenomenon in history, not only because life and goods are sacrificed with cold fury, but also because terrorism endeavors to accomplish by mass murder what is inherently impossible. Terrorism is the summit of contradiction in the course of a social revolution. When this summit is reached, the tide is reversed, and the counter-movement begins.

For, in order to secure its dominant position, the proletariat must at least have the power to do so. But it does not have this power. It can only rule temporarily; lower in numbers, intelligence and personal energy, it will be swept away by the first serious attack of the possessing class, and this happens rarely without the latter taking bloody revenge. The victory of the property-owning class is inevitable; but, since it also is gained by force, force . . . eventually occupies an independent position above the two classes of society. This independent position by which force as such rules, not in the name of any social idea, is called *dictator-ship.* The really successful revolution, therefore, always leads to a dicta-torship . . . The dictatorship declares itself to be the independent state and invests itself with the right, the task and the dignity of the state.

This is the end of the social revolution. From out of the turmoil of the social struggle there re-emerges the idea of the state, detached from the power of the various social classes, founded on itself and ruling by itself. And thus the thought that the life of the community consists of thrust and counter-thrust between society and the state, between dependence and freedom, becomes reality . . .

Social Reform

. . . If it is true that property and acquisition of intellectual and material goods entail the realization of the idea of personality, conditions ought to be conceivable under which, despite all imperfections, this ideal of social life is at least approximately attained. This ideal is not identical with the realization of the idea of equality . . . Equality of all people is just as inconceivable as it is unreal, in the past as well as in the future. Even though people are equal in general, this generic equality represents only one aspect of every human being; but at the same time, he is more; he is also . . . an individual. No matter how we conceive of the origin of individuality, differentiation always remains a fact . . . Therefore, the purely philosophical assertion of the equality of men contradicts not only reality, but also the very concept of equality. . . . If neither the inorganic nor the animal world produces equality, even between two of its most subordinate units, if the whole world, from the planetary system to infusoria, shows differentiation, how could it be conceivable that the highest order of life—personality—constitutes the absolute opposite? And if the concept of life is derived from the concept of variety and organism, how then could one conceive of a living world of personalities deprived of the basis of all life and striving, which is differentiation of development and individuality? . . .

The realization of the idea of personal fulfillment, though, does not depend on the mere elimination of poverty, any more than it does on the concept of equality. We may consider it a generally accepted fact today that poverty and the proletariat, though closely interrelated, are totally different entities . . . Poverty arises when the ability to work is lost, or when labor is unable to satisfy the natural, common human needs. The proletariat, however, emerges when labor is unable to produce capital, although the worker strives for it. The poor can and ought to be helped by giving them assistance, the proletarians by offering them opportunities to acquire property. There may be poverty in a nation without a proletariat, as well as the other way around; the major concern of a social movement is not the problem of poverty.

The social problem which social reform tries to solve is the result of the laws which determine the relationship between capital and labor and thus also govern society, the constitution, and the development of each individual personality . . . We have shown that the contradiction in the situation of the proletarian consists in his dependence on the property-owner because he owns only labor and no capital. Is it this dependence, then, the consequence of the laws of acquisition, which ought to be eliminated by social reform? . . . Is it the very existence of these two classes, whose complete abolition is the aim and the driving force of the social problems of our time as well as of the future? . . .

If one considers the nature of capital and labor, it seems undoubtedly true that the division of society into property-owning and laboring classes, and the dependence of the latter upon the former, is *not* in contradiction to the concept of personality or of personal freedom, as long as capital remains the fruit of labor. In this case, capital ownership is merely a higher stage of development of personal life . . . As long as the inherent nature of capital and labor remains unchanged, this differentiation and dependence are inevitable. It would be a complete misinterpretation of the nature of social life to consider the abolition of this differentiation as the aim of social reform . . . The wealth of mankind rests on the developmental potentials of labor to transform itself into capital . . . Indeed, the abolition of this differentiation is not at all the aim of the proletariat . . . The proletariat wants to be able to acquire capital. Here is the core of the problem. By conquering nature and submitting it to his service, man becomes free. His freedom rests on his ability to dominate the outer world by his own effort, the realization of his personal and continuously reasserted self-determination. In the acquisitive society, capital is the symbol and the reality of this domination. Personal independence in this society rests on the ability of even the meanest worker to acquire capital.

This provides an opportunity for everybody to break through the traditional pattern of social classes and of the ensuing dependence . . . As long as this opportunity exists in the form of a rule also extending to the worker, no contradiction is apparent, and the social order is stable, no matter how great are the dependence and the differences between the two classes.

The essence of the social question and of social reform in our present society is therefore clearly indicated. The problem is whether it is at all possible, in the acquisitive society, to provide labor with the necessary opportunities and corresponding institutions for the acquisition of property commensurate with the accomplishments and standards of labor. The social reform movement consists of the work, the activities, the suggestions, the attempts, the laws, and the institutions which aim to create these opportunities for the working class . . .

We have seen that all social movements are necessarily controlled by interests . . . If society is to accomplish its own reform, such reform has to be in its own interest. Let us not deceive ourselves; social reform would and could never be accomplished if it were not in the interest of society.

No doubt this is the case. The harmony of eternal laws guiding mankind would be completely destroyed if the principle which gives rise to the social order would destroy social independence within this order. Interest must be able both to demand and also to establish liberty.

To prove this lies beyond the scope of this book . . . But it is now clear where the principle of any true social reform lies. It is the awareness of the property-owning class that its own highest and clearly understood interest forces it to work for social reforms unfalteringly with the greatest exertion of its social power and with the full support of the state . . .

A FINAL CONSIDERATION: GERMANY AND FRANCE

. . . It has been our task to compare the concept of society with the concept of the state, to regard the social order and the social movement as the main determinants of political life, and to interpret the contrast between the ideas of personal independence and dependence as the very essence of social life and social changes . . . We have answered only the first of the three questions which present themselves: What is society and what is the nature of its dynamics and its contradictions? The second question, not less important, is the following: If the organization of society rests on the principles indicated, if its development is determined by the laws which have here been outlined, what then is the social condition, the social danger, and the social question of Europe or the various European countries? This raises the third question: What are the means for coping with the antagonism between the two classes of society, and what is the social future of Europe? . . .

Up to now, Germany has not yet made an original contribution to the social sciences. The experienced scholar has to admit with embarrassment that our social-intellectual movement to date has been only a very weak reflection of French thought . . . If we want to achieve great things going beyond the accomplishments of our neighbors, we must now try to penetrate to the very core of human order . . . While the French remain involved in questions of social theories, subject to the danger and weakness of a merely subjective interpretation, we should develop a *science of society*, an objective analysis of social elements and phenomena . . .

In order to do this, we have to look for a starting point which raises us above the French. Would not this point of departure emerge precisely from the social movements in France which, during the last fifty years, appear to us to have attempted at various points and at different stages of development to grasp the specific problem with which we have to deal? This being indeed the case, our point of departure is exactly the one at which not only this or that social theory, but the very concept, the nature, and the supreme life of society reveal themselves. This life has its eternal unalterable laws, since personality and property are its eternal elements. If all of nature, if the solar systems as well as the smallest wheel in their movement, if the human body in its growth, if even chance all have their predictable laws, how could it be possible that the highest form of earthly life, the community of men, in its different forms, in its changes and in its progress, is not subject to laws? . . . At a time when most people search only for theories which would provide a solution to social antagonism, I have ventured to develop the theory of the concept and the nature of human society . . .

Whether what has been developed here as a basis for scientific knowledge is only logically consistent, or whether it also reflects objective truth embedded in the reality of human life, can only be decided after solving the second major problem, namely, the presentation of the history and the present structure of European society . . . Our investigation should not merely relate political history to legal history, but should also view both from the aspect of the idea and the laws of social development . . . We have confined ourselves to the most recent historical period; in more than one respect this is predominantly the era of social movement. For this period we have chosen to concentrate our efforts on one nation, the French, as the representative of this movement.

Germany, seemingly closer to us, caught our attention first. But Germany is a peculiar case in this respect, as in many others. Germany is divided into different states, but the Germans are nevertheless one people. With all her will power and her enthusiasm she strives for political unification as a prerequisite of freedom. But she has been unable to attain unity so far . . . The national movement considers the present social movement as secondary, and has used a good part of its strength to keep it in check. The social movement has partly despised, partly misjudged, the political one and has moved away from it. As a result, the best forces of both have been dissipated . . .

If our law of the movement toward freedom is correct, political change has to precede social change. Therefore it is certain and inevitable that in Germany the social movement must and will be pushed into the background as soon as the German people rise again; then it can and will first of all solve the purely political problem of German unification, since this is the natural and necessary precondition for the solving of the social question. The next revolution in Germany, therefore, will be a political one, and will determine the political form of Germany. However, just as inevitably the social movements will follow this political revolution; so only when Germany has become politically united will the question of social freedom arise . . . Because of the intermingling of two historical phases in our time, the movement in Germany cannot very well be used as an illustration of the concepts above; rather they can be used in explaining the social movement in Germany. In France the situation is quite different.

France is, above all, the country where the general movements of Europe tend to take a specific form, quickly and decidedly so. In all public matters the interest of Europe is focused on this country of action. For it is recognized that she is chosen to provide the testing grounds for the validity and truth of all those principles which dominate public life . . . The history of French society, more than any other, has been full of serious consequences and lessons. Her contemporary condition reveals a peculiar and far from stable picture. Here is a rich soil to capture the attention of the educated and privileged classes, for the interest of the historian and for the research of the scholar, if they want to explore the reasons for the social struggles in contemporary European society . . .

It has frequently been stated that the French history of the last decades has been copied by Germany almost step by step. The Germans have been reproached for this, and the reproach has been used as a weapon. This is not justified. What has happened in France was not due to the specific endowments of the French people. French history from 1789 to the present is not a great deed of the country; it is nothing but the purest manifestation of the laws unhampered by other influences which rule the movements of political and social life. The development during these decades, the single great events as well as the most important legislative acts, . . . have been necessary phenomena. The revolutions of 1789 and 1830 were unavoidable; it was inevitable that social ideas emerged; it was inevitable, too, that social democracy made its first appearance with the revolution of 1848. It was not necessary for all this to happen exactly in the years it did happen, nor was it necessary for it to happen under the specific circumstances it did.

But the events as such were necessary. The history of France is the best justification for the emergence of the science of society. The development of freedom is everywhere essentially the same, even though it may appear in different forms, as it did in the cases of England and Germany . . . Therefore, historical research dealing with society will first turn towards France and her revolutions . . . Everything that has been said and thought during the last half-century with reference to the great questions of our future may be found there in embryonic form . . .

If it is true that France represents the basic model of the history of society, this history is reflected in three quite natural phases: the first phase, stretching from 1788 to the July revolution, includes the purely political revolution, the victory of the acquisitive but legally dependent class over the merely owning and ruling class. The second phase will show the origins of the working class as an independent and unified part of society, or of the proletariat, and its opposition to the owning class or to capital; it will also trace the social ideas and intellectual movements which emerge in it out of the idea of liberty and equality. Finally the third phase shows the struggle and the victory of social democracy and its present condition . . .

THE SOCIAL HISTORY OF THE FRENCH REVOLUTION UNTIL 1830

THE ELEMENTS OF THE FRENCH REVOLUTION

The Condition and Inner Contradiction of French Society before the Revolution

. . . During the 18th century, a movement which took not less than a thousand years to reach its full limits came to its end. This was the formation of feudal society, which was essentially the same for all of Europe, so that in speaking about France we are speaking about the other European countries as well.

The old empire of Charlemagne had disintegrated as a result of the ever recurring fact that the most courageous and powerful warriors were invested with landed property conveying to them the sovereign rights of the state over it; in other words, that the authority of the state became their private property. These rights were inherited by their families; by these rights they ruled the families of the tenant farmers, the burghers and the peasants—all in the name of the state. There developed a ruling class—determined by birth—which considered itself exclusively called upon to participate in the administrative function of the state. This social class within society was the aristocracy.

When the Kingdom of France and the principalities in Germany arose, both had first to face a hard struggle with this aristocracy. After the aristocrats had been defeated, they openly aligned themselves with the throne. As ruler, of a large part of the land—in France more than half of the whole territory—experienced in warfare, brave, skilled in public affairs, wealthy, brilliant, chivalrous in manners, they were received with open arms by the reigning princes. The previous enemies now became the pillars and the glory of the throne. In order to govern their dependent people without state interference, they allowed themselves to be ruled by the absolute princes; absolute rulers on their own domains, they became absolute servants at the court.

The aristocracy was joined by the clergy, which was almost as powerful. The clergy had undergone a peculiar development. Originally, from the 10th to the 13th century, it was recruited from all parts of the population; the serfs as well as the barons found in the church the equality of all as human beings, which the Christian religion had held out to all souls before the Lord. The highest position could be reached by the most humble, and these highest positions were almost equal in power and splendor to the princely thrones. The clergy, therefore, offered an opportunity to members of the lower classes to achieve a powerful and brilliant future by their own efforts; at that time, only personal ability determined promotion among the clergy. It was this natural interrelation between the upper and lower classes that contributed to the great power which the Church held over the whole populace.

But when the clergy slowly gained extensive landed property and became a powerful influence, the aristocracy expected to get the better part of it. Their younger sons joined the church, and, as a result of powerful connections, they succeeded in securing the higher positions almost exclusively for the aristocrats. The proper work of the church was left to the lower ranks, the priests and subaltern clergy, while the honors and the benefits were reaped by those who did the least for the holy mission of the Church. As early as the 16th and 17th centuries, the two main elements within the Catholic Church began to separate: the aristocratic branch, represented by prelates and definitely aligned with the nobility from which it came; and the democratic branch, the priests, siding with the population at large to which they belonged. This was also the state of affairs in the 18th century.

Anybody who was neither nobleman nor clergyman belonged to the third estate. It encompassed very diversified elements of the population. It included the wealthiest merchants, the biggest manufacturers and entrepreneurs, the well-to-do peasants, the scholars, writers and artists, as well as the smallest shopkeepers, the hired man, the worker, the serf, the idlers—for the members of this estate either owned no property or else their property, no matter how large, was such as not to give them any legal privileges. They were excluded from all higher positions in the state, from becoming officers in the army or state administration, excluded from the whole social stratum of the upper classes. Only total subservience to the rule of the latter provided for the unifying bond of this estate. However, they formed the large majority of the total population, which became dominant as commerce and trade developed during the 18th century, as education spread and wealth accumulated in their hands. While the nobility in France ruled and the clergy belonged in part to the ruling class and in part to the ruled class, the whole remaining population was one huge class which possessed almost no rights.

Such was the situation in French society during the 18th century, and it is well known that in other countries similar conditions prevailed . . . The nobility had become an independent estate through the privileges based on property . . . The possessions of the aristocracy were almost exclusively landed property . . . This property was not gained by work but in most cases by force of arms and had been transmitted to the present generation through inheritance. It was a traditional property, the original acquisition of which could not even be proved in thousands of cases. This fact alone made it distinctly different from any other property. Still more important was another factor. The landed property of the nobility was not maintained by the labor of the families owning it. The big as well as the small landlords considered it beneath their dignity to cultivate their own land. Instead of gaining benefits for themselves as well as for society through competent agricultural management, they considered it their right and duty to live on the services of their serfs without working themselves. In addition to their property, which had not been acquired by labor, they also had an income which did not result from labor. They lived on the labor of others . . .

Since the property-owning nobility did not work, it had to secure its possessions and the unearned income derived from it by privileges . . . There were two main types of privileges: First, that the traditional landed property of the nobility could not be acquired by labor or by wealth gained through labor; it had to remain under the control of the aristocracy. Second, that this property could be taxed only within narrow limits in order not to affect seriously the unearned income of its owners. Both privileges were in contradiction to the nature of things . . . Since labor could never gain property, work was done poorly; and since the unearned income was to be derived from labor, the revenues of the nobility decreased constantly while their wasteful living continued. This resulted in large indebtedness of entailed landed property, and thus into a new social contradiction: the value of the land was transmitted into the hands of the creditors who, however, were not allowed to seize the possessions. All these contradictions were maintained by law, and because of that they first appeared as privileges and later as injustices. . . . French society was founded on the contradiction that the historical property, whose owner did not work, ruled unrestrictedly over labor on this property, and that this rule was preserved not by the nature of things but only by privilege . . . Thus, the relationship between the nobility and the third estate was contradictory in its very nature . . .

The laborer was not the only one who belonged to the third estate.

Capital had developed simultaneously with industry as the by-product and prerequisite of industry. Capital consists of the accumulated surplus of values over and above the costs of production. Under the given conditions, capital could not develop in the countryside; it grew in the cities. Capital is essentially different from traditional property. As a product of labor, it is acquired, and as such available to anybody. It is rarely denied to anyone who has courage, zeal and good luck . . . As a rule, capital is the manifestation of personal ability, and entitles its owner to an appropriate social position. It also carries with it the right to be disposed of freely by its owner. This is the nature of capital . . .

The traditional property of the nobility is the direct opposite. The nobility excluded the acquired property, capital, completely from participation in government, and assigned to it a subordinate social position. At the same time, taxes were almost exclusively imposed upon capital owners, who, as a result, carried the heavy burden of public expenses without deriving any benefit from it. In this fashion, the nobility came into sharp opposition to the second important element of the third estate.

A similar attitude toward the rights and position of the aristocracy prevailed among a third group of this estate. It included the scholars, the artists, all the highly educated whose life, income and significance rested on their intellectual possessions. The nobility, holding the highest station without working, despised the sciences. Vaguely aware that the free movement of the mind might lay a basis for a struggle against dependency in society, the nobility persecuted the propagation of ideas wherever possible. Where is the opposition to freedom stronger than under conditions where even free thought is not tolerated? What would free thought have propagated if it had been permitted to do that under these conditions, and what did it propagate despite the existing restraints? That no prerogative is genuinely justified if it hampers the achievement of the eternal goal of the free personality, of its development towards the realization of its individuality . . .

The Position of the State in France before the Revolution

Under such conditions, it was natural that the gloomy feeling of general discomfort spread more and more. Slowly, pressure built up against the prevailing order, and a search for remedies began. With the growing tension, the reasonable and the thoughtful turned first to the authority which has the function and the power to intervene in such a case of emergency—to the state.

We have shown that under the existing conditions of French society, the wealth of the nation had to remain at a low level. The finances of the state gave an accurate picture of this fact. While expenditures rose, revenues declined quite out of proportion. Distress—long since prevailing in the cottages of the laborers—now knocked at the door of state administration. Nobody could deny that the administration moved towards an abyss. The financiers had been aware of this for a long time; finally the government too could deny it no longer.

It is undoubtedly true that the degree of the state's welfare, wealth and statesmanship is definitely determined by the extent of the well-being and wealth, and by the vigor, of the majority of the population. The state is, therefore, by virtue of its interest as well as of its principle, called upon to help the population with all the power at its command. The population at large senses this, . . . so that at first it always addresses its demands to the state, which has a specific responsibility. If the form of the state is such that it hinders the promotion of welfare, the state has to sacrifice its form of government in order to save itself. The form is nothing but the existing public law. The state must, by its supreme power, do away with the existing law and develop a new one which the suffering society demands. If the new law emerges, it will promote the participation of the new elements in society; it will destroy the old society by first attacking the privileges of the ruling class. If the state refrains from doing so, it acts contrary to its own interests. It uses its power, which is designed for the well-being of all, for the preservation of the well-being of the few at the expense of all; it thereby deprives itself by a fallacious use of its power of the means of its existence. If this happens, the state becomes the enemy of the majority of the people; it becomes partisan. But if it sides with the people, it strengthens the basis on which it may rest permanently, the general welfare and the firm conviction of its citizens that the state is the guarantor of true progress. This choice is inevitable. The state has to choose between a constitutional reform and the corresponding order of society on the one hand, and involvement in the social struggle on the other; if the state chooses to take a partisan position it will either be defeated or will establish a despotic rule.

Such a situation prevailed in France when Louis XVI ascended the throne. The finances were completely ruined, and the deficit increased from year to year; the revenues declined, and the expenses grew. The state was powerless as a result of a lack of funds; it had lost its old glory without giving up its despotism. The disorder of the finances was in fact not primarily a result of mismanagement; although there was mismanagement, it did not prove to be the source of misfortune but rather the result of the general conditions of a society built on privileges and monopolies. To a clear-thinking mind there was no doubt that there was no salvation without the establishment of a new system of social rights and privileges . . .

France, the center of Western Europe, felt as well as any other country the pulse of the new life; it was significant that the population hailed the young King at his ascendency. It expected from him nothing less than to begin developing a new position of the monarchy in France. The conditions were such that there was no time to be lost.

Since the beginning of the 18th century, France had a number of excellent men who pointed out the inescapable necessity of change. Louis XVI had honest and virtuous advisers when he became King. Turgot became minister of finance, which was the key position in the state, and he succeeded within two years in cancelling more than 100 million francs in debts and anticipated taxes. The country sighed with relief. But all this did not touch the roots of the misery; it was only an improvement in administration, not in social conditions. Turgot knew this very well, and he turned his attention toward the latter. He submitted to the King a financial project, the basis of which was free corn trade, abolition of guilds, and finally the distribution of the land tax on *all* landed property, which meant equality of the traditional and priviledged property with acquired property, equality and liberty of commerce and industry, and the establishment of competition in trading.

French history would have appeared in a different perspective if proper importance had been attached to this crucial turning point. Indeed, the developments of the subsequent period were completely dependent on what the King was about to decide. Turgot's proposal represented a challenge to the throne to take charge of social reforms without which the state would perish. The road towards the union between the monarchy and the third estate—the life of the whole population—was open, indicating the possibility of progress without a revolution. If one privilege of the landed aristocracy was cancelled, there was nothing to prevent the others from being revoked by a far-reaching legislation; one would have to assemble the old estates and, by establishing self-government of the people, give support to the crown. Monarchy would thus have been the savior of the apparently insoluble social contradiction. If this did not happen, the people would necessarily give up the hope of gaining freedom through their rulers after they had reached unity through them. What could one possibly reply if people said: "We are going to perish unless conditions are changed, our ministers admit it; the King is able to help us; he does not want to; he would rather preserve the aristocracy than save twenty-five million people from certain ruin; he upholds the abuses. This is only conceivable because the monarchy itself is an abuse." The confidence in the monarchy could have been strengthened for centuries to come by *one* powerful act. But for the first time—and this was a unique example in Europe of that time—the court was victorious over the monarchy, and both were lost.

Louis XVI had the right instincts. He established free trade in corn, . . . he even yielded to Turgot in dissolving the guilds . . . But the court instigated the Queen's intrigue against Turgot; the whole aristocracy revolted; in vain did the King state emphatically: "Only I and Turgot love the people." The aristocracy reproached the King for impairing the sacred heritage of his children and for disgracing the throne by bourgeois institutions. If Louis XVI had shown as much strength in carrying out the good proposals as he did later in bearing adversities, he would have been saved. But he did not resist. When Turgot handed in his resignation he said to the King: "The fate of kings ruled by courtiers is that of Charles I." The King mourned, but the Court rejoiced. The ordinances were rejected. Clugny, who then became secretary of finances, wanted to save the finances by credit, which no longer existed. Malesherbes left for his country seat, later to accompany his King to the guillotine. The nobility had won a decisive victory. It was the year 1776. . . .

Ever since Turgot's resignation, France knew that there was no hope of changing the existing order by way of legislation. The third estate, deserted by the state, turned toward the new ideas. What it needed was a systematized expression of its convictions and demands; it found it in the doctrines which the social contradictions had already produced.

The Origin of the Ideas of Liberty and Equality

. . . There was only one way of solving these contradictions. Progress had to be justified by replacing traditional rights with new ones. The theoretical basis for the new rights could provide the moral justification of the struggle against the old ones. The most able scholars entered the new field, the philosophy of law, which was in search for a principle of absolute rights independent of all historical conditions. In this way, the laws of the coming new order were confronted with those of the traditional order, and the arguments set forth to justify the rights of the new order to dissolve the old were exalted as a science, traceable to the ultimate roots of human knowledge. In this fashion, philosophy of law became a revolutionary power in the interpretation of the law and of all its social institutions; it heralded the dawn of the new century.

The philosophy of law developed in the 16th century, during the

Reformation. It was transformed into a science during the Thirty Years' War by Hugo Grotius. From there on it continued to develop in accordance with its acknowledged task. At the time of its origin, the old Church and its law had been repelled. The new world needed a new law. The foundation of the old idea of law was the absolute commandment of God; the new era had to search for a new legal foundation, and since it could no longer be discovered in faith, it was found in philosophical concepts. Since all law is rooted in the individual and exists for his sake, legal philosophy, in spite of all its deviations, was bound to pay attention time and again to the individual. Aside from many errors and half truths that had cropped up in legal philosophy, this one tenet, namely, that the individual is the source of all laws and rights, had remained unchallenged. . . .

The importance of this idea can be summed up in a few words. The Absolute in any man was necessarily common to all men. The concept of personality did not allow for inequality. The philosophy of law, therefore, even if it came to different conclusions, could not choose a point of departure other than the one of theoretical equality of men.

Hobbes, often quoted and seldom understood, determined the direction of this interpretation as early as the 17th century. . . . Since his appearance, the idea of a *status naturalis* remained the basis of any philosophy of law. Natural equality as a starting point was generally accepted, but not Hobbes' conclusions concerning the war of all against all. Through him the philosophy of law received the name of "natural law." For one century, the philosophers continued to be concerned with this problem area. The last, very important and much too neglected representative of this line of thought was Christian Wolff, who elaborated it in an impressive system, and through whom it came to a close. . . .

According to him all people are first in *status naturalis;* in it "the laws of liberty and equality rule, the right to make use of everything which is necessary to human beings, the right of inviolability and the right to worship prevails." [Jus. Nat. et Gent. (1748) Praefat. to Part I. "libertas and aequalitas"]. In the state of nature "all people are equal", because "according to their nature" (which is identical with the concept of personality) "no person has more rights than any other", nobody has "more obligations than any other, nobody has any praerogative over any other." [*ibidem.* Part I Ch. I §§ 89, 92, 94, 105, 106] . . . Wolff adds [*ibidem.* § 130] "If people had remained in this original state, general equality of all would have lasted. . . . But after stepping out of this original condition, they have become unequal, as regards rights as well as obligations because property and the state were instituted." These were the results of a contract determined by human nature which established a state of law, the *status civilis*, whose function it is to promote human welfare. . . .

It is important to keep the theories of Wolff in one's mind in talking about the conditions of society at that period. Wolff was a most distinguished philosopher known not only in Germany; his logic was taught in France and to some extent in England; . . . he was the personification of the philosophy which attempted to reconcile the abstract concept of personality with the contradictions of the contemporary socio-political situation. This was the very reason he has been so quickly forgotten without leaving a trace. The existing law was in fact no longer reconcilable with the highest needs of the personality. People, longing for a change of social conditions, were searching for a different philosophy to bring about such a change. The logic of Wolff had had the function of explaining contemporary conditions philosophically. With this its mission ended. . . . Indeed, the statement that all men are free and equal corresponded to the needs of the new era; this proposition is the connecting link between the old and the new philosophy of law. However, why was it unavoidable that the transition from the state of nature with liberty and equality should have brought about thralldom and inequality? If the supreme essence of the personality consists in freedom and equality, was not the supreme right that which established liberty and equality, not only in the state of nature but also in society, and hereby maintained the harmony between the consequences of the social system and the principle? The philosophy of natural law did not answer this question, and here the thoughts of the old and the new philosophy diverged.

In their despair over the abuses of the state, the people first embraced the general statement that human rights are rooted in the nature of man. Social conditions were different from natural ones. Whereas nature taught equality, society preserved inequality. The difference between the ruling and the ruled classes in society appeared to reflect a contrast between nature and social development, i.e. civilization. With the unfailing instinct of the common people, the idea of a natural state became part of the common tradition, while the concept of equality slowly permeated their thoughts. Historians acknowledge that the education of children became more natural. Lavallée states: "The morals became less corrupt, there was less ostentation of vices; virtue was no longer considered ridiculous and people became afraid of the reputation of being immoral. Egotism lost its validity. Charity, humanity and sensibility were in everyboday's mind, permeated all publications and accompanied all projects, especially those of the governments." "The French," states

Lacretelle, "had only peaceful plans. At no time were they more peacefully united to fight all evil imposed upon men by nature and affecting social conditions in a thousand ways." Country life and agriculture became attractive, rural happiness was praised, and the peasantry was believed to be embued with the highest virtue. When Louis XVI, at the advice of Voltaire and Necker, liberated the serfs on the domains, a storm of applause broke out. Men were looking for confirmation of the inner nature of men in the external world; sentimentality and simplicity were nothing but a weapon against the frivolity and luxury of the upper class. However, this quiet opposition against an aristocratic society was not enough to create a new system of law. Out of the prevailing sentiments a clear and solid principle had to be developed. The new philosophy in France undertook this task.

The Principle of Equality and the New Ideas of Political Liberty

When the new philosophy turned toward the great question on which the future of France depended, one thing became quite clear: If a new principle of social order was to be found, it had to be discovered in man outside of society, in man proper. Man as such, the natural man, or in other words the concept of man, became the basis of the new philosophy. It followed from this principle of social order that one natural man is equal to any other natural man, a necessary basic statement upon which further requirements of the new society were to be founded. In this way, the ever-recurring principle of natural equality in the French movement, of *égalité*, entered from the theoretical plane to that of social reality. There is no use trying to describe the distinct meaning of this idea for the people who were willing to live and to die for it. In the public consciousness it first started as a vague notion, continued as a negation of the existing order, provided the basis for the struggle against the given form of community life, eventually including state, administration, law, church, society and property; it was a movement unable to determine its own goal. On this basis, a considerable literature—powerful in view of the circumstances—developed in France. It destroyed the belief in the right of birth as the basis of social stratification; such was its mission; it was essentially negative as the beginning of a new epoch usually is. Voltaire was the foremost representative of this movement. Voltaire did not have political convictions, but he had the right instinct regarding general social conditions. He prepared the way for freedom of thought by destroying with scathing sarcasm the belief in tradition in all areas of human life. To be convinced beyond doubt became ludicrous; this was a terrible weapon against a social order whose main support rested on the conviction of the people that the status quo of society was God-given. . . . Without Voltaire, the representatives of traditional thought would not have lost quite so quickly their self-confidence—the source of unshakeable resistance against dangerous thoughts; and without him the younger generation would have perhaps gained too late the necessary self-confidence in the struggle for new ideas. Voltaire was not primarily interested in politics; nevertheless, he tried to formulate some basic constitutional principles. . . .

More significant as a man of science was Helvetius. He was the psychologist of the idea of equality. In his most important work, *De l'Esprit*, he shows that all men are equally endowed with reason and that only society makes people unequal. . . . Rousseau stands next to him and above him. There is almost no event in the whole Franch revolution in which we do not discover traits which he had impressed upon the French mind. His treatise "On the Origin and the Foundations of Inequality among Men" had appeared as early as 1754. The Academy of Dijon had offered a prize for an essay on the subject: "What is the origin of inequality among men, and is it authorized by the law of nature?" Rousseau traces the origins of inequality to property and states that inequality is not in harmony with the law of nature. He did not receive the prize; the influence of the paper was perhaps even greater as a consequence of this fact. . . . Rousseau's *Émile* is nothing but the application of the philosophical principle of the *status naturalis* to education. . . . Equality of education will make all people free and equal. Inequality is rooted neither in man nor necessarily in the social order, but rather in the inequality of the conditions under which both live. This was a weighty conclusion. . . . From then on, the thought persisted that inequality is not an inherent necessity as taught by German philosophy, but that only external power imposes it upon men. It seemed irrelevant now to find out how this power had come into being. It was obvious that the state was the power which upheld inequality—in contradistinction to the inherent equality of all human beings—and that the state constitution prevented the state from fulfilling its function of preparing the ground for a return to equality. In this way, all feelings and thought converged upon the necessity of reforming the constitution; common grounds between pure theory and practical life were established.

We have now reached the point where the principles of the philosophy of law, after being merely a subject of philosophic exploration for a whole century, turned toward reality. The philosophy of law had expounded the need of a new state for the emerging new society; the question was what this new state was supposed to be like. Two different views prevailed.

The first line of thought may be called the practical or historical. Without denying the value of theoretical thinking, it sets itself a main goal which is attainable in practice. . . . It turned towards England, where it believed a form of government existed which seemed to correspond to its highest hopes. Thus an admiration for the British constitution developed. We still suffer under the one-sidedness of this view.

This school of thought was working for a reconciliation between present and future social conditions. It wanted to incorporate the remnants of the feudal estates into the newly and necessarily transformed state. It approved of the aristocracy but only on the basis of its usefulness; it wanted to preserve the monarchy, and assumed this could be done only by preserving the nobility and its privileges. It wanted to destroy despotism, but only by dividing organically the existing power of the state, because it saw the basis of despotism not in the political principles of absolute monarchy by divine grace, but in the concentration of excessive power in the hands of one person. It wanted to put an end to the suppression of the people not by a reduction of this power, but by balancing its various elements. For this purpose, it developed the concepts of judicial, legislative and executive powers, . . . but it did not understand that the democratic ideas were something other than a mere form of the highest power of the state. . . . It did not come up to the highest ideals of the time; . . . it reflected the opinions of the older generation and died with that generation. It would have shaped the future of France if the change had occurred without a revolution, but it was powerless in the revolutionary development. It did not have a conception of a free society based on free property rights, because it was attempting to build the political constitution on the well-understood basis of the estate society. . . .

The main representative of this school of thought was Montesquieu. His main work—*Esprit des Lois*—is well known. It is the political science of Aristotle applied to a monarchy and to an estate system. . . . Montesquieu merely showed what the old constitution might have been, not what the new one was to be. He had many and powerful followers, so that his ideas only disappeared with the monarchy itself.

Indeed, if the state were nothing else but the monarchy, and if the monarchy could only have been protected by the nobility and by privileges, there could have been no other alternative for society. Another concept of public authority had to be developed to justify freedom within the state. This idea was represented by the second school of thought. Its basis was not historical traditions but the concept of free man. Its principle was the *social contract*.

The idea that the state had been established and organized on the basis of a contract was first expounded by Hobbes; from him it came to Germany via Pufendorf and was accepted by all philosophers of the 17th and 18th centuries. One of the characteristics of this earlier theory was the assumption that the people had divested themselves of public authority by contract and that the state consequently would be absolute and inviolable in its form. . . . But is it possible for a power which is based on an independent will to be absolute? This is impossible; the idea of the contract is either completely wrong or has to lead to a different conclusion. State power established by popular will and contract is not absolute; rather it is the will of the people itself that is sovereign. The will of the people remains sovereign, and the state power acts only in its name and on its behalf. . . . The state therefore is identical with the people. Because of this, no nation is bound to a specific form of a state; rather, any nation remains free to establish a new constitution at any moment and to withhold its mandate if it considers this appropriate. . . . This version of the idea of the social contract was the one accepted by French society. . . .

Popular sovereignty was not an abstract term during that period. It meant nothing less than the authorization of the state to abrogate the privileges of the nobility and of the clergy. The right of reason was set against historical rights. By contrast to this superior right, the traditional system appeared to be one of sheer arbitrariness based on the rights of the stronger and upheld by force. Who could find fault with the people who used their own power to oppose the right of the mighty? Thus the new form of the state was legitimized, and the revolution became sanctified.

It is well known, that J. J. Rousseau was the main representative of this theory. The *"contrat sociale"* is the codex of popular sovereignty. . . . According to this theory, right was no longer on the side of the throne, which could arbitrarily call upon the consent of the people; neither was it divided between the two; rather, the people were the only true source of all rights. . . . The consequences of this proposition accounted for half of the revolution; they were directed first of all against the sovereignty of the king, the protector of the nobility and its privileges. If the king would not obey, were the people then obliged to obey him? No. . . . Says Rousseau: "If a brigand overtakes me, am I obliged to hand over my purse?" Certainly not. If those who hold the power are victorious, the result is the rule of force but not of right. The subjection of the real sovereign under his representatives is a misfortune, not an obligation.

These are Rousseau's general principles. They were applied . . . by Sieyès, whose pamphlet *Qu'est-ce que le Tiers État?* . . . was published in 1789 and went through several editions. It became the basis of the Revolution. Sieyès for the first time expressed who, according to Rousseau, was the sovereign representing the "general will," namely, the third estate. . . . "What is the third estate? Everything!" . . . What does the nation which the third estate represents really want? Here begins the specific task of Sieyès. First, it aims at the complete abolition of all privileges, exemptions, status-differences—not only of the tax privileges of the aristocracy; second, after the estates have thus been abolished, it aims at the representation of all the people in one body. Sieyès applied the ideas of Rousseau to the problem of popular representation. . . . Through him, people of action were won over to the theories of Rousseau. Consequently, the revolution had made a big step forward. At the same time, the news of the rebellion in North America arrived in France; Lafayette returned across the Atlantic Ocean, as witness of the victory of popular sovereignty over the "legitimate" power. The independent states prospered, and, as a result, the philosophers were able to contrast the example of old aristocratic England with that of North America. The enthusiasm was great, but it did not concentrate on North America. Rather it focused on the hope that the victory of the people over the holders of power would also come true in France. Thus the wrong position which the ruling power had taken toward society turned the minds of the French people against the power of the state. Different as the two schools of thought were, they both agreed on the necessity of changing the existing conditions. . . . It is evident that the revolution could not limit itself to changing only the institutions of the state.

Part One, Chapter One

THE FRENCH REVOLUTION

THE RULE OF THE THIRD ESTATE

The Notables of 1787 and 1788

. . . We have described the new element within the French population, the third estate, its size as well as its cultural life. Until 1789, this element had that quasi-rudimentary existence which is visible only at close scrutiny and apparent more on the basis of a general feeling than on the basis of distinct independent facts. Although the state acknowledged its existence, the third estate had no position in public law, and the monarchy was neither detached nor foresighted enough to value its importance. The third estate could become a political power only as a separate organization with specific functions within the state administration. The rise of such an organization was unavoidable, but the question of how this goal could be reached had remained unsolved.

The simplest and most natural solution would have been for the state to have taken over this task at the right time. But none of the public authorities was willing or courageous enough to grant the right for such an organization and the personal representation to the third estate. A dismal feeling spread over France. The leading men of the country definitely predicted the approach of a terrible revolution; the impression spread that France was in a state of tremendous, apparently insoluble, contradictions. Even the Court had a foreboding of a tumultuous period to come; on the surface, however, everything appeared to be quiet. . . .

The theory of society shows that the social order, according to its unchangeable nature, determines the constitution of the state. Wherever a new social order develops under the rule of an old constitution, a contradiction necessarily arises between society and state. This contradiction is part of social life, spreading to the life circle of every individual; it affects every commodity, all pleasures and any ability; it spreads to the constitution and administration, which becomes estranged from the people. . . . It is this contradiction which manifests itself in the feeling of discontent, of anxious expectation of new and powerful events. This hazy premonition reflects merely the absolute necessity for a harmonious relationship between constitution and society and the certainty that this harmony as an unalterable law has to reassert itself at any price. The harmony is broken whenever a new class of society is added to the established ones; and the uneasiness therefore indicates—according to the law of political change—the rise of a new social class and its demand to share in the power of the state. Such was the situation in France during the last half of the 18th century; the same was true again during the 1840's. If the true nature of society were known to the same extent as were the various forms of the state, good intentions could have avoided many evils, then as now. But good intentions especially were lacking. Those who ruled the state did not want to share their power with the other classes. Besides, there was in fact nobody who demanded such sharing. . . . It appeared as if one needed only to refuse representation to the third estate in order to render it powerless. . . . It seemed as if the sheer act of refusal was sufficient. However, the tension grew.

Meanwhile, the financial distress, the immediate sore point of the situation, grew progressively more serious. . . . It was the privilege of the nobility not to be subject to taxes. The whole power of the aristocracy rested on this prerogative. Turgot's main idea, originally concerned with the national economy, was now applied by Necker to the public finances. It was publicly acknowledged . . . that the social order had to be broken to preserve the state. But the aristocracy still possessed absolute power, and Necker, like Turgot, was dismissed. . . . Yet the stress was not relieved thereby. Not only were the reserves of the state exhausted, but so was its credit. . . . Even the King's aristocratic secretary had to admit that either the state or the privileges of the nobility were lost. Money finally accomplished what the lofty ideas of philosophers, the urgent admonitions of statesmen, and the greatest suffering of the people had failed to do. This was the first occasion when money exerted immense power; it forced the state to initiate the new social order. . . .

The main point of the *Memoirs de M. Calonne au Roi*, written in 1785, was the suggestion that the land tax ought to be extended to all landed property and that the third estate be relieved of the most oppressive imposts, the *taille* (head tax), the tax on salt and the compulsory services. Without such measures there was no way out of the difficulties. To be able to inaugurate these laws the King was asked to convene the Notables.

The Notables were originally understood to be the representatives of the people. Their origin is obscure: the high point of their importance was in the 14th century, when they became known under the name of "*Etats Généraux.*" Since then, they had become more and more tools in the hands of the King. . . . The Notables, predominantly composed of the nobility and the clergy, were but an advisory board without any legislative powers. In fact, the king, who continued to be absolute, had the power to manage and use them as he saw fit. . . .

Historians have largely neglected the two assemblies of the Notables. It is true that these assemblies changed nothing, but nevertheless they are of great importance and should have taught an important lesson to future generations . . .

The Notables represented the old feudal society; therefore they seemed acceptable to the nobility and the clergy . . . The state gave the Notables the choice of voluntarily yielding their privileges for the benefit of the state; it asked them to derpive themselves voluntarily of their privileges and of thus to recognize as equals the new elements of society. It was one of the solemn moments when an opportunity exists to avoid a violent revolution by a voluntary sacrifice. But the old society rejected the offer. The Notables of 1787 and 1788 exemplified the statement—which almost possesses the validity of a law—that a society which controls the state rarely abandons a social order without compulsion and that it usually risks a revolution in preference to letting the lower class, at the expense of the hitherto privileged take the place to which it is entitled. This proposition, applicable to the analysis of the source of all revolutions, proved to be true during those two years in France . . .

Before calling on the *États Généreaux,* the state made another attempt to obtain the approval of the Notables. In 1788, the Notables were called upon to voice their opinions concerning the best method of convoking the Estates General. . . . It was the last attempt to give an opportunity to the old society of giving a friendly hand to the emerging new one . . . Necker, a representative of the ideas of the third estate, was called upon once more. Necker belonged to the school of Montesqieu; he could conceive of a state without estates. He requested the doubling of the votes of the third estate, in order to set up a lower house as against the upper house of the two privileged estates. The Notables voted five to one against this doubling of the votes of the third estate. This amounted to denying the new estate an adequate position within the government. The Notables were dissolved. The state was deserted by the old society; it had to accept the fact that only a representation based on the principles of the new society could save it. What neither reason nor sympathy had been able to accomplish dire need did. It forced the state into its natural and only appropriate position of putting itself at the head of the development towards a new society. The short history of the Notables—often overlooked in spite of its importance—has been summarized by the clever statement of a statesman, as told by Sieyès: "What did the Notables do in 1787? They defended their privileges against the throne. What did they do in 1788? They defended them against the nation." [Chapter IV §11].

The Estates General and the Constituent National Assembly

. . . On January 1, 1789, the King issued a resolution, according to which, "in consideration of the opinion of the minority of the Notables" and of public opinion, representatives of the people ought to be called together in such a way that the third estate was represented by the same number as the total of the two other estates . ..

These *États Généraux* assembled on May 5th, 1789. This day marks a new epoch in history. It is necessary to look carefully at this assembly which was supposed to rule France . . .

The representatives of the third estate included everybody who—without belonging to the two privileged groups—excelled in competence, scholarship and character. No other assembly had up till now gathered together such a number of excellent minds and personalities. It represented the most valuable part of the people, few of them young but also few who would not have been willing to sacrifice their lives for their convictions. They were conscious of the fact that the future of the country depended on them. Everybody who had taken part in the formation of the new set of ideas, was present among them. Excellence was without question on the side of the representatives of the third estate.

The representatives of the two other estates were understandably nothing but the sequence of the Notables, with all their prejudices, their stubbornness and their persistent defense of every prerogative. Only the lower clergy was favorably inclined toward the third estate . . .

What, then, were these *États Généraux* which were thus composed? Indeed they were a strange phenomenon never encountered before; there they were, the two big classes of society, represented at their best within a limited space, as one body and not as enemies confronting each other; assembled rather to decree either the destruction of the state with the preservation of the old privileges or the survival of the state with the abolition of these privileges . . .

The task of these *États Généraux* was to legislate the annulment of the supreme and sanctified rights of the two all-powerful estates, a task which even the state itself had been unable to accomplish. This in itself was already an accomplishment that usually takes places only after a long struggle. The power of the state was really in the hands of society; the government had succumbed to the representatives of the people; the decisive step had been taken with the convocation of the *États Généraux*. Now the three estates stood together. Necessity and reason forced the Court to support the third estate against the other two. The third estate was represented in equal numbers as the other two estates, and its representatives were superior to those of the other estates. It also knew how to be victorious. With surprising tact for so young an assembly, the third estate requested that the three estates should jointly undertake the legitimation of the deputies. The question on which everything depended, whether the votes were to be counted by persons or by estate, would have been thereby decided. The other estates opposed the motion. The quarrel lasted five long weeks . . . The count of votes by estate according to former rules would have amounted to nothing but an approval of the old feudal society by the *États Généraux;* the counting of votes by heads meant the acknowledgement of political equality of all members of the state. Finally the privileged estates had to give in . . .

Was this a parliamentary victory? Such an interpretation would indicate a crude narrow-mindedness. In fact it was much more. By the the decision to vote as individuals rather than as estates, the third estate took the supreme power originally resting with the three estates into its own hands. Beyond this, the decision implied equality of all the members of the *États Généraux;* it destroyed the principle of feudal society. . . . As soon as this new principle became accepted, the whole concept of the *États Généraux* was changed. They no longer represented merely the three estates as such, but, since all members were considered equal, they now also represented the nation, the community of equals. It therefore followed naturally that the representatives did not consider themselves any longer as an assembly of the three estates, but as representatives of the nation. At the suggestion of Sieyès they constituted themselves as the National Assembly.

What was, in the nature of things, bound to happen had become a fact: the downfall of feudal society and its supersession by a society of equals. One thing remained to be done. The government had challenged the *États Généraux* to break the law of the old society; it had raised them above itself and made them a legislative body. The Estates General had been transformed into a National Assembly, representing the third estate. Consequently, this body had to set itself up as the true legislative power, and they did what the situation demanded with enthusiastic conviction. They declared the Assembly to be an indivisible unit, set up the principle that no taxation was legal unless approved by them, and issued a declaration of the King and the nation to justify and explain these steps.

This powerful Assembly rose in a few days to the summit of the Revolution. It had destroyed the social opposition within its boundaries and demonstrated the equality and unity of the nation. The law of reason was victorious over the historical law. It was more than an administrative reform . . . A completely new state had to emerge with the new society established by the Assembly.

The brief interval of time which we are considering here has been poorly understood and often misinterpreted. It has often been considered as a parliamentary struggle only. But the very fact that a revolution followed shows that it was much more than that. That the French Revolution was a social revolution had already been indicated by the preceding analysis. This first victory of the third estate, in fact, implied already the whole transformation of society. The full import of these steps will become clear only when a history of society is written.

With the establishment of the National Assembly, only the principle of equality in public law had been accepted. The third estate, the nation, had only made a first step into a sphere that had slowly to be conquered . . . So far, the National Assembly had only cancelled the privileges of the estates. What were the essential characteristics of the rule of the estates? . . . The privileges of the nobility and the clergy had developed from circumstances inherent in landed property; the various privileges were nothing but an application of the principle of feudalism according to which landed property is affiliated with the sovereign rights of the state. By eliminating the special representation of the two privileged estates, the Assembly actually dealt only with the consequences that arose out of the principle of the territorial domain. This included the individuality and the entail of landed property, which caused the great differences in the distribution of land. It included further the services and the variety of other burdens imposed on the serfs. It truly reflected the dependence of the people upon the aristocracy. It further included such sovereign rights as that of police and of jurisdiction. In short, it was the very core of the feudal social order. As long as this principle remained untouched, a parliamentary rule of the third estate meant very little. The Assembly knew all this very well. By establishing itself as a National Assembly, it had not yet solved the old contradiction; it had only replaced it by a new one. The representatives of the third estate remained subservient to the other estates. The third estate held the power within the state, but the first and second estates held the power in society. Again the state constitution and the social order contradicted each other. This contradiction could only be solved by annihilating the basis of the feudal order, namely, feudal property. Out of necessity, the new power of the third estate now turned towards its most difficult, but also it greatest, task. This is the history of the years that followed.

Meanwhile, the people arose. The fatally deluded government did not understand what it had started to do: it had convoked the *États Généraux* to abolish the main privileges of the two superior estates, and to accomplish this it had given to the third estate the greatest chance of commanding the maporile vote. It did, however, consider the legitimate use of this power as a revolution against itself. For the first time, the true nature of a monarchy based on nobility became apparent. The King declared himself in favor of the aristocracy and used military power to interfere with the new developments. The King closed the Assembly, gathered troops around Paris and attempted to quell the movement in blood. People were seized by rage. Revolt broke out. The Bastille was stormed. The old state showed that it no longer had even military power. The people were victorious in the streets, as the third estate had been in the Assembly . . . This struggle was of the utmost importance in one respect: it drew the masses into the dispute about principles and imbued the intellectual conflict with the violence of passion . . . From then on, the Assembly and the nation were one body. The subsequent steps of the Assembly strengthened this bond.

The Declaration of the Rights of Man, the First Principle of the New Society, and the New Order of Property Rights

. . . The new society demanded a completely new legal foundation; in order to provide it, the Assembly had to state its principles . . . The victory of the people in Paris was not an ordinary revolt; it was the first heartbeat of the new life. Next to the establishment of the National Assembly it was the greatest political event at the beginning of the Revolution . . .

Everybody felt that something extraordinary had happened. There came a moment when no single person dared to fall behind the all-powerful movement. This moment was the famous night of August 4th. No distinct step had yet been taken against the prevailing differences of rank by the new Assembly, which was based on the still embryonic concept of "the nation". The youthful courage of some members of the privileged estates anticipated the new law. The young Count of Noailles suggested the redemption of all feudal imposts and the abolition of personal services. He blazed the trail. All the privileged rushed to the tribune, everybody brought a sacrifice; within a few hours the hunting privilege, the tithe, the right of jurisdiction, offices for sale, tax exemptions, inequality of taxes, pensions, privileges to town and villages, the guilds—all were abolished . . . The still uncrystallized idea of equality and unity of the nation had for the first time acquired a practical meaning.

During this night the Assembly had the experience, as people who have long been searching for a truth, of suddenly seeing themselves confronted with the goal of their search through an inspiration. Without further inquiring about the consequences of its statements . . . the Assembly adopted all these principles. There was universal rejoicing; it resounded all over Europe . . . Mirabeau summarized the decisions in a common declaration; after a short debate it was accepted on August 26th by the Assembly. It was the well-known Declaration of the Rights of Man.

The Declaration, submitted to the King and accepted by him, was the basis and the beginning of the Constitution of 1791 . . . Its contents can be summarized in three main points: First, it abolished the privileges of birth and stated that all people in society are equal with regard to power, acquisition, occupation and property. It declared liberty, security of property, and the right to resist oppression as inalienable rights of Man . . .

The second and not less important principle adopted by the Assembly . . . established equality within the state. It stated in Article 6: "All citizens have the right to cooperate personally or through their representatives in the process of legislation. All citizens, knowing that they are equal, can equally share the enjoyments of all dignities, public status and public offices according to their ability and without any other distinction than their virtue and their talents." . . .

Thirdly, the principle of the sovereignty of the people was set forth . . . To secure the sovereignty of the general will, the press was set free, and the right to assemble and to petition was formulated. According to this principle, the general will is formed by the effective participation of all citizens, and the law thus becomes the expression oft he common will to which everybody submits.

This is the essence of the Declaration of the Rights of Man. Its logical connection with the trend of history can easily be understood. It is not a law in the traditional sense, nor is it simply a measure taken by a legislative body; rather it represents the first acknowledgement of the principle which secured in public law exclusive power to those elements from which the third estate had emerged and through which it had become powerful. The principle which made the Declaration the foundation of the new society was the development of the free individual personality unhampered by the feudal privileges of the past. The Declaration reflected the essence of the demands of the third estate, now fully aware of its own wishes. From now on, the movement of the people towards a new order of society had a solid foundation, and it has not been abandoned since. The ideas of liberty and equality had changed by being applied to actual conditions. Until then, these ideas had been conceived merely as political maxims. Now it became clear that they were social principles. From then on, the revolution, by setting up the Declaration of the Rights of Man as the first social principle of the nation, showed its true character in terms of a social reorganization of the total population.

Yet, the Declaration is nevertheless wholly negative. It does not establish anything. It does not contain anything but a systematic destruction of old feudal rights. A new society cannot be formed by a sheer negation; the Declaration was merely the beginning of the new social order. Here we have to refer to a series of decrees of the National Assembly which have not been properly evaluated because of ignorance as regards the concept of society . . . These decrees are the actual foundation of the new social order; they have continued to be in effect since the beginning of the Revolution. They are the true cornerstones of the transformation, which would never have lasted without them.

The Declaration of the Rights of Man had indeed asserted the equality of men as an inalienable principle. But what was it that had made three quarters of France so miserable, so dependent, and so unequal by comparison to the upper class? It was not the law; the law was only a consequence of something else, namely, the distribution of land. As long as two-thirds of it remained in possession of the aristocracy, as long as millions were dependent on the landlord, equality was a principle and a wish, but not a fact . . .

The night of August 4th did not bring about a change in the legal conditions of the peasant class; it only proclaimed principles. What mattered was the application of these principles . . . First, there was a large class of completely dependent serfs . . . Louis XVI had liberated them on his domains by the Edict of 1779, but the powerful feudal lords had not followed suit. There were still millions of serfs; . . . in a society where serfdom exists the principle of equality is an empty phrase. The Assembly immediately decreed that all these privileges based on power and contradicting liberty were to be abolished without compensation

. . . This declaration marked a true and impressive progress. It meant not only that the whole class of serfs could now breathe freely under the new law and could pursue the acquisition of property by labor; it also meant as a consequence that the new order of things gained most fervent supporters. Only this law explains the enthusiasm of the lowest classes for principles, the beneficial influences of which they probably experienced while they first heard about them. Equally important was another series of relationships based on all irredeemable feudal taxes, which were abolished by the Assembly . . . In removing these, the Assembly acted on the assumption that they were contractual, and interpreted them by the decree of August 11, 1789 as regular assessments subject to redemption . . . Finally the principle of irredeemable rent was abolished, and all rents were declared to be redeemable. (Dec. 18, 1790). By these decrees the Assembly laid the basis for the development of a peasantry and an agricultural economy in France. Without them the population would not have supported the revolution nor borne its burden. Their influence has been tremendous; they derived from the principle which, from then on, determined the future of the whole economy. They opened the road to well-being and independence for the farmer by making him free, personally as well as financially.

However, these decrees were only a step towards independence for the small landholders. Aside from this there continued to exist—in spite of the night of August 4th—the tremendous estates of the aristocracy . . . As long as these remained, equality was only a phrase, because the free peasants amounted to little by comparison and the estates presented a source for new dependence and new privileges. The Assembly was well aware of this. It used the only method which would unfailingly destroy this fortress of inequality on a legal basis in the name of equality. The permanence of these aristocratic possessions had been secured by the fact that they were transmitted undivided to the eldest son of the family . . . On April 8th, 1791, a decree was passed by which all heirs in the same relationship of consanguinity were to receive equal parts of the property. Every death of an aristocrat, therefore, led to the division of his possessions into as many parts as there were heirs. The large land holdings met unavoidably with dissolution; by continuously becoming smaller, the sons of the big landowners were brought with each generation a step closer to the small farmer. In this fashion, excessive land-ownership was reduced, while the small landholder, who was now free, was enabled to expand his possessions. Few laws have had a more powerful effect on the social development in France; this decree had become the basis of equality in an agricultural economy . . . It also won over the whole group of younger descendants of the upper classes for the cause of the Revolution, because it gave them hope for a share in the landownership of their families.

One thing still remained to be done. A great number of citizens were as yet unable to get hold of land because no land was available for sale. Here a political expediency contributed towards the solution of the problem . . . In order to reduce the government's debts, public domains had to be sold . . . The sale had two grave consequences. First, it gave rise to a great number of new estates, small and large, which now all contributed to the rise of well-being and the development of the economy. On the other hand, all these proprietors, who became owners in the name of the Revolution, were totally dependent on the victory of the revolutionary principle. Thus they became the main representatives of this principle within the agricultural sector of the society, so that each step they took to strengthen their position and their new possessions also contributed toward the stabilization of the Revolution . . .

The above are the most important decrees by which the abstract principles of the Declaration of the Rights of Man were transmitted from the .Assembly into the reality of social life: into the cottage of the peasant, the family of the aristocrat, and in the relationship of the new landowner towards the soil. They were the real roots of the Revolution which made it possible for French society to withstand internal terrorism and the attack from without . . . Only by these laws were the foundations laid for the new society of France, and only now the revision of the Constitution became an inevitable necessity. At the very time when the Assembly drew the consequences of the events of August 4th did it become aware of the fact that the new order of the state first had to be placed on a firm, well-protected social foundation. The Declaration designates the state as a "social body" (*corps social*) and states in Article 16: "Any society which does not provide a guarantee of rights does not have a constitution." For the first time in history, it was stated that the state constitution is conditioned by the social order . . .

The Third Estate and the two Elements of the New Society.
Its Contradictions. The Introduction of Property Qualifications.

The French Revolution had started when the third estate declared itself to be "the whole nation," according to a statement of Sieyès. What was this third estate? What was it that made it into a unified whole? Scholars, artists, merchants, shopkeepers, farmers, workers, even hoodlums and vagabonds belonged to it; they did not share a common way of life but only the purely negative opposition against the two privileged classes. This is what held all its members together in one unit. It is understandable that the question of whether there were differences within the third estate was not raised, so long as only determined solidarity could lead to victory over the privileged. The equality among its members was the equality resulting from the absence of rights, the equality of being suppressed; the freedom aspired to was the freedom from the yoke of privilege. The third estate was united on this matter and had been victorious in this respect . . .

Now it had become the only estate. But a single estate ceases to be an estate, it represents society itself. After the aristocracy was destroyed, after the clergy had become state functionaries and all privileges had been abolished, the third estate had replaced feudal society; there was no other society left.

However, a single estate is not only a unit, but necessarily homogeneous. As an estate it consists of a multitude, or perhaps a community of individuals sharing equal rights. Society, however, is more than a mere community; it is a specific order of its various members, a system of classes, interests and activities. An estate cannot be a society. If an estate takes the place of society, it either disappears or carries within itself the elements for the emergence of a new society . . . The appearance of the third estate is not so much the beginning of its reign . . . but rather the first step towards an altogether new social order whose seeds were already present in this victorious estate.

Such was the position of the third estate after its quick victory. It had so far acted only in a negative fashion; it had considered a new constitution but not yet a new social order. Now it was challenged to develop a new society. How could that be done? A new constitution can be created by one stroke, because it is an act of the will of the people. To create a new society is beyond a deliberate decision, because it is the creation of the social life of the people. A sudden establishment of a social order by the third estate was unthinkable. It had to grow slowly and organically. This is what makes that time so significant . . . In order to mold the forms of the new society it had to discover the elements which the third estate contained . . .

The third estate proceeds on the assumption that everybody has the right to participate equally in public decisions. But it is impossible for everybody to rule simultaneously. People have to choose representatives. The choice should fall on the most able and most influential. But who are they? Obviously those who have the means for the best education and for the most powerful support of others. All those who dispose of these means will, by the nature of their position, be called upon to represent the state by those who lack these means. What are these means? Evidently, first of all, the superior faculty to administer public affairs, knowledge and education. To acquire these, however, certain conditions have to be presupposed. What are these? There is no doubt that property is the condition without which the individual rarely or never acquires a higher cultural status and practical influence. It is property which singles out within the community of citizens those who can administer the state; and since they should be and are superior, it is property which in a society of equal rights creates differences and transforms the community into a society . . . Although the third estate appeared to be quite unconcerned about the social order, the contrast on which the future society was based developed all the same, almost unnoticed. It is again the contrast between the property owners and propertyless. But their relationship has a completely different character from that of the past.

The feudal society was also based on property. But it was the historically conditioned and privileged land ownership which could not be acquired by work. The concept of the new society is based on labor, and the new society makes acquired property the basis of its order. The feudal society absolutely excluded equality. The socialist society makes equality the ruling principle; the third estate, while demanding equality of opportunity, accepts the right to the acquisition of property and the resulting difference in education and prestige as a principle of differentiation . . . True, the new constitution was not concerned with these differences and their consequences. However, if it is true that society determines the constitution, there has to be at least one point where social reality is reflected in the constitution . . . In the case of the French constitution such a point was provided by property qualifications . . .

The introduction of property qualifications—no matter whether large or small, simple or differentiated—marks . . . the intervention of the acquisitive society in constitutional development. Once society is based on property, property qualifications are of necessity established. The question whether this is practical or not is nothing but a variation of the question whether a society based on property rights is the most desirable . . . Strangely enough, during the first months of the French Revolution, events confirmed this kind of interpretation. As early as September 29th, 1789, Thouret submitted the Commission's report on the voting system. The Commission was aware that it had to reconcile the structure of the new society with the theoretical demands for equality. It was also aware of the fact that this could not possibly be done. It stated: "It is not necessary to make a contribution in order to be a member of the Assembly, since this would destroy personal equality and establish an aristocracy of the wealthy"; nevertheless the commission suggested a system of property qualifications . . .

A violent debate arose around this problem, illustrating that here was the very center of the struggle between the principle of equality and the principle of civil society. The left side of the Assembly started to talk about a new slavery, the right would have liked to add landowner-ship as a prerequisite of eligibility for office. . . . Nevertheless—even though with a slim majority—the suggestions of the Commission were accepted. For the first time, society won a victory over principles. The vehement attacks against the Assembly indicated—already at this point —the approaching cleavage. . . .

According to the concept of personality, everybody who was of age and a resident of the country ought to be a full citizen. The Constitution, however, states: An active citizen is one who has made a direct con-tribution, the equivalent to the value of three working days; everybody who works for a wage in a household (*"serviteur à gages"*) is excluded from active citizenship. The concept of a full citizen in this constitution is thus dependent upon a criterion which is not—like age—an attribute of each individual. Completely excluded from all participation in public action is he who does not own anything, namely the worker; he cannot meet the necessary requirements, regardless of his personal qualifications and his intelligence, which might deserve highest honor. There is no equality of all individuals, but only of those who own a certain amount of property. This establishes an insurmountable difference between two kinds of members of the state, citizens and subjects; the difference in estate is replaced by the difference in wealth; from then on there exists a new dependent class. . . . The first period of the French Revolution, the constitutional period, ends at this point. It had fulfilled its task, but it had not completed the revolution. . . .

We have seen that the fight against the feudal society established the principle of equality as the basis of all progress. We have seen further-more that equality during the downfall of feudalism became the motto for the basic laws of the Declaration of the Rights of Man. We have seen, finally, that the Constitution of 1791 considered equality of all citizens as fundamental and the will of the nation as sovereign. But how did the Constitution apply this principle of equality? At the same instant when all differences were supposedly eliminated, when all members and classes of society were brought into a close relationship, when all barriers sanctioned by law and customs were destroyed, in the midst of this liberated populace the constitution erected the barrier of property ownership in order to attain liberty. How was it possible that the contradiction between the principle and its application remained concealed? What was the justification for separating active and passive citizens, after the declaration (Article 1) had stated: "men are born and remain equal in their rights"? How was it possible to exclude the large masses of non-owners from the legislation and yet state, in Article 6, that the law was an expression of the "general will"? Was there any justification for excluding from the sovereign nation those who did not pay direct taxes but who, on the other hand, contributed by excise taxes and were also under obligation to bear arms? Or how was it possible to justify the contradiction whereby Part I Article I stated "that there is no other difference between citizens than that of virtue, of character and of talents", while on the other hand the differences of ownership were stipulated in the very same document as a basis for the rights of active citizenship?

A contradiction was hidden here of which, up to then, nobody had been aware; . . . it is this contradiction which was taken up and elaborated during the following decades. This contradiction between the idea of the free and equal personality and the differentiated distribution of goods was destined to determine the social development of the whole 19th century. To gauge the importance of this contradiction and its influence on the historical events in France, it is necessary to analyze its specific characteristics.

The contradiction which exists between the distribution of property and the free personality is by no means a temporary one. It is an absolute contradiction, due to the boundless ambitions and the external limitations of all mortals. This contradiction did not originate through the laws of the new society, but it emerged for the first time during this period. The great thinkers of the 18th century had long recognized the dilemma. . . . However, to understand the revolutionary movements, one has to keep in mind that the contradiction at the beginning was neither great nor oppressive. Its gravity was mitigated by the notion that property is a result of labor and thrift and that everybody is capable of acquiring it. The oppressiveness of the contrast develops only through the large accumulation of capital and the competition between its owners, a competition which tends to lower wages and increase investments necessary for any enterprise. Thereby the acquisition of property, even under favorable circumstances, becomes possible only in the course of several generations.

With reference to the social conditions in France, it follows that the struggle between capital and labor was an inevitable consequence of the principle of equality; its sudden appearance, however, was not so much a result of the inner development of society but of the pressures of extraneous circumstances. It is a generally acknowledged fact that the changing course of the French Revolution was brought about by the aggression of foreign powers. Only from the vantage point of social history is it possible to prove the full truth and the significance of this statement. We claim that the transition from the constitutional to the social stage of the early revolutionary period, in spite of all the unsolved contradictions of the former, was made possible only through aggression from outside. We shall consider it our main task to trace the development of this contradiction.

TRANSITION TO THE DEMOCRATIC - COMMUNISTIC PERIOD

*The Gradual Separation of the Two Classes. The National Guard
    and the Clubs. Their First Clash.*

The great reformers of this period started out with the conviction that the concept and rights of citizenship could provide a basis for an order of a state and a society of the free and the equal. But together with this principle there emerged the new social order based on property. This transpired not only in society but also in the Constitution. . . . At the beginning of the Revolution, when the close unity of the whole third estate had gained victory over privileges, reference was made exclusively to "the nation;" the individual was the "citizen." Nobody took notice of any differences. Not even the concept the "people" *(peuple)*, even less that of the "bourgeois," was being used. The general opinion prevailed that state power was in the hands of the whole nation.

The public becomes aware of the existence of classes in society, no matter how sharp the distinctions of class are, only when one class is in control of the state. . . . Property qualifications may make people aware of class differences. . . . But the rulership of a class becomes noticeable when sudden events crystallize elements of the different classs into independent institutions. This is what happened in France.

After the fall of the Bastille, . . . after the destruction of the old state order and the annihilation of traditional authorities,—when the monarchy and the Court were left without real power—it became clear that it is impossible to remain without any ruling authority. But on what should power be based? It should be very enlightening for all those who are still unwilling to see the true meaning of the notion of popular sovereignty to consider seriously and objectively this particular development of the French Revolution. What could popular sovereignty mean except that the whole people held whole power over the nation? Such was exactly the case. The "nation" ruled, and it ruled absolutely. It ruled as a homogeneous mass of citizens. . . .

History shows that whenever sovereignty of the people is proclaimed as the highest principle, immeasurable confusion in state and society follows. Such a confusion indicates an inner contradiction. The concept of society explains this inner contradiction. The concept of "the people" applies to a unity only in relation to the outside world, in contrast to other people. "The people" proper is nothing else but a social order ruled by social elements which determine relationships of super- and subordination, dependence and differences of interests. Sovereignty of the people actually comprises the concept of the "sovereignty of society."

Since any society contains major opposing forces which are hard to reconcile, . . . the acceptance of popular sovereignty implies the sovereignty of these specific elements within society. Each tries to subdue the other; each, imbued with sovereignty, aligns itself against the other. The intrinsic presupposition of the concept of sovereignty—unity of personal will—thereby disappears; the struggle of antagonistic social elements legalized by the vague notion of popular sovereignty takes its place. . . .

With the breakdown of the old feudal state, two highly interesting institutions emerged: The National Guard and the Clubs. The storming of the Bastille . . . appeared to be the beginning of greater trouble. . . . In anticipation of more serious difficulties, some distinguished citizens met in Paris, . . . divided the city into sixty districts and established an organization consisting of all citizens able to bear arms. They were supplied with uniforms and munition, chose their own leader, and bore the name of *Garde Nationale*. Lafayette became its Commander. Nobody had made preparations for such a plan, . . . nobody had issued an appeal; . . . but in three days, 40,000 men were mobilized. Whom did they represent? What was the importance of this new impressive power which suddenly appeared in Paris like a completely natural phenomenon without causing a great sensation and spread from there over all of France? . . .

If, in the course of a revolution, the state opposes the demands of the new elements of society, the danger exists that they will be suppressed through an external power, represented by the army. The army cannot possibly support an idea or society at large, . . . it can only support the state. If a new society wants to be safe against the power of the state, it has to provide an organization corresponding to the army. In civil society this organization is the National Guard. The reason for its appearance is always fear of state power. . . . This was the reason for the establishment of the French Guard. It was the weapon by which the new victorious third estate counter-balanced the power of the monarchy and defended itself against the standing army. However, there was a second element represented in the National Guard. After the fall of the Bastille, the military power of the monarchy was already broken, since state power had been transferred to the third estate. Immediately after victory, the third estate disintegrated into opposing groups. Nominally, equality prevailed, but in reality owners ruled over non-owners. The new Constitution was in the hands of the ruling class. This state had no army. It needed one. The National Guard, composed of active citizens, offered its services; and, by upholding the Constitution, it became the military power of the ruling class of society.

The National Assembly had excluded the whole class of non-owners, the passive citizens, from participation in sovereign action. Full citizens were meant to rule half-citizens; particularly, the workers could not own property. In upholding this law, the National Guard upheld the rule of the legislators, the active citizens. In defending order, it defended the political power of the owners over the non-owners. Since the law split the "nation" into two social classes, the National Guard maintained the rule of one part of the nation over the other, the owners over the non-owners. It therefore—without even knowing or wanting it—determined the course of events on the domestic scene in France. . . . It represented the armed organization of the ruling class against the masses which were excluded from power. Thus it developed from a semi-police and semi-military force into a social power, into the embodiment of a social contradiction, into a social institution. . . .

The opposing forces developed a representative organization in the form of clubs. The nature and the destination of the clubs is determined by the needs which created them. No constitution can satisfy everybody. But everybody is well aware of the fact that improvements can be made by way of discussions if freedom of speech is guaranteed. The dissatisfied were looking for contacts and concensus; this is what the clubs provided. Clubs develop whenever the constitution or the administration do not meet the demands of a part of the nation; it is their function to formulate the thoughts which reach beyond the existing order, if it is believed that these thoughts can be realized. . . . Therefore, clubs are unnecessary if the general will essentially prevails; they whither away as soon as this is accomplished, and they reemerge if this is not the case. . . .

While the National Assembly carried on its activities, misery in Paris grew. There was no work and no bread. . . People, though free, suffered terribly. Whose fault was it? Did the sovereign nation not even provide the means to avoid famine? . . . Obviously there was something wrong with the planned constitution, which did not correspond to the demands of the people. Whenever the masses suffer they look for an enemy. They are willing to submit to leaders and easily become a tool of demagogues. The clubs represented these two elements: those who were not satisfied with the Constitution because of its inner contradiction became the leaders of the masses who suffered because they had no property. The clubs promised help; they became the organizations of the propertyless class.

Such was the state of affairs in 1790. The main trends are clearly distinguishable. . . . It is the division of the new civil society into two classes which represented the contradiction legalized by the new constitution. The classes of owners and of non-owners are standing side by side, clearly distinguishable and as yet peaceful. Through the National Guard and the clubs they have become aware of their respective position.

The concept of the "nation" already appears to be divided into two, the cleavage increased from day to day. And we ask: What was the meaning of popular sovereignty now? That is to say, who held state power proper, which is by definition indivisible? The monarchy became weaker from day to day; the zeal displayed by the clubs did not leave any doubt that, already by 1790, the race between the two parts of society for the conquest of state power had begun. . . .

Shortly after the Assembly had moved to Paris, the starving people had slain a baker. The Assembly was extremely indignant and wanted to intervene with the strongest measures. A law against revolt, the first "martial law" was suggested. . . Already at this point the deeper significance of the whole question became clear. Robespierre said: "The Commune"—at that time yet ruled by respected citizens—"requests bread and soldiers—and what for? To suppress *the people*." For the first time, this now widely accepted term was used in a way distinctly different from the concept of "nation", a concept which had not been questioned until that point. Here was the core of the conflict. The citizenry felt endangered by the unknown power; the Assembly, guided by a vague anxiety, issued on the very same day the law against revolt, the so-called "Martial Law": "If the masses do not disperse upon request the armed forces will open fire." . . .

This law is of great importance; from now on, the class of *bons citoyens* was officially at war with the *peuple*. It is never wise to apply such a law at such a time and even less wise to issue such a law. The masses—willing to be reasonable—do not want to be condemned to silence by sheer physical force. They want to participate, even if only by being informed. Their normal relationship to the upper classes was disrupted; hate and mistrust began to be rampant. . . .

While the Constituent Assembly continued its work under such circumstances, the clubs developed with an unusual energy; particularly the Club of the Jacobins, which seemed to represent a sort of second assembly. The best speakers at the Assembly, even Mirabeau, made their appearances there. . . . Reasonable people set their hopes upon the acceptance of the Constitution.

Suddenly the news spread that the King had fled. If martial law represented a partial declaration of war by citizens against the workers, the flight meant a total war by the King against the Constitution. There was no doubt that the King had betrayed his people. Inevitably the question arose whether liberty could be assured by preserving the throne. . . .

Now the clubs became more active. If this King switches from being a secret to an avowed enemy of liberty, how is it possible for the Constituent Assembly to defend him without betraying liberty? The undertermined position of the two classes of society became finally clear through their different relationships to the King. . . .

On July 15, 1791, the Assembly passed the decree which ordered the *Non-déchéance* of the king, in spite of the fact that he had attempted to flee. The Club of the Jacobins had entered a strong petition for dethronement. . . . The Assembly decided to address the whole nation; it defended its decree forcefully and succeeded in persuading the Club of the Jacobins to withdraw its own petition. The leaders of the people were alarmed, but after having lost the majority support of the Jacobins, they withdrew to establish the new Club of the Cordeliers which was also joined by Danton and Desmoulins. It was this club which now took the lead in instigating the masses. On July 17th, great masses of people marched to the Champ de Mars to sign again the petition against the King. The Assembly lost its composure; the National Guard was called in and marched against the unarmed masses, which did not take any measure to defend themselves. . . . The martial law was read; shouting and stone-throwing followed. Then Lafayette ordered his men to fire against the masses. Several hundred fell dead or were wounded, the rest dispersed. . . . It was the first blood shed by citizens. The Assembly had been victorious. . . . Paris was in a distressed mood, altogether different from that after a victory.

Indeed, great things had happened. The two classes of society, long in existence, had visibly begun to oppose each other. The blood of the victims brought the conflict to light; war was declared; nobody had any illusions that this was only the first act of a terrible struggle. Had public order actually been threatened? No. . . . The Assembly had taken notice that the masses strove to take over the state. By ordering the National Guard to fire at the people, it defended public authority . . . invested in the upper class of society. The Assembly had issued a decree, the masses had dared to petition and had been shot down. Obviously the Assembly wanted *complete* exclusion of the masses from political power, although this power was supposed to be based on popular sovereignty and on complete equality. The contradiction became clear; . . . this event showed for the first time the inevitable consequences of the hazy concept of popular sovereignty. Apparently, the law had been defended; in reality, however, the events indicated that the social struggle which necessarily develops on the basis of popular sovereignty had already started and that the new social order was threatened.

Ever since that time the Assembly had one irreconcilable and terrible enemy: it was the contradiction between the acknowledged principles and their consequences, manifested in the hatred of the people against the National Guard. . . . Either the Constitution had to be abandoned or the power of the people had to be broken. The Assembly was well aware of this. . . . At the last session, after a prolonged struggle, it decided to close the clubs and prohibit their contacts with other associations; significantly, on the same day, the decree pertaining to the final organization of the National Guard was sanctioned. . . .

Nevertheless, both classes of society were to act in unison once again, but only to gain freedom of action against each other.

The Downfall of the Monarchy

Monarchy in the Teutonic European world is one of the most remarkable and at the same time the most peculiar phenomenon of history. It is almost inconceivable that historical research has accepted the institution of monarchy simply as a fact. Under the strangest adversities it has shown a greater vitality than all the other political institutions. . . . It has formed and maintained states; it has survived many changes of constitutions; wherever an attempt was made to destroy it, it returned with almost elemental force. It has been attacked and insulted, it has been fought with intellectual weapons; kings have been executed, and in some cases kings themselves have contributed more to their own destruction than all their enemies—and yet monarchies have always reappeared. Such an institution must have an important function which must be considered in an account of the fate of monarchies. . . . The unit called "the state," which is equipped to make decisions and act independently, is an absolutely indispensable institution, whether we consider it from the point of view of history, of need, or of philosophy. Even the doctrine of the social contract interprets the contract on which the states rest, and thus the state itself, as necessary. It is not true that a society without authority or without a state is conceivable, just as it is impossible to envisage a condition where popular sovereignty prevails. The state is an independent life, and, like everything alive, it has a personal life. As an entity composed of people, the state has a variety of organs and elements; none of them represents it completely; the state is more than just the relationship among its elements; it governs them all, therefore it transcends them as an independent unit. . . .

The concept of the state manifests itself ideally if it is represented exclusively as a personality and if it is independent of its various elements and organs. History has attempted to solve this greatest problem in a variety of ways. First by the caste system of the Orient where the idea of the state is incorporated in one specific caste; then by the Republics of antiquity, where the idea of the state was finally dissolved to the extent that it was identified with the elements and organs of state life; only in the Germanic world does the monarchy appear in such a way that . . . the person of the king represents the personality of the state. . . .

Since the state embraces all the various elements of the population, its strength and welfare depend on the strength and welfare of all these elements. These elements are identical with society. . . . In society, inevitably divided into classes, the tendency prevails for one class to gain power in order to further its interests at the expense of the others. Only the state has no specific interests. The state has to keep itself aloof from the social struggle. If the state takes sides it contradicts itself; if it participates in the struggle it destroys itself. . . .

With the onset of the French Revolution it was clear that the third estate revolted against the privileged. The monarchy, holding on to the old notion handed down through centuries, conceived of its sovereignty as the basis of the existence of the state. Since the privileged estates defended it, the monarchy sided with the privileged against the people. As the struggle between the social elements broke out, the monarchy committed the grave mistake of aligning itself against liberty. But liberty was victorious, and the state was transformed. Two new social classes began to struggle for control. Monarchy had changed; it had to adjust to its new role.

The class of capital owners, still in its infancy, was supported by the new Constitution, and it was aware of the fact that the masses of the laborers were in opposition. It, therefore, turned to the monarchy, which still represented the state, with the demand to protect its rights; in exchange it also had to protect the monarchy. We discover here for the first time the natural coalition between monarchy and the bourgeoisie which is the basis of constitutionalism. The class of non-owners always feels weaker than the class of owners. It observes that after privileges have been abolished the rule of property owners begins. The non-owners know that this will be a rule of proprietary interests. The only hope of the lower class is that element of the state order which has no interest in property, the king. This explains the centuries-old connection between the lower orders and the king. . . .

Since both parties were dependent on it, the monarchy had an unusual power. . . . During a brief period the monarchy still stood between the two powerful classes of society. Not so much by the measures it took as by its mere existence, monarchy prevented the final conflict; by still holding state power, it made the direct control of one class over the other impossible. It was the last, though weak, partitioning wall.

For, indeed, the monarchy of the Constitution of 1791 was no longer a true monarchy. The idea had taken root that the king was merely a representative of the people; to consider him as an independent authority would have contradicted the concept of popular sovereignty. On the other hand, one did not dare to disregard his independence altogether because of the awareness that popular sovereignty, as Montesquieu had already stated, tended to transform personal despotism into a despotism of the masses. At the beginning of the revolution the republican party was very weak; but those who wanted to preserve the monarchy were in a self-contradictory position. The monarchy of the Constitution is a result of this contradiction; it was neither monarchy nor merely executive power; for the former it was not enough, for the latter it was too much. What, indeed, was the meaning of Title III Article 4 "The government is a monarchy" if there was nothing left to the king but the simple and strictly limited execution of the will of the people which was considered to be sovereign? . . .

An unfortunate interpretation developed here which has frequently contributed to revolutionary eruptions. The monarchy refused to be merely a representative of the people. . . . It wanted to reestablish state power independently of the mandate of the people. Neither of the elements in the new society was willing to support this claim, since each accepted the monarchy only in order to paralyze their social opponents.

If the King wanted to regain his old position, he had to ally himself with the foreign enemy and put himself in opposition to the whole society consisting of his people. This meant to risk everything, because it came close to treason and a declaration of war against the people. It destroyed the basis of the Constitution of 1791 and the possibility of defending the institution of the monarchy. It provoked hatred in the masses of the people, because the King had identified himself with the aristocracy; it also provoked animosity in the bourgeoisie, because their newly acquired rights thus became endangered. . . . In this way the monarchy deliberately undermined the new legal order, for it wanted the old feudal society to rise from the ashes of the new constitutional society. The monarchy dug its own grave. One may very well ask: How was it possible to be deceived on this issue? Others have tried to explain this big mistake in terms of trivial factors. Something much more important than sheer, cold expediency was reflected in this bold venture of the King. . . .

The French Revolution had, beyond all hopes, spread the idea of a new social order all over Europe. The enthusiasm which welcomed the victory of this thought was great. Other countries felt that they, too, contained the elements of a new society and that the struggle against privileges and absolutism was approaching. A two-fold current flowed from France into the countries of the West; one of new ideas and hopes, the other of emigrants with claims of the past. Wherever they came they were welcomed by each country in its own fashion. Suddenly it became clear that, besides the political balance of power, there was a second, perhaps even more powerful bond, a strong solidarity in the whole present life of the people, the homogeneity of all European society. The different estates began to recognize the similarity of the struggle, the companionship in victory and defeat, in progress and limitations. The concern of the emigrants became the concern of the privileged classes in all of Europe, the cause of the third estate that of all suppressed people. The development of European history had finally led to the discovery of that element which established the community of all people—the social conditions.

Before the Constituent Assembly had finished its work, the privileged estates of all Europe—in England, Germany, Italy, Sweden, Spain—had united for defense and attack against the third estate. But the third estate, on the other hand, also joined hands all over Europe. The whole Western World was now divided into two camps; an altogether new phase of history was about to begin.

Here, indeed, and not in wars, victories, and changes in state boundaries, can the present be distinguished from the past. Through the uniformity of European society and the awareness of its solidarity, the meaning of the proposition that state constitutions depend on the social order had become yet more comprehensible. . . . Subsequently the history and order of Europe became dependent on the social order; not material power, but the structure of society in any state, was bound to be the factor which determined its position, its prestige, and its function within the newly developing balance-of-power system. . . .

The privileged estates, frightened by the victory of the citizens' state in France, were soon aroused in all European countries. They considered war indispensable to stem the revolutionary tide, because they identified their privileged position with the monarchy. In complete agreement, they pushed and worked powerfully until they had united the ruling powers of the West against France. This was not a war against the state of France, even less a war against the King. It was the first European war of the organized feudal society against the emerging civil social order. The French court realized this. It had to take sides in a conflict which was not merely French but European in scope. An honest identification with the new Constitution would have meant that a king for the first time in history would separate himself completely from the traditional system, that he would dissociate himself from all former European relationships, royal friendships, and all legitimate support. In exchange he would be offered in France a future full of mistrust and dangers, full of deprivation, and yet without glory and honor. That was the choice with which the court of Louis XVI was confronted. . . . Officially he declared war against the European coalition of feudal societies, but secretly he allied himself with them. He broke forever with the civil society: he identified himself with the feudal society and perished with it. . . .

When the legislative Assembly met, everybody in France was convinced of the treason by the Court. The unfortunate flight of the King was a clear indication of the nature of the conflict, and many other circumstances had also helped to correct the misconceptions of the people. One important clue consisted in the fact that the emigrants and the foreign powers had always presented the King as yielding to sheer force. It did not help him that he declared war against Austria and Prussia; it was obvious that he had done it only under pressure and that, as a result, the war was not adequately prepared for and was poorly pursued. Thoughts favoring abdication and the establishment of a Republic appeared. At this moment two events occurred which, by uniting once more the two opposing classes of the new society, were destined finally to destroy the monarchy.

We have shown how the Revolution, under the Constituent Assembly, had already effected the distribution of landed property, partly by liberating the peasant owner, partly by the new inheritance law, and finally by distributing state property. Nevertheless, there had remained two major types of landownership which, if undivided, were bound to perpetuate inequality in society. These types of landownership were, moreover, of political importance inasmuch as the owners identified themselves with the interests of the feudal estates, thus preserving remnants of the old order and also an opportunity for the old order to re-establish itself. The new society could not be considered safe as long as the huge landed property of the Church and the aristocracy continued to exist. The legislators, therefore, took the first opportunity to break up these remnants of the old order. . . .

Early in 1790, the Constituent Assembly had decreed that the catholic religion would not be recognized as a state religion; later, the church organization was adjusted to the new civil administration, and it was decreed that the clergy had to take the oath to the Constitution. By these decrees the clergy ceased to be a separate estate. In addition, these decrees were intended to make the landed property of the clergy subject to sale. This project succeeded to a certain extent. Money owners began to buy church properties and to parcel them out. Again a new group of land owners developed. The first step towards a radical transformation of the church, towards a consolidation of the revolution among the clergy, had been taken.

The priests, particularly the High Church, opened a fierce battle against these measures. They stirred up civil war in the French community; they identified, as usual, their private claims with religion; disorder broke out in the name of God; the measure taken by the Constituent Assembly, which had been intended to strengthen the Revolution, seemed to endanger it more than all the demagogues and all foreign interventions had done.

The new owners, however, were just as unwilling to part with the new property as were the old ones. They identified their rights with the idea of liberty and turned to the newly established state power for protection. A link was established thereby between the new society and the monarchy. . . . The King, as highest executive, needed only to uphold the law in order to ingratiate himself with the entire powerful class. He did not do it. Suspected by the democrats, he made himself unpopular with the new class of owners as well. They turned away from the King and allied themselves with those who were hoping to gain by the parcelling out of the landed property of the aristocracy. . . .

A large section of the aristocracy, more wealthy yet than the church, had emigrated and used the revenue of their property to lead the war against their homeland. . . . According to international law, the Assembly was entitled to take measures against this. But at this point the Assembly trespassed the limits of the law and of moderation in order to abolish forever the privileges of the aristocracy and of the clergy in the new society. Two decrees were passed which definitely tied the class of the new owners with the Revolution. The first decree was directed against the emigrants: all Frenchmen who had left French soil were declared under suspicion of conspiracy unless they returned by January 1, 1792. Unless they returned by that date they were guilty of treason, and their property became subject to confiscation for the benefit of the nation (Nov. 9, 1791). The second decree was directed against the clergy who refused to take the oath of the Constitution. They lost their salaries and were placed under the authority of the secular administration (Nov. 29, 1791). Both decrees were submitted to the King; these decrees were definitely more important than the Constitution, because they actually abolished the aristocracy and the clergy as specific estates by disowning them. It was apparent that the emigrants would not return, nor would the majority of the priests take the oath. By submitting these decrees to the King, the Assembly was in effect asking whether or not he wanted to align himself with the new order of society. But the King rejected this challenge to accept constitutional monarchy. He vetoed both decrees. From now on, there was no other way to success open to the newly propertied class except the one of overthrowing the king.

From this time on, the National Guard disappeared from the scene of the revolutionary movement. The property-owning class yielded to the masses. The clubs were reopened. The King had for the last time used his constitutional rights to fight against the natural growth of the new society; even the Constitution could not be upheld. The monarchy could not be saved. . . .

The president of the Gironde made the decisive motion in the Assembly: he proposed the convocation of a new National Assembly to draw a new constitution and to suspend the King. The motion was accepted unanimously. Both decrees concerning the aristocracy and the clergy were put into effect. The property of the landed aristocracy was confiscated and sold, 4000 clergymen were deported . . . and the King was taken prisoner. This happened on the famous night of August 10th, 1792. Just as the night of August 4th, 1789 had realized the ideas of a civil society, this night realized the ideals of the republicans. . . .

Looking back, one may pose the question: What had really happened concerning the development of society? It is evident that, with the abolition of monarchy, the last institution which could claim to be a representation of the state's personality standing above the people had disappeared. . . . Only now did the concept of popular sovereignty become a reality; the people were their own masters. The corresponding form of the state was the republic. This was a logical consequence of the events of August 10th. This republic encompassed two distinctly separate parts of a divided society. We have seen how they had come to form an alliance against the king, each motivated by its own interests. After the fall of the monarchy they parted again. The fall of the monarchy was the signal for the battle between these two parts of society for the final conquest of state power. . . . In fact, the republic represented this struggle. For the first time it became clear that the dangers of the republic lie in the self-rule of society, which will always result in the rule of one class over another.

The ruling class had changed as a result of the actions of the King. The bourgeoisie, after having ruled for two years, lost power because it was unable to take constructive steps. Its work and the principle of its existence was the civil Constitution of 1791, which contained everything that the concept of citizen could do for society. A tremendous and very important sphere had remained practically untouched, namely, that of possessions and property. The masses of non-owners now started to rule; they attacked the problem of property and tried to establish a new society rather than a new state. The history of the republic coincides with this attempt. The fall of the monarchy had opened the way for it.

The destruction of monarchy in France had for all of Europe one momentous consequences: henceforth the institution of the monarchy, which in the middle of the 18th century had taken the lead in reforms, became opposed to social reforms. The death of King Louis threw the other kings openly into the arms of the aristocracy. This more than anything else blocked the road of a normal and peaceful progressive development. . . .

A new world emerged.

THE DEMOCRATIC - COMMUNISTIC PERIOD

The Two Interpretations of Equality. The Downfall of the Gironde.

The phase of the French Revolution that followed is, without any doubt, one of the most important in world history. . . . This assertion is made particularly with regard to the main topic of our inquiry: society in relation to the state. . . . Here, too, we presuppose an acquaintance with the main historical facts. The moving forces of history, however, have not yet been fully understood.

The monarchy, insensible to the turn of events, had taken sides with the old feudal soicety. It had been destroyed and, by its down-fall, had crushed the first manifestation of the civil society based on property and acquisition; it had also compromised itself and destroyed the basis for constitutional rule. The exploding forces of the people had been victorious. The people ruled. The next questions were: Who are these people? What do they want to accomplish through their power?

Towards the end of the Legislature, the expression "the people" had come to denote the masses composed mainly of non-owners. However, we have seen that the opposition to the King brought together the propertied and the masses. Thus, at the beginning of the National Convention in 1792, the ruling "people" did not consist exclusively of the non-owning masses; it included both elements of civil society. The main question of the future was whether, in sharing the power of the state, these two elements would be able to come to an agreement.

At this period all public authorities were completely dissolved. There was no legal or traditional order to speak of. The military were at the frontier. The National Guard, having shed its essential characteristic, had also lost its power. It was only through the multitude that order could be established. The multitude, however, is the body of the nation. Like every body, it is destined to follow the thought emerging from public debates and thus to receive its stimuli and its orders. Speeches and pamphlets, therefore, at this time commanded a power so far unheard of. Rule of the masses is, and was then, the crudest form of the rule of ideas.

Watching the course of events, one is irresistably thrown back to the ideas of those who were the leaders of the people. Their ideas . . . were the true rulers of the social movement in France; the coming events demonstrated this soon enough, with disastrous consequences.

All points of view among all the parties had one common core, the idea of equality. Nobody doubted the truth and realization of this idea. And yet, it was the consequences of this concept which provoked bloody discord within a few months. . . .

The concept of equality can be interpreted from two essentially different points of view. One of these is altogether negative; according to this interpretation all men are equal before the law. Equal rights as viewed in terms of this concept imply merely a guarantee that everybody is entitled to develop his individuality without interference and by his own initiative. "Negative equality" presupposes the possibility of inequality among individuals; it accepts the fact that inequality is justified if it is the result of the free development of the individual; the negative concept of equality, therefore, is not necessarily in contradiction to practical inequality; it does not struggle against it but accepts it. Among those who demand this type of "equality," natural inequality is usually recognized; indeed, it is frequently even considered to be indispensable. The practical enforcement of absolute equality in social life seems therefore inconceivable to them; they accept the fact that there are good and bad people, and consequently different elements within society. Consciously or unconsciously they demand and strive, as a consequence of their interpretation of equality, towards a rule of the better elements over the others in state and society. Negative equality views inequality in state and society as a result of innate differences among individuals.

But there is also a second interpretation of the concept of equality, which we call the positive. Positive equality is derived from the principle that individuals are equal and that the inequality among men is the result of circumstances, predominantly of property and education. Existing inequalities, natural according to the notion of negative equality, are from this point of view contrary to nature. It is man's task, according to this interpretation, to abolish these unnatural conditions. Since these conditions derive essentially from property and education, which also contribute to preserve them, the positive notion of equality necessarily leads to the abolition of property and to the destruction of differences in ownership and work. . . .

Regarding the use of the state's power, the proponents of the first interpretation will aim at preserving the existing society and at passing a constitution based on it. The proponents of the second interpretation, however, will struggle against the alleged unnatural character of existing inequality and draft a constitution in such a way that the reappearance of inequality is precluded as much as possible.

The practical results of the two principles of equality differed widely; they tended to bring about diametrically opposed usage of the state's power. Since both views had adherents in France at that time and since, in the absence of any established authority, ideology and propaganda (der Gedanke und das Wort) ruled the masses, and a life-and-death struggle became inevitable. The outcome was destined to determine the future of France. . . .

The Gironde represented the first, the Montagne the second, of these principles. Together they had overthrown the monarchy, because its power was contrary to both their interpretations of equality; now they shared the power of the state, and internecine war could not be halted. We know the fate of the Gironde. . . . It is not our task to retrace the history of these days. But we have to ask ourselves how it was possible for the principle of positive equality, with all its contradictions, to gain a victory over the negative concept of equality at this precise moment. Not the parties, but the law of social dynamics, gained the victory over men.

When, in 1792, the European princes saw the downfall of the monarchy in France, they united all their strength to suppress the Revolution. At the same time, the flame of revolt within France became intensified. General misery increased from day to day. Common remedies were of no avail. At this moment the leaders of the movement in Paris decided with great daring to take an extreme last measure. It was proclaimed that the Fatherland was in danger; all France was declared to be under siege; everybody able to bear arms was called up, and the people did their utmost to save the country. What was it that the nation could offer in the greatest emergency? It was the life and property of every individual, the complete submergence of all specific elements of personal life into those of group life, the sacrifice of the person. Here one saw that the love of one's country really has the power to make all people equal with reference to the most precious good.

The salvation of France at this moment depended entirely upon absolute dedication of all the people; the nature and the results of this dedication were such that complete equality ensued, followed by the disappearance of all individual differences. Whoever, at this solemn moment, wanted something special for himself or even for his class betrayed the community. There was no other way to save France from complete annihilation but by this unconditional devotion for the sake of the Revolution. All documents and reports testify to this end. One should not believe that the conservatives thought differently. Even de Maistre, in his *Considérations*, states "After the revolutionary movement had gotten underway, France could only be saved by Jacobinism." Everybody who knows the history of the period agrees with him.

In this way, through the powerful attack of foreign countries, positive equality of all Frenchmen at this particular moment became the basis of the future of France. The external circumstances gave this idea of equality a power which it otherwise would never have attained. Consequently, any theory or any attempt to destroy this basis was viewed not only as reactionary propaganda, but generally as a danger for France, a symptom of shortsightedness, or even treason.

It is impossible to understand the unfortunate position and the fate of the Gironde, to understand how a nation succumbed to the rule of a few who sacrificed the prime of the revolutionary generation, or to explain the change in the power of the parties during 1792, unless one keeps in mind these specific conditions. Only the highest enthusiasm of the masses could create an army and gain victories, and only the conviction that all as equals, and in equal measure, fought for the highest common good could bring about this enthusiasm. What, on the other hand, did the Gironde want to set against this absolute demand? It wanted doubtlessly, something very reasonable, the creation of conditions which would favor the development of natural inequalities. The Gironde took a position deviating from the Revolution; in times of peace the highest hope of freedom, the Gironde now seemed to endanger it. . . . Having sacrificed the monarchy to the idea of negative equality the Gironde was aware of the fact that the idea of the state was now threatened. "If the Revolution takes one further step, it cannot do this without danger. The time has come to put an end to the Revolution. It should be terminated at the moment when the nation is free and all Frenchmen are equal". This serious statement of Barnaves [Lamartine, *Histoire de Gironde* L. III, 6.] in 1791 had passed unnoticed; the Gironde expressed the same views to the Montagnards; but it was in vain; it had to be in vain. In order to find support, the Girondists attempted to prevent the condemnation of the King; they did not succeed. From the beginning of 1793, they were directly opposed to the Montagne, who attacked them as traitors and called them secret allies of tyranny. Suddenly Dumouriez developed the ill-considered plan of using his army in order to save the constitution of 1791. But the army deserted him, because it consisted of the strongest elements of Republican France. At this moment the Montagne had a powerful instrument against its enemies, and it vowed the destruction of the Gironde. . . . Only the tyranny of liberty was able to save liberty from tyranny. . . Open warfare broke out, and on June 2nd, the twenty-two leaders of the Gironde were arrested. The Montagne ruled unrestricted.

Looking backwards, we may ask ourselves: Did this mean nothing but the destruction of one party in the Assembly and the rule of another one? Was this only the victory of the masses over the intelligentsia? It is impossible to interpret the meaning of this great event by referring to such secondary features. What had taken place was the victory of the principle of positive over that of negative equality, of a society of equals over the preservation of social inequalities. The rule of Robespierre and Danton was but a symbol of the fact that the power of the state of a great country in turmoil was now gripped by the idea that the external conditions of society, by fostering the inequality of equals, are unnatural and ought to be fought to the end as the enemies of man's true destiny.

This is the true character of the movement. . . . Here, for the first time, we are confronted with the great problem of whether the state is able to enforce equality within society which, by its very nature, is a structured entity. From this perspective, the year of terror of the French Revolution may become a source of valuable experience.

Pure Democracy and the Constitution of 1793.

. . . The principle of positive equality had been victorious. The first question which arose was: what will the constitutional law in a society of positive equals be, and to what extent does the civil constitution differ from the constitution of equality? After the fall of the Gironde, the Montagne, now in power, had to proclaim its aims, other than the one of abolishing monarchy, and beyond the guarantees of the Constitution of 1791.

Whenever the socially valid principles are applied to the constitution, they usually take on new names; this fact has made the understanding of the mutual relationship between state and society more difficult. The principle of social equality, as applied to the constitution, is called the democratic principle. . . .

The decisive victory of positive equality should have brought about a governmental organization which was the purest expression of this principle, that is to say, the most democratic constitution. To most of those who believed in absolute equality everything seemed to be accomplished by such a new constitution; therefore, it was adopted as early as June 24, 1793. As the first legal document of the rule of the masses over the state, it deserves special attention. It shows, unlike any other historical document, the real content of the two concepts "Republic" and "Democracy."

Most people assume that a republic is sufficiently characterized by the mere absence of monarchy so that popular sovereignty is established as soon as the monarchy falls. . . . How obtuse this interpretation is becomes evident after the monarchy has disappeared. . . . The state, in accordance with the concept of being the general and highest personality, . . . is definitely the highest authority, responsible only to itself. It will necessarily give to its representatives, acting in its name, higher dignity and more power. Absolute equality, therefore, if it shall recognize the existence of a state at all, has to raise some individuals over others; . . . it has to impose great differences among the people by endowing some with governmental power. The first principle of any democratic state is established through the interrelationship of this necessity with the never-theless retained principle of equality: that anybody sharing public authority has to be elected by the people, and only for a limited time. Election is the act by which governmental power flows back to its originator, the people, from which it re-emerges. The identity of the people with governmental power, or, in other words, popular sovereignty, is manifested by this election of all officials.

The second principle of political democracy is easily understood: Everybody has to share the sovereignty, which resides in *all* the people; there can be no differences based on property or qualifications; there is equal voting power; there is no difference between the active and the passive citizen; person and citizen are identical. There is no other legisla-tive power except the people, that is to say all citizens; only the decision of the original assembly turns the popular will into law. The *Acte con-stitutionel*, presented to the people on June 24, 1793, had carried out these principles. . . .

. . . Here the principle of equality had apparently reached its climax. The state does not recognize any inequality among its citizens; neither does it recognize the existence of a governmental decision other than the people's will. The Constitution of 1793 is the first clearly conceived, purely democratic constitution in European history. . . . What, then, remained to be done for equality? While drafting the constitution, the legislators felt already that it would not suffice to establish equality. Shortly after this Constitution was put into effect, it had to be suspended again. . . . One realized that this Constitution, by itself, would be unable to control its opponents, unable to function by its own power. The immediate suspension was already a suspicious symptom. Where was the enemy? Basically this Constitution was not so very different from the earlier one of 1791—yet, while the former had been supported by the whole nation, the latter could scarcely gain nominal acceptance even with the aid of terrorism. There seemed to be an insurmountable difficulty. What was its source?

Hegel had already stated that the French Revolution was thought transformed into action. The truth of this interpretation refers to the situation with which we are confronted now. Not the French Revolution, but the Constitution of 1793, is indeed an act of thought. This was its strength but also its weakness.

We have shown how society and the constitution, according to their very nature, are mutually interdependent. The form of the state has to be based on the social order. . . . The structure of society may be temporarily determined by the form of the state, but it will always reassert itself irresistibly and force the state to adjust the constitution accordingly. Wherever a constitution prevails, it does so by the power of society; wherever it fails, it does so through the contradictions with society. The basic tenet of the new Constitution of 1793 was absolute personal equality. Public law, the right to vote, public representation and legislation were established according to this principle. The state did not want to recognize, still less create, any differences. This state form, according to the law which determines the relationship between state and society, is based on the assumption that society too is not differentiated. But did social equality really exist side by side with political equality? We do not simply want to deny it. To eliminate any doubt we ask whether it was possible that equality really existed.

Certainly there was no trace of equality before 1789. If it had developed since, it would have been brought about by the power of the state. What had been done to further social equality during the intervening year?

Nobility, privileges, monopolies and guilds were abolished. Every individual was to be evaluated according to his own merits. However, nobility and privileges not only represent inequality, they also create inequality. Individuals become different because of them. Privileges not only grant property and income, they also transmit education and prestige. They deposit something in the individual, something which becomes an integral part of him. At the same time and by the same token, they are the conditions of personal inequality. By their removal legal inequality was destroyed, and the conditions of personal inequality were attacked. But the consequences of these conditions, the inequality of personal development based on pre-revolutionary conditions, could not possibly be removed. Society was not composed of equals. To the extent that inequality was independent of privileges it had not even been attacked; differences based on privileges were only abolished for the future. Therefore, society, in 1793, was an organization of very diverging groups and classes.

Upon this existing inequality was imposed a Constitution based on absolute equality. This created a contradiction between society and constitution, two institutions which are mutually interdependent. . . . It was a constitution on paper only. That it was not applicable was not a result of specific rules but a result of the contradiction with the existing and emerging social order. But if its acceptance by society was impossible, it could not have been created by this very same society. Who had conceived of this Constitution?

For the first time, we meet here an element of all democratic trends regarding constitutional law, an element which, though imparting rigor and keenness, is their most deadly enemy. Democracy presupposes the equality of men; however, this is not interpreted as a fact upon which one can build but as a conclusion drawn from the concept of personality. A democratic constitution is but a systematized consequence of this concept. It is a constitution based on principle. Among all possible constitutions it is the one which springs from an idea; it assumes the reality of principles. The state, therefore, becomes a mechanism, and society becomes nothing but the nondescript multitude of people. Such a constitution is an abstraction of the reality of mankind and of real society; it is a doctrine in terms of a state constitution; the French, quite appropriately call it an ideology. Wherever it rules without qualifications it places state and constitution in opposition to society. The principle is its truth; and while this gives to its adherents the courage of convictions, it deprives the institutions of an operating basis. Pure democracy is therefore unable to rule; . . . a result of thought, it is valid only in the realm of thought. . . .

This was the state of affairs in France after the downfall of the Gironde. There was no peace possible under this insoluble contradiction. . . . Terrorism, with all its horror, had to demonstrate to the amazement of Europeans of that time what the power of an abstract principle is able to accomplish and also what it is not able to do.

Terrorism

There is no other period of the French Revolution besides the period of terrorism which has been traced and retraced back so decidedly to the furor, the madness, and the power of certain individuals. All traditional interpretations and rational explanations seemed to fail. Such bloody scenes may be comprehensible in a country which is sorely afflicted, where the victors rule over the defeated, where retribution is carried out and dangers prevail. But up to now, the fact that made it possible for thousands of peaceful citizens to be cold-bloodedly sacrificed with the sincere conviction that this was done in the name of truth and justice have rarely been explored. And yet terrorism was in fact the necessary consequence of the situation in which state power was exclusively in the hands of democratic extremists. Terrorism, for most people an excess of mad bloodthirst, was quite a natural result of the revolution, comparable to a crisis during serious illness. Its explanation rests on the foregoing analysis.

We have shown that the state form of political democracy presupposes equality—an equality which did not exist. If it is true that the structure of society determines the constitution, either the constitution of 1793 or the society was doomed. There was no other possibility. . . . The state power based on that constitution had to begin a life-and-death struggle with society. Every trace of inequality had to be annihilated. This was the function of terrorism: the use of state power against any differences in society which might lead to differentiation within the state.

In order to understand the position of the rulers in a pure democracy, one has to have the strength to figure out intellectually the inevitable necessity of these terrible consequences. It was one of the most solemn moments in the course of history when the cruelty of thought reigned over the whole life of the people and the blood of thousands of its citizens did not stir any human sympathy. . . .

A dismal period followed. The three representatives of the Montagne —Marat, Danton and Robespierre—began to sense what they had done with that Constitution. The principle of equality, realized in the state, now turned toward society; since it was sanctified through the form of the state, any offense of this principle in society became a crime. The mere fact of being different, to be distinguished by education or property seemed now the danger; in fact, it meant danger and irreconcilable opposition against the purely democratic state order. That was the basis on which these men stood. . . . This principle enforced man's inhumanity to man. . . .

How these three men acted in this situation is of more than just historical importance. The first, Danton, that powerful Mirabeau of the marketplace, wanted liberty and equality; but mainly he wanted to enjoy them. He relished them partly as a fighter against the old regime, surrounded by the rejoicing masses, but he was also intoxicated by the enjoyment of riches. . . . He wanted everybody to share in it, but did not want to forego anything. He did not understand the need for equality of work nor for equality of restraint; he indulged in the liberty of complete licentiousness. When the "party of virtue" around Robespierre took offense, he broke with Robespierre and fell. He did not have the courage to accept the fact that restraint is the first source of authority. There also exists an aristocracy of pleasure hunting. After having destroyed every other aristocracy, he plunged into this one. He fell because he had become a nuisance to all those who did not want this kind of aristocracy either. Nevertheless, he was a powerful and an unusual character. All those who wanted to preserve a differentiated society by acknowledging genius, superior ability, and extraordinary personality had put their hope in him. But unfortunately a number of people had attached themselves to him who looked upon the Revolution as a mere venture and simply wanted to indulge under his protection. The last stronghold of anything that aspired to be superior to the ordinary went down with his fall. . . .

Another terrible and revolting character was Marat. He represented the personification of resentment against anything superior. Lamartine has characterized him best by the statement: "Equality was his obsession because superiority meant his martyrdom." Marat represented all those who supported the revolution because they wanted to destroy excellence and to establish the rule of mediocrity. This part of the intelligentsia is not negligible; and no matter how much it weighs in the scale of events, it grows on poisonous soil and has but ill effects. With the acute instinct of envy, Marat first pointed out the germ of all differences in a civil society, the true enemy of pure egalitarianism. He for the first time pointed to differences in property as the true enemy of liberty as he understood it; but his thoughts did not reach any further than to the sheer annihilation of the propertied class by the masses. He wanted to persecute the wealthy, he wanted their houses to be destroyed; he did not want anybody to gain status by virtue of his property. During the Constituent Assembly, his newspaper,*Ami du peuple*, had been the voice of mass antagonism against upper-class society; there we find for the first time the statement that "it is a poor victory to defeat nobility in order to succumb to an aristocracy of money", that "the favorites of fortune" ought to tremble, and that the poor "to whom active citizenship has been denied because they are too poor, will make an end to their poverty by confiscating abundance." He further develops the idea of equality; he denounces all superior people and for the first time acquaints the worker with the idea that equality before the law is not enough, but that "equality of rights leads to equality of enjoyment and only here the thought of equality finds its fulfillment." It was he who pushed the arrest of the Girondists; he was not satisfied with the annihilation of leading individuals; he asked "whether it would not be of great benefit for the innocent millions to execute hundreds of stubborn enemies of liberty;" everybody was denounced to be a traitor unless he belonged to the general populace. Nobody has ever popularized blood and murder as Marat did in the *Ami du Peuple*. Marat, just like envy, was altogether negative, and negative exclusively against the specific. He never rose to the heights of communism, to the negation of property, even less to a positive concept for society. . . . It was his mission to instigate the lower classes to a pitch; then he suddenly died. Had he lived longer, he would doubtlessly have had to fight with Robespierre for his survival. After his death, the fall of the Hébertistes, who represented pure nihilism, by the hands of the defenders of virtue, was unavoidable. Soon after the death of Danton and Desmoulins and those few endowed with genius who had kept their heads above the revolutionary waves (March 1794), the other group, which had no principles at all, was also doomed (April 1794); and now Robespierre ruled all by himself.

To most people, Robespierre is nothing but the bloodthirsty madman who, after having sacrificed all his friends, seemed set to destroy one part of the nation by the other. There he stands, a frightful phenomenon, cold, hard, consistent, not being afraid of any means, surrounded by henchmen in front of an assembly trembling with fear, ruling all France, defying all Europe. He is neither orator nor statesman nor military commander; he has no ability to incite the masses, to inspire the doubtful, to pardon the opponents; he has left no legacy, nobody has ever loved him, few respected him, most hated him, but everybody obeyed him. He is an enigma to all who look at him as an individual in the history of France. But the riddle dissolves as soon as one considers the history of social development in France. . . .

It was Robespierre who for the first time tried to establish real equality by his actions and by the use of state power. For the first time, this principle came to be considered more important than the form of the state. While up to now society had determined the structure of the state, from now on the state was supposed to rule society. Robespierre's life, work and death converge upon the line separating these two principles.

Robespierre, of course, could not possibly have thought of the relationship between state and society in the same terms as we today are able to do. His basic concept is more of an ideal than a logical conclusion; we discover traces of the poetic spirit of Rousseau in the concepts of this exponent of democracy. Let us try to disentangle its essential elements. Even the most abstract concept of equality has to be based on a corresponding phenomenon in society. The question of when people are supposed to be equal had to be answered. It is possible arbitrarily to conceive of the archetype of man as a standard of equality; but arbitrary concepts do not arouse any enthusiasm. In order to pursue such an ideal by tyrannical measures, it had to spring from a determined thought; Rousseau had conceived it and thrown it into the history of France.

He starts from the Supreme. The Eternal Being cannot possibly be evil, nor has it created anything essentially evil. Man is by nature good. . . . The external circumstances, also a creation of God, cannot possibly make man, who is good by nature, wicked and unhappy. What corrupts man is man himself.

If one wants to establish happiness for mankind according to his destiny and the will of God, one has to approach the class closest to the original state of nature and least deprived of nature by external circumstances. The natural man represents the ideal of equality; he is the expression of true humaneness; to return to him is the task of society.

Is this "natural man" completely extinguished among men? Is there no sector of society where the paradise lost has been kept alive? There is. To find it we only have to go back to those members of the human community who have been the least spoiled by the riches and temptations of human society. The natural, the true man, lives in the lowest classes of society; he is the genuine representative of the state of nature. "The people" . . . with their direct and innocent emotions, their natural strength and their natural kindness of heart, are the source of all goodness, the model for society. . . . This interpretation raised the rule of the masses from a mere fact of political life to a moral principle of democracy. . . . All humanity ought to behave as "the people" behaved, any refinement would be dangerous to human nature. "They did not think of instructing, of improving, or of raising the moral standards of the masses; they regarded the masses as the source of justice and power." [Lavallée IV, 165]. And from this it followed that everybody who was not one of "the people" was suspect as its enemy. . . . The new Declaration of Rights—at the beginning of the Constitution of 1793—omitted the important sentence of Article 1 of the Declaration of 1789 that men have "equal rights"; and that "social differences should only be based on general utility"; equality of rights and social differentiation is replaced in Article 1 by the statement that: "the purpose of society is the common good"; and Article 3: "All men are equal by nature and by law." The tremendous difference between these two declarations is clear; they are two completely different ideas of human society and therefore two equally different principles of the form and usage of state power. . . . The time of Robespierre's rule is the only period in the history of Europe during which the radical principle of equality was pursued to the extreme.

If "the people" were the true exponent of unspoiled human reason, it was the task of the state to establish an unrestricted rule of "the people" within the state. A constitution—although important—did not suffice, because it had to endow certain individuals with public authority and place them more or less outside the people's realm. Therefore, it was necessary to keep the people in a state of permanent and vigilant control of political power. Out of this need emerged a principle which is perfectly appropriate and natural to all true democracies. In order to avoid an alienation of the state from the people, the clubs were developed as an organic part of the state, a watchful guardian of the whole. The clubs were supposed to guarantee that the state never became separated from the rule of the lower classes and could never aim at and pursue an independent goal; through them the state had to be an absolutely obedient servant of "the people," in the new meaning of the word. But this only secured the democratic form of the state. The task of the state went a step further. If only "the people" are good, loyal and truthful, everything has to be brought down to the level of "the people." Equality is no longer equality before the law, but the negation of all social differences. The destruction of everything superior in society is the condition of the rule of "pure democracy," and that has to be done for the sake of the highest principle of the realization of true humaneness which can only be found in the "people."

These are the main ideas on which the rule of Robespierre is based; they gave him the courage to carry out his terrorism; his convictions regarding the genuine kindness of the lower classes provided the bond which tied him so closely to this part of society. In this sense Robespierre is the first true democrat; even though the communists go beyond him, nobody among the democrats has yet reached him. For his principle did not stop with the rule of the people; he desired, at the same time, the destruction of all classes of society who had set themselves apart from the people.

However, for the renunciation of all goods and enjoyments which society offers to the individual, there had to be at least one substitute. This brings us to the point where the higher ethical element of this type of democracy is revealed, an element which accounts for more of its followers than its hard, logical consistency and its terrorism. . . . If that return to the lowest class of the people finally meant the realization of truth and humaneness, God's highest commandment, man would have to find in this fulfillment of his divine aspirations the reward for what he had to sacrifice. The awareness of executing the will of the Deity by renunciation of external goods provided another but greater happiness. This is the source of the powerful concept of "republican virtue," which presented the positive content of the new democracy. The democracy of this period was well aware of the fact that the last stronghold of all positive equality was specifically this virtue; this was the secret power by which democracy during this period attracted the noblest hearts. Even Napoleon was an admirer of Robespierre for a short period! . . . The freedom of the future was transplanted into the inner life of man, in the liberating act of the mind, into the limitations imposed by one's own will. "We want," said Robespierre in a report of February

5th, 1793, "an order of things"—he ought to have said "of society"—
"in which all the low and evil emotions are enchained and all the
good and generous ones are encouraged by the laws, where the
Fatherland assures the well-being of any individual and everyone
enjoys prosperity, where distinctions only arise out of equality itself.
We want to replace egotism by morality, honor by integrity, practices
by principles, customs by duties, the tyranny of fashion by the empire
of reason, the scorn of misfortune by the scorn of vices. We want, in a
word, to carry out the will of nature, to accomplish the destiny of humanity, keep the promises of philosophy and abolish the long regime of
crime and of tyranny." . . . That was the goal by which Robespierre,
Couthon, and St. Just, aware of the aimlessness of this movement up
till this point, "wanted to establish a purpose of the revolution." And
society really bowed to their absolute power. People greeted each other
as "Brother" and "Citizen"; they signed themselves, officially as well as
privately, with the formula: "Salut et fraternité." . . . They searched
for the Republic in republican virtues; for a short time these men could
maintain the belief that the new society would start with their reign.

But they soon felt that something was opposed to them which they
could not conquer because it was somehow intangible. . . . Such an equality was only a deception; it was not a reality; the upper class remained
the upper class and the more powerful. This made these men angry,
and, as is the rule with abstruse wielders of power, they attacked the consequences instead of the causes. They began a crusade against the upper
class of society; they expected that what their principles had failed to
accomplish would be performed by the guillotine. The society of France
became drenched in blood. Instead of trying to raise the lower classes
in order to establish equality and "the common good" of which nobody
had a clear conception, they annihilated the upper class. The danger
to the country, the proximity of the foreign enemy, the fear of treason
were used as pretexts to destroy the upper class without discrimination.
The Society of Equals was to be built with the blood of the superior.
The super-human principle became inhuman; this was the period of
terrorism at its worst.

This movement was bound, of course, to reach a point of reversal.
Who was, after all, superior? Who could be sure that he was safe?
Where was the dividing line to be drawn? And was it possible that
murder raised to a principle could go on? Some energetic men finally
summoned up their courage, and Robespierre fell with his followers and
his system, a victim of his own law; had they not singled themselves
out as the better and more virtuous among equals? . . .

It was not an external enemy that brought Roberpierre to the fall. It was the result of the victory of his opponents among the representatives. . . . The high tide of equality had been broken on an indestructable rock. . . . What power was it which even Roberpierre was unable to master? What was the deadly enemy of positive equality as well as pure democracy?

Indeed, there could be no doubt that this enemy was wealth. The boldest legislation could not secure more than liberty for everybody to develop his abilities; it could not secure more than the acknowledgement of equality amidst existing differences. Equality in the practical world, however, is subject to one conditioning factor. This factor was and remained the amount of property owned. . . .

Nobody had yet grasped the function and the importance of ownership, . . . nor did the Constitution of 1793 take sufficient cognizance of it. Looking backward from the present on these unfinished ideas, the basis of this constitution seems strangely contradictory. It guarantees (Article 2) as natural and inalienable rights, equality, liberty, security and property. It defines the meaning of liberty, security and property, but not that of equality. It sanctifies equality, but, at the same time, without attempting to reconcile the contradiction, it justifies the inescapable consequence of human inequality by glorifying property as a human right. . . . The principle of positive equality was overruled because it was incompatible with property rights. . . . And no sooner had Robespierre been defeated than the property-owning class reappeared on the scene. The revolutionary laws were already repealed in August, 1794; the Jacobins were persecuted by the *Jeunesse Dorée*, their club was shut down; the Gironde was reinstalled and the Faubourgs disarmed; even the royalists turned up again; the well-to-do quarters of Paris united, and reaction became a victory of the property-owning class over the non-owners who later, in the Constitution of 1795, attempted to re-establish their rights. . . .

Thus ended the short period of pure democracy in France, the epoch of Robespierre. Was the principle of equality finally exhausted? Had this been its last appearance? No. There were men with a sense of reality who had perceived that a democracy of virtue is an illusion. Following carefully the course of events, they had learned a lesson. They remained loyal to the idea of equality, but they now saw clearly that equality can never be realized as long as it is applied only to the abstract person and only to the form of the state. During all these years, neither the character of men nor the lot of the people had changed for the better; the explanation appeared to be that the last stronghold of inequality, the unequal distribution of property, had never been challenged. The realization of this truth was a result which the defeat of pure democracy had brought about. . . . It was the beginning of the victory of social over political ideas, the beginning of the problems with which we are confronted today. . . .

The Forerunners of the Idea of Communism and of Social Democracy

. . . The principle of equality of men in the state of nature—first presented by Hobbes—had been incorporated into a systematic philosophy mainly by Christian Wolff. He had already recognized that this equality . . . had been destroyed by personal property. This was as far as the German philosopher went and from where French philosophy took over.

Those who advocated the principle of absolute equality soon discovered that differentiation of ownership eliminated equality, even though equal share in political power was granted. Even abstract ideas which had developed under feudal conditions, tending toward liberation, came close to this final conclusion. It is of great interest to trace the development of these ideas.

The first group of men who connected causes of dependence with the distribution of goods were men of the legislature and administration, lawyers and officials. . . . Necker, who was foremost among them, stated in his brochure, "Corn Laws and Corn Trade" (Th. 1. c. 25) that the state, unless it is willing to abolish the laws according to which property is distributed, has to assure the people "of the barest necessities which is all that is granted it according to these laws," in order to secure public order. He further showed how "property owners determined wages and food prices in order to retain their power over people without any property." In a similar fashion, Linguet emphasized, in his *Theory of Civil Law*, the great contrast between the two classes of society; he demonstrated that the rule of the property-owning class over the non-owners is secured by law; but he did not know how this could be changed. "Justice is the eternal and the persistent will to grant everybody his due. But the poor have nothing but their poverty. The laws cannot give them anything; rather the laws try to protect those who live in abundance against the attack of the deprived." . . . "The laws are set up by the wealthy who draw the greatest advantages from them. The laws are like a fortress built by the well-to-do who are the only ones in danger." (Book 1 and 5) It is "the nature of society to relieve the wealthy of toil;" however, the philosopher of law had not explored the possibilities by which this might be changed.

Of equal importance was the appearance of the Physiocrats, with Turgot at the lead. They introduced the concept of a *"classe stérile,"* a merely consuming class living at the expense of others. Their theory of a single progressive income tax suggested the levelling of differences in ownership through the power of the state. Other similar notions among economists and political scientists during the 18th century are not difficult to find. They illustrate how the ideas of liberty and equality turn slowly toward the great problem of property and property laws without, however, achieving any positive results. While describing and deploring the contrasts, they are unable to dissolve them.

A second group consists of those which are usually classified as the Utopians. They are distinguishable from the foregoing group inasmuch as they do not consider the factual conditions but construct a community on an arbitrary basis without concerning themselves with the methods of its realization. . . . Their influence has never been, and could not be, of great importance, because they have only created a social fairy tale. All the more important was the impact of the third group, the philosophers proper.

Pascal, the great adversary of the Jesuits, had already stated (Pensées P. 1. Art. 9 § 53) "This dog belongs to me, said these poor children. . . . This is the beginning and the illustration of the usurpation of the whole earth." It was Rousseau who picked out this quotation from the works of this powerful mind and explored its meaning. In his *Discours sur l'égalité,* he states that civilization, with all its inequality and vice, has come into being through the institution of property. "The first one who enclosed a territory stating 'This is mine,' and found people naive enough to accept it was the founder of civil society. How many crimes, wars, murder, how much misery and terror could have been avoided if that man pulling out the stakes and filling up the moats, would have called out to his fellowmen: 'Don't listen to this imposter; you are lost if you forget that the fruits belong to everybody and all and that the land does not belong to anybody.' ". . . Thus Rousseau is confronted with the question of the relationship between the idea of equality and the idea of property. . . . What was more obvious than to negate property if it presented the only source of anything unnatural? But Rousseau foresaw that it is not possible to eliminate property without invoking contradictions; however, he is unable to account for this. The consequence of this confusion is evident; he had to sacrifice equality to preserve property; his position is basically identical with that of the Constitution of 1791. He demanded the recognition of equality as an absolute principle but added that (*Contrat social* L.II, chp. XI) it should not be absolute. "The supreme good for all is liberty and equality." . . . Concerning equality, the term must not be interpreted as meaning that the amount of property should be absolutely equal, but that nobody should have enough to buy anybody else and nobody so poor as to be forced to sell himself." He added in a note: "If you want to give consistency to the state, eliminate the extremes as far as possible; do not tolerate opulence nor pauperism; these two states are naturally inseparable and they are equally disastrous to the common good; they traffic between them with public liberty; the one buys and the other sells it." All his statements about property and equality are equally inconsequential; he never became aware of the fact that they cancel each other out. . . . Although Rousseau, restrained by the right instinct, never advocated the abolition of property and community ownership, he is the first one to characterize wealth as the enemy of liberty and equality. This is the point at which he paved the way for communism. A similar viewpoint was taken by Helvetius. . . . The only one who came to the conclusion that private property had to be abolished and a community of goods established was Mably. His work *De la législation* (1776) presents the first theory of communism and the only one during the 18th century based on scientific methods. But even here communism is based predominantly on observations rather than ideas, and the work contains more attacks on private property than exploration of its nature. However, he sees clearly that "equality cannot exist in conjunction with private property which is the source of all our social evils (L. I. Ch. III). I am at a loss to explain why property rights have been established. I have only conjectures to offer which do not satisfy me completely." . . . His whole second chapter proceeds to prove that "the inequality of wealth and of conditions decomposes man, as it were," and that "the human race will continue to indulge in vices which are always brought about by inequality. If complete equality is not attained, the spirit of revolt will not be extinguished" and he continues prophetically: "it is only hidden under the ashes and you may expect that it will be kindled again." . . . Mably concludes his first book by attempting to prove that the re-establishment of absolute equality is met by "insurmountable obstacles," the two main unconquerable enemies of equality, the two main pillars of private property being avarice and ambition. From here he comes to the main subject of his work, in which he does not advocate communism but tries to demonstrate that, "under the prevailing conditions, legislation has to prudently turn all its power against avarice and ambition." . . .

In this fashion, even for the most radical thinkers, the idea of abolishing property is as yet outweighed by the vague notion that such a move would not be advisable. Very few went beyond the limits set by Rousseau and Mably. . . . Several small brochures by Brissot are remarkable through the pungent criticism of property which he calls an "outrage on nature." He states that originally everybody has an equal claim to land, he acknowledges the existing difference between owners and non-owners, and he explains that a thief in the state of nature is the one who has more than he needs, while in a civilized society the theft is the one who steals from the wealthy. [Brissot *"Recherches philosophiques sur le droit de propriété et le vol." 1780*].

. . . It was natural that under the prevailing circumstances of that period the question of property in its relation to equality was raised; but the spirit of the time, even though it had to attack the distribution of property, particularly of land, has never really called into question the institution of property as such. This was left to the following decades. . . . The Convention of 1793 represents mainly the ideas of Mably and Rousseau; it attempts to abolish too great great differences in property, and yet it attempts to sanctify property as such. . . To establish happiness is the task of the state; . . . Robespierre states in the Report of the Committee of Public Welfare: "Opulence is the way of life of a rather large number of people who are enemies of the Revolution. The needs of the working population make it dependent upon its enemies; let us not tolerate that there is anyone unhappy or poor in this country—happiness is a new idea in Europe." And the Convention decreed: "All the communities of the Republic shall set up a roster of indigent residents. The Committee shall make a report about the means available to compensate all these unfortunates with the goods of the enemy of the Revolution." This was still merely an application of the principle established by the Committee of Public Welfare: "The way of strengthening the Revolution is to make it work for the benefit of those who support it and for the ruin of those who fight it." It was anything but communism. Even Condorcet, who went farthest in the direction of communism, favored only the use of ordinary means of public power as a means of levelling the differences in possessions, but certainly not the abolition of property. His *Tableau des progrès des connaissances humaines* express most distinctly the hazy viewpoint of that time and of the means which were considered useful for a reconciliation of property and equality, namely, making everybody a property owner. "The existing inequality, which is almost exclusively a result of the imperfection of social institutions, must be lessened continuously to give way to factual equality, the final end of social action." . . . After the basis for political freedom has been established, Condorcet next desires to secure civil liberties. He suggests the abolition of inheritance rights and the provision of means for the greatest possible personal development . . . by free and equal public education toward "real equality among all citizens." He demands, therefore, like Rousseau, Mably, and Helvetius, not a community of possessions, nor a complete equality of property, but rather the use of state authority to conquer misery and to put into practice step by step the greatest possible real equality. . . . He is the most doctrinaire representative of the social idea, to the extent that this idea is distinguishable from the political struggle at that time . . . Attention of the popular leaders was called to the fact that political institutions alone were insufficient to cope with the two great concepts of the time—liberty and equality. The sphere where the eternal inequality of man manifests itself, the sphere of property rights, had been discovered in its significance with regard to the idea of equality; one had raised the question whether property was justified and had given the state authority over this right; one had asserted that factual equality could be attained only by a redistribution of goods. One had confiscated without compensation, redistributed or sold the land of the nobility and the clergy; one had attacked property for the benefit of society; one had called for progressive taxation and therewith also threatened movable acquired property, the latter also for the benefit of the Republic. At the same time, one identified the greatest common good with the realization of equality and liberty, well aware that this implied a redistribution of property. After all this, how could one avoid reaching the conclusion that the goal could only be attained by the complete abolition of differences in property ownership and that the state was not only entitled but committed to carry out the abolition of private property?

It is obvious that here the idea of collective ownership had been developed on the philosophical as well as the administrative level as never before. And one almost wonders why common sense has delayed the proclamation of the abolition of private property for so long. In any case, the climate of opinion was such that the last step towards absolute and positive equality was inevitable. Only a slight incident was necessary to let the Revolution take its full course.

Robespierre fell, and with him fell the representative of the hopes of the people; the Jacobins and the Faubourgs were suppressed; the conservative sections of Paris ruled again; poverty and the working class were derided; the *jeunesse dorée* dominated even the streets. The Constitution of 1793 was abolished. Reaction raged as blindly as the masses had done before. Once more the masses rebelled, but the uprising of May 1795 was suppressed by arms, and the political role of the Faubourgs was annihilated.

Who was it, then, who ruled? Who was causing the suffering of the working class, the people? There could be no doubt that, with the fall of Robespierre, reaction of the owners against the non-owners had become more conspicuous from day to day. The new *Directoire*, in all its insignificance, was only the beginning of what the remaining friends of liberty had foreseen; any new revolt or a renewed terrorism would only lead to a second Thermidor, unless the foes of liberty were attacked at their very roots. He who wanted the destruction of the newly emerging bourgeois society had not spotted his adversary, personal property. The negation of the ancient privileges necessarily led to the negation of private property, and thus to the idea of a society of positive equality. Or another possibility was to submit to the laws which the new society began to adopt, irrespective of the Revolution.

The second alternative was unacceptable to those supporting the Revolution. Nothing remained but a desperate attack on private property as such, the natural final course of the deeper elements in the preceding struggle. This became the last phase of the revolutionary development. . . . The equality of communism is the natural outgrowth of the French Revolution, as well as of all other revolutions based on the concept of equality.

Babeuf and the First Manifestation of Communism

. . . When terrorism finally ended in the blood bath of its own making, with Robespierre . . . being scoffed at and cursed by the same people who had glorified him only a few days earlier, many people thought that this really meant the end of the Revolution. They hoped for a final and stable order even at the price of a bloody reaction. However, the power which had ruled society lately was, though broken, not yet destroyed. The first revolt against the new command which had risen from the ashes of terrorism broke out on May 20th, 1795. But the people, having lost their best leaders and being abandoned by many of their partisans, were soon completely defeated. . . . The last representatives of the revolutionary principle who survived were either killed or fled, or were dragged into prison. Popular sovereignty ("pure democracy") was a lost cause. . . .

In the stillness of prison, however, a new form of life began. Supporters of the common cause, living together, began to exchange their views and to develop their rigid principles into formal systems. They attempted to clarify what they really wanted; while public authority assumed that it had subdued its enemies, they found in prison a new incentive for a last and systematically conceived attempt to establish the principle of the Revolution, which was "equality." It was here and now for the first time in French history that the basic difference became clear between the two movements which had grown out of the same principle and of which, up to now, only one had come to power. . . . These two movements were the democratic and the communist movement. No matter how close the two were in principle, they led to quite different consequences.

In the revolt of May 20th, all parties had fought for one common purpose: the acceptance and the implementation of the Constitution of 1793. As the leaders of those parties now in jail were reconsidering the situation, the question was raised whether their supreme goal of achieving complete "equality" was really guaranteed by this Constitution. The divergence of the answers will be easily comprehensible.

To those who adhere to the idea of political democracy, the form of the state is of supreme importance; they believe that equality is established by the assurance of political equality. They are indifferent to society, because they hold the opinion that the principle of liberty realized by the state constitution will generate and preserve the principle of liberty in society. The communistic-egalitarian view, on the other hand, assumes that society determines the form of the state . . . and that in order to secure political equality, social equality has first to be firmly established; the basis of this view is the negation of property. To the democrats the Constitution of 1793 was the terminal point, while those who were more radical wanted to use it to establish an egalitarian order of society. . . . These two groups, which differed with reference to the principle of equality, were distinctly separated in the beginning. . . But the split could not last long; both parties were too much dependent upon each other, and, once released from prison, their members began, though reluctantly, to approach each other. It needed but one man who, by the power of his personality, was able to unite and inspire them to a common victory. This man was Babeuf.

We know nothing about Babeuf except for Buonarotti's long forgotten book which has now become famous (*Conspiration pour l'Egalité dite de Babeuf. . . .* par Ph. Buonarotti, Bruxelles, 1828. We owe all information about the conspiracy of Babeuf to this book, written twenty years later during the Restoration. It is the best work as a description of . . . communism during this period.). . . . After the fall of Robespierre, Babeuf first aligned himself with the victors; for unknown reasons he later went over to the opposition and was arrested. . . . During his stay in prison, his hatred against the enemies of Robespierre who obviously had mistreated him grew. He allied himself with several of the most radical republicans and embraced the idea of a conspiracy in order to establish absolute equality. After his release he became, due to his keenness and his versatility, the center of the new alliance. Babeuf was decidedly a bold and ingenious, but also a very ambitious, man. He was the first who understood the weakness of political democracy at a time when the masses began to grasp that they could gain very little by political liberty alone. But the Constitution of 1795 satisfied him as little as it satisfied the people, because it robbed . . . the absolute-democratic element of all hope of ever establishing a new ochlocracy. He therefore vowed to destroy it. This united him with the republicans proper. At the same time, he was audacious enough to acknowledge and spell out the final consequence of the egalitarian principle: complete equality of possessions and abolition of all private property. He thus became the main exponent of the ideas with which the masses were preoccupied. . . . Toward the end of 1795, after the new constitution had dashed all the hopes of the ochlocrats, he rallied a small group of like-minded persons and began to lecture and discuss the true principle of society. He quickly gained an increasing number of followers; in a short time they numbered about two thousand, and a society was formed under the name of "*Société du Panthéon.*" This society used to hold its meetings in the neighborhood of the Panthéon, along the line which divided the Parisian bourgeoisie from the people, the suburbs of the south and the east. According to the customs of his generation, Babeuf adopted a name from Roman history, . . . calling himself Gracchus, and began to publish a periodical with the significant title "*Le Tribun du peuple.*" It is easy to guess what the members of this club thought and wanted; its secret name was "the Society of Equals," and the

Le Tribun du peuple gave it an aggressive twist. Justice and law, constitution and society, state and property were attacked in the name of equality. With unscrupulous fury, the masses were urged to remember what they had lost and to consider what they might gain; the benefits enjoyed by the propertied classes were contrasted with the advantages of communal property, emphasizing the righteousness of the idea of equality. This was done in such a way as to arouse desperate revolutionary passions among the people. The people were challenged to live up to the legacy of Robespierre . . . The club grew more powerful from day to day. The people, overwrought, were inclined towards a frightful course of action.

The growing danger could not have escaped the attention of the Directory. The police searched for Babeuf; however, he succeeded in hiding and remained at the helm of the club and of the journal. The Directory now took more drastic measures. The *Société du Panthéon* was closed and membership proclaimed illegal, after the society had dared to publicly defend Babeuf and his principles. Even this might have been of no avail if another factor had not come into play. In the public meetings of the society, the number of voices which in crucial points deviated from Babeuf's egalitarianism grew, although all accepted the principle of absolute equality. Babeuf knew full well that skepticism within his party was his most deadly enemy and that the success of - a revolutionary act depended on complete agreement. He therefore welcomed the suppression of the society and its public discussions, which he was unable to control, because it was impossible for him to speak altogether frankly. Perhaps the society could have continued to operate underground, but Babeuf preferred to abandon it altogether. The most determined representative of the principle of equality was, at the same time, the unrestricted ruler of his followers, and at no price was he willing to renounce his position. Only now—after all other organization of the revolutionary movement had ceased to exist—did it become possible for him to take the unchallenged lead to which he had aspired. The *Société du Panthéon*, therefore, terminated its sessions first temporarily, then permanently. Babeuf was now the supreme ruler of his party.

A decisive step towards his goal was thus accomplished. *"Le Tribun du peuple"* continued to be published; it had now become his mouthpiece. To the masses he was a martyr for their holy cause, and his doctrines were accepted on the sole basis of his prestige. But there remained two more difficult steps to be taken. . . . Babeuf had to establish a Central Committee which could decide on doctrinal ques-

tions as well as on a course of action. He called upon the most determined members of his party, who established themselves as "the Secret
and permanent Directory," and tried to convert and organize the
masses. Next to Babeuf, the main leaders were Darthé, Maréchal, and
Buonarotti; they succeeded beyond their own expectations. The masses
were ready to believe and to act. The Directory defined the role of
the masses as that of the "insurrectional power of the people." Now
there remained just one more step to be taken.

In addition to the actual rabble and to the pure egalitarians, the
opposition consisted further of the radical Republicans, the remnants
of the Montagnards, once the mainstay of Robespierre. There were
some points of contact between the egalitarians and the Montagnards,
but no real cooperation. Therefore, it was impossible for the egalitarians to bypass the Montagnards, and it was equally impossible to
oppose them. . . . A way toward consolidation had to be found. . . .
The communists had spread slowly over all parts of Paris. The Directory took all necessary measures to allow the local members to participate in shaping and directing future actions. Ninety members of
all sections were chosen as representatives of the Departments. They
formed the secret National Assembly. The Republicans had constituted themselves in a similar fashion, also under a leading committee.
The confession of Buonarotti to the effect that the committees of the
two parties were decidedly on bad terms with each other is of particular interest; but circumstances pressed, and Babeuf arranged a common meeting . . . which ended with the fusion of both parties into
one large corporation. The Republicans, with about sixty members
of the National Convention, joined with the ninety communist representatives, entrusting themselves to the greater power. The preceding
discussions had provided the occasion for Babeuf to present his
ideas systematically. Buonarotti has reported on them and their
ultimate consequences in detail. It is difficult to judge, however, how
much Buonarotti has added of his own thoughts after speculat-
ing on the subject for thirty more years; there is no doubt that the
clarity and assurance on the question at hand which Buonarotti
shows had not yet been attained at the time of the fusion. The main
points and principles, on the other hand, must have been laid down
at the time in a way similar to that which Buonarotti describes.
Here is the first document of a communistic system to be put into
practice. It was the final consequence of the principle of equality.

The first question raised between the democrats and the egalitarians
(they did not yet call themselves "communists") concerned the Con-

stitution of 1793. The egalitarians appreciated its value but only as a road to equality. They saw its main mistake "in the articles of the declaration of rights which by defining the right to property sanctioned it in all its frightening scope." The *"Comité des Egaux"* stated its own principles in criticism of that Constitution. According to this principle, inequality is the cause of the eternal and absolute misfortune of men. The source of this inequality are property rights. . . . No half-measure is of any help against this basic evil; even progressive taxes are not sufficient. Only the community of goods and of work can be the true goal of mankind, and only such a community will guarantee a perfect society.

Some of the democrats appear to have been won over to this principle; others must have raised serious opposition, since Buonarotti relates that agreement between the two groups was finally accomplished by agreeing on the following two premises: first, that the Constitution of 1793 was acceptable, and second, that "true equality was to be worked for as the distant goal for which one should strive." The republicans accepted these premises, but they were decidedly in the minority, as is shown by the decrees of the egalitarians, who now began to develop a minute system of true communism.

The principle of absolute equality requires first of all the abolition of all property and equal distribution of all goods. "Ownership of all commodities is indivisible, it belongs to the people." At the same time, the principle of the common good has to be upheld. Therefore, the community accepts the principle of the "right of everybody to a happy life", to realize that it specifies work as a general obligation for everybody. If work and happiness are considered to be inseparable, it is inevitable that the decision to work is no longer left to the individual. Work will be regulated by law, which—in order not to endanger the general happiness —should guarantee that "labor never degenerate into fatigue", but "that everybody be encouraged to it by habit, by devotion to his country, by pleasure and by the approval of public opinion." The sciences are called upon to cooperate toward that goal, and all citizens are called upon to participate in turn in disagreeable jobs that have to be done. On the other hand, complete equality in consumption ought to be secured, and everybody should be entitled to everything. Universal work is apt to produce universal abundance. The basis of all wealth is the exploitation of the soil. The political administration determines the total produce of each district to secure the correct use of the land. The adversity of work, however, requires—and this in the midst of absolute equality!—an arrangement of the citizens into classes, each of which is assigned by law to a

particular type of work according to the supreme principle of equality.
. . . On the other hand, there is a fear of equality exactly because of
abundance, the very abundance which the system is expected to provide.
Although the citizens shall be well off, they shall all live and dress simply
and uniformly. Why have different colors of clothes or different furniture?
Why have a well tailored dress for one and a shabby one for another? . . .
"It is essential for the happiness of all individuals that the citizen never
experiences the slightest degree of even apparent superiority." Here
communism is already lost in the particulars of clothing regulations.
Even with this complete process of levelling all differences there was
one serious danger for absolute equality, namely, the difference in mental
ability which manifests itself in the arts and sciences. Here also radical
measures were proposed. It is true that "some arts are indispensable for
the happiness of society," but shall one "let the human mind roam in
the vast areas of imagination without leaders and without restraint
under the pretext of refinement and improvement? Shall one tolerate
that a world of artificial wants, inequalities, quarrels and wrong concepts
of happiness is instilled into society?" Certainly not. Says Buonarotti:
"Our committee had unanimously consented that works of art and artisans
had to be of such kind that they could be easily communicated to everybody." "Convinced that nothing is less important to a nation than to be
conspicuous and famous they wanted to do away with every pseudo-
scientific pretext for withdrawing from common obligations and for
providing a different happiness to the individual than the one of society.
They were determined to abolish all basic discussions right from the
beginning and were convinced that as soon as it became obvious that no
special compensation would be available the mania for displaying aes-
theticism and for writing books would abate". In this way the all powerful committee imposed its control also upon science. And lest the unalterable nature of things would reassert the dreaded inequality in the
children, education, of course, was under no condition permitted to be
left in private hands. Only the state was to have the right to educate
the children. "The more domestic education there was the greater would
paternal power become." All children will be placed in a huge institution,
and here, without regard to intellectual qualifications, all will receive a
simple and absolutely equal education. But what will happen if later the
indestructible difference would appear anew, for instance in the press?
Here was a new danger which the Committee had to acknowledge. To
prevent the eternal living spirit from reasserting itself and shaking off
the fetters hampering it, restrictions had to be imposed. The idea of
abstract freedom thus led to the establishment of the most rigid censor-

ship. The whole press was to be kept within the narrow limits of republican principles; any violation was to be severely punished. Indeed, we are overcome with dread while reviewing these ideas. "Nobody is allowed to utter opinions which contradict the principle of equality, no pamphlet whatsoever is permitted to publish a report on a discovery, nothing is allowed to be printed and distributed unless it is officially approved as being favorable to the Republic." . . . Can the human race, under the rule of the most terrible despotism, possibly be more deprived than by what the idea of equality threatens to realize? . . .

As one reconsiders the principles presented by early communism, it becomes clear that it is definitely opposed to all previous conditions but that it has nothing to offer beyond this negativism. The tyranny of equality attains nothing except the complete elimination of everything which may threaten equality. The true character of communism is already apparent from the beginning: it is the negation of the social order based on the inequality of property. This was true for communism in 1795, and it is still true today.

But even the early communism of that period could not possibly be satisfied with negative criticism alone. It was all right to use such formulas as "abundance," "general welfare," "community work," etc.; some new social order had to be constructed which might be able to produce the necessary conditions for the achievement of general happiness. . . . Whenever the adherents of the idea of equality should gain power, they would have to create a positive basis for the new socio-economic order. Communists rarely have an opportunity which forces them to do so. Therefore, many people think that communism does not have any constructive concepts, but this is not necessarily the case. . . .

The inescapable contradiction inherent in communism will necesarily lead to its dissolution. This can be predicted on the basis of the following analysis:

Property is not an inherent necessity of human society, but society cannot exist without goods. The satisfaction of needs makes survival possible, and goods alone accomplish this. However, the availability of goods is not enough; they have to be distributed to the individuals living in society. Everything depends upon this distribution. Since the personal life of the individual depends upon the share of goods he receives, since he is either rich, well educated and influential, or poor, frustrated and deprived, depending upon whether he receives many or few goods, his freedom is dependent upon the power which determines the distribution of goods.

In feudal society, privileges were the determining factor for the distribution of goods; in bourgeois society, it is the invested capital; both lead to inequality, even if there originally existed no property. Communism, having eliminated the latter, is confronted with the question of how to preserve equality in its system of distribution, even if property has been abolished. There are two possible ways of doing this: One may use labor as the basis of distribution, so that the amount and quality of work determines the share to be allowed. (Later we will see that this is the principle of distribution favored by socialism.) Even Babeuf acknowledges the fact that labor is a factor of differentiation. A distribution of goods based on labor is necessarily unequal. This is precisely the kind of difference which had been eliminated by the aboli-tion of property, and which therefore should not be re-established through income. What was one to do? It would be necessary to adopt the other alternative and assign the distribution of goods to public authority. The right of the state to distribute goods is a specific characteristic of communism, which distinguishes it from socialism. The feasibility of communism depends upon whether or not the ideas of freedom and equality can be safeguarded in a society where the distribution of goods —and consequently also the correlated distribution of labor—is carried out by public authority. It immediately becomes evident that the opposite, namely an unlimited despotism of those in power, is inevitable under communism. This does not yet doom communism to failure. Three basic rules for any communistic society are necessary to give public authority the monopoly of the distribution of goods: All private exchange among members of the communistic community has to be abolished; . . . all products have to be delivered to a public warehouse in order to separate the individual from the product of his labor; and each individual's share of the goods produced must be obtained exclusively from these warehouses by public authorization. These are the necessary prerequisites of a communistic economic order. The fourth rule, the compulsion to work in order to increase the amount of goods to be distributed, is a consequence of the demand for affluence. It may be emphasized or omitted, depending on what type of communism is desired, one of wealth or one of poverty. . . .

Obviously, the distribution of goods which has just been described refers to the form of distribution only; the essential question pertains to the principle according to which this distribution is to be carried out. The answer already conceived by Babeuf is: that everybody shall receive according to his needs. The decision as to how large this need is can obviously not be left to the individual; it will have to be made by public authority in charge of distribution. This authority will have the power over everything that possessions can do for men. It will take the place of property, and the recipients of goods will be dependent on the power of individuals instead of on the eternal and unchangeable laws of economic relations. The relationship which at present exists, often enough on a small scale, and in accordance with which the distributor of wages is also the superior of the wage earner, will be made into a general principle of the whole communistic social order. Whoever does not admit that this dependence of the consumer upon the distributor leads to complete despotism of the latter over the former and therewith to a complete destruction of all personal freedom, is either totally ignorant or altogether insincere. And yet communism claims to be the realization of freedom.

Let us also consider another approach, according to which the needs of all individuals are equal, so that the distributing authority hands out completely equal shares and is deprived of the power of arbitrary decision through distribution. Even assuming that wants are equal, it is doubtlessly true that man can control his needs and therefore restrict himself. He who receives more than he consumes must appear to be superior to the one who has more needs than he is able to satisfy, although both receive equal shares—especially since physical needs, as well as bodily strength, are unequal to begin with. Equal distribution, therefore, leads—in view of the different needs—directly and inevitably to inequality. And yet equality has been the guiding principle. . . . Even the most radical communistic system can attain neither freedom nor equality when it tries to apply its principles in practice.

The early representatives of pure communism did as yet not visualize these consequences. They considered their mission accomplished by the attack on personal property. They took, however, one further step by devising the first system of positive communism, and this system is in some respects of great historical importance. For the first time, we discover the blueprint for the organization of the national labor force, even though only in a formal sense; there is no reference made as yet to a classification of types of labor or the conflicting interest of capital and labor; secondly, we see the principle of the restriction of wants established as the basis for the economic order; and finally, we see the despotism of public authority established over the workers with reference to their labor.

At the same time, this system is important, because it places work in the center of the whole economy and indicates the road for later socialist systems. Lacking any concept of capital and its importance—an importance upon which the whole social life of the following historic period rested—early communism could not have gained a deeper insight into the significance of labor problems. Instinctively it had put its finger on a problem which gained great importance in the future. . . .

. . . It is unlikely that the Republicans supported the principle of absolute equality. Furthermore, the blueprint for a communist society was by no means complete. But it remains, in spite of its inner weaknesses, an important historical document of social conditions of that time. In spite of the emphasis on a complete community of goods, we do not find a trace of either national workshops or nationalized industries. Babeuf's communism is definitely an agrarian communism. It is further evident that—while the question of the distribution of goods is treated in great detail—the problem of labor is cut short, and this in spite of the fact that Babeuf's type of communism derived its main support from the lowest, propertyless class of society. The neglect of this problem was only possible because there was as yet no proletariat, properly speaking—although there were enough non-owners—with definite demands as to the distribution of profit between labor and capital. The great difference between this early form of communism and its later manifestations is not one of principle but of differences in the social order. . . .

It is evident that what we call industry today did not exist at that time, and therefore was not considered by Babeuf's type of communism. Instead of "fraternities" and "national workshops," the economy of early communism was concerned with war and agriculture. Babeuf's doctrine is one of Spartan virtues. If he had grown up in the period of large scale industrial enterprises, he probably would have developed a different theory of labor. However, the striking fact is that in Babeuf's theory the idea of equality reached its extreme in the demand for the abolition of private property. The first great cycle was thereby completed. The greatest enemy of equality had been located, and for the first time the organizational principle of all forms of communism—distribution of goods according to needs by public authority—had been formulated. Irrespective of whether Babeuf was to succeed or to fail, it was through him that the basic idea of the whole Revolution was confronted with its final task.

In spite of the apparent scope of the conspiracy, its strength and chance to success were very limited. It was too easy to detect the conspirators and their plans, and one needed only to know them in order to get them out of the way. One single serious attack of public power sufficed, and the communism of the first Revolution disappeared for more than a generation from the history of French society.

The Fall of the Alliance

When the Committee of the New Revolution believed that it had worked out its principles satisfactorily, and when the alliance with the Montagnards—or "pure democrats"—seemed to be sufficiently stable, its next goal was to gain the support of the masses for the insurrection. It therefore became necessary to present these principles to the public. This created difficulties which were likely to raise doubts among the leaders. Sylvain Maréchal wrote a "Manifesto of Equals" which the communists wanted to submit to the Democratic Committee for acceptance as a program for the insurrection. This manifesto was nothing but a simple summary of communistic principles concerning private property. It did not contain anything beyond that. There was no mention of political conditions, of a constitution, of government; government was condemned as such, even the Constitution of 1793 was rejected by implication as being detrimental to the happiness of men. . . . This manifesto was unacceptable to the Democrats; they knew that it could not possibly gain public support and that the pure Republicans would be repelled by it. Babeuf, who considered it his mission to unite democratic and communist elements and whose name was already well known to the people, drafted a new manifesto intended to satisfy both factions. This "analysis of the doctrine of Babeuf" was actively discussed and finally accepted. It is reprinted here unabridged, since it was widely read at the time and because it presents the point of agreement between the Democrats and Communists:

1) *Analysis of the doctrine by Babeuf*

Article 1: Nature has given everybody an equal claim to the enjoyment of all goods.

Article 2: It is the purpose of society to defend this natural equality, often threatened by the strong and the wicked, and to increase the common enjoyment through concerted effort.

Article 3: Everybody is obliged by nature to work, nobody can avoid labor without committing a crime.

Article 4: Work and enjoyment must be shared.

Article 5: Suppression exists if one person is overworked and lacking in everything while others indulge in luxury without doing anything.

Article 6: Nobody has ever appropriated the products of the soil or of industry without committing a crime.

Article 7: In a true society there should be neither poor nor rich.

Article 8: Wealthy people who are unwilling to forsake abundance in favor of the needy are enemies of the people.

Article 9: Nobody is entitled, by accumulating all requisite means, to deprive another person of education indispensable for his happiness. There ought to be a common education.

Article 10: The purpose of the Revolution is the abolition of inequality and the establishment of general happiness.

Article 11: The Revolution is not completed, because the rich devour all goods and rule alone and the poor work like real slaves, languish in misery and play no part in politics.

Article 12: The Constitution of 1793 is the true law of France because the people have accepted it solemnly; because the Convention had no right to change it, because in order to do so, it has massacred the people who wanted the constitutional law to be carried out, because the Convention has persecuted and murdered the deputies who defended it loyally, because fear of the people and the influence of emigrants played a decisive role in the draft and alleged ratification of the Constitution of 1795, which did not get one-fourth of the support that the Constitution of 1793 did; because the Constitution of 1793 has upheld the inalienable rights of man: to have a voice in the legislative process, to exercise his civil rights, to assemble, to demand what he considers appropriate, to be informed and not to starve—all rights which the counter-revolutionary act of the government of 1795 has publicly and thoroughly violated.

Article 13: Every citizen is obliged by the Constitution of 1793 to re-establish and defend the will and the happiness of the people.

Article 14: All authority based on the Constitution of 1795 is illegal and counter-revolutionary.

Article 15: All those who have violated the Constitution of 1793 are guilty of the crime of offending the people.

This manifesto, distributed in Paris in April, 1796, read by the people everywhere with great curiosity and fear, created a sensation; opponents began to fear a revolt; anxieties on one side and hopes on the other developed anew. . . . Everybody knew that the Directory in its secret sessions had gone much farther than was publicly admitted. Everybody felt that his own way of life and the basis of his social and political existence were threatened; but nobody knew how to ward off the approaching and growing danger. . . . The time of terrorism was still too recent to be disregarded. The Directory took notice of the situation and mustered all available forces. The whole city was agitated. The conspirators continued to work in secret. Babeuf hid at a safe place; the meetings taking place in those dark streets of the Faubourg St Antoine and St. Marceau remained undiscovered; the number of supporters—according to Buonarotti—was estimated at about 16,000. . . . On the 8th of May, the revolutionary committee of the Montagnards solemnly renewed its pledge of loyalty to Babeuf's communist party; the two main elements of the insurrection were united, and victory for the most terrible revolution seemed certain. At this moment, the conspiracy met the fate of many similar organizations; it was betrayed. . . . Barras had offered his services as a secret agent. . . . He was successful. On May 10th, the main leaders got together to determine the day for the revolution. . . . They neglected to take extreme precautionary measures; the police succeeded in arresting sixty-five of the leaders, in seizing the most important documents, and in leaving the alliance without leadership and counsel. The members dispersed, courage and unity were gone, and the cause of communism was hopelessly lost with the fall of Babeuf. The Directory displayed determination and care. It did not want to deny to the conspirators a regular judicial procedure, although the documents gave a clear enough testimony. . . .

The details of the proceedings are of no importance here. Originally, the conspirators were willing to confess and claimed to have a legal case; later they attempted to present the whole plot as merely an abortive attempt. But this was in vain. They did not command any moral support, they had no satisfactory explanation, and could not deny the facts. The judges punished them for their bloodthirsty plans by a relatively mild sentence, considering the customs of the time and the dangers which the plot presented. Of the 65 defendants, only Babeuf and Darthé received death sentences; seven others, Buonarotti among them, were deported; all others were set free. . . .

Another act of the tragedy of the Revolution came to a close, to make room for a figure who soon would drown republicanism, love of liberty, communism and ochlocracy in the one great wave of the glory of his victories.

THE TRANSITION TO THE NEW PRINCIPLES OF SOCIETY

*French Society after the Reign of Terror and the
Constitution of 1795.*

Our history of communism has to a certain extent run ahead of the sequence of events. The conspiracy of Babeuf was opposed to the

Directory and the Constitution of 1795. But since this conspiracy represents, above all, the ultimate consequence of the principle which until now had dominated the Revolution, we have discussed it in conjunction with the period of terrorism to which it essentially belongs. We have seen that it had no genuine appeal to the people, it was not capable even of staging a revolt. It was condemned to impotence not so much by its inner contradiction but by the much more powerful fact that French society did not as yet provide a fertile soil for such a doctrine. Changes in a constitution can be made in a single day; changes in society require generations. The newly established society of France had not yet moved beyond the sphere of the general law which had been established in 1789; the doctrines had not yet affected individual life. This development is part of the history of the following period.

We now turn back to the analysis of French society at the end of the reign of terror.

The laws of the Constituent Assembly had established the principle of complete legal equality with respect to acquisition and property. This had become an accepted fact in the life of the people; on account of this principle they had been willing to endure even terrorism. For one moment all persons were aligned side by side as equals. The thorough destruction of all status distinctions, as well as of all privileges of property, had erased all differences. The fall of the party of Robespierre had not affected these principles in the least; . . . the 9th Thermidor had been directed against the misuse of this principle but not against the principle itself. And yet we discover that at this moment a great change takes place, affecting the whole life of the French people. . . . The violent storm is followed by calm. Slowly the law and the administration get organized; a certain stability, so far unknown, replaces the revolutionary unrest; a new Constitution is adopted; a new, not particularly outstanding power takes over the government. The recent years, barely passed, seem to recede into the distant past. Things start to move again as if by themselves, just as before the Revolution; they gain stability on the basis of the new principle, which so far had not been able to achieve anything whether reasonable or unreasonable. This calm is not a result of lack of strength: France fights foreign powers with the same energy, and the government is just as strong at home as it had been during the Revolution. Such conditions require an explanation.

The explanation points to the fact dominating the whole period, namely, that the old society of France had been completely dissolved, but a new one had not as yet taken its place. . . . No period in the history of a nation can demonstrate better the absolute necessity of social order for the life of the nations and the states than that in which social order is absent. This is always the case after a great and successful revolution. If a nation could exist without an ordered system of society, this condition would become permanent. However, at this point the same phenomenon always reappears. As soon as an old social order is destroyed, people make every effort to lay the foundation for a new one. It is so indispensable a condition for human existence that the nobler impulses of the people relegate the demands of the state into the background in order to devote themselves to the rebuilding of society. They are instinctively aware that society—although not the absolute prerequisite for the idea of the state—is indeed the absolute prerequisite for state constitution. During these periods the life of the nation seems almost to have ceased, because all activities are concentrated in the sphere of individual life; therefore, dreariness in public life prevails, mediocrity rules, and any kind of administration is tolerated because one knows that the yet unfinished order of society has to be fully established in order to give direction to the state and form to its power. In such a period the revolutionary states are most vulnerable to foreign aggression. If this period passes without disturbance, the new society will be strong enough to take care of its own future, the danger from outside interference disappears, and the only source of its destruction then rests with its own composite parts.

Such conditions prevailed after the fall of Robespierre. The years from 1795 to 1798 will always remain unexplained periods in the history of France unless one sees them in terms of the nature and dynamics of society. There was, at this time, great poverty in France: in the midst of the country where the happiness of the people had been established as the principle of the constitution and of the administration, famine and despair threatened the cities and the countryside. Comfort had disappeared, and if there was any wealth it was not visible. Industries were laid low; the worker had nothing to eat because he had no work. Those who were better off discovered that they were threatened more by the despair of the propertyless than by the armies of the enemies. Was there no way of avoiding a second reign of terror?

There was—but only one: to give the people, by means of social changes, what they had tried in vain to gain by governmental authority —namely, work and bread. The road to this goal was clear enough. More than half of France was lying waste, practically without proprietor. . . . In order to improve conditions it was necessary to let the rich resources which had been made available through the redistribution of land be used by the working population. This was the price to be paid for well-being and order; at this price, general well-being could certainly be established.

Why had the French people not started earlier to utilize these possessions taken away from the nobility and the church, although the high prices of agricultural products threatened the welfare of the country as well as the well-being of all individual entrepreneurs?

The whole movement of the French Revolution appears in a new light as soon as this question is raised. The labor of the farmer does not yield immediate gain as does that of the manual worker; agricultural produce requires time to bloom and to ripen, and every harvest represents a year's period in the farmer's life. Successful farming is therefore only possible if security of land-ownership corresponds to the time-consuming labor which farming demands. Security of property rights is as important as is property itself, which remains useless without it. . . . The former owners were still living in the country, and there was no certainty that, with a sudden change of political circumstances, they might not lay claim to their former property, which others had bought with assignats. Therefore, the soil was not well cultivated, and the assignats remained valueless. . . . The salvation of the state and of the people required that any doubt concerning the finality of the redistribution of land be eliminated. To accomplish this, all those who pretended to have any present or future claims to these estates on the basis of the legal rules of the old society had to be literally annihilated; they were those who in one way or another were attached to the old society. The misery of the people, therefore, put political power consistently into the hands of those who did not hesitate to obliterate the remnants of the old regime. They were the representatives of the idea of absolute equality. We have described their role in the area of the history of ideas. Their mission in the area of practical social life was to guarantee the security of the new land distribution through the annihilation of the former proprietors, in order to make the cultivation of the newly acquired farms economically possible and to establish a new basis for the new acquisition of property through labor and capital. This notion transpires in several sources, especially the reports of the Committee of Welfare. The Convention tolerated terrorism, which not only saved the Republic from foreign enemies but also finally established the new system of land distribution; . . . the same Convention condemned terrorism and its adherents as soon as it began to fear that it threatened the possessions of the new owners as well and that the return to normalcy was endangered by the constant threat to those who were better off. This caused the fall of Robespierre; after his fall the new economy developed. It could not have grown without terrorism, but neither would its growth have been possible if terrorism had continued. Those who know the tremendous influence exerted by landed property on society will understand that the practical importance of terrorism for the domestic life of France lay in safeguarding the new system of land-distribution as a permanent institution. With the end of terrorism, the property owners demanded above all that public authority should protect work and the utilization of the newly acquired property. It is curious that the same Convention which first abandoned the Girondistes to allow terrorism to take its course later put an end to terrorism in order to introduce the Directory. During the period between September, 1792, when they first convened, until October, 1795, when they dispersed, the Convention consisted of the same deputies. But conditions turned out to be more powerful than men. It was the task of the Convention to prepare the new society, and this it had carried out. The history of the Convention consists of three stages. During the first six months of its existence it witnessed the fall of the monarchy and the Girondists. From May, 1793 to July, 1794 it supported the reign of terror. Until then the Convention was a powerless tool of its leaders. It might have been expected that when all those who had had a reputation and power in the Convention had perished, the rest of the Assembly would be an indecisive mass of people. However, instead of a group of representatives without leader and easily swayed by every change, we see a Convention which formulated its goals correctly, clearly and steadfastly, and which opposed the revolt of pure democracy on May 20th, 1795 with fearless energy worthy of the greatest acts of the original Constituent Assembly, which with the same energy, on the 13th *Vendémiaire*, contained royalism by its military power. We see a Convention which, after the fall of the terrorits, allowed a certain latitude to reactionary forces to make the reappearance of conditions favoring absolute equality impossible by annihilating its main representatives, but which then, when the reactionary forces felt almost victorious, suddenly turned around, forgave and calmed, abolished death sentences almost completely, reintroduced class differences, and finally created a constitution which, although not based on principle, corresponded to the requirement of the prevailing conditions. . . . What was it that gave the Convention the courage and the power? What was it that made stormswept France obey this Convention?

We believe we have given the explanation: The elements of the new society wanted to be left alone. The Convention acknowledged the fact that, in spite of legislation and military measures, the basis of a new social order was still missing . . . A stable order of society is the necessary basis of a stable state. The riddle of this period consisted in the fact that France, although it had a nation, a community, and a system of property distribution, did not yet have a society. . . .

In what respect did the domestic conditions in France differ from those of a true social order? . . . It is not enough that the various elements of society, property, and law do exist; it is necessary that these elements bring forth a permanent order of things. Even the individual had not yet adjusted to the new conditions. The soil had not yet been cultivated for one whole season, manufacturing not yet geared toward regular needs; the education of the people was even less oriented toward the new system with its new customs. The last and most important element of society was also missing in France; the new order of things had not yet been integrated within the families and had not yet grown into an order of society through the family. That was the process which now began. This process, although it took considerable time, had no history in the usual sense of the word. It took place naturally in line with Rousseau's statement: "The more time the events need to take place, the shorter time it takes to describe them." The period of war was terminated with the abolition of the rigidly separated class system; class domination had been destroyed. Says Mignet: . . . "The Revolution displayed its second characteristic, the one of order, of creativity and of peace. The parties, none of which had an exclusive and lasting claim on liberty, were discouraged and threw themselves from public into private life." This describes the consequences without explaining the causes. The cause was the lack of a new social order. Only a well-established society struggles for state power, never the people as such. But France at this time was made up only of "the people," the total of its population which was not socially structured.

This is why the period is of such interest as regards the problem of the true relationship between society and state. The mutual dependence of these two forms of human life was reflected in a new light through the establishment of the Directory. It had just been formed under the most dismal circumstances when, although almost without means, it immediately became sovereign. . . . No more revolts in the streets, no clubs, no siege by the masses, no fierce competition for the highest positions, no applicants for public favor, nobody who dared to take action against these conditions. . . . The whole terrible insurrection of Babeuf, which claimed 17,000 followers, was disposed of by a few policemen without a shot. The chaos of unparalleled power was followed by the chaos of powerlessness; the corpse of the Revolution lay stretched out on the soil of shattered France. The power of the Directory did not rest on the enthusiasm of the people, nor on the powerful armies, nor on its excellent personalities; it rested solely on irresponsibility. This is the criterion of any state power which presides over a dissolved society. Responsibility is not a consequence of a law; it is not a prerequisite of the ideal state; . . . responsibility is a result of an awareness that two classes of a society struggle for the control of the state; responsibility is the means by which one of these classes does not allow governmental power to yield to the other class. The period of responsibility came only later. . . . At the time, the classes had not yet evolved, while the estates had disappeared; the lack of a social order became the basis of the irresponsibility of the rulers. . . .

What were the main features of the new Constitution? . . . It is not necessary to go into detail here. It was similar to the Constitution of 1791, but without provisions for a king, and with two legislative chambers. . . . It provided for a separation of state powers; the Directory was given the executive and the representative chambers the legislative power. The first chamber was the "Council of the Aged," whose members were to be over forty years old, married or widowed; it was given the right to accept or reject the decisions of the second chamber, the "Council of the Five Hundred". . . . Citizenship was granted to all who were 21 years of age, were settled in France for at least one year, or who were registered as having been born in France and who paid direct taxes, either personal or on landed property. . . . The Directory seems to be an altogether new creation, but it is easy to see what is hidden behind the *pouvoir éxécutif* which the directors held. . . . It is the need for a strong authority which can support the laws appropriate for the new society. Under the Directory, liberty was hardly fostered. The people had thrown their rights carelessly into the arena of the social struggle; they knew now that freedom as an abstract concept differs from freedom in a specific social context.

The Constitution of 1795 has often been compared to the one of 1791; the question suggests itself of why the latter was not reintroduced and the monarchy reinstated. It was not possible to answer this question clearly till a later date. Monarchy in Europe was still the true representative of the old society, of the former proprietors and the old legal system. Kings were rejected because privileges and estates were rejected. The Republic of 1795 differed essentially from the Republic of 1793. It was not, like the latter, a true democracy, and its Constitution clearly indicated that it was not intended to be that; it aimed only to dislodge, with the monarchy, those elements which might become dangerous to the emerging society based on the new principles of distribution of property. If the monarchy had been able to abandon its old principles, a reform might have been possible. But such a monarchy was unknown in all of Europe, and France would have been unable to hold its own when confronted with the forces of feudal Europe. Therefore, what was wanted was a Republic. This is the meaning of the statement by Mignet: "The goal at this moment, was a Republic without a revolutionary government, a moderate regime without counter-revolutionary tendencies." What was wanted was public peace. There was a fear of disturbances from above as well as from below, and therefore a constitution was drafted which excluded the masses from power. . . .

This explains the course of French history up to 1815. The same society which wanted the Republic of 1795 abandoned Napoleon and greeted the new king. In 1795 it would have been necessary to subdue society to reinstate the king; in 1815 he was accepted almost voluntarily, although the power of the king was three times as great as before. Society did not change, but monarchy in all European countries had definitely changed. The history of Napoleon is unrivalled in its glory, unprecedented in the vicissitudes of life, fabulous in the magnitude of actual events; it is unprecedented in the scope of political revolutions and the changes imposed upon countries and their boundaries. All these changes took place within one generation. . . . The actual significance of Napoleon in European history is reflected not in the history of individual states but in the history of European society. He was the man who spread the seeds of the new French society over Europe; . . . this man, whose greatness overshadows everybody else in both the 18th and 19th centuries, saw his life work fall into ruins; though much of what he had created was against his own intentions, it gained predominance over all Europe directly after his death—the ultimate victory of civil society and constitutionalism over feudalism. . . .

Part One, Chapter Two

THE EMPIRE

THE FOUNDATION OF THE ACQUISITIVE SOCIETY

Let us review the development of society from the vantage point where it clearly begins to constitute itself. What is apparent so far? The collapse of the old feudal order, its complete obliteration, and consequently the necessity for the establishment of a new social order. Up to this point, the principle of this new social order had been established. This principle evaporated completely in its abstract demo-cratic-communistic form; it was preserved only in its merely negative form as the demand for equality before the law. We see furthermore that, on the basis of this principle, the elements of the new social order—the new system of the distribution of goods on the basis of new laws and assignats and the new system of free trade—assert themselves. But we do not yet see the structure of a society evolving. No definite chance for the individual, no clear formation of classes and interests, no definite new forms of community life are as yet discernable. They are, however, indispensable. What will this new society be like, arising as the most recent form of social order on the basis of the negative principle of equality before the law and the new system of distribution of goods now evolving in France and spreading over all of Europe?

An analysis of the Empire, its origin and its history, will answer this question.

ORIGIN OF THE EMPIRE

*The Last Elements of Feudal Society and the
Emergence of Moneyed Power.*

. . . With the establishment of the Directory and the Constitution of 1795, things quieted down in France. People retreated into private life and began to busy themselves with their property, the real basis of all social development. "The Revolution proceeded successfully to consolidate its gains; after first having created a nation of sectarians, it now produced a nation of laborers," stated Mignet. The people who had taken possession of the newly distributed estates began to make use of them. While engaged in economic activities, they left all political decisions to the rulers of the state. They began to be indifferent toward decisions which did not seem to be of immediate economic advantage. The influence of the masses on the state had accomplished what had been humanly possible. While until then the state had been the center of all activities, personal well-being now became the focal point for all individual actions.

Many historians have seriously reproached the French people for having allowed this short interval between the Revolution, with its grandiose concepts, and the Empire, with its brilliant victories. Used to the interpretation of history on the basis of political action only, they were unable to explain the inertia and the decline under the Directory except by assuming the complete decay of all the noble and superior impulses which had made France great. Even Mignet, the most profound interpreter of the Revolution, exclaims: "After the Directory had been established, nobody believed in anything anymore; everything seemed to be lost, the virtue of the bourgeoisie and the virtue of the people." This verdict has been almost generally accepted.

And yet, this state of affairs was altogether natural and necessary. Man has only limited abilities, he can only live for *one* purpose. This one purpose now became the acquisition of material goods; after the land had been acquired it now had to be utilized; this, by its very nature, had to be done by individuals, not by the government. The only demand made upon the state was not to interfere in the economic affairs of the individuals; otherwise, state power really was of no consequence, because it could not assist the individual in his house and home, field and ground, shop and factory. If such was the case, it was necessarily reflected in the indifference of the people toward the constitution and the administration. The unsurpassed devotion of the people in former years to the fight for new public law had been as natural as was its indifference now. . . . Public life subsided, and private enterprise became the center of activity.

This was obviously a propitious time for the survivors of the feudal society to wage a last decisive battle for the restoration of the old order. Only eight years had passed since 1789. There were still hundreds and thousands of people whose existence depended upon the old system, who neither wanted nor were able to adjust themselves to the new order of things, who had never understood this new order nor accepted its high validity. The issue to them was not one of specific privileges but an issue of their whole social existence. They had learned during recent years that it is highly dangerous to have recourse to violence. They had rejoiced in seeing the reign of terror and its aftermath dispose of the leaders of the Republic. Then as now, in their short-sightedness they believed that only the leaders of the Revolution represented the power of the new ideas. After those individuals had been eliminated, they imagined that they would be able to gain control of the apparently abandoned battleground, by way of the latest Constitution. For the complete silence of the people in public affairs made them believe that they no longer had to deal with the people but only with a weak and stupid government.

The remnants of the old society began a systematic constitutional struggle for the usurpation of the power of the state. It is the only outstanding feature of this time and later led to the coup d'état of the 18th Fructidor. This development is all the more important because it illustrates the close relationship of feudal elements with the newly developing groups of society which in later years partly cooperated, partly fought, with each other. . . .

Since the first appearance of the assignats, there had developed a great confusion in all economic relations which in the course of several years caused large-scale unemployment. . . . The assignats . . . were remittances for future cash made available by the sale of the estates, which guaranteed their value. Their value went up and down depending on the expected returns of these estates. During the years 1793 and 1794 the estimates for the expected returns dropped to almost nothing, because the dissolution of society, and particularly the threats to property, discouraged everybody from acquiring property. Nevertheless, the state needed money. . . . Since the assignats had no value whatsoever, the state had to use other means to obtain money. It had to buy cash in coins, in exchange either for land or bonds. . . . During these years, coins still in existence had been withdrawn from circulation. Many people hoarded them. All those who possessed cash in coins had become wealthier during the Revolution without any effort on their part, simply because cash money had gained tremendously in its market value. Since the government needed that cash money at any price, it had to buy it back in exchange for something which was infinitely more valuable but had a lower market exchange value than cash; it paid the money owners with huge tracts of land or with large numbers of state bonds. In this way, the mere possession of coins suddenly turned into great wealth without the investment of labor. The possessions of the state were transferred to the money owners.

Naturally such shifts in wealth were accompanied by a new kind of speculation. All those to whom money and possessions meant everything played the market. . . . Ignominious bargaining increased. . . . Unbelievable values were offered for little cash; once, not less than twelve millions in state bonds were exchanged for 300,000 francs in cash. Many public servants participated in these speculations. "All the departments and especially the war department were taken over by a mob of looters of whom Barras was the patron; they made a mockery of the orders of the Directory and of the laws of the Councils, they supported each other and had become the sole power of the Republic" (Lavallée T. IV.). "The new fortunes date back to this period. All of a sudden one saw a swarm of parvenues emerging from the mud, children of stock jobbing and immorality, attached to the camps of unrestrained luxury and of the most counterrevolutionary spirit. All the sacrifices of the exhausted Republic were rendered impotent by their dirty hands" (Report of Joubert de l'Hérault to the *Conseil des Cinq Cents*). These nouveaux riches of usury began to indulge in the luxury of times past and in mockery of the principle of equality which had been the basis of the Revolution. The rage for pleasure reappeared, accompanied by a rage for wealth. Old customs of the old regime came into fashion again in the midst of the Republic of Equals. Says Mignet: "Everyone threw himself frantically into the pursuit of pleasure; balls, banquets, debauchery, sumptuous carriages, were more fashionable than ever before. It was the reaction of the members of the old regime." It was the counterpart of the Republic of Virtue during terrorism; it also left deep scars. The inconsistency with principles for which the whole country had fought was too striking; for the first time, the power of money, which later was frequently mistaken for the power of property in general, appeared on the scene of French history; at the same time, an intense hatred developed against the power of money, a hatred which found its first expression in Babeuf's communism. The instinct of the common people was a good indicator, because this money power was the first and loyal ally of feudal reaction which arose anew with and within it.

All these wealthy people knew very well that the Republican principle stood in natural opposition to their position based on moneyed property, all the more so since their money was acquired at public expense. They knew furthermore that they would never be able to enjoy their possessions peacefully as long as the principles of equality and of the virtues of devotion and frugality prevailed. They could feel safe only where inequality was the basic principle of the social order. . . . For this reason, the huge capital funds grown out of the Revolution made their owners determined opponents of the Revolution and allies of the remaining representatives of the old feudal society.

These two parties of the new society devised a plan for future action. According to the Constitution of 1795, new elections were due for one-third of the Council. The reaction began its work in the provinces. It undermined the weak authority of the Directory, instigated particularly the South, and almost succeeded in reinstituting the monarchy. . . . Pichegrou, the head of the whole conspiracy, was elected President by the Council of the Five Hundred. Direct and indirect attacks on the Directory grew more numerous. Five thousand emigrants were back in Paris; the situation had deteriorated to such an extent that being called a "Republican," a respected and feared term abroad, became an insult and a cause for proscription at home.

The victory of reaction seemed almost secured. What stood in opposition? A weak and divided Directory, the practically dissolved state, an impoverished population. In favor of the reaction was a strong party alliance and even the law, since their representatives were in the majority in the Council of the Five Hundred. And yet a single daring decision of the Directory could have destroyed it completely and definitely. Actually, it was not constitutional power to which the party of reaction aspired; it wanted the destruction of the Constitution and a return to the old law. The existing law, however, was a reflection of the new society based on the principle of equality and the redistribution of land and other property. An attack on the Constitution meant an attack on the whole society, whose common interest was opposed to the reaction. The reaction could not expect any assistance from the population at large; ideas as well as interests were opposed to it. Its only chance was the use of sheer power; strangely enough, it deceived itself into believing that even this was not possible for it.

The Position of The New Army

. . . A new factor made itself felt in the life of society; this new factor was the Republican army. . . . It is true that the very nature of the army presupposes obedience to the ruling power, but the powerful course of revolutionary events had changed this. The French Republic had been attacked from all sides but was almost always victorious. Victory was assured partly through excellent leadership, partly through the enthusiasm for the Republic. The army identified itself with the ideals of the Republic; its fame and its future were the fame and the future of the Republic. The fall of the Republic would have left the army isolated between France and the monarchies of Europe. The abandonment of the Constitution would have meant the dissolution of the republican army and the abuse of republican victories. In this fashion the Army identified itself with the Republic, and the furious hatred of the monarchical armies had only endeared the Republic to the French soldier. In addition, the glory of the republican victories had been gained with great sacrifices; the tremendous deprivations and exertions resulted in a sense of power and of pride which can only be understood in terms of a victorious campaign. The army knew that the dissolution of the Directory would mean its own dissolution. How could the army which had won victories over Austria and Russia be expected to submit to a faction of the Council to whom, in addition, all the people were opposed? The army itself had adopted the republican principle of equality, a fact of great importance during that period. Before the Revolution, the gulf between the common soldier and the officer had been enormous. The rank of officer in the army had been reserved for members of the privileged estates, the relationship between officer and soldier was based essentially on feudal law. During feudalism the feudal lord used to set up his own army corps from the vassals of his estate. It was his own corps, and the military leader stood just as high above the soldier as the feudal lord above the peasant. This had been changed later only to the extent that the officer was installed by governmental authority but he continued to be a member of the aristocracy; a rise from the lower grades was practically impossible, even on the basis of great gallantry and military prowess. . . .

All this had been completely changed as a result of the Revolution. The soldiers had not been enlisted by order of the king or their landlords; most of them had answered the call of the fatherland voluntarily. The rank and file, therefore, consisted to a large extent of the superior elements of society. The military machine had been replaced by an institution which was mentally alive. The officers no longer came from the nobility only; they came from the rank and file, and everybody was entitled to promotion. A companionship devel-

oped between officers and soldiers which was renewed and strengthened by the sociability of camp life, the common effort, and common
deprivations. At the time when Napoleon marched into Italy, the
army was without sufficient clothing, food and pay, equipped with
nothing but confidence in an apparently impossible victory; the position of an officer was far from being attractive. What it meant to be
an officer is illustrated by a document quoted by Buonarotti (ibidem.
pièce XX p. 273); the most revealing passage states: "Except in the
higher ranks the entire officer corps consists of former soldiers who
have only their wages on which to live. For a major this amounts
to about eight sous in cash per day. This obliges the majority of
officers to eat in the soldiers' mess and consequently to become
very intimate with them. This equality of destitution of the common soldier and the officers brings about a mutual friendship, an
attachment and mutual confidence which differed widely from the pre-
revolutionary relationship between officer and man." Such were the
conditions under which the young army of the Republic had won
its victories. And what did the reactionary forces demand? The
re-establishment of the old law would have meant the return of the
old order of the army. It would not only have undermined or even
destroyed the life nerve of the young army, that close community of
all the comrades-in-arms, but at the same time destroyed the positions
attained by the republican middle-class officers and the hope of the common soldier for advancement through good fortune and courage. The
reactionary forces threatened not only the Directory, not only society, not
only the new owners; they also threatened the very life of the only
power which then existed—the army. If the army did not want to
destroy itself, it was forced to uphold the Republic even against the
Directory, the state authority to which it owed allegiance. It is almost
inconceivable that the royalist reaction nevertheless counted on victory; only complete ignorance of the army made this belief possible. The position the army was to take during the approaching revolt
was definite and irrevocable. . . . It was sheer stupidity to believe
that the army—with its greatest general, the already world-famous
Bonaparte, and after the decisive victories it had won for the Republic—would have been willing to renounce this Republic. The Directory
could trust society and the army: the army, supported by the new
society, would have been able to maintain the Republic alone against
all antagonists. The appeal of the Directory to the army was nothing
but the legalization of the army's original approval of the new order
of society; a great European future lay ahead of it.

Most historians, particularly Thiers in the ninth volume of his History of the Revolution have interpreted the subsequent events as though the Directory and the republican party had thrown themselves "into the arms of the military power," out of fear of the counter-revolution. This opinion is generally accepted. But it is one-sided. The Directory or the new society did not have any choice but to call upon the army for the defense of the Republic; the army was the natural and necessary defender of the Republic, which meant to it the glory of France in foreign relations and equality within the army itself. In defending these achievements of the Republic, it had also to defend the rest. Royalism was the exponent of the opposition to these principles; therefore, the army was the necessary opponent of reaction. This was the true relationship of the new army to the new society and the new Constitution.

When the first news of reactionary machinations reached the armies, a universal outcry, particularly in the Italian army, arose against royalism. Soldiers, officers, and the General Staff issued appeals to the Directory, not any more as obedient servants but as independent parts of society. "Tremble, royalists," the soldiers stated, "there is just one step from the Adige to the Seine. Your injustices have been counted and you will find your punishment at the points of our bayonets." "It is with indignation," stated the General Staff, "that we have watched the intrigues of royalism threatening liberty. We have taken the oath in the name of those who died for the nation, to fight implacably against monarchy and the royalists. Such are our feelings, they are those of patriots." The opinion, the will, the oath of the army came to predominate over the will of the constitutional power! The Directory, backed by the army, watched the goings-on of the reaction undisturbed, but action finally had to be taken.

The Coup d'État of the 18th Fructidor of the Year V.
(September 4th, 1797)

According to the Constitution of 1795, the two councils were the only judges of their own action. The royalists had a decisive majority in both. Legally a disregard of the majority was impossible. When Bonaparte took Venice, he captured the papers of the Count Entraigues, which disclosed the conspiracy. He sent them to the Directory and advised a coup d'état. The Directory asked for a general; he sent Augereau; troops were gathered around Paris. . . . Twelve thousand men and forty cannons stood in front of the Tuileries, where both Councils were assembled at midnight of the 18th Fructidor. The three republican members of the Directory had called the republican minorities to the Odéon. Upon their order the troops took over all important positions, dissolved the Assembly and entered the city victoriously without one shot. The minority condemned the two members of the Directory, Carnet and Barthélemy, and fifty-three deputies to deportation; the laws against emigrants were reactivated; all noblemen and priests were exiled by the threat of death; even the owners and editors of not less than forty-one journals were deported en masse, and civil rights were suspended for all those who formerly had been members of the aristocracy. The victory over the last great conspiracy was decided in a few hours; the people approved, and the fate of the Republic was again secured. That was the coup d'état of the 18th Fructidor. On the surface the event had few consequences; for the development of the Republic and of the new society it was of the greatest importance.

The order and content of any new constitutional law is determined by one of three factors: by the changes within society, by a new principle which reflects these changes, or by the requirements of political prudence. There is no doubt which of these three factors determined the Constitution of 1795, which had been rejected by the 18th Fructidor. Sieyès, with his keen and well-balanced intelligcnce, was always of the opinion that one could satisfy all social needs by a prudent distribution of powers and a carefully organized state. The Constitution of 1795 is mainly his; it differed in major points from its two predecessors. The Constitution of 1791 had been the result of the struggle between the two social orders and of the victory of the new society. The Constitution of 1793 was the creation of a grandiose, though one-sided, principle; the Constitution of 1795, however, was solely the product of political expediency. Seldom has a man understood and judged his time and his people better than Sieyès; as never before the circumstances were favorable for a stable constitution; therefore, this Constitution offers a striking illustration of the proposition whether a constitution created in the art of politics is viable at all.

We are living at a time when political theory carries an even greater weight than formerly in founding state constitutions. . . . Therefore, it is important to prove by this first example that no constitution which is conceived only in theoretical terms is able to survive. Even if devised with supreme intelligence, it will necessarily be overthrown and changed by those powers which actually determine constitutions, namely, the elements of society. . . . Even if such theoretical constitutions may be enforced for a while, the first percussions will blow them away like a dry leaf gone with the wind. Only the constitution based on the social order is able to withstand inner conflicts. Does not the strength of the British Constitution in contrast to the ephemera of Germany suffice to prove the point? . . .

The Constitution of 1795 certainly was a masterpiece of expediency. Everything fitted most beautifully; all principles seemed to be adhered to; one could have lived excellently under such an order of the state. But if we ask what kind of a social order it reflected, which social elements were represented by the two main political organs, the two Councils and the Directory, we do not find an answer. It was characteristic that the Constitution did not represent anything, while it precluded nothing. Consequently, one party used the organs created by the Constitution and attempted by strictly legal and constitutional means something that was contrary to the development of society, namely, the re-institution of the old order. In this way a revolution, which usually develops against an existing constitution, was brought about *by* the Constitution, and the Constitution was destroyed. The question arises as to what kind of constitution was possible at that time. Indeed, no constitution at all was as yet possible. This may sound like a daring statement, but it is true. Where was the order of society which the constitution was supposed to reflect? There was no such order yet; there were at that time no classes, no provisions for the inheritance of social status, for education, for special interest groups within the framework of the new principle of freedom and equality; the constitution expressed only the general principle of the Revolution but not any of the social elements. And whatever is valid with regard to the French Revolution is also relevant for any similar revolution. Wherever a doctrinaire constitution has to be created, no adequate condition exists for a genuine constitution. But what could be done under the prevailing circumstances? What were the needs of the time which could support neither a purely social constitution, such as the one of 1791, nor one based entirely on principles, as the one of 1793, nor a purely doctrinaire constitution, as that of 1795?

Napoleon

During the preceding years, the third estate had adopted new property rights, particularly the rights of landed property. This began with the legislation of 1790 and 1791 and had been secured through the reign of terror. The various proprietors began to get used to their newly acquired property. But the role of proprietors was still new to them. Thousands of landowners had settled on portions of the subdivided large estates; they started to erect buildings, to buy livestock, to till the soil; the liberated peasants had to reorganize the management of their farms; in the cities all guilds had been dissolved; the journeymen became masters and shop owners. The old guild masters had to replace their lost privileges by new efforts. Trade, liberated from monopolistic control, took a different development. In brief, the various elements by which the Directory had replaced terrorism continued to expand. There was no time for political activities. The Constitution had opened the new roads to acquire property; it was powerless to do more. The drive for monetary acquisitions took the place of the drive for political changes. The government was left to itself, provided it did not interfere with the pursuit of economic interests, except by protecting and furthering them. . . . If none of all the Constitutions was able to offer sufficient security, as the experience of 1797 had shown, if any law could be manipulated in order to attack and destroy the basic principle, where then could security be found? Which form of state could . . . provide external security and at the same time exclude all elements of the old order?

There was obviously only one answer. If the Constitution, by its very nature, had to tolerate the ambitions of reactionary elements and therefore to permit the peaceful development of the new propertied class to be threatened, then individual security could only be protected by the absence of any constitution or by extra-constitutional powers of the state. Two things were necessary for the latter alternative: a strong state, and a state which ruled according to the principles and laws on which the new distribution of wealth was based. These objectives could no longer reside in the representatives of the people but had to be invested in one man: he had to identify himself with it in order to forestall any revival of the popular movements and of the conflicting parties, representing different social factions.

Napoleon was such a man. Formerly a follower of Robespierre, the victor over Austria, the most glorious name in the Republic, he was admired for his extraordinary administrative talents, his aversion to the disturbance of state order, his concern over foreign policy; he was the only rallying point not subject to any controversy. Napoleon was known to uphold the principles of the Revolution, but yet wanted the Revolution as such terminated. He had saved the Convention on the 14th *Vendémiaire*, he had crushed royalism while in Italy; he provided security from foreign enemies and from domestic turmoil. In him one could find what was most needed at the time: a powerful defender of the power of the state, without tendencies towards feudalism.

Napoleon was the man of France; yet he was more: he was also the man of contemporary French society. This aspect of Napoleon's role has been neglected, although, at least at the beginning of his career, it was the most important one. It was because he dared to replace the people's will by his own and not despite it, that he became the master of the new revolutionary state and the ruler in the name of the new society.

Social history must revise its judgment about Napoleon. He has been stigmatized in France as well as outside of France as a despot. He has been condemned, and his country has been deplored; he has been accused of using his power to suppress freedom; it has been stated a thousand times over that his fight against liberty and his tyranny over his country, barely recovered from the wounds of the Revolution, destroyed his power. It has been stated that having gained the throne by abolishing the Constitution he might have saved himself by inaugurating a new constitution. . . .

And yet Napoleon was not born a dictator; he became one through the power of circumstances. It is interesting to watch how he himself attempted to understand the factors that drove him to absolute power. Sometimes he accused England of not leaving him alone, sometimes he was angry with Austria; sometimes he was convinced that freedom and happiness of the people could be established by this or that expedient. If it had been possible for one man to control the elementary power of social forces Napoleon would have been able to do so. But his fate illustrates the force of the elements whose history is our main subject.

The abolition of the Constitution after the 18th Fructidor and the resulting absolute power of the state were not the result of Napoleon's political ambition, nor of the success of his armies, nor even of the growing French nationalism which has been referred to so frequently; it was the necessary consequence of the underdeveloped state of society, which needed protection and could find such protection only from outside forces. Neither choice nor character made Napoleon a dictator; the needs of society forced him to become one. This society had no use for a politician like Sieyès or for a diplomat like Talleyrand, or for a compliant character like Moreau. It needed a man who had the courage to put himself in place of a constitution. . . . Without despotism Napoleon would not have had the support of all the people, nor would he have served his country as well as he did. Society gave him absolute power. . . .

The rise of Napoleon and the subsequent history of France illustrate clearly that the despotic rule of one man is conditioned by social changes, as is any other type of constitution. This is particularly confirmed by the fact that whenever laws of social change seem to give way to one man's arbitrary rule this is accepted with enthusiasm by the whole population.

Therefore, a phenomenon like Napoleon is by no means unique in history. The power of circumstances is so strong that similar conditions produce similar personalities. There are some dictatorships which have little or nothing in common with that of the French Emperor; those are dictatorships which are set up on the spur of the moment and are due to either administrative or military expediency. They disappear after a brief period, since they serve a single cause. But those which grow organically out of the life of a nation are altogether different. They persist because they correspond to a definite condition of society. This type of dictatorship grows out of preceding dissolution of a social order; the beginning of a new social order usually coincides with the beginning of dictatorship. We might call it a social dictatorship. The most striking similar example of such a dictatorship is that of Cromwell. There is no doubt that any country under similar conditions will bring forth a dictator; it is an inevitable consequence of the laws of social development. Even the greatest historical figures are subject to these laws of history. "Freedom" has little meaning in this context.

Napoleon was the very cornerstone of the new society. His career serves as an illustration of the condition under which social growth can only be accomplished by the complete transfer of all political power to one individual. But it is not sufficient that such a dictator take control over the state. The prevailing social conditions are of specific importance and, in turn, determine the task of the dictatorship.

After the struggle between classes or estates has come to an end, the struggle between parties develops. A party distinguishes itself from other social groups primarily by the fact that it has specific goals which it desires to attain; the nature of these goals depend upon personalities, principles, or interests represented in the parties. The party is aware of the fact that its goal can be attained only by control over the state, and therefore it attempts to gain this control. . . . Parties appear to be most powerful whenever the new state is not yet consolidated. This always occurs after a social revolution has been successfully carried out. Thus in France, after 1795, social changes were overshadowed by the emergence of political parties. The victory of the 18th Fructidor had been a victory over one party. It was the beginning of inter-party struggles. . . . State authority, in order to be stable, must display an ever-present and comprehensive power. This is the very nature of the state. Only then do the differences between the state and the party become apparent, and only then . . . is the state safe against the attack of the parties. This is what determines the course of any social dictatorship.

A social dictatorship usually finds the state in dissolution. To cope with the various parties, it must attempt to reorganize the state in such a way that all power is concentrated in the hands of the dictator. Only then is he secure against party attacks. Dictatorship by its very nature must accomplish what society has attempted to do in vain, namely, the establishment of a well-ordered administration and of a constitution legitimizing the rule of the dictator over the whole population. This is the natural development of any social dictatorship. The needs of society explain the otherwise inexplicable phenomenon that the people, who had just taken extraordinary risks to establish self-government, suddenly transferred their rights unanimously and without resistance to the new sovereign. This also explains why a social dictatorship, even one adorned with greatest military glory, will never rule for any great length of time unless the dictator has outstanding administrative talents. . . . There is no other way of coping with party politics in newly emerging societies except by the establishment of an able and uniform administration. The history of Napoleon strikingly proves this point. He conquered Europe with his armies, but France submitted to his administrative skill rather than to his military power.

After the 18th Fructidor the development of French domestic life is quite distinct and easily observable. We distinguish two spheres of development. One is the establishment of a constitution, by which society deprives itself of political power, and by which the dictatorship of Napoleon, slowly and organically, and without recourse to violence, establishes itself and spreads over the whole society as well as the institutions of popular representation. The other is the sphere of administration, in which the whole organization of the state, with all its institutions, becomes centralized in the hands of the dictator. . . . The victories of Napoleon until the establishment of the Empire have had only the function of barring any of the foreign enemies from interference with this new order. . . .

The Transition from the Constitution to the Actual Organization of the State. The 18th Brumaire Anno VII (November 10th, 1799). The Constitution of 1799 and the Senatus Consulte Organique of 1802.

The 18th Fructidor had indeed crashed the reactionary party. However, by violating the Constitution for the sake of its own principle, the confidence of the people as well as of the representatives in this

Constitution had been destroyed. It had been demonstrated that the army, and no longer the people and their appointed representatives, was the true exponent of the new developments. The army confronted the Directory with the alternative of usurping the power of the state or of being crushed by pressures of the parties. To take over supreme power presupposed an enormous administrative change in order to replace the moral strength and the constitutional power of the people by the personal will of the rulers. Members of the Directory took over this power, but soon it became evident that they had neither administrative ability nor moral independence. They left everything unchanged. This did not help France.

Consequently, the indifference of the people toward the Constitution and the representatives grew. Some already voiced the opinon that popular representation was the source of all misfortune. The antagonism against reaction turned against a constitution which more and more tolerated the reaction. The indifference of the people, together with the ineffectiveness of the administration, favored the resurrection of the old parties; the Royalists appealed again to the Vendée; there were insurrections in the South; the armies of the Republic, poorly supported and poorly guided, were beaten everywhere. Conditions were becoming more critical from day to day. The self-propelling forces of the Revolution had become exhausted; unless an altogether new and strong element appeared on the scene, France was lost.

Meanwhile Napoleon had gone to Egypt with the core of the army and had completed his fabulous but rather useless campaign on the shores of the Nile, which had made him famous. He learned about the situation in France from the newspapers which a British admiral gave to him, and he decided to return to France. He was not quite sure what to do, but he felt that he should act. . . . On his return to Paris he found a complete chaos. He immediately saw that the principles of self-administration had lost their force and appeal and that the Constitution could no longer be the answer. It is true that Napoleon was a born ruler; it is not true that his lust for power suppressed liberty in France. While in Paris, the sight of the complete disruption of the two Councils—the Council of the Five Hundred and the Council of Elders —the absolute incompetence of the Directory, the complaints of the people, the breakdown of the administration, the decline of the authority of the state, the opposition of all social classes against popular representation all convinced him that the continuation of the revolutionary conditions was impossible. He had to overthrow the Constitution in order to save France. This conviction led him to disperse the Council of the

Five Hundred with his grenadiers on the 18th Brumaire (Nov. 10, 1799). When the Council, this last truly popular representative body, resisted him seriously, he answered them with the profoundly intuitive statement: "I do not want any more factions." With this statement he won over half of France. . . . Lavallée states correctly: "There was not the slightest opposition against the attack of the 18th Brumaire." Everybody felt that Napoleon would express the opinion common to all parties. It was new for France when, a few days after his victory, Napoleon announced the principle of his administration, namely, "that there should be no more Jacobins, no moderates, no royalists but only Frenchmen."

The Constitution of 1795 was swept away by the 18th Brumaire. It was the last of the series of Constitutions proper. With the new Constitution of December 13th, 1799, swiftly conceived by Bonaparte, a completely new era of public law began. The constitutional state was now replaced by the administrative state. A constitutional state establishes the identity of the will of the individuals and the general will; the administrative state considers the individual and his will merely as a part and an organ of the personal state. The constitutional state always assigns to the constitutional organs the task of participating in the determination of this will. In a mere administrative state, on the other hand, the task of the state organs is restricted to their specific domains. In a constitutional state the attitude of the individual, as well as of all constitutional groups, toward the state is always determined by the individuals themselves. . . . In contradistinction, in the administrative state, the will of the state, independent of the individuals, holds the power to control the behavior and the activities of the various organs. While initiative in a constitutional state moves from the lower level—the variety of individuals—to the upper, . . . the reverse is true in an administrative state. Fully developed, the former represents the free formulation of the will of the personal state, the latter mainly the organic execution of this will. . . .

The Constitution of 1799, in which the principle of the administrative state was virtually developed into a system, is of great interest in the history of constitutions, but only of minor importance in the present context. After the necessity of a one-man rule had been created by the existing social conditions, the form in which it emerged developed almost independently. The Constitution of 1799 was the first step, the Constitution of 1802 the second, toward the administrative state; the third and last step, the complete elimination of all popular participation, was no longer embodied in law but was a mere fact. The Constitution of 1799 differs essentially from the three preceding ones in that it does not contain a preamble with a "Declaration of the Rights of Man." This was a symptom of progress because it indicated that most of these rights appeared to be secure without specific legal acknowledgement; on the other hand, it was a sign of retrogression because the Constitution had lost one of its dynamic elements. The Constitution establishes the *Sénate Conservateur* as the main organ of popular representation. It has three members who are appointed by the legislative body, the Tribunate and the First Consul (Art. 16). The Senate, however, appoints the members of the legislative body as well as of the Tribunate (Art. 20). . . . Pending legislation is first submitted to and criticized by the Tribunate of 100 members; however, laws can be approved only by the legislative body (300 members). The Tribunate is obviously supposed to represent the element of change, . . . but only the Consuls have the power to initiate legislation. . . .

There was one element in this Constitution which endangered its existence, and this was the Tribunate. The Tribunate was able to oppose the wishes of the Consuls so energetically that the legislative body could reject the proposals of the executive. Under such conditions the executive could either give in to the semblance of popular representation or violate the Constitution. This was the point where the inner contradictions of the pseudo-constitution became apparent. To gain absolute power it was necessary to take one further step to definitely change from the constitutional state into the administrative state.

This step was taken by Napoleon through the establishment of the "*Sénatus-Consulte organique de la Constitution*" on the 16th Thermidor (August 4th, 1802), according to which the Consuls were appointed for life. However, its main importance lies elsewhere. Napoleon had already understood that the element of freedom in the Tribunate, reminiscent of the old Constitution, was the last source of opposition against his absolute power. Powerful circumstances had made him, the former follower of Robespierre, an unrelenting foe of all independence except his own. From hatred against factions which had inspired him to carry out the *coup d'état* of the 18th Brumaire he had finally developed a hatred of free actions, even of free speech. . . . He was the embodiment of the need for a strong state power; he assumed that this desire for power was his own personal characteristic, while in fact it reflected a need of society. . . . Thus he turned scornfully against the Tribunate, banished by Senate order all speakers of the opposition, and replaced them by his followers (1801); the last remains of a constitution proper were abolished, and its provision, the form of which had been preserved in the Constitution of 1799, pertained to functions compatible with the essential characteristics of an administrative state. All this was carried out by the *Sénatus Consulte organique.*

The *Sénatus Consulte,* which was not called a constitution but an organic law, preserved the traditional forms; this is why it was deceptive with regard to its true nature. It determined that the choice of district officers, department officers, and members of the *Sénate* was the function of the First Consul; that the *Sénate* could not inaugurate any laws; that the Tribunate was to be reduced to 50 persons; and finally, it was explicitly ordered that the assemblies of districts as well as departments should only deal with such issues as were submitted to them by the government. This was the last and final indication that popular representation had been replaced by state organization. From this moment on there was no longer any direct participation of the people in state affairs; the representative body became an administrative organ, and the sovereignty of the government was secured.

At the same time . . . a principle was revived to which little attention was paid at the time, but which nevertheless became important. It had to do with the slates for the caucuses of the departments, which were to be chosen from a group of 600 persons who paid the highest taxes. . . . The regulation is of importance, because here, for the first time, property rights again made their appearance in public law. Almost as a reminder that theirs was the future, they were specifically mentioned in the new law; and while their rights had formerly been part of the state constitution they asserted themselves here in the administrative state with their negative attitude toward the propertyless. It is only an indication, but one of significance. The contributions of the propertied classes were still made in the economic rather than in the political sphere.

With the establishment of the *Sénatus Consulte organique,* legislation in French public law came to a halt. Napoleon's rise to the status of Emperor belongs to another phase of development. But there is a series of laws which we have to describe briefly in their relationship to society and to the new state power as the application of the new principles in public law. . . .

The Organic Laws. The Code Civil and its Social Implication.

These laws fall into three groups. . . . The first group includes all the laws relating to administrative action and central organization. . . . Napoleon subdivided the country into *Départements* under the head of *Préfects, Arrondissements* under *Souspréfects,* and *Municipalités* under *Maires;* each of these officials had full responsibility for the execution of orders from Paris in his district. In order to secure the execution of these orders, the officials in charge had to be kept in direct submission to the highest office. This was accomplished partly by the fact that the official was subjected to dismissal, partly by the fact that he was well paid, and partly by the omnipresence of the government, which supervised the execution of its orders. On the other hand, he had almost unlimited power in his own district as far as the execution of the governmental orders was concerned. This law and its continuous application guaranteed the authority of the French government in all parts of the country. By providing powerful instruments to carry out its will, the government doubled the strength of the country and its people by a rigid centralization. . . . It is this organization which has made France great; it is the highest form of consolidated state power spread over a whole country.

After the new administration was established, steps were taken to rearrange the judiciary. These laws constitute the second of the above-mentioned groups. . . . Each *Arrondissement* obtained a civil court, each *Département* a criminal court; and in addition 29 courts of appeal were established. In this fashion the people's courts were replaced by state courts. The centralization of France, which has distinguished that country among other European countries, was carried out under the guidance of Napoleon. One has to recognize the powerful mind of this man, who wanted to build a state in order to control party politics. The brilliant example set by Napoleon has affected European developments distinctly. It is he who first solved the great problem of centralization. . . . France was never stronger than under these laws. What was the secret by which Napoleon made the nation submissive and strong at the same time?

The need for the unhampered development of the individual and for the growth of a distinctive social order was the tacit presupposition for the growth of absolute and organized autocracy. Until now, the state, in almost all of Europe, had stifled individual development. . . . The people needed a state, but they equally needed unrestricted freedom for individual growth. The question was whether the two were compatible with each other. . . . The solution of this problem is the secret of the greatness of Napoleon and of France during his lifetime.

The third group of organic laws include the whole codification of French laws. It is altogether wrong to consider the Napoleonic codes as part of the process of centralization. They are just the opposite of a centralizing force: all these codes, particularly the *code civil*, erect a stable wall of civil law protecting the individual and his social position. . . . This code is not so much an event in legal history as in the history of society.

Civil law is a system based on a definite and accepted principle. . . . The principle of all civil law is the rights of the individual personality. . . . The development of a true personality can only take place in society. . . . If society—as during the feudal epoch—bestows different status to different persons, there has to be a different civil law for each such different category of persons. The principle of feudal civil law was not uniform; it contained as many different systems as there were different social classes. The peculiarity of feudal civil law was not so much the right of the person as the right of property held by persons. Feudal society, with the three estates of clergy, nobility and third estate had three different principles of civil laws: . . . there was one for the clergy, . . . one for the nobility, and one for the members of the third estate.

The multiplicity of civil law had been broken by the Constituent Assembly. . . . Equality before the law involved the acceptance of the principle that the individual, without regard to his social position, should be the basis of the civil law system. This is the meaning of the term "equality before the law". However, the consequences of this principle had not yet been drawn in all instances. The old civil law was abolished, but there was as yet no new one; a situation of almost complete lawlessness in private affairs prevailed. The fact that judges were elected by the people aggravated the situation. The judges were no longer chosen from the experts of law, since the law they were versed in was in contradiction to the principle of the new law. Judges were chosen from the rank and file of the people. These judges, however, confronted with the vague principle of the new law, made more or less arbitrary decisions depending on which class of society was stronger at any particular moment. This arbitrariness seriously endangered the new society; it made the new proprietors dependent upon the judgment of the experienced and the security of their new property dependent upon arbitrariness and chance. The basis of individual development was threatened, because property rights were not secure legally. . . .

This was the point whose importance Napoleon immediately recognized. Right after the 18th Brumaire he initiated preliminary work for the *code civil*; . . . its origin is one of the major monuments of this extraordinary man. The *code civil* deserves a place of primary importance in the history of French society. It incorporated into a system of established law the principle of equal and free individuals whose rights are independent of social difference. The facts of the new economic order and legal equality became transformed into a system of laws which at all points fostered and guaranteed equality among the people; it was the consolidation of the social revolution in the sphere of civil law.

From this point of view the codification gains a new significance. The comparison of the Code with old feudal law is not only a comparison between two different forms of law, but it entails a comparison of two different stages of social development. . . . The deep gulf between the old and the new law is unbridgeable, because both represent two completely opposite orders of society which have no common roots but which necessarily cancel each other out. . . . We in Germany have particular reasons to account for the conditions of such a legislation. For thirty years we have been listening to arguments about the ability or inability of our country to develop such a codification. It is an endless dispute which cannot lead to any result because our approach to this problem is wrong. The indispensable prerequisite for a codification is the acceptance of a free and individual personality liberated from legal status differentiations. This is what is lacking in Germany. . . . The lack of uniform German legislation is not a consequence of the diversity of the development of local law. . . . The whole problem of codification in Germany is a purely social problem and will remain such according to the nature of private law. France has its code of law not as a result of a better training of her law-givers but as a result of an acknowledgement of absolute equality of individuals and goods before the law. There is no doubt that a code of law in Germany will be developed only after the abolition of differences in status; . . . but it is also undoubtedly true that a German code of law will never be developed as long as status differences prevail in German society.

The *Code Civil* is the first of a series of other codes of law. . . . One may differ on specific regulations of the *Code Pénal*, the *Code d'Instruction Criminelle* and the *Code de Procédure Civile*. There is much to be criticized; but with all their faults, they have fulfilled a higher mission. Each in its sphere has elevated the principle of legal equality of all individuals in a systematic order. The systematization of French law, the task set by the Constituent Assembly, was thereby accomplished. This legislation has been accepted and preserved as a great treasure, whose validity and excellence is beyond questioning, during the following decades, because it embodied the principle of legal equality in civil society. Only through this step had France moved from the revolutionary period, the period of the destruction of the old law, to a new state with a specific and consistent legal framework.

The legal equality of persons in their mutual relationships was thus guaranteed. There remained one more sphere of equal social importance, the application of the laws and the rules of the courts. The court is an organ of the state; . . . in court action the will of the state comes in contact with the rights of the individual. This is where the question is decided whether the individual is really free; only the respect of the state for the independent individual provides full recognition of that independence. The decision of this question is safeguarded mainly by one principle—the irremovability of the judges. If the judges are subject to dismissal, those who hold the power of the state are considered to be superior to the judge who executes the law. . . . Just as the law guarantees the independence of the person from arbitrary actions of another person, the irremovability of the judges protects the individual against arbitrary actions by government. This principle, which made the codification of supreme importance, was accepted by Napoleon without qualifications. Although the Constitution of 1799 declared that the judges are appointed by the First Consul, Art. 41 states that the Consul does not have the power to dismiss them. The last point of the codification deals with the independence of the judges. . . .

To sum up: as we look at the new administrative state, a twofold development is discernible. On the one hand, an organization and centralization of the state has taken place which is without precedent in history, . . . it became the source of tremendous strength. An almost perfect organization of the independent personality of the state had been achieved. On the other hand, a concept was developed of individuals equal before the law and protected by courts which were assisted by the state in all matters except with regard to political activity. Side by side, independent and separated, . . . are arrayed the two main component parts of the state, the general will and the individual person. Each has its own life circle, its rights and its organs. . . . The separation of citizenship from state power brings about the concentration in the government, of all the noblest strengths of the nation, which by their nature belong to the community as a whole, and focuses the interests of the individual on the personal sphere of life. Napoleon had separated state and society to allow each of them to develop freely, or rather: the law of social dynamics had driven the state power out of the sphere of society so that a new social order might develop unhampered by political demands. This condition could not prevail for long. The constitution of the state is essentially the reflection of the social order. As soon as the new society had secured its order by persistent labor, it was inevitable that it should make demands on the state; the time for the collapse of Napoleon's system had to come. . . .

After order had been established in France, Napoleon's European history began. The Empire marks the closing of the French social revolution and the beginning of the social transformation of Europe.

THE EMPIRE

Napoleon's Constitutions

. . . As we review the attitude of France toward the rest of Europe during the first revolutionary decade, it becomes evident that a development was taking place in France which was in basic opposition to the foundations on which European public life still rested. All of Europe was at that time an estate society, and public law was shaped by this society. A civil society based on the principle of equality before the law was still unknown in Europe. As soon as the new order of things had been consolidated to a certain extent in France, there began that series of wars which is the content of the external history of this period. . . . Never before had the nature of Europe as an organic entity been so much in evidence as during that decade. All those wars were definitely a struggle of the European organism against this one member of that organism; at no time during this period did any state take up arms alone against coalitions of the remaining European states. . . . It would be wrong to interpret these coalitions as mere alliances; alliances may be formed at will. The coalitions, however, were inevitable responses, deriving from the nature of those states, of the whole organism against the incompatible elements of one of its parts. These states fought for their common foundation, which was threatened by France. They sensed that either their own traditional social order or France had to perish.

The first period of this struggle terminated with the appearance of Napoleon. The French movement had withstood the attack of the remaining old organism; the new France had become a recognized power. It is possible that Napoleon did not try to deceive himself when he stated that he sincerely wanted peace for France and for Europe after the treaty of Amiens, which marks the end of the first period, and that he hoped to lead a new France peacefully along the road she had chosen. It is also true that England did not leave either Napoleon or France at peace; undoubtedly a national antagonism going back many centuries continuously rekindled these tendencies. But the true reason for the new outbreak of the European war lay beyond all political machinations. The peace treaty of Amiens recognized a feudal Europe and a civil France, a part which was essentially different from the whole—an absolute contradiction—as the foundation of a European peace. This is the reason why permanence and peace were impossible. The organism of Europe was torn, . . . the necessary and natural cooperation of all European states became impossible. . . . The real problem had not been solved. The struggle had to begin anew. It now took on a different character. France, which had so far been on the defensive, now began to interfere actively in the affairs of Europe. . . .

This was the second period of the transformation of Europe by France. . . . If European life was truly an organic entity, it was inevitable for Napoleon—whether he wanted it or not—to plunge into a European war incalculable in its effects. It is his name which, in world history, marks the point at which the whole European organism, defeated by France, detached itself from the old political and social system to build a new one on the basis of constitutional, public and private law. . . . We are going to talk about European history only to the extent that the powerful interplay between the two struggling elements affected the society of France.

The events that took place after the peace of Amiens had been broken and the new war had started can be arranged into two major categories. The victories of Napoleon appeared to be victories of his armies, but in fact they were the victories of French society over European society. A society, however, cannot be subjected like a state. The real victory over the old society . . . consisted in the creation of a new society. Napoleon was well aware of the fact that he had accomplished little through the military conquest of the feudal states; he knew perhaps better than the French people that he fought for one type of society against another. Only if the old social order could be broken would his France be victorious; the struggle of the armies was only the outer manifestation of a much more vital struggle. Thus an altogether new war started. The effects of this war on Europe outside of French society belong to the first category of events. These phenomena are summed up by historiography under the title of "Napoleonic Constitutions;" . . . these constitutions have been very differently evaluated; their real importance can only be gauged in their relationship to the international situation of that period.

The antagonism between France and Europe was based not merely on the struggle for power but on social contradictions. It was evident that France, with her victorious armies, could be secure against this powerful opponent only for the moment and not forever. She could secure her position only by transforming the societies of the conquered people. The true allies of France would be those countries which . . . had accepted the social principles of the new France. How could that be accomplished? It is true that some elements of the new order were powerful and alive side by side with the feudal order in these countries. But in war one could not wait for a slow and peaceful development; Napoleon needed, in the name of France, a definite declaration that these states would adopt the French social system. How could a valid declaration of this kind be given without the consent of the individual princes? . . . France, fighting against feudal Europe, either had to force the conquered powers to enact constitutions in conformity to French law—or else she had to do it herself in the newly conquered territories.

This is the true importance of the Napoleonic constitutions from Spain to the Russian frontier. They spell the victory of the new European socio-political order, and they finally put an end to the isolation of France. The entire war cycle from 1803-1814 thus acquired an original and grandiose character. Napeoleon was justified in assuming that his European position depended on these constitutions rather than on his armies; he was therefore justified in giving to his brothers new kingdoms whose constitutions were to provide the essential link between the new France and the rest of Europe. He was right in considering Prussia, Austria and Russia as unconquered, because they continued to uphold the old law. He expressed these thoughts when he addressed the Spaniards in Madrid: "I have abolished the tribunals of the inquisition to which the spirit of the century and Europe are opposed. I have suppressed the feudal laws; the selfishness, wealth and prosperity of the few did more damage to your agriculture than the furor of the poor (*sans cule*). Just as there is only one God there should also be only one justice in a country. All the various privileges have been usurped and were contrary to the rights of the nation. I have abolished them. Your children will bless me as your benefactor." This interpretation explains, better than the inner weakness of the constitutions themselves, the hatred which they aroused and their sudden abolition after the fall of Napoleon.

The struggle of Napoleon with Europe establishes his lasting position in the history of European society. During these wars, which threw all the old states into confusion, rebuilt them, and destroyed them again, the fate of the states proper is only of secondary importance. . . . The Napoleonic constitutions are the great boundary marks which history had erected at this crossroad; they are the first manifestation of a basic social change which is determining the history of the world in the 19th century. . . . Their mission is independent of their political expediency, their influence is independent of their short duration. The fact that they did exist and were accepted as valid had changed the social life of Europe, and had proven that the laws and movements of society were to determine, not only the constitution of just one country, but of all Europe.

However, such a powerful impact of one country on a whole continent had to have strong repercussions in France as well. By her interference with the internal affairs of other states, these states, in turn, gained an influence upon the social conditions in France. Most states might not have accepted the French social system except for the fact that Napoleon had supported certain important and powerful social groups of the conquered countries and thereby built a bridge from the Revolution back to the past. These are the elements which later participated in the struggle for restoration. . . . Through them Napoleon turned anew toward society and established a bond between society and his original rigid state organization.

The Imperial Order of French Society.
The Nobility of the Empire and the Entails.

. . . When France wanted to impose a uniform social order upon Europe, it was soon understood that even new constitutions could accomplish this task only partially. In Italy, in Spain, in Germany, in Sweden, even in Poland there were certain institutions, . . . particularly the principalities and the nobility, which resisted an adjustment to the social development in France. Napoleon had an opportunity to experience the power of these two elements particularly during his wars against Austria, but also in Italy and in Germany. These elements had withstood the impact of time. They were deeply rooted in the imagination of the populace. It was impossible to wipe them out without destroying the people themselves; they held all the power in their hands; they were the more irreconcilable enemies of the French rule; they symbolized the tremendous rift between the society of France and the rest of Europe. If the war against France grew out of these differences with such elemental power, the danger persisted that the war and the isolation of France would never end.

Such were the thoughts which Napoleon entertained, animated by ambitions which increased with each victory, when at the end of 1803 a third large coalition was formed against him. He considered himself powerful enough to accomplish anything in France, but not powerful enough irrevocably to subjugate all of Europe. Unless he was able to do this he had to make concessions to the European tradition in France. . . .

Napoleon never conceived of a greater and more comprehensive plan than the one which placed him on the imperial throne. By re-establishing the imperial tradition in France, he hoped to be able to reconcile Europe to the French Revolution. . . . He wanted to do what Louis XVI had attempted in vain, namely, to combine the principle of monarchy with those of the new society . . . and thus to prepare a common ground for the new social developments. In his person the idea of monarchy, with a tradition going back beyond recorded history to the Teutonic tribes, was to be reconciled with the idea of legal equality of recent origin. Through replacing the old royal family in France by a new one, he believed that he would be able to build a bridge between France and the traditional European principalities. To him his coronation as Emperor before the outbreak of the war was an act of European importance; and yet the consequences of this step only aggravated the position of French society. For the new imperial power based on elections by the people could not deny the right of the people for a new election. This Emperor was not "His Majesty by the Grace of God" who could take away the right of the people to new elections. . . . The French Emperor could not attain equality with the European rulers. Napoleon was well aware of it. And here, due to the tempting glory of the old principalities and to his aversion against all parties, he committed an error which endangered his throne more than the victories of the European armies. . . .

If the French Empire . . . could not possibly gain equal footing with the traditional monarchies, what could Napoleon still do? He had to win over to his side those elements of society from which his monarchy had emerged. His empire had been established through the participation and by the consent of the people. . . . Instead of aiming to become the equal of other European principalities, he should have sustained, strengthened and organized the specific social classes which supported him. He had to become a truly constitutional monarch and strive for a transformation of Europe by his example rather than by conquest. Instead, Napoleon assumed that he could find permanency for his dynasty by imitating the old European monarchies. . . . He re-installed the nobility in France, thereby destroying the unique social configuration of French society.

Already on May 19, 1802, Napoleon had established against vehement opposition, particularly that of the Tribunate, the Legion of Honor. Through this institution he wanted to adjust French society, which was based on equality, to the highly stratified societies of Europe; but it remained in spite of all efforts a purely military honor. . . . After his coronation, and after having defeated Austria, Russia and Prussia in two more memorable battles, he conceived the idea of "reorganizing the nation." The Tribunate—the only organ representing the revolutionary principles and defending equality against differentiation introduced by the Empire—was simply abolished on Sept. 8, 1807. Then Napoleon turned toward the basis of all social differences, to property, particularly landed property. We have shown how the old estate had been destroyed, particularly through those laws which introduced the division of large estates. These laws had been incorporated into the codes. But now Napoleon re-introduced the old inheritance laws . . . that "those estates which are the basis of a hereditary title which the Emperor may grant as a favor to a prince or the head of a family shall be hereditary." This decision was incorporated in the code in 1807 (Art. 896). It remained in force until 1835. It was simply the revival of entails. The groundwork for a new aristocracy was now sufficiently prepared. On March 1, 1808, the *Sénate Consulte* issued a complete order of the nobility re-introducing the old titles derived from feudal law. At the head of the nation there were again princes, viscounts, barons and knights; an imperial court with a rigid and brilliant etiquette provided the center for the new nobility; unable to assimilate Europe, Napoleon wanted to excel it, not only militarily, but also by his new social order.

France accepted all these spectacular experiments of her Emperor and the complete destruction of her liberties with equanimity. Without grumbling she tolerated the suppression of the press; she obeyed quietly when Napoleon changed the university to an institution of learning ruled and administered by him, and when he made loyalty to the Emperor the first article of faith in the education of children. It seemed as if he had gained his purpose with these risky regulations, as if he had mastered not only Europe but what had appeared more powerful than the whole coalition of European princes, the revolutionary society. . . . He appeared to be the absolute ruler, not only of the state, but also of society. The amalgamation of the old and the new world now seemed to make a European peace possible. It was not only love of glory which motivated Napoleon; his vision and farsightedness were understood only by very few. His true aim was the unification of Europe. This is why he re-established the aristocracy. He stated: "I have created different imperial titles to prohibit the restoration of feudal titles which are incompatible with constitutional law, to reconcile the old with the new France, to put French institutions on an equal basis with those of Europe." This was what he considered indispensable, and he was right. The only question was whether his method was appropriate.

Indeed, if these institutions had actually played the role which they attempted to suggest to feudal Europe, namely, a reconstruction of the old society, the whole society from which the Emperor and the new, powerful France had arisen would have to dissolve. . . . All these new institutions, however, did not attack the basis of the new society, the principles of wealth, the distribution of goods, and civil law. Only in appearance did they put the social structure of feudal Europe and Civil France on an equal footing; only in appearance did they re-institute nobility and social differences. . . . Nobility in a feudal society distinguished itself from other social classes not only by its closeness to royalty, not only by its large possessions but essentially by the fact that the nobles as well as their estates enjoyed specific prerogatives and that private property in the form of land carried certain sovereign rights, particularly the right of manorial jurisdiction and manorial police. These were the functions which gave power and status to the noblemen, many of whom considered the royal families nothing more than the most powerful members of the nobility. . . . An estate which was not entitled to these rights, for all its advantages, was not a privileged estate. Although distinguished from the rank and file, its members had nothing in common with medieval nobility, no marks of honor nor property rights could possibly make them equal to the nobility. . . . If Napoleon had reintroduced the medieval order of nobility he would have destroyed legal equality and the administrative unification of the state; the code civil would have been nullified and the new administrative system would have been crippled. It would have meant the dissolution of modern France. This was practically impossible, and Napoleon himself did not even think of it. He simply bestowed titles and distributed property, rights of etiquette, emblems and uniforms—all the status symbols of feudalism—but he did not give the new title-bearers one single privilege.

What, then, was this "imperial aristocracy" of which Napoleon boasted? It was anything but real nobility; it was only a status group of large landowners under a different name. The whole scheme was a complete failure, one of Napoleon's great misconceptions. He antagonized society based on legal equality by making it fear a return of the old privileged estates, without creating a new estate which would support the throne. From this time on, people no longer looked at him as the personification of the new social order. From the time that Napoleon attempted to establish a new aristocracy, he no longer differed from the old monarchy except through his military victories. This was one of the major reasons why France gave him up quickly and almost unanimously after his military defeats.

There was one other point which seemed to favor the future of the new aristocracy, the entails. . . . All the vague notions about the nature, value and influence of the entails result from a failure to recognize the basic difference between feudal and civil entails. This error is due to the fact that both institutions are designated by the same term. . . . In a feudal society, any large landed property bestows a legal authority on its own. The rights of landowners are property rights, but the endowment with state rights transforms landed property into territorial domain. This bestows legal independence on the landowners. This is the true reason for the original indivisibility of the entails. Since each feudal lord had his own court, his own administration, police, laws and customs, even partly his own military service, the property could not be divided without upsetting the system of public administration. The very nature of these conditions made it necessary to transmit the land undivided. . . . The purpose of this rule was to preserve landed property as an independent legal entity (Rechtskoerper).

In civil society, property rights are not only equalized, but all administrative and legal authority is vested in the state. Even the huge estates are nothing but economic units. To preserve them as units means to secure revenues from these possessions. Indivisibility of entails does not create a new class whose members have superior legal position, but only a class with a definite, secure income. . . . The feudal entail preserves a legal estate within society, the civil entail only a social class; the former establishes absolute, the latter only relative inequality; the former is a logical consequence of the feudal principle of identity between property and public authority, the latter is an exception to the principle of the division of inherited land. The feudal entail preserves nobility, the civil entail only the large landed property. As an economic measure, the latter was subject to justified criticism; as a social institution, it had no influence whatsoever upon the re-instatement of the old nobility. The essential attributes of the old nobility—privileges and territorial domains—was lacking; . . . the true amalgamation of the new order in France with the old order of the rest of Europe remained an illusion which deceived nobody except Napoleon. . . .

It will have become clear by now why French society tolerated all this silently. The basis on which this society rested had remained intact. . . . The true elements of French social life proceeded side by side with the imperial orders. . . . The future belonged to these elements, they knew it, and they waited undisturbed for their time. . . .

Concept and Origin of the Acquisitive Society

At this point we have to review the concept of society and the changes that have taken place since the Revolution.

The French Revolution in all its phases always re-emphasized one principle: complete equality of individuals before the law. This principle was so firmly established that even the Empire with its despotic institutions was unable to break it: equality before the law continued to be the basic principle of French society. . . .

Napoleon had coped successfully with a chaotic situation. The establishment of a new and stable order of society had been indispensable. Could France expect the new society to develop on the basis of legal equality? . . . If this was not the case, what other stabilizing forces could be mustered?

Equality before the law is essentially a negative principle. It denies privileges of one individual over another; it further acknowledges the individual as an independent unit of the community. The function of the law based on equality is only to protect the independent individual. Equality does not acknowledge any legal differences among individuals. . . .

All the institutions and organizations of the past had been based on differences in legal rights; it was the law which determined the structure of society. The new era had changed this. Legal inequality would have been contradictory to the new social order and a return to the former. It is, therefore, understandable that the principle of legal equality has been regarded as the main source of the whole Revolution and also as the basis of the new order. One has characterized—as Louis Blanc did in his history of the Revolution—this era as the epoch of individualism. Rarely has a greater and more deceptive error been committed. The prevailing opinion was that the new order of society which emerged from the Revolution was based on legal equality. This opinion is the result of a misinterpretation of society. Society is an order and therefore a system superordination and subordination.

Equality before the law refers to the independence of one individual from the other; therefore, it is the exact opposite of the principle of organizations; it refers to the factor which posits the independent individual outside the order. It is the negation of privilege as well as of subordination. Legal equality is incapable of establishing a social structure, . . . although such structure is indispensable to the human community. Equality before the law contradicts a social order of legal differentiation. It forces the community to accept differentiation by another element which allows stratification without endangering legal equality. What was this other element?

The impact of the French Revolution on Europe was in the first place directed against legal inequality and against a society based on status differentiation. As long as nothing was sought but the abolition of these differences the movement had a merely negative character. This inevitably leads to the question: What shall and will be the order of society if all are legally equal? This is the question of the immediate future; the answer will have to refer to the factors on which contemporary society rests.

Equality before the law abolished all individual or class prerogatives, which had, after all, been a matter of chance. If differentiation was to be re-introduced, it would have to be based on an element invested in the people and attainable by everybody. This element had to have the quality of uniting people and of organizing them. It had to further individual abilities while producing and preserving differences among individuals. . . . All these qualifications applied to property: it was available to everybody and yet unevenly distributed; it was in accord with the principle of legal equality and yet created differentiation.

With the introduction and acceptance of legal equality—no matter when and where—a new era for the role of property begins. As long as the social structure is determined by law, property serves only for the satisfaction of wants. As soon as legal equality is established, property rights are the only institution through which inequality, and thus a structured society, may develop; they become the formative elements of social organization. A totally new type of society comes into existence at this point.

If property has the function not only of satisfying needs but also of conveying social status, it must transgress the private sphere and must become generally accepted. . . . The individual must utilize his property because his social position is supposed to be based on it. Individual acquisition manifests itself in individual enterprise.

An enterprise cannot be run by a single person; it unites laborers and entrepreneurs into smaller or larger economic units; the unity of purpose of the various productive functions becomes crystallized in an organization encompassing managerial and operative groups. Private enterprise thus creates a difference between the two main elements, the entrepreneur and the laborer. Since this differentiation exists in any enterprise and thus permeates the whole economy, . . . it is the basic characteristic of acquisitive society.

At the same time, another economic difference develops which is of equal importance. Factories cannot produce for a single consumer, but only for large groups. A relationship develops among the various enterprises, which become mutually dependent. An acquisitive society thus develops a whole network of exchange, and the effective functioning of enterprises becomes dependent upon a rigid order of this exchange. . . . Gains and losses on the market may occur which are beyond the control of the entrepreneur; individual wants as a determining factor of the economy almost disappear; property is merely the basis of an acquisitive market economy. As such it is called capital. All other things being equal, a large amount of capital guarantees greater and more secure gains and tends to control the small enterprises so that a differentiation develops within the entrepreneurial class itself. The bigger capitalists make the smaller ones dependent in their business, subjugate them, and usually control the market. With the emergence of an acquisitive society, two entrepreneurial groups, whose relationship is not dissimilar to that between the factory owner and the laborer, usually emerge: the capitalists and the small entrepreneurs.

In a society of legal equality, property rights are the natural medium through which the individual can assert his worth. Therefore, the stages in the acquisition of property become the basis of differential individual prestige. Equality before the law is nothing but protection against any other difference except that of acquired property; it is the prerequisite, not the regulating principle, of society. . . . Possessions and property rights develop a new quality; by determining the social position of the individual, they become the basis of the social order of any acquisitive society. In contrast to a society characterized by legal status, we call this society the acquisitive society. Regarding the history of society, it follows that equality before the law, which follows abolition of legal differentiations, produces a social order determined by economic forces . . . The abolition of monopolies, privileges and guilds is followed by a rapid increase in entrepreneurial activity. The former dependence on the privileged is replaced by a dependence on the owner of capital. . . . The acquisitive society, by making equality before the law its only prerequisite, is necessarily opposed to any political power which would favor inequality before the law. But beyond that, the acquisitive society is indifferent to constitutional law as long as legal equality is preserved. . . .

Now let us go back to the realm of social life . . . and ask ourselves: what was the basis of the social order against which Napoleon struggled in vain with his nobility and his entails, and which nevertheless . . . was not acceptable to the old order? . . . There is no doubt that this society was the new acquisitive society. . . . When Napoleon first appeared on the scene there was but a multitude of individuals; a condition of pure legal equality prevailed without a social structure. It was Napoleon's mission to leave this situation undisturbed, to eliminate the interference of public law in society, and to monopolize public authority. The new society continued to grow under his rule; naturally and slowly, but firmly, the new acquisitive society, the organism of the human community, developed side by side with the organism of the state. His power was finally limited by the new social order, which he did not understand, although he had given it more support than any other ruler. It was the new social order which opposed the creation of a privileged new nobility as well as a transformation of the entails into territorial domains; it reduced titles without an economic basis to mere words. This was the society which Napoleon feared while he was trying to recreate elements of the old order which would support him. He served the acquisitive society as long as he was powerful; it finally dethroned him because he threatened its existence. This new social order, which appeared negligible and weak, was in fact, very powerful.

However, the new society under Napoleon was still young; if one sets its beginning with the Constitution of 1799, it did not yet extend over half a generation. . . . During this period, the first decade of our century, three groups of the acquisitive society were still closely affiliated with each other. The worker could become an entrepreneur, the entrepreneur in turn a capitalist; tremendous chances of industrial growth opened an opportunity for everybody, and the government endeavored to assist all enterprises by all means. . . . The Continental system practically forced the people to develop new enterprises. Spinning mills for wool and cotton were introduced, the beet root sugar industry was established; in fact, industrial production in continental Europe began only at this period. The Emperor supported it wherever he could, while he attempted in vain to re-institute nobility; actually, he was the most powerful patron of the elements tending to destroy forever nobility and privilege. . . .

It is of great importance that the very war which Napoleon waged against the foreign enemy favored the growth of the new society in France in a peculiar way. The new social order was not so much threatened—as will be seen later—by the foreign powers or internal despotism, as by the opposition between labor and the property-owning entrepreneur. This opposition was effectively counteracted through the war. Any war has to make use of the larger part of the property-less population. On the other hand, anybody who is willing to risk his life for what he wants to attain can force his way to the top: fame, wealth and opportunity are offered to everybody who is bold and strong enough to act. Under the flag of a great commander, anybody who is not bound by property to a definite domicile finds what he wishes. By fighting for himself he, at the same time, fights for the glory of his nation. Neither Napoleon nor his marshals forgot that they, too, had come from the lowest ranks. In this way, the property-less during the war led an existence in which the class antagonism of the acquisitive society did not exist. The factors which unite the propertyless into a class—the large number of competing workers and the lack of opportunity for improving one's lot, the source of hatred against the property owners—were missing.

This was true for the soldiers of Napoleon's army. By withdrawing them from industry, competition among the remaining workers was reduced. Whoever remained could dictate the price of his labor because he had become indispensable. He now had a good chance for making a profit and for the acquisition of property. . . .

These circumstances contributed a great deal toward the realization of the law of social development, the steady growth of the acquisitive society evolving from the principle of equality before the law. Usually it takes a whole generation to build a new society from the ruins of the preceding one; here it was accomplished during one decade. Although during the period of Napoleon's brilliant reign there was not yet any chance for the new society to participate in politics and in extending its activities beyond the sphere of economics, France was, according to the unanimous opinion of all contemporaries, internally strong and flourishing as never before.

Transition to the Next Period

The acquisitive society based on free economic activity was the new social order growing out of the principle of equality before the law. The future of Europe was to be determined by it, its problems were to become the problems of our own generation. . . . This is inevitable according to the law of social dynamics. . . .

If it is true that the order of society is necessarily reflected in the constitution of the state, the question arises as to what kind of constitution is appropriate to the acquisitive society. Under Napoleon the new society had only begun to crystallize. Later, however, it could not possibly remain neutral toward political developments without contradicting itself. The assertion of the acquisitive society in the constitutional and administrative sphere is usually called the period of Restoration, thereby adopting the name of the defeated rather than the victorious element. It would be more appropriate to call it . . . the period of citizenry. . . . The contradiction of the acquisitive society to the Napoleonic system began to show, after this society had grown strong enough, by the very despotism it had called for during its infancy and which finally became intolerable. The era of citizenry was established by the July monarchy. Only then, during the reign of Louis Philippe, the theoretical problem became a practical one: whether the acquisitive society provided the satisfactory framework for the fulfillment of man's destiny. . . . Socialism and communism are the theoretical attempts toward solving this problem. The history of the Second French Republic records the practical effort to cope with the emerging contradictions.

Part One, Chapter Three

THE RESTORATION

ORIGIN, STRUGGLE AND VICTORY OF CIVIL SOCIETY

The social implications of the era of the Restoration have been understood more clearly than the period of the Empire, of which usually only the external events were recorded. The reason for that may be that with the Restoration the new market economy had become an established fact and determined the course of events, while during the reign of Napoleon the new elements had only begun to take shape. But nevertheless, the most important institutional principle, which later spread all over Europe, had not yet been formulated. This is the concept of citizenship. During the ensuing period a specific, though not yet clearly discernible, social life developed. It is the era of the Restoration, which led to the emergence of a clear and distinct concept of citizenship in France unparalleled by any other nation. . . .

*The Acquisitive Society and the First Principle
of the French Constitution.*

. . . In the growth of the acquisitive society a principle other than that of being conditioned by equality could be discerned; it can be explained by the events of the period. An acquisitive society develops when the abilities of the individual, stimulated by the processes of acquisition through business and enterprises, finally also determine the order, not only of these abilities, but also of the personality structure of the individual. The specifically economic activity, or the participation of the individual in acquisitive pursuits, e.g. in mechanical labor or in the management of enterprises, changes from a temporary activity to a specific occupation determining the whole social existence of the person. It affects the totality of his life; it focuses all his thoughts on one center; it teaches him to rate all his abilities with reference to their suitability for this particular economic function; some elements in his personality useful for this purpose will be highly developed, while others—although they may be of a more noble nature—wither away. The individual becomes in a way the servant of a specific task. . . . The occupational role of the individual will affect him and his family throughout his whole life. It causes the father to educate his children in a specific manner. Depending on economic success, the family may offer to the children a better or more limited education and develop or thwart their abilities. Because it is easiest to teach what one knows best and because it is extremely expensive to hire teachers, the family creates a situation in which, as a rule, the children will be educated to the business and profession of their parents. In this way the order of acquisition is already consolidated within the family. The social position, the skill, the intellectual orientation as well as the economically determined environment, eventually become hereditary. Slowly but irrevocably a stable, secure and almost self-propelling society develops out of the mere order. The emergence of such a society becomes inevitable as soon as acquisition has been accepted as the basis of social life.

Obviously this society is not a society of complete liberty, and even less a society of equals. Yet, having grown out of the concepts of liberty and equality, it is indeed closely related to these concepts. . . .

The complete domination of the personality over the forces of nature is the aspiration of man. . . . This can only be accomplished if the community of men, by an intricate method of division of labor, cooperates for the exploitation of the available raw materials. . . . Only the common effort of all men will enable the individual to control and enjoy the resources of nature to an extent to which he could never have done it alone. Nor does he work only for himself; his work benefits everybody else. As a single person he is a negligible entity in the acquisitive process of the whole society, and yet he gains more in the distributive process than his isolated efforts would have ever made possible. . . . The wealth of the individual is the result of the labor of all, and, . . . at the same time, the basis for reaching his inner destiny, his intellectual development. This development is dependent upon the organically operating, acquisitive activity of all the people; it is secure and complete only when the order of acquisitive powers changes from a casual and transitory order into a steady and permanent one. This happens when the order of acquisition is transformed into a social order, the acquisitive society. The acquisitive society . . . represents a stage of development where man, in fact, accepts the "community of wealth" as the condition which enables him to gain control over nature.

The law of acquisition to which society submits during this period appears to the individual as a state of greatest personal freedom and independence. Not only is he free to choose his occupation, his profession; the rule of acquisition actually demands that he follow the calling most suitable to him, because one does best what one likes to do, and what one does best will be most valuable and remunerative. Moreover, this law does not bar anybody from his chosen profession. If ability is assisted by good fortune, even the lowliest person may be able to reach the highest social position. Everybody is on his own, and social prestige depends entirely upon the individual himself. . . .

Such was the general character of the society which took shape under Napoleon's regime in France. It spread farther and farther over the rest of Europe, partly through France's aggression, partly because, in the other European countries too, the elements of the new society were already present. In retrospect, one recognizes the close relationship of these changes to the very beginning of the social revolution. When the legal privileges of status had been abolished by the Declaration of the Rights of Man, property became the main principle of the new social order. . . . As such it affected the individual owner but not yet society. The potentialities of property develop fully only in the acquisitive society. . . . The social order of a market economy represents the unfolding of the principle of free property rights as the basis of the social order.

This society has also its inner contradiction, which is as yet unsolved. However, before it becomes noticeable the new social order must be fully developed; it must extend beyond the sphere of individual life and must have subjected the constitution of the state to its own laws. . . .

The constitution of the acquisitive society has its own peculiar character. It depends on the guarantees of civil law and on the security of acquisitive activities. In the acquisitive society, with its rigidly interlocked parts, a strong conflict of interests develops, as well as an interminable struggle between all competitors. The first constitutional principle of an acquisitive society is determined by this contradiction. All enterprises are built on one commonly accepted principle: the inviolability of property rights. Property thus determines the social position of the individual. The non-owner is therefore excluded from entrepreneurial activity and becomes the opponent of the property owner, who controls his personal and social life. If these two basic social forces of the acquisitive society were to confront each other in isolation, a struggle for property rights, a disruption of the acquisitive process, and the downfall of this type of social order would be the inevitable result. If the owners were to completely control the non-owners, liberty, the basic prerequisite for acquisition, would be destroyed; on the other hand, the rule of the non-owners would abolish property, which is the very basis of the acquisitive society. The first task of a constitution corresponding to an acquisitive society is to solve this contradiction.

Secondly, it is quite natural that each individual considers his specific occupation to be the most important. Everybody, therefore, will want to promote his own interests at the expense of his fellow man. As a result of this . . . innumerable contradictions will arise. The victory of any one economic group may by its selfishness undermine and ruin all others. . . . A solution can only be provided by a stable state power which is independent of all particular interest groups. . . .

Only the state, being neither owner nor non-owner—although related to both groups—is the representative of the inviolable law. Only the state is able to safeguard property and acquisition; only the state stands apart from the struggle among the various economic interest groups, it cannot ignore one group for the sake of others, because the disadvantage resulting from such partialities would harm the whole and thus also harm the state itself.

This describes the position of the state within the acquisitive society. The first principle of the constitution has therefore to be above everything else the independence and stability of the supreme political power. One may also reverse the above statement and say that wherever people demand an independent and stable state power, an acquisitive society has emerged. The specific form of the state is relatively unimportant for the social order. . . . The acquisitive society is neither dynastic and monarchical, nor aristocratic, nor republican. All it wants is a state independent of the influence of particular interests. . . . This explains the origin of the July Revolution. If the state identifies itself with a specific section of the people, the whole society is bound to become its enemy. . . . The outbreak of the revolution is not so much the consequence of one particular state act but of the consolidated existence of an acquisitive society. . . . French society was willing to tolerate Napoleon because a sovereign ruler has seldom done more to support this social order; seldom has a state supported all sections of the economy as fairly and impartially as did the Emperor and his administration. However, this is not the only quality which society demands from the state.

*The Concept of Citizenship, of the Civil Constitution
and of Civil Society.*

It lies in the nature of the supreme political power, in order to safeguard the individual, to regard all elements of society as subordinate to the needs of the state. No matter what its form may be, the state is the master of the whole external life of man. The nature of this highest temporal personality is so powerful that . . . the individual, in times of danger, does not hesitate to sacrifice all his belongings, his health and his life for the sake of the state. It is a misinterpretation of the concept of liberty to assume that this condition changes through the establishment of freedom. Free nations especially bring the greatest sacrifices to the state; the state is their unrestricted master, just as it is the master of a subjugated nation.

If liberty nevertheless does have any meaning, this meaning must be found in the fact that the will of the state is no longer independent of the individuals but rather reflects the organic unity of the reasonable wishes of the people. . . . Liberty is not freedom from government; it is self-government. This abstract principle of liberty had already been considered during the last century by French as well as other European ideologists. However, the actual life of the state is determined at every point by the social order. The French Revolution illustrates the fact that the abstract principle may be capable of ruling temporarily; the final course of the Revolution, however, showed that a permanent order of the state has to be based on a permanent order of society. What kind of society is it which of its own accord demands the realization of the principle of freedom?

The pursuit of profit forms the basis of the acquisitive society and is, therefore, at the center of the life of each individual. It is the end-in-itself to the individual, because it determines individual development and his enjoyment of life. If another independent will exists, it threatens individual independence, which is the basis of the free pursuit of gain. Such is the case when the state, as under Napoleon, is merely an administrative state, altogether separated from the people.

The contradiction arising out of the separation of society and the state constitution, which characterizes the Napoleonic era, manifests itself in the dependence of the free economy upon the state. This contradiction can be dissolved only by popular participation in the political decision-making process. A free economy remains free only if the acquisitive people rule the state. The organism which safeguards their participation in government is the constitution. The free market society requires, by its very nature, a constitution that guarantees the organic self-government of the people. However, popular participation in government should not endanger the sovereignty of the state. The acquisitive society, as a specific social order, has a particular character which expresses itself in the constitutional principle. The acquisitive society needs, above all, a strong state, a need which in turn conditions and limits the need for a constitution. The constitution should guarantee the political rights of the people while also upholding the independence of the state. The constitution of an acquisitive society, therefore, differs on the one hand from an absolute monarchy and, on the other hand, from political democracy; it attempts to establish a system of popular representation without violating the independence of the personal state.

Two principles peculiar to this type of constitution may be derived from this fact: the inviolability and sovereignty of the head of the state—regardless of whether he is a monarch or a president; and secondly the responsibility of the ministers. . . . No civil society is conceivable without these two features. They reflect the relationship between constitution and state authority. Another problem is the relationship between the constitution and the populace. Since it is the principle of free acquisition which reigns in a representative state, free acquisition ought also to be the condition of participation in this representative government. Any acquisition depends on two factors: labor as well as capital. . . . Only labor combined with capital secures a social position; only by combining both is it possible to attain the ultimate goal of individual development. In such a society only the combination of labor and capital can secure the right to participate in public life. In such a society the mere laborer cannot possibly be accepted as a fully valid member of society. Equality in public law . . . can be bestowed only upon the laborer who owns capital. . . . By acquiring, on the basis of this principle of acquisitive property rights, the right to participate in the decision-making process of the state through the election of representatives, he becomes a full-fledged citizen (Staatsbürger) a participant in state action instead of a mere subject. Citizenship is a concept according to which ownership, the acquisitive unit in a market society, entitles the individual to equal participation in the decision-making process of the state. . . . There is only one method by which acquisitive ownership can be recognized, i.e. by the taxes paid to the state, because only through taxes does property acquire a reality for the state. . . . The principle was established as soon as the acquisitive society became stabilized; the tax return, as a symbol of acquisitive ownership, became the condition of participation in popular representation. . . . It is the evaluation of people on the basis of their tax returns which reflects the identity of this society with the state. . . . This is the main difference between this type of constitution and the purely democratic one. The democratic constitution is based on equal voting rights. It thus unconsciously makes labor into the only decisive factor in society. In most respects it is quite similar to the constitution of an acquisitive society. It differs essentially through one major aspect; this difference in principle is indicated by the tie between voting rights and tax return, no matter how small the latter might be. . . . Through the divorce of labor from capital, and through the property requirements, the citizens in the acquisitive society are divided into two essentially different classes, one participating in the government, the other composed of mere subjects. Although it is possible for anybody to cross the dividing line, this line nevertheless does exist. . . . This separation . . . gives the acquisitive society a new and peculiar character. A deep schism develops within the organism of work and of acquisition, and the whole, thus split, is characterized by a new concept. While the acquisitive society envisions all its various elements as one unit, in which all parts belong together, it becomes, divided into a ruling and a dependent class on the basis of property and taxation, a civil society. This, however, is apparent only after the civil constitution has been established. . . .

We now return to the history of France under Napoleon. . . . Under his reign the acquisitive society had become an established and stable order. . . . It was inevitable that this society should finally enforce the enactment of the civil constitution in France. . . . Once the acquisitive society was securely set up, Napoleon's unique historical mission was fulfilled. The time was ripe for the downfall of his system; . . . contemporary events facilitated such a development. This explains a number of otherwise obscure facts concerning the period of the decline of Napoleon and the establishment of the new monarchy. If Napoleon had been victorious in Russia, he might have possibly postponed the establishment of the civil constitution for a few years. But it finally had to come. . . . Napoleon laid the foundation for the acquisitive society, the end of his regime brought the civil society to power; the history of the civil society in France begins with the retreat of the great army.

The Fall of Napoleon, the New Monarchy and the Charter of June 4, 1814.

The great army of the Emperor was destroyed by the winter of 1812. Europe had arisen. Napoleon was defeated; the allied armies entered France. The Empire was in serious danger. But Napoleon himself was not yet discouraged. In fact, France had faced more serious situations before; when the Convention had declared a state of emergency, the frontier had been more vulnerable than it was in 1814. At that time half of France was in revolt, while it was obedient now; in those days the army was neither a strong organization, nor was it led by a great general, nor was it well supplied. Napoleon was the greatest commander of his time, and his army was the best in Europe. What was it that made France—wealthier, stronger and more flourishing than ever—drop her Emperor and surrender to foreign powers?

Two factors which will now be well understood caused the change. Napoleon, whose power had been built on the greatest rigidity of the principles of absolutism, was a declared enemy of popular representation. He knew that popular representation would make the state the servant of the ruling class within the new society. He would rather surrender France than his absolute sovereignty. The members of the new society, which was thus far without political power, knew this very well; they had to press for political rights in the framework of a civil society. There was only one man who opposed this development. The nature of society was stronger than even the emotions of national honor and Napoleon's popularity. Napoleon had to rely only upon his army, and the army alone could not defeat the Allies. French society abandoned the man under whose auspices it had grown up.

On the other side, the old European feudal society was deeply shaken by the war. The victories of Napoleon had demonstrated the impotence of state power based on feudalism. There was no hope for the defeated states of regaining their former position on the basis of the old social order. They had to call upon the elements of the new society in order to defeat Napoleon. They had to promise to their populace a civil society, which means a system of public law corresponding to an acquisitive society. The proclamation of Kalisch was the great event by which the German states dissociated themselves from the old society and accepted the new one. This proclamation had, especially for Germany, the same importance as the Declaration of the Rights of Man had had for France. Napoleon was defeated in the name of the Constitution. On the basis of this hope the German people abandoned the cause of Napoleon; the fight against Napoleon became the struggle of the emerging civil society against despotism.

What was it that France desired to accomplish? Indeed, it was nothing else but what her enemies had fought for when they had fought against Napoleon. The secret opposition against the Emperor was animated by the same ideas which permeated the German armies. The course of events depended upon the strange fact—which illustrated clearly for the first time the deep difference between state and society—that French society was the natural confederate of the Allies against French state power personified by the Emperor. Napoleon had defeated each of these two adversaries separately. When they came to realize that they had a common cause, he recognized his error too late. A feeling of complete isolation, leading to despair, befell him. Napoleon abdicated. The cause of the acquisitive society had been victorious, and the era of civil society dawned.

After Napoleon's abdication the problem of the new power in France became acute. Two facts had a decisive effect at this point. The new France had to establish a new state in harmony with the other European countries; and the interests of the acquisitive society had to be safeguarded. Only the former could re-establish the friendly relationship between France and the other European states, and only the latter could provide a secure basis for the new state at home. At the time, these considerations were not discussed theoretically; the politicians, however, fully appreciated them. They demanded the enthronement of Louis XVIII as King and at the same time obliged him to issue the Charter, the new constitution of society. It did not make any difference whether or not he himself had formulated it. The decisive fact was that the constitution transformed the acquisitive society into a civil society, accepting the monarchical form of government combined with a system of popular representation, whose organs became the two chambers of the legislature. The restoration of Louis XVIII brought peace with Europe, while the Charter brought peace with the French people.

Only a lack of understanding of the social movements can explain the fact that the enactment of the *Charte constitutionelle*, which is one of the most important and magnificent events of European history, is usually mentioned only incidentally and that no great importance is accorded to it. Actually, a completely new era in European history had been inaugurated by the *Charte constitutionelle*. All former constitutions of revolutionary France, as well as the constitutions imposed upon defeated countries, had been considered antagonistic to the traditional state order. The *Charte constitutionelle*, however—the price which Louis XVIII had to pay for the throne—constituted the formal acknowledgement that Europe had relinquished feudal society and was entering the era of civil society. What up to this time had been enforced by French military power was now accepted voluntarily and as a matter of course by European diplomats; the Charter of Louis XVIII is the beginning of the constitutional epoch in Europe.

On the other hand, the new French Constitution was also deeply influenced by events and developments in the rest of Europe. Feudal society had been undermined in the other European states but by no means destroyed. Civil society was accepted there, but it was not the only existent form of society. The society of Teutonic Europe presented a strange picture, which must be visualized in order to understand not only the Charter but the whole development of European public law. This society consisted simultaneously of two essentially different systems. It included elements of feudal society and feudal rights, property rights in public domains, privileges of the aristocracy and the estates—social distinctions which were quite conspicuous—side by side with elements of civil society with a free, growing industry, with acquired property, with equality in the field of civil law and the claim for popular representation. It is this mixture of elements which has characterized the condition of Europe since 1815. Two such contradictory elements cannot possibly coexist permanently. Sooner or later the struggle for supremacy was unavoidable. However, during those years, the great common effort had for the time being covered up the differences. It was assumed that the coexistence of the incompatible was possible. Those who knew better and who were aware of the inevitability of coming events demanded only a period of public security. Peace prevailed on the surface of a society which carried the seeds of war in its foundations but not yet in its consciousness.

A problem arose which was to test the viability of this situation. It is society which determines the constitution. Up to now, the intrinsic similarity of the social order had brought about similarities in the constitutions. The latter had changed with the former, but each constitution had been an organic whole. Now for the first time it became necessary to represent two essentially different social systems by the same constitution; it became necessary to draft a constitution which reflected both a society of estates and a civil society. This was the task of the European countries which wanted to adopt constitutionalism. If France wanted to cooperate harmoniously with the rest of Europe, she had to accept a constitution which recognized both these systems.

The Charter of 1814 was designed to accomplish this. It was the beginning of the bicameral system characteristic of the new era, which was soon to demonstrate its inner contradiction in France. France was different from the other European countries, because it had no remnants left of the feudal order. To establish a common social foundation with the rest of Europe, she had to facilitate the re-emergence of a hierarchical society by means of the constitution, while, in reality, the given order of society ought to determine the constitution. This peculiar attempt, altogether new in the history of constitutions, was reflected in Article 24, which established a Chamber of Peers which shared the legislative power. Originally, the king was authorized to grant lifetime peerages only (Article 27). But this was in contradiction to the principle of differentiation by rank and hereditary status. The ordinance of August 19, 1815 rectified this situation by declaring peerage to be hereditary according to the laws of primogeniture. Membership in the Chamber of Peers was determined on a completely different basis than membership in the Chamber of Deputies: the deputies were elected on the basis of property qualifications. The coordination of both chambers seemingly represented the unification of both social systems into one constitutional body.

However, this attempt to reverse the natural course of events proved to be a complete failure. The Peers were supposed to replace the nobility, but a nobility without privileges and legal authority was a nobility in name only; landed property and privileges were its true foundation; this foundation had been destroyed by the new inheritance laws. Neither the few remaining entails nor the institution of Peership could prevent the final disappearance of the nobility. The Chamber of Peers never had any influence on the course of events in France. It was too weak to maintain a rigid status differentiation, and too strong for the unhampered rule of a civil society. With regard to the rest of Europe, the Chamber of Peers was nothing but a concession of civil France to the feudal elements of its neighbors; it was a handicap for France's development without actually being an important antagonist of the new society. Its history and its downfall provide a striking evidence of the fact that constitutions cannot shape societies and that no part of the constitution will endure and exert influence unless it is representative of specific elements in society.

Another factor of the new Constitution was of far greater importance. In discussing the early stages of the acquisitive society, we mentioned the emergence of an independent social element, the moneyed classes. Although capital accumulates only within the acquisitive society, it acquires specific characteristics which place it in opposition to the interests of labor. This antagonism develops only when the acquisitive society is fully established. Little knowledge about social relationships is required to comprehend the relationship between capital and the emergence of a class society. Once citizenship was accepted as the principle of the new constitution, a hierarchy within the acquisitive society had to be established which gave capital the right to participate in governmental decisions to the exclusion of the two other factors of the acquisitive society—labor and entrepreneurial activity. The method of accomplishing this was the institution of property qualification. Articles 38 and 40 of the new Charter stated that only those who paid a direct tax of at least 1000 francs could be eligible for membership in the Chamber of Deputies, and that only those who paid at least 300 francs in taxes had the right to vote. Such a tax could only be paid by actual capitalists. The new property qualifications, unlike those of the Constitution of 1791, were not designed to grant full citizenship to all members of the society who represented either labor, entrepreneurship or capital. It did not, like the Constitution of 1791, attempt to make civil society identical with the acquisitive society. The new property qualifications were rather supposed to bring about a deep and far-reaching cleavage of society by identifying citizenship with capital ownership only, while all other elements of the acquisitive society were excluded from political representation by the new Constitution. The expectations placed in the new property qualifications were not only of a negative nature; they were intended not merely to exclude the population at large from politics; rather, it was hoped that the new representative government, being the agency of a single class of the acquisitive society, would make common cause with the status society and with the reaction. However, this kind of reasoning had not taken into account the power of the monarchy.

If one applies the laws which determine the relationship between social classes and the constitution to the Restoration period in France, one can predict the inevitable course of events. Once the new French society had been fully established as an acquisitive social order, the Chamber of Peers would have to be discarded as a useless institution; in addition, the contradiction embedded in the fact that only capital owners were full citizens would eventually force the small entrepreneur into a close alliance with the laborer in order to reduce the property qualifications to a minimum. The time for the attack on the Constitution could not be predicted, but it was approaching. The elimination of property qualifications would mean the final victory of the acquisitive society. Since the attack was bound to accentuate the opposition between capital and labor, it was inevitable that the deep inherent contradiction of the acquisitive society would become evident. The later this happened, the greater would be the chances of the laborer to become an entrepreneur and the chances of the entrepreneur to become a capitalist. This date drew closer as the chance of individual advancement within industrial society diminished. In any case, the struggle between these two sectors of the acquisitive society could not be avoided forever. The excessive property qualifications would become the immediate cause of the conflict which would destroy the harmony of the new social order.

Nevertheless, there was no trace of any struggle for the next fifteen years. Quite to the contrary, all parts of the population were unanimously opposed . . . to the supreme power of the state personified by the king. The reason for this cannot be discovered in the social order. It is the monarchy itself which, by completely misinterpreting its natural function, generated the antagonism of the whole population; in its struggle against the contemporary trend it demonstrated the compelling force of a social order striving for an adequate constitution indispensable for its survival.

The era which covers these events is the Restoration Period. There is not much to be said about it. It did not create anything; it has enlightened only a few. It could have demonstrated the power of monarchy if, according to its true function, it had dissociated itself from the opposing forces in society, and if it had supported the natural trends of society with wisdom and strength; it only demonstrated what monarchy cannot accomplish if, in conflict with the social order, it wants to force the government to take sides against the population at large. The era of the Restoration had only a negative function. It delayed the full emergence of a civil society and the manifestations of its contradictions; but it did not affect them. We have to start our discussion of the Charter of 1830 by asking the same question we asked when we completed our discussion of the Charter of 1814.

The Restoration and the July Revolution

If Louis XVIII had returned to France alone, history would have taken a different turn. But with him, and mostly against his wishes, both the emigrants and the old concept of monarchy—which had given rise to the Restoration and brought about the July Revolution—also returned; both have been sufficiently described although not sufficiently interpreted. Their true significance lay in their relationship to civil society.

The emigrants had been brought up within the framework of the feudal law. According to this law, the basis of social differentiation is the accident of birth rather than the merits of the individual. The civil society is basically uninterested in the prerogative of birth; personality and success, the rise from laborer to capitalist, constitute its standard of value. These two principles and the social orders based upon them are irreconcilable. . . . The concept of feudal law subordinates commoners to the nobility; it cannot tolerate equality established by constitutional law. . . . Since nobility cannot exist without privileges, public law based on status—if not in its conception, then certainly in its consequences—necessarily had to re-establish the principle of inequality before the law. Legal inequality has to begin with landed property. Side by side with landed property, subject to parceling by inheritance, indivisible large estates have to be established in all sections of the country, not only as an exception as was the case with scattered entails, but as a rule. In order to avoid a situation where, as in England, differentiation is only a matter of size, landed property has to be endowed with sovereign rights, particularly judicial and police power. Only then does a basis for a true aristocracy exist.

Social conditions in the new France depended, as we have shown, precisely upon the dissolution of legal prerogatives. The Chamber of Deputies, although representing, due to the restrictive qualification of voting rights, only the capital-owning class of the new society, was nevertheless the natural defender of the new civil society against any attack. If the emigrants wanted to re-establish their rights, a basic attack on the constitutional position of the Chamber was inevitable. Restoration of former conditions was possible only after the destruction of this institution.

A direct attack on this institution was impossible. The assault had to be made at its weakest point, at a point where the authority of the Chamber of Deputies was not clearly delineated. This weakness presented itself in the relationship of the Chamber of Deputies of the king.

Every civil constitution accepts as a first principle the absolute independence of the state; another accepted principle is that of popular representation. Every civil constitution—in contrast to a democratic one

—tends to subjugate the state to society as far as this is compatible with individual freedom. Where is the dividing line between these two principles? Who has to resolve the case in which the king considers his independence threatened by a decision of the deputies? Who, furthermore, has the decision-making power if the king considers it necessary to expand his own authority while the deputies hold the opinion that such a measure threatens the basis of a civil society? . . . It is obviously here that a discrepancy between constitutional law and practice develops. . . . The danger grows if the king is convinced that the stability of his state power is secured only by the re-introduction of status differentiations. . . . In this case the monarchical principle merges with the principle of a status society. Through this alliance the latter gains a foothold in civil society. . . .

This coalition and its manifestations, which had already appeared, though rather unintentionally, during the early phases of the Revolution, represent one of the most important developments of Teutonic history; it had a greater impact on modern history than anything else. . . . It is this alliance to which the often used as well as misused. . . concept of "reaction" refers. Reaction is identical with the principle of feudal society and feudal monarchy with their law and glory, the inevitable fact of their existence fighting civil society. The power of reaction depends on the fact of whether the status-seeking elements represent merely the demands and hopes of a party or whether they formally represent part of society. The reaction in France is distinguished from the reaction in other European countries by the fact that, while the nobility in other European countries had been preserved, it had to be newly created in France.

Related to the concept of reaction is the concept of "constitutional opposition," which also derives its true significance from social contrasts. This opposition is also based on principles; . . . just as reaction represents the feudal principle, constitutional opposition represents the civil principle. In a clear cut civil constitution—just as in a democratic one—there is no opposition. The function of the opposition is to fight by constitutional means the still existing feudal elements inimical to the constitution. . . .

If the nobility were to oppose the civil elements in society, civil war would follow. Civil war is not a war between citizens but a war against the class which is in power by a social class excluded from and suppressed by power. . . . To avoid civil war, or at least to postpone it until victory seems certain, the nobility has to identify itself with the monarchy and let the crown lead the attack against civil rights. An increase in the power of the crown will increase the chances of success. The first necessary task of all reactionary movements, therefore, is the removal of monarchy from the control of popular representatives. If the crown stands above the constitution, the status society will re-emerge from the ruins of a civil society.

The battle begins when the crown takes sides in the struggle among the various elements of society. As soon as this happens, the constitution is threatened, because it cannot tolerate any power besides its own. The survival of civil society is inextricably linked with the preservation of the constitution, which is a reflection of the social order. As soon as the constitution is attacked, the struggle can only be determined by the force of arms. Any reactionary movement, as soon as it has won over the crown to its side, necessarily leads to an open revolution.

This was the case when Louis XVIII ascended the throne. As a brother of Louis XVI and a man of the 18th century, he nursed a deep aversion against the new society, and still more against the principles on which it was based. The goal of his aspirations was the revival of the old feudal monarchy. But he was also well aware of the fact that only at the price of restoring the old royal power would the Holy Alliance keep him on the throne. His inclination, as well as his life's history, put him altogether on the side of the reaction. But at the same time, he was a shrewd politician. He knew his people better than did either of his brothers; even though he hoped that the reactionary system would finally be victorious, there was nothing he feared more than the sudden outbreak of an open hostility. This was the spirit of the reaction under the first Bourbon of the restoration. Louis XVIII convoked the famous "*Chambre introuvable*" which, in a true reactionary spirit, immediately made a heavy attack upon civil rights, suppressed the press, encroached upon individual liberty, and even suggested the revision of not less than 13 articles of the Charter of 1814. Doubtlessly this revision would have re-instituted royal sovereignty by suppressing the rights of the Assembly; the Constitution would have been annihilated, and France would have been driven to the brink of a second revolution. Louis XVIII did not permit this to happen. To the great distress of the royalists, he dissolved the Chamber on Feb. 5, 1817 and issued a new election law announcing the new elections to be held according to the regulations of the Charter. This step gave at least a certain latitude to the civil society. But opposition, though weak, continued. Ruthless intervention of the police was in vain; having only a repressive function, it was able to crush a revolt but could not interfere with the principle and the various group activities of society. Other less obvious means of coercion were applied. On the basis of the assumption that the moneyed class was the natural ally of the feudal elements, money was given a broader representation. (June 1820) . . . But the opposition was by no means broken; on the contrary, it grew from day to day in numbers and strength. The rise of the Carbonari indicated that the suppressed class of society was preparing an attack against the forces of reaction; the constitutional means of the government to interfere were almost exhausted. Louis XVIII, who due to his intelligence had avoided extreme measures, began to view the future with pessimism. Before he died at the Tuileries in 1824, he put his hand on the head of the young Duke of Bordeau and said prophetically: "May my brother manage the crown of this child." His apprehensions were altogether justified.

Charles X came to the throne at a time when all Europe was certain of the final victory of reaction. France alone still had a citizen-state. Charles X considered it his task to subject France again to the ancient law. Proud and firmly convinced of his principles, he made no secret of his conviction. All the elements of the new society saw in him the enemy of the new social order and the principles of this order. Sensing that such a contradictory situation could not endure, they prepared for a showdown by organizing all elements opposed to a status society. The King, on his part, decided to use power in order to strengthen his position. The Constitution itself offered him an opportunity for that.

We mentioned that every civil society leaves one point in the constitution necessarily open to interpretation. This happens as a result of the conflict of the two main constitutional principles, according to which the king is subject to the constitution and yet the institution of monarchy is preserved. This lack of clarity is reflected in the various constitutions in various ways. The Charter of 1814 contained, in a final statement in Article 14, the following passage: "The king issues the necessary regulations and edicts for the execution of laws and the safety of the state." This was an area where royal power could exercise supreme power without the participation of the representatives of the people. According to the nature of things, the king could enforce certain measures independent of the legislative body; but where were the limits of his authority? The limits of his authority could not be imposed by the deputies. It was up to the king to decide what he dared and what he did not dare to do.

King Charles was convinced that he could not increase his power by traditional constitutional means. On the basis of Article 14, he ventured openly to challenge the Constitution. On July 25th, 1830, he issued three executive orders cancelling freedom of the press, dissolving the chambers, and publishing a new election law. This act has been interpreted in a variety of ways. There is no doubt, however, that it is ultimately based on the Constitution and that its consequences correspond to the nature of civil society. By acknowledging the personal power of the king, the civil Constitution authorized him to act independently. However, by making the king solely the executor of laws dependent in any of his actions upon the approval of his secretaries, the Constitution deprived him of this personal element of independence. By asking the king to stand above the parties of society to control their competitive activities and to prohibit excesses, it put him above the popular representatives as the . . . independent element of the community at large. However, by legally acknowledging that the king was allowed only to execute the will of the majority, the Constitution made the king into a tool of those groups in society which could win a parliamentary majority. By laying down the principle that kingship is inviolable and the source of all state power, the Constitution deprived the popular representatives of the right to avenge the misuses of power; . . . by requiring the king to confirm the Constitution by oath and accept it as an expression of the rights of the people, the Constitution gained an inviolability of its own which coincided with the inviolability of the king. . . . This cornerstone of the Constitution was poorly and imprecisely formulated and contained a grave contradiction. . . . No ingenuity was capable of solving it and giving it non-contradictory legal interpretation. We have to admit without reservation that the Constitution contained this contradiction. . . . But we claim that it was not a unique case and that every constitution contains such contradiction, because it is the contradiction between the general will and the individual personality. It is impossible to draw up a constitution without such a contradiction; . . . constitutional monarchy is only a specific form of the contrast between the state and society; whether it is a workable form depends on the willingness of both elements to accept the nature and the value of each other . . . in order to preserve the living unity of the state. The strength of a constitution rests on this awareness and not on the legal framework. The dangers of the constitutional state also arise from this. . . . Wherever one of the elements attempts to overpower the other, the contradiction becomes visible and a revolution results, the struggle of society against the opposing state power.

The executive orders did not go beyond the limits to which the King and the Chambers had agreed upon in the beginning of the Restoration. Freedom of the press had been frequently restricted. The election laws had been changed several times. It was not the content of the decrees which sparked the revolt but the fact that the decrees represented the first instance in which the King legislated without the consent of the Chambers. The evidence that the King considered absolute state power as his prerogative and the control of civil society as his task was the occasion for the uprising. French public life was characterized by the juxtaposition of state and society; the decrees tried to destroy one element by the other. Therefore, these decrees represented not only a violation of the Constitution but a declaration of war against the accepted public law.

But they represented more than this. The monarchy of Charles X represented the hopes and claims of the old feudal society. Though subjected to the civil society by the Constitution, the nobility had found in the monarchy the necessary power which could re-establish their former rights by means of state intervention. The decrees assuming the right of the king to represent public law without due regard to the Chamber were a declaration of war against civil society; they were the last desperate attempt of the feudal system to regain power. After they had been enacted a final decision was imminent.

The decrees were published; Paris took to arms; all the various elements of the free society joined forces under the attack, and after three days the revolution was completed. The King was dethroned, the people had been victorious. Feudal society had met its final defeat in France.

At the basis of the social movement from 1788 to the end of the July Revolution we have found one great contrast and one powerful driving force: the opposition of the old feudal society based on privileges of birth to the new acquisitive society which led to the final victory of the latter. This antagonism was now dissolved. The new society had overcome, step by step, first the feudal estates, then feudal rights and the feudal distribution of landed property, then the contradition of absolute equality, the attack of feudal Europe, the dissolution of the state in France and the despotism of Napoleon, and finally the last attempts of feudal restoration and even the monarchy itself. . . . The new society had won a complete victory; universal citizenship was a result of a forty-year movement, and civil society ruled supreme and unhampered by opposition over the nation and the state. Will this be the terminal point for several generations at least? If this is not the cases, . . . why is it that civil society and the Constitution are also finally not satisfactory? Does it contain in itself, just like feudal society, deep and unsolved contradictions? And if this contradiction is as powerful as that of feudal society, and civil society is yet capable of progressing toward freedom, is it possible that freedom perhaps is in contradiction to state and society? On what is the contradiction within the fully developed civil society based, and where does its solution lie?

Here a new series of problems faces us. Concealed up to now by the effort to establish itself and by the struggle against the common enemy, the elements of the new society have now in their unchallenged position full freedom to develop their own antagonism and inner struggles. . . . With the July Revolution, history of the old order is completely and finally closed; with the history of the July Monarchy, contemporary history begins.

Part Two

Industrial Society, Socialism and Communism in France 1830-1848

THE CHARACTER OF THE NEW ERA

The July Revolution was the beginning of a completely new era. For a long time, it was commonly believed that political developments were the main characteristics of this era. Its connection with the first Revolution was sought primarily in the constitutional questions and the struggle arising over them, the antagonism between monarchy and republic. . . . But the July Monarchy is merely a framework in which a completely different picture of much greater importance presents itself. . . . The period of the July Monarchy is a new chapter in the fierce antagonism between society and the state. Here, too, without doubt, the changes in society are the more important ones; all political events are subordinate to them. . . .

The July Revolution was not directed against one particular point of the Constitution, even less so against any specific decree. Resistance was directed against the attempt to re-establish the elements of feudal society by means of state authority. This attempt was doomed to failure; it miscarried. With the victory of the people, feudalism, to the extent that it had survived the first revolution, was banished from France forever. What was the nature of the social order which became dominant after this victory? . . . Its foundation had long been laid, and the history of the first Revolution shows distinctly enough the nature of its principles and its order. It is the acquisitive society, the society of free enterprise. The legal principle of this society is the premise that the right and the qualification of each individual are equal to those of any other individual. There are no differences of personality and no restrictions by any one on any other, no subordination without free consent. Associations among individuals in civil life—to the extent that they are not comprised and formed by the state and its order—are based on free contract only. No contract should be powerful enough to bind the free will of free men forever; since external conditions give rise to contracts, an interminable contract would forever subjugate men and their free development to external circumstances. There is a socially conditioned law even in this society; but as a consequence of freedom and equality, the individual has free choice whether or not to accept them in each individual case. This legal equality is also central to constitutional law. According to the principle of this society, nobody is excluded from the highest state positions; there is no difference of birth, no nobility and no third estate; citizenship is the common attribute of all members of society. Thus, the highest principle of the Revolution, equality, has been realized here by the very nature of society.

While equality was the accepted principle in law, freedom was the principle of the new society in economic life. There are no more privileges of acquisition, no monopolies, no special rights. Any economic activity is open to everybody and may possibly lead to the ownership of property. Hence, everybody has to rely upon himself and his abilities. The personality is principally accepted as the source of individual development. . . . Individual liberty prevails in the economic sphere as long as the rights of others are not encroached upon.

From these two principles emerges the third one, the real order of society. Since the law recognizes only equality, inequality, as the prerequisite of all organization, must grow out of the economic order. It is acquisition, therefore, which coordinates and subordinates the legally independent and personally free individuals. This demonstrates the great importance of the economy. It extends the necessary order of economics to men themselves. The organism of production becomes the organism of individuals, and subordination, indispensable to mankind, nevertheless preserves freedom because it is the outcome of a contract between free individuals. According to the same principle, the ultimate position of individuals in this social order is dependent upon acquired property. On the surface, it seems that, in accordance with the inner principle of the acquisitive society, the highest possible standards have been established for justice, acquisition and society. The goals for which the first revolution had striven in vain at the cost of tremendous intellectual and material efforts thus seemed to have been realized after all. . . .

The social order of the acquisitive society developed slowly out of the aspirations of the people. This social order represented the fulfillment of the basic idea of the first great movement which had begun to crystallize under Napoleon. The people could be expected to accept the new social order with great confidence; what they had aspired to for so long seemed finally realized, legally secured and firmly installed. A final settlement of the long and violent movement appeared within reach.

And yet—what were the consequences of that revolution? Neither peace, nor quiescence nor satisfaction with the very social order which had grown out of liberty and equality. The July Revolution was but a signal for a series of new bitter battles, followed by a condition of permanent war.

How was that possible, and what was the character of these new movements?

Most people . . . have interpreted these struggles as nothing but a war between the parties about the constitution, particularly a struggle of republicanism against the monarchy. But few will dare to deny that the real basis of these movements was social rather than political. The following analysis proceeds from this point of view.

Every constitution is a reflection of the social order. If not only individuals but whole classes rise against a social order, such a social order must contain within itself an unresolved antagonism. The constitution must, in such a case, provide the state with authority to suppress this antagonism. According to the law of social movements, the ruling class must have taken possession of the state and therewith transformed social dependence inherent in every society to political dependence also; the lower, subjected class, unable to call upon the assistance of the state by constitutional means, has to resort to arms in order to seize the power of government. . . . Wherever there is an attempt at a revolution, social antagonism and the subjugation of the state to the interests of the ruling class unquestionably prevail again. . . . If, in spite of the great social victory of the July Revolution, one revolt followed another, if . . . the country continued to be in a ferment, if the best informed and most unbiased leader of the nation declared openly that France was living on a volcano and that its future would be stormy and perhaps tragic, . . . it was evident that an unresolved contradiction was clearly imbedded in its social order. . . Instead of the destroyed feudal dependence, it now contained the germ of another social dependence, instead of the rule of the privileged estates, another domination, no less rigorous, no less contradictory to the development of the highest personal aspirations. . . . The society which inevitably produced these contradictions and struggles was the social order based on free acquisition, the society of free enterprise. Was it by chance that this society followed upon the feudal society, and was this an accidental sequence? No. . . . According to the nature of things a market-oriented society will always grow out of a social order based on estates. . . . People who strive to rise from their assigned position in society to social liberty will always be caught in these contradictions.

The free enterprise system, which was established in France through the July Revolution and which was the natural sequel of feudal society, is the freest conceivable form of society. . . Neither the human mind nor the history of mankind has so far discovered a superior form of free society. If it nevertheless results in dependency, if a subjected and a ruling class immediately emerge, if the latter again succeeds in usurping the state, excluding the former from power, is, then, a really free society and a really independent state conceivable? The social revolution of 1848, which marks the end of the epoch beginning with the political revolution of 1830, has not provided an answer to this question. The society of free acquisition has not only survived that revolution; there is no doubt that it will continue to last for a long time to come. No other configuration of society which guarantees social peace is so far discernible. But if the acquisitive society is the basic type for present and future societies, and if it necessarily leads to dependence and conflict, what can be done to avoid this struggle? . . .

This is the question of the present and of the near future, and here and nowhere else can we discover the root of future danger. Here we encounter the first as yet negative version of the problem of the social question. Here begins an altogether new movement in society never before encountered in history, a movement which permeates more and more thoroughly all conditions, all principles and convictions. The historical picture which the eighteen years since the July Revolution present is more profound and richer in powerful, intellectual, though futile, effort to solve the question than that of the first Revolution. In the latter, men had attempted to force the state into recognition of an established order. They now wanted to resolve an existing contradiction which had grown unbearable, and yet neither the facts nor the principle of this contradiction were as yet understood. In the hothouse atmosphere which had settled over Europe, the competitive society has been pushing the elements of its order with great energy toward full development; however, step by step, the inherent contradiction followed. The antagonism against the new society appears in a great variety of forms and carries on its attacks in the most diverse ways; society fights back with the sword as well as theory, scorn as well as contempt. But the antagonism emerges always anew, ready to erupt. It becomes progressively clear that true social peace is unthinkable without a solution of these contradictions; but as yet, even the wisest do not know where a solution may be found. The antagonism finally crystallizes. Society is split into two great camps, the interpretation of social relations reflected in two opposing social theories, and social history in two power movements which are mutually exclusive and ready to engage in an open struggle. The great, universally important, historical significance of the July Revolution is that it represents the turning point in this development. It was of much greater importance for society than for the state; without its social implications this Revolution cannot be fully understood.

The July Revolution definitely established industrial society by destroying the last remnants of feudal society. Inasmuch as the industrial society had to emerge from the first Revolution, gaining more power from day to day since 1795, under Napoleon as well as during the Restoration, the July Revolution spells the end of the first Revolution. And inasmuch as it belongs to the historical era which began around the middle of the 18th century, when the first theories of liberty and equality were formulated, it represents the terminal point of that era. However, by putting into effect . . . the social order of free acquisition, the July Revolution represents at the same time the turning point at which the inherent contradiction of this society evolves. It is at this very moment that the question is raised whether the idea of liberty for which mankind had struggled during the last century has become a reality. The July Revolution is, therefore, also the starting point of the actual social movement.

This is how we see the history of the main events of social life during the subsequent eighteen years. We are not suggesting that there is to be found a solution to the problems in the events of this period. The true significance of the era of the July Monarchy is the natural growth of the antagonism, inherent in the acquisitive society, between the two classes of this society, in practical life, in theory, and in the process of organizing for militant action. All struggles for cabinet posts, all revolts, intrigues and political convulsions of this period dwindle to nothingness in comparison with this development, which alone is the key factor of that time. Nothing that otherwise happened has had any lasting importance except to the extent that it is related to this development. . . .

What was only vaguely indicated and ill understood during the first Revolution by the communism of the "Republic of Virtue" now develops into comprehensive systems; what formerly presented the truth only for a desperate thinker is now elevated to the creed of a whole class of society. What formerly was executed by power and force now attempts to gain victory as a scientific system. . . . After the proclaimed social revolution actually took place in 1848, nobody can seriously doubt any longer that the French developments up to that date were essentially social movements. . . .

Part Two, Chapter One

Industrial Society, its Domination and its Contradiction

INDUSTRIAL SOCIETY AND THE RULE OF CAPITAL OWNERSHIP

. . . The society of free acquisition has prevailed in France since 1830. If there exists a contradiction and a struggle which affects the whole population as well as the country, . . . it must be due to the inner nature of this society. Only from this vantage point can the history of the July Monarchy be understood. Since a specific form of society comes to predominate with the July Revolution, the whole series of movements following it are nothing but movements of the constituent elements in this society. . . . In which way does the society of free acquisition develop an inner contradiction, and what are its effects on state and society? . . . We have shown in the section on the theory of social movement that any human community develops into a social order of men and their activities. It is supported by laws and family relationships, and it is thus that the ruling class and the dependent class come into being. The emergence of classes leads to social dependence which contradicts the essence of personality; social dependence is aggravated by the rise of estates. Therefore, any social order contains this germ of social dependence; the revolt against a social order is always a revolt against this social dependence. . . .

The concept of the acquisitive society does not yet contain a concept of class, even less one of estate. In the society of free acquisition, the acquisitive personality is the organism of acquisition. If opposition, movement and struggle are to develop, a ruling class has to emerge first within this order. And since this ruling class has to grow out of that order, one element of free acquisition has to develop within and through the ruling class, as a basis of its rule which makes it superior to the other classes of society. . . . What is the nature of this element, growing out of free enterprise economy, which is destined to rule? . . . In what manner does the urge for liberty in the dependent class manifest itself? In brief, what is the shape of a society which grows out of the economic order of the entrepreneurs, and how does the ruling class of such a society exert its power? . . . If it is property which determines the final shape of society, the inevitable laws of distribution of wealth by free acquisition will also determine the shape of society in an acquisitive economy. . . .

The more highly developed form of economy begins when . . . the production of goods goes beyond the individual needs of the owner of material and of the laborer and is geared toward the satisfaction of needs of others. The use of material and labor thereby changes in character. The well known and usually fixed . . . personal needs are replaced by calculations of human needs in general, . . . and production . . . is geared by the entrepreneur for this purpose. . . . Those who have the ability to run an enterprise hold a position different from those of the two traditional classes of laborers and owners; their acquisitions are not due exclusively to the possession of material and not limited by the amount of physical labor power. They are the ones who have the best chance to become owners through personal effort.

Entrepreneurial activity first breaks down the rigid barrier between owners and non-owners. It therefore becomes the source of material independence, and thereby leads to a new era in the life of nations. . . . As soon as industry begins to grow, the value of things takes on a different character. Industry satisfies needs, but also produces them. Before industrial goods, for which a need has been created, can be bought, other things have to become marketable commodities. The extent to which things or skills are marketable constitutes the measure of their value. This value is expressed in money. Because of the impact of industry and the commerce related to it, everybody has to assess the monetary value of his property. Although money existed before industry and always exerted a certain influence, with the industrial age it becomes the conditioning factor of the whole industrial economy. . . . But money—although the element of industrial growth— is not available to all. It is always in possession of individual owners. . . . The accumulated quantities of money, indispensable for the entrepreneur, are called cash capital; to provide capital for industries is the function of a special type of enterprise, the bank. To the extent that industry grows, enterprises become more dependent upon capital. . . . Since the manipulation of capital becomes an enterprise of its own, the efforts of entrepreneurial ability without capital are handicapped; even though the establishment of new enterprises is not restricted, capital is not always available. This indicates the basic relationship which affects industrial growth: capital rules over industry to an increasing degree, and the available amount of capital determines the condition of industry, its existence and its profit.

The essential element which stands out in market society and in its acquisitive efforts, and which determines the processes of acquisition, is capital. Two factors signalize the beginning of its rule: the appearance of bank business in support of industrial enterprise . . . and the appearance of capital in industrial enterprises proper. . . . As a consequence of this development, the market economy slowly loses its essential characteristics. Market economy changes from an economy based on common striving for acquisition by efforts and hopes, and becomes a representation of the powerful ruling element, which are capital and the owners of capital; . . . entrepreneurial activity and labor become subjugated to capital and have no hope of regaining independence. This schism, the new version of the ever recurring separation of owners and non-owners, of material and labor, of ruler and dependent, characterizes and determines—if fully developed—the industrial society. The essential characteristic of the industrial society slowly but necessarily emerging from the market society is the rule of capital ownership over the whole economic life and all economic processes. . . .

We now have to consider the movement which evolves within society through the rise of the rule of capital. Its origin may be traced to labor but by constituting itself independently and making labor in its various forms dependent upon it, it develops a peculiar opposition to labor as well as to acquisition through labor, an opposition of which one has to be aware in order to understand the profound antagonism which extends through industrial society. . . . Capital, once gained, provides a secure existence and a superior social position even without work; it is the source of unearned income similar to landed property of feudal times. It is, therefore, the main factor, the first condition of worldly enjoyments and personal development. It provides security of existence, of enterprise and of future prosperity.

Through these elements capital has a twofold effect in any society in which it comes to predominate. In the first place, it disparages practical activity in the eyes of those who strive for possessions; labor, being dependent on capital, appears to be the occupation of dependents, and laborers appear to be inferior to capital owners. . . . During the period of transition from the market to the industrial society, while the role of capital increases in importance, the most efficient and aggressive entrepreneurs, who do not as yet own sufficient capital, try to gain profits for the amortization of investments; they search for new markets, . . . new combinations of various kinds, new inventions and cost saving devices, they struggle against obstacles, take risks, experiment and expand the frontiers of industry and commerce. This is the youthful period of industrial society. An industrial middle class constitutes itself, strives for, and usually succeeds in gaining capital ownership by entrepreneurial activity. This class differs from the middle class of farmers and the petty bourgeoisie, whose property and acquisitive powers are rather limited. With the growing importance of large investments, this traditional sector of the middle class becomes crushed and finally also dependent upon the industrialists. This marks the end of the first period of industrial society. Powerful firms grow up with whom it is impossible to compete. . . . The frequent occurrence of bankruptcy is an important symptom of social development; enterprises without capital easily fail in competition with big enterprise. This trend indicates that enterprises can no longer acquire capital ownership without taking extreme risk. . . . This is a symptom of the transition to industrial society.

Later, capital exerts its influence on the life of the individual. Since the administration of acquired capital rarely inspires the superior and noble qualities in men, it does not provoke higher moral and intellectual interests. The income is used for the satisfaction of a lower category of wants. . . . Ostentatious display of possessions, consideration of usefulness and the lack of good taste begin to prevail; enjoyment is valued according to its price, and artistic performances by money earning power. Abilities are assessed . . . according to their acquisitive capacity; and professional performance is appreciated to the extent that it serves the money-earning interests. All of human activity,' human capacity, even human hopes and dreams become concentrated on money-making; money-making comes to absorb the superior vigour, the most noble personalities and the most generous impulses. The most powerful human interests become subordinate to money interests. Unearned money income becomes the goal of life, and all other challenges to men become secondary in importance. . . . The power of capital directs affection, love, and social life; it ties the bonds of the young and dissolves the friendships of the old people; it becomes the general element of all spiritual and material movements. . . . The condition of culture where money exerts social power, where its enjoyment presents the peak of satisfaction, where the acceptance of its importance has come close to a veneration of money, and where the striving for possessions has made everything purchasable, is called materialism. Materialism is not to be confused with respect for labor, or with a striving for acquisition, or with the enjoyment of material goods or with a lack of higher ambitions; the savage primitive man, the uncultured, or the busybodies are not materialists. Materialism is a definite state of the human mind in society and is directly tied to the rule of money. . . . Materialism is a consequence of the rule of capital, and as such a natural and necessary stage of development of the market society; it must be considered among the cultural changes which are independent of national characteristics. . . .

The second trend is more easily comprehensible. . . . Since all enterprises and investments can continue to exist only by producing at the lowest possible price, a new series of symptoms develops. . . . In order to be able to maintain a low level of prices, the enterprises have to turn against labor—all the more so if the prices of raw materials increase through growing competition. The unemployed will be subjugated by the entrepreneur, and consequently, labor, which has already declined in prestige in comparison to capital, will be exploited. . . . A system of production develops in which the laboring class is forced to accept the lowest possible wage. Exploitation of labor by capital, the material dependence of the laborer in addition to his social dependence, prevail, and even profits tend to decline to the wage level. It is unreasonable and perhaps even malicious to blame individuals for these consequences of the social system. These consequences are unavoidable in the process of growth. But it is equally unwise and dangerous to overlook or to underestimate the misery and the danger of such conditions. These conditions represent a contradiction to the most natural urge of free human beings to become independent through work. . . . People who are willing to bear this contradiction unconditionally are not equipped for a higher cultural life, because here freedom in its most tangible form—work and acquisition through work— is destroyed. The period which follows will illustrate what happens if this contradiction leads to an explosion.

In this fashion, capital becomes the ruling power in what is called industrial society. . . . In this kind of society there are two large classes, one consisting of those who own capital or are able to acquire it, . . . and the other of those who are unable ever to acquire it in the natural course of events.

. . . Another important problem for the people who have entered this era of social development is the problem of their relationship to state power.

THE RELATIONSHIP OF INDUSTRIAL SOCIETY TO THE STATE

Constitutionalism

As long as the elements and the nature of the social order are unknown, the existence and security of the state will usually be sought . . . in the proper relationship of the various organs of the state. Since Montesquieu this relationship has been known as the balance of state powers . . . The Restoration in France and the development in Germany, however, have shown that the external balance of powers is unable to protect either itself or the political liberty of the individual. There is another factor which is of decisive importance here: the rule of the upper social class over the state. Capital and capital-owners rule in industrial society. What is the most general principle of the state which this society has to strive to realize, and what are the means of realizing it?

The industrial society, just like the society of free acquisition, is based on the principle of equality before the law and on freedom of enterprise; its order, however, is dictated by ownership resulting from acquisitions. The emerging ruling class must subject the state, but in order not to contradict itself, it has to build its rule on elements corresponding to the social order.

The principle of equality as applied to the state is essentially negative: no privileges are to be granted and guaranteed by the state; authority is based on the free consent of the parties; administration of the law does not tolerate any legal differences. The principle of freedom of enterprise and acquisition presupposes the independent administration of the private as well as of the public budget. The principle of prevalence of private property makes property ownership the determining conditions, not only for realizing a superior social status, but also for the exercise of political rights. The general principle of the acquisitive industrial society in its relationship to the state is, therefore, the principle of self-government, interpreted particularly as the control of the state budget. . . . The constitution and the administration of the state according to this principle are based on two major rules: parliamentary representation based on property qualifications and the right to control taxation. These general principles suffice as long as the acquisitive society has not yet developed a ruling class; practical politics then circulates narrowly around the relationship between parliamentary representatives and the main organs of the government. . . . Since the acquisitive society is as yet without a ruling class, and since its members live under conditions of equality, the organs of the self-governing administration are free of the element which directly strives for control of the state. . . . As long as the acquisitive society persists and the rule of capital has not yet developed, the activities of parliamentary representatives are limited to participation in public administration through tax control, while the more important decisions of the state may be made by individual members of the legislature but never by that body as a unit. . . . During this period the government still controls the positive power of the state to the exclusion of all others; society merely determines the limits of its actions. But as soon as the ruling class of capitalists appears, it inevitably attempts to seize the actual power of government regardless of the specific form of that government, whether it is a republic, an aristocracy, or a monarchy. Since this class is the product of the acquisitive society, its method of governing always utilizes the same basic instruments. . . . The nature of the capitalist class is such that it always usurps the power of the state by means of the two basic instruments of power: parliamentary representation and tax control. . . . Without destroying the state, it subjugates each of its organs. This is an inevitable consequence of the development of any nation after free acquisition has been acccepted as the basis of the social order. . . . The resulting form of the state is known as constitutionalism. . . .

Mere parliamentary representation is of minor importance in the formulation of the concept and the description of the essential features of constitutionalism. . . . Any attempt, however, to check the growth of constitutionalism is in vain, once the acquisitive society has changed to an industrial society; however, the latter usually develops slowly, because the social order of free acquisition cannot grow without the accumulation of large amounts of capital. Constitutionalism necessarily becomes the form of the state, because large capital is a necessary element in industrial growth. . . .

Even though the July Revolution resulted in a complete revolution of the state, we observe the apparently striking circumstance that there was almost no change in the existing legislation. . . . Until the July Revolution, French society had been essentially an acquisitive market society. Only the July Revolution, by establishing the domination of industrial society through the final destruction of the feudal monarchy, compelled society, as it were, to produce a ruling class. This could only be the capital-owning class. By sudden change the July Revolution created the industrial society out of the acquisitive society; this is its true social significance. By taking over the government, the ruling class could not essentially change the established rights of the Charter; only the spirit of the constitution and the administration could be reformed, and came to bear the impress of the rule of capital over the state. Such is the character of public life in France since the July Revolution. This period is the period of constitutionalism in its most clear-cut form, with all of its strengths and all of its dangers. One question remains: How did the new ruling class of society take possession of the state through popular representation? Constitutionalism established itself on the basis of the new position of the Chambers and through the new principle of monarchy.

Constitutional Parliament and its Position within the State

The first practical application of the rule of capital over the organs of the state consists in the formation of the institutions by which society controls the state; this is the Chamber of Deputies. The relevant laws acquire a specific character under constitutionalism which had already been suggested but not fully developed in the acquisitive society of the preceding period. Now the upper class is no longer based on potential but on accomplished acquisitions, which become the prerequisite for actual participation in politics. . . . Only direct taxes paid indicate capital ownership, and that is now what matters. This social order, therefore, imposes property qualifications on the basis of the amount of direct taxes paid; the minimum amount of paid tax required for voting is not set as high as under pseudo-constitutionalism, because the whole property-owning class is supposed to be represented; neither is it put very low, because only true ownership—wealth proper—and not the aspiration to acquire wealth is to be represented. Furthermore, a direct vote is stipulated in order to insure a clear representation of the interests of property and to exclude personal interests and influences. . . . In addition, voting is carried out under the supervision of the voters themselves in order to avoid the influence of any other element. These are the principles of industrial society; the clearest expression of these principles is the April 19th, 1831 election law of the July monarchy. Since the propertied class is supposed to rule, the upper chamber is either eliminated or becomes subordinate to the lower chamber; this is achieved by the abolition of hereditary membership in the former. The upper chamber acquires an intermediate role between that of a status and that of an administrative institution and is prevented from ever gaining political significance, because it does not represent a specific status element of society, nor does it have an administrative function. The acquisitive society leaves the upper chamber untouched only to protect the monarchy as an institution which it needs; . . . but the upper chamber, as well as the king, are made powerless against the will of the lower chamber. This has been for eighteen years the position of the Chamber of Peers in France; it disappeared without leaving a trace when the Revolution broke out; it was not even worth the effort to dispose of this burden of constitutionalism by special action.

These are the principles by which the ruling class of industrial society takes over state power. Among these, property qualifications are the most important ones. . . . The ruling class acquires control over state administration through the rigid application of two principles which characterize true constitutionalism: majority rule and ministerial responsibility. Popular opinion considers majority rule as decisive, because it is the only method of reaching a common agreement. But this interpretation with reference to life in society is inadequate and unconvincing. It suggests that majority rule implies a rightful decision, through actually in industrial society it reflects the rule of a specific power—in fact, the only power. Property qualifications based on tax contributions reflect the interests of property ownership and of acquisitiveness. The legislative chamber is, therefore, above all a representative of the interests of society. Its power is based on this and on nothing else. The majority of the Chamber, although it represents arithmetically the majority of individual votes, must be seen as the majority of the general interests. Interests rule in an industrial society, the majority of which can be discerned by the majority vote. The majority rules unconditionally, because it is the manifestation of the rule of the upper class in society. In no other state order, nor in any other constitution, is majority vote accepted so unconditionally; . . . nowhere is it applied as concisely as in a social order where the ruling majority is identical with the majority of interests instead of the majority of convictions. . . .

Majority rule determines the form and the content of constitutional responsibility. . . . The ruling class not only insists on the inviolability of the constitution; it demands that the whole administrative process be carried out in the spirit of the prevailing majority. . . . Since interests dominate the chamber, harmony between the government and the majority is secured only if the principle of administration requires state action in favor of the interests of the ruling class; the majority of the chamber, being identical with the majority of interests, know best what these interests are; therefore, the administration is expected not to pursue any objective other than those in harmony with the predominating interests. Only if the majority finds itself fully represented in the administration is the system of constitutionalism complete. . . .

Since the majority represents the ruling class of society, it is part of all true constitutionalism that the ministers have to resign as soon as differences develop between them and the majority. A different group of ministers acceptable to the majority takes over the administration. Since they are appointed with the understanding that they are to act in the spirit of the majority, the very nature of their positions and their right to these positions would be invalidated if they were to remain in office against the wishes of the majority. Opinions may differ regarding the value of majority rule. But genuine constitutionalism requires that ministerial power abdicate if it is opposed to the majority. To remain in office against the will of the majority is unconstitutional, even though a violation of the letter of the law has been avoided. Wherever this happens, it would mean not only—as is often stated— that the principle of parliamentarism is violated, but also that class rule, as represented by the majority in the chamber, is destroyed and with it the law according to which the social order rules the state. . . . Constitutional responsibility is a system of administration in harmony with the majority; . . . this is the principle of true constitutionalism as distinct from pseudo-constitutionalism. This principle alone ties the constitution to the administration by constitutional means.

This system cannot be enacted by legislation; it has to be established through the all-pervading power of the ruling class. This class had been victorious in the July Revolution; therefore, no specific laws were necessary to establish its rule. The ministers depended on it. This answers the question of how this revolution, in spite of the fact that it produced only negligible changes in public law, nevertheless produced a completely different type of state from the one which had preceded it.

Constitutional Monarchy

. . . During the July Revolution we saw a dynasty swept away, the masses of the people persecuting the royal family in blind fury, hurling curses and imprecations at them, and yet, incredible as this may seem, only a few days later by common consent putting another prince of the same line on the same throne. How was that possible after such a revolution? The king had been the representative and pillar of pseudo-constitutionalism, and yet another king was put on the throne which had just been overturned. . . . What, then, has become of this monarchy, formerly the pinnacle of feudal society, in the period of free acquisition? What is it in true constitutionalism? . . .

It has been shown that interests are the moving force anywhere in industrial society; furthermore, it has been shown how interests get in conflict with the idea of universal freedom and individual development because some individuals have to be subordinated to others. The state is the personal representative of the idea of freedom; but it is in constant danger of being subjugated to the ruling class of society and of becoming serviceable to its interest rather than to freedom. If the state loses its independence and its supreme position, a state of dependence is established, because one class rules absolutely. . . . Wherever this happens liberty can be acquired only by way of a ·political or social revolution. . . . To avoid this extreme in the life of human community, the idea of the state has to be personified by an institution which stands above all interests and is the manifestation of the pure personality of the state. . . . The classes of society should be unable to get control of it; it should have no interests of its own; the struggle of society with the government should be of no concern to it. Such an institution represents the principle of the state, the idea of freedom; the state has what no constitution can give it, a representative who can withstand social conflicts and thus be able to overcome the principle of dependency embedded in society. This institution is hereditary monarchy. . . .

The thought motivating the ruling class was the following: If we remain without a king the aroused masses will continue against us the struggle now directed against the king; either we are victorious and through our victory make an irreconcilable enemy, or we are defeated and have to live under a terrible tyranny. Only monarchy can build the bridge between us and the other class of society. It is the only form of escape from the attack of the non-owners against the owners. The July Monarchy was the result of these considerations. . . .

However, with the inauguration of the July Monarchy—representing what Benjamin Constant calls the "neutral power"—only one aspect of its role was determined. Soon a new form of relationship developed between the king and the majority group which led to the emergence of "constitutional monarchy", a new type of monarchical rule. . . . Since the ruling class tends to usurp the state, it demands that the king, to the extent that he represents the state, forego any independence. The king has to submit unconditionally to the majority of the Chamber. . . . Constitutional monarchy does not grant freedom of action or decision-making power to the king personally other than in conformity with the wishes of the majority.

One may ask what would follow if the king refuses to submit to the requirements of the constitution, if he wants to remain independent. How is it possible to create a monarchy which is reconciled to constitutionalism at all? If the right to the throne is a supreme right and beyond the control of society, the monarch cannot legitimately lose his throne even in the most bitter battle waged against the latter. This right, therefore, sets him in absolute opposition to the social order. Society can succeed in maintaining its natural domination only by destroying the legitimate claim to the throne and by expelling the dynasty in power. This is the reason why all revolutions at the time of the rise of the acquisitive society result in a change of dynasty. The subsequent dynasty will be put on the throne only by and with the consent of the ruling class. . . . The act of enthronement . . . will always show that the royal prerogative depends on the consent of the ruling class. Through a new prince, a new type of monarchy is established which cannot aim to be anything but constitutional. As a rule, constitional monarchy can be created only by a change in dynasty. Such was the case in England, in Belgium and in Norway. . . .

The July Revolution, by establishing the rule of the acquisitive society, had subjugated the state to the ruling class of this society and to its interests. It had replaced pseudo-constitutionalism by true constitutionalism and sealed this change by the change of dynasty. This is the deeper meaning of the statement by Louis Philippe: "From now on the Charter represents the truth". . . . In this spirit the new prince accepted the crown; in this spirit it was given to him by society, and in this spirit the July Revolution marked the beginning of a new life in the state of France and in French society.

The July Revolution is an important European event, which marked the beginning of the victory of industrial society over the monarchy and other remnants of the feudal society on the continent. A new era begins, which is nowhere developed more clearly and consistently than in France. . . .

THE DEPENDENT CLASS IN INDUSTRIAL SOCIETY

The Origin of the Antagonism

. . . Capital is not only an external factor. It is property, but also, as a result of individual activity, the essence of real personal freedom as well as the necessary prerequisite of freedom. Property plays this role in every form of society, because this is its very nature. It is only the type of property which varies with the different social orders. The form of property in control of industrial society is capital. To be excluded from capital ownership is not merely to be excluded from the ownership of property. It also means to be excluded from the conditions providing a full development of personality and the enjoyment of civil liberty. The industrial society, by creating a class without capital and without a chance to ever acquire it, has established an element of bondage. . . . Bondage also differs in form from one social system to the other; in industrial society it appears as the improbability of becoming a capital owner. The non-owning class thus becomes the dependent class. The originally free market society has made dependence an integral part of the social order within the industrial society.

How is it possible that the acquisitive society has, as a result of the idea of personal freedom, brought about dependence of a whole social class? And if the general principle of freedom is the very basis of life in industrial society, does this not mean that the idea of freedom will aim to devise new forms of expression and new forms of organization in this newly developed class of dependents? Will the inner social impulses not attack the conditions which create a relationship of dependency and proceed to struggle for the principles on which the industrial society is based? If lack of capital implies material dependency, and if the demand for and the awareness of liberty remains alive, industrial society may emerge but may not be able to survive. The class of non-owners, dependent and lacking freedom, becomes the decided enemy of capital; what happened in feudal society is now repeated again under different circumstances, a struggle of the lower class with the upper class over the right of determining existing social order.

The Proletariat—The Emergence of the Industrial Working Class

During the last century, when the ideas of liberty and equality had for the first time appeared in Europe, most people were bound to the soil and were dependent on agriculture even if they were free. The needs of the overwhelming majority were satisfied by the domestic economy or else by the products of artisans in the towns. . . . There was almost no trade except for domestic exchange between town and country. . . . The limits of production and trade were so narrow that it is hard to visualize the frugality of life prevailing at that time. . . The needs were restricted to what could be provided from the surrounding country; wages were mostly paid in kind. Home produce was the principal means of exchange between employer and employee. The worker consumed whatever he earned without further trading. . . . In consequence, he had little money and few opportunities to dispose freely of his wages; to a certain extent the fact of his being a member of the family upon which he depended was more important. . . . The low wages and the working conditions restricted considerably the free development of the working man. . . . The payment of wages in kind has contributed more to his dependence than all laws and all suppression of the worker. It has completely subjugated the individual worker to the individual master and to his family. . . .

A general change of circumstances was not possible unless an altogether new force were to affect production and consumption. Since all work was done by human hands, too large a share of this productive force was consumed in the process of production. Hence the surplus of labor available for trading was negligible. Industry based on human labor could not supply sufficient products for the markets in order to provide enough goods in exchange for wages, even if wages were paid in cash. For this reason, the laborer had no vital interest in money since there was no opportunity to profitably exchange it. There was neither an incentive to give nor a need to receive cash in payment for labor.

Suddenly, and strangely enough, at the same time as the ideas of liberty and equality appeared in France, the first machines were produced in England. With them a new era began for the economy of the whole world, affecting production, consumption and trade. The machines became a truly revolutionary power in the material world, which they now dominate and whence they deeply penetrate into the realm of the mind.

The growing number of factory workers and the nature of their hourly work made a personal relationship between factory-owner and laborer partly impossible and partly unnecessary. The factory worker—until then kept under strict domestic control— . . . became a free person in the factory. When his work was finished nobody cared about him. He got paid in cash and was able to spend it as he liked. He had to set up his own household. No matter how modest it was, it made him self-reliant and independent of any individual control. Only labor was his master.

This step from the traditional dependency of his household to independence was of enormous consequence. It is comparable only to the dramatic event when the son leaves his father's home to set up his own household. The whole class of laborers took this step wherever machines were introduced. . . . By making the laborer independent, the machine laid the basis for the independence of the working class. . . . This elemental development was nothing else but a thorough separation of work from property, manifested by the parting of laborers and owners, who until then had lived in a close and natural relationship, though unaware of its importance. The separation of the two elements of all material development had been caused by the machine.

Only at this point did it become apparent that the interests of the owners are essentially different from those of the laborers. This separation has given rise to the indifference of the laborer toward the enterprise as such, be it agricultural or industrial, and has gradually suggested the question of whether the money wage is equivalent to the contribution made by the laborer to the total product. Only when the laborer stands separated from the enterprise, weighing his money wage, do the conflicting interests of capital . . . and labor . . . become discernible. From the separation between labor and property to the antagonism which develops between them there is but one step. And this step, too, had to be taken because of the machine. . . .

Under the preceding economic conditions the laborers had been dispersed; it had been difficult or impossible to establish a direct contact among members of the laboring class, all the more so because the leisure time of the worker had usually been spent with his family. But now, when hundreds of workers worked in the same shop and were free after the day's work was over, the equality of conditions as well as the community of work created a common way of life, a community of thought and feelings. As long as wages were satisfactory this new community was only of small importance. But when wages went down and the misery of wage earners became apparent, while at the same time the capitalist class indulged in an evergrowing display of wealth and pomp, the laborers began to consider themselves as a distinct group, a specific element of the industrial world subject to certain not yet clearly discernable laws. The laborer had a family; if he did the work which sustained his family well, he had little time to spend with his family. The laborer had no chance to accumulate capital and raise his children to become members of the property-owning class. On the contrary, it was desirable that the children start earning money as early as possible; their education consisted in following their father's occupation. And if they in turn had children, the same rule remained valid. In this way the laborer's position became hereditary, exactly like that of the owner. This hereditary character of labor, in conjunction with the fact that it was difficult or almost impossible to change the position of the family, transformed the working class into a status group. This class was altogether separated from the capital-owning class. It was dependent upon it; it became aware of its antagonism against the rule of capital, and considered itself a powerful opponent by virtue of its numbers and its concentration. With the appearance of the industrial laboring class, which was joined by more and more workers released from the bonds of their former masters, the difference between the propertied and the non-propertied class had been clearly established. . . .

The Proletariat (continued)—*The Wage-relationship. The Dependence of the Working Class.*

The appearance of the working class seems to be a mark of progress as compared to former conditions. The personally dependent laborers had become . . . personally free laborers through the factory system and the introduction of money wages. Generally speaking, legal equality entitled everybody to establish his own enterprise on the basis of his savings. The road to capital ownership was open. Independence made everybody depend upon his own devices, his abilities, his industriousness and his thrift. This became the source of his self-improvement. . . . This, however, was only the negative side of liberty; its realization depended upon the fact of whether the laborer had any real chance of acquiring capital. Without this possibility the working class was, in spite of its independence, excluded from the rule over society and from developing a free personality; without this opportunity the principle of freedom was a delusion, even a mockery for the working class. . . . The question of the future, of real freedom for the working class, became identical with the question of whether the industrial laborer could ever acquire capital or not. . . . The wage level was therefore at the core of the whole problem. . . . And the laws which determined industrial wages were decisive as far as the freedom and independence of the industrial working class was concerned. . . .

At the beginning of the industrial era, wages had been relatively high because of the great profits of the entrepreneurs and the limited number of workers. But this could not last. . . . In accordance with the laws of the economy, wages became reduced to the level of subsistence. As soon as industry, at the beginning of the century, had advanced and a working class had emerged, the wages went down; during the second decade of the century it became an established fact that the average industrial factory worker was receiving a wage just high enough to satisfy his basic needs. . . . It was impossible for him to accumulate capital. . . .

Competition played a twofold role for the laborer. It operated among laborers due to their concentration in specific places and their growing number. . . . Since the worker is dependent on wages for making a living, he has to accept work at any price. . . . A second form of competition, competition among entrepreneurs, then ensues. Since they can compete successfully only by keeping the price of products at the lowest possible level, they will try to keep the costs of production down. . . . The laws affecting the wage level make it impossible for the working class, in general, as well as for the individual worker, to acquire capital. This answers the question concerning the idea of freedom in industrial society.

It does not, however, take full account of the position of the industrial working class. Since the worker is dependent on his wage, it remains within the personal power of the entrepreneur to hire him or not. This power increases as the labor reserve grows. It is true that the worker is legally free to accept or reject the job. Nobody is forced to accept work, and wages are not legally regulated. Therefore, the laborer is, in relation to the employer, legally free. But since he is dependent on the wage and the wage in turn on the employer, in most cases he, and his wife and child as well, depend in reality on the arbitrary decisions of the entrepreneur. The laborer submits to the factory owner with the same inevitable necessity that he submits to his own needs. In spite of all legal liberty he is in fact not free. . . . The material dependence of the laborer upon the employer is the second main fact in the life of the industrial working class.

Dependence, wherever it appears, tends to bring about adversity and discord by the ever increasing pressure it generates. Even the generous individual can hardly resist this power of evil. Laborer as well as master soon sense this dependence and accept it as part of their mutual relationship. The worker becomes either obstinate and malicious, or a dull-witted tool, or else a subservient servant. The pride of a free human being begins to waver and to disappear; he, the laborer, does not have the power to defend his independence against those who have power over his and his children's daily bread. On the other hand, the master, whom everybody obeys, becomes presumptuous, haughty, and cruel toward those who serve him and indifferent about their sufferings and their future. The unalterable law that submissiveness spoils the master more than does innate wickedness operates on a small as well as on a large scale. The factory becomes a place of misery for all, work begins to look like a punishment for the worker; the master is dreaded and hated; to pass the day without brutal and cruel incidents is all people can hope for. Although the days of slavery with all their horror are remote in free Europe, slavery reappears here in a more destructive form because it is imposed in the name of freedom. There are examples to the contrary, of course, where humane masters try to make work pleasant and the worker happy, but this is entirely a matter of chance; only the individual personality of the master may make working conditions bearable. . . . Life may be relatively comfortable with a good factory owner; but usually the master is indifferent to anything not directly related to the process of work, and this indifference permits intolerable working conditions, which could only be eliminated by strong counteractions of the master, to lead to the ruin of the worker.

Such is the personal relationship resulting from the material dependence of the laborer on the factory owner. But dependence, once established, does not remain restricted to personal relations. The only area of independence left to the laborer is his money wage. No matter how small, it is his own; as long as he preserves it he has some independence. But the interest of the employer does not permit him to enjoy it. The laborer has to buy shelter, food and clothing. The master offers these for sale, thereby reducing the cash wages earned. He can buy wholesale and without any risk, and be satisfied with a small profit or no profit at all. He really is able to provide goods for the workers more cheaply than anybody else. And is it not . . . in his greatest interest to provide things cheaply and well in order to raise the incentive for better work? In this fashion the master also becomes the tradesman and the landlord of the worker. He builds apartments and rents them; he sells self-manufactured goods; he erects little trade centers for shopping. This may not be wrong in itself. But the dependence of the worker enables the master to force him to live in his cottages and to accept his wares instead of wages. . . . In consequence, money wages which are just sufficient to provide for the basic needs tend to disappear; with the so-called cottage system and the truck system, working wages tend to relapse into the feudal stage of payment in kind, from which the very same factories had raised the laboring class by cash payments.

The circle, which begins with the invention of the machines and cash wages, thus seems to have completed its course, and yet something altogether new has happened at this point. A working class has developed which begins to think of itself as an independent unit. In spite of freedom of acquisition, it is impossible for their members to accumulate capital; their work relations are based on free contract, but their needs make them dependent on the class of employers, who use their dependency to reduce wages to provision of subsistence in kind. Even the acquisitive society, based on the two great principles of liberty and equality, has thus re-established the principle of dependency inherent in any society. The property-owning class, which owns or can acquire capital, has become the ruling class. The non-owning class, in spite of all liberty and equality, is not free but totally dependent. . . . The objective observer has to admit that the dependence of the laborer on the employer is similar to the conditions of the serfs in their relationship to the manorial lord.

Most people are willing to be dependent if, in return, they are assured of well-being. The peace of the new society which had again reproduced dependence depended on whether the laborer received comfort and security in exchange for his dependence. This leads us to the other most disheartening part of the situation.

The Proletariat (continued)*—Pauperism, its Nature and Consequences*

There have always been poor people in every society, and usually they have been supported by their fellow men. Whoever is unable to work and does not own enough property to live on is poor. Loss of ability to work may be a consequence of any number of factors for most of which the poor themselves are not responsible. . . . The causes of poverty - lack of ability, or unwillingness to work - are of a personal nature. In times of war and epidemics, a large portion of a country may be temporarily afflicted. . . . But the general conditions, having their origin in individual circumstances, can be ameliorated by taking care of the individual cases. . . .

The situation is totally different when poverty is a consequence of a general cause. In this case the social order itself brings about poverty. Every society, to the extent that it contains an element of dependence, produces it specific type of poverty. . . . This socially conditioned poverty differs with the order of society. The poverty of the Indian caste system rests on the principle of propertyless pariahs; their misery is the inevitable consequence of their total social nothingness. Poverty of slavery results from a degradation of men to mere tools. Poverty of feudalism results from a lack of incentive to work when the lord of the manor receives most of the returns. But industrial society—the society of liberty and equality—also has its specific type of poverty, which results from the same principles on which its order rests. We call the poverty of industrial society pauperism, which is industrial or mass poverty. . . . It is an inevitable consequence of industrial society; it is necessarily part and parcel of the conditions of the laboring class; while dependence and lack of capital arouse the opposition of the laborer against the capital owner, this form of poverty definitely makes the laborer and the capital owner into inevitable enemies. . . . We have shown how factory work and the power of competition lower industrial wages to the subsistence level for the largest part of the workers. As a rule, the laborer is not in a position to save. . . . His working capacity is his only possession and his only safeguard against pauperization; this working capacity supports him and his family; the average wage equals the average level of consumption. As long as his working capacity is intact and an opportunity for work exists, the worker's well-being is secure without savings. But as soon as his working capacity is impaired or the opportunities for work disappear, pauperization immediately sets in. . . . If the inherent nature of the working class or industrial society can destroy permanently or temporarily the laborer's opportunity or capacity for work, then impoverishment and poverty are the inevitable concomitants of industrial society and a perennial scourge to the working class. It is easy to illustrate the truth of this proposition.

The first and less serious case is the one where, through no fault of the laborer or the employer, temporary unemployment occurs and wage payments cease. . . . The rapid spread of machinery in all fields of production has the effect of bringing about unemployment in those areas and localities where new machines are introduced. . . . This kind of pauperization is usually incurable, and only the subsequent generation, which has been trained for different skills, can again improve living conditions. More comprehensive but also less enduring is the unemployment due to the business cycle. . . . The laborers, suddenly deprived of income, are forced to dispose of whatever small reserves they may have; . . . privation, hunger, and misery result. . . . These deprivations break the power of resistance against the other, more powerful kinds of impoverishment, the destruction of the working power itself through work in industries. This occurs in the first place through old age and its consequences. . . . The working man is not in a position to save for old age. As soon as his earning power declines, pauperization ensues; poverty and age become identical in the industrial world. . . . But no matter how hard old age may weigh upon the laborer, it is not his greatest enemy. What really undermines his working power is the work itself—and partly the wage. This touches upon the sorest spot of the life of industrial workers.

Industry is based on the division of labor. Division of labor assigns to each individual worker a specific task which he has to perform throughout his whole working life. The constant repetition in the application of the same skill affects the equilibrium not only of his body but also of his mind. . . . The industrial worker loses perspective and becomes merely an instrument without a will of his own. He loses the ability to understand and to manage an enterprise composed of a diversity of elements. The full development of his mental capacity is arrested; he is deprived of capital acquisition by the very process through which he is supposed to acquire it. . . . Work—the source of all strength and blessing—is perverted in industry, it becomes the antagonist of its own resource, the ability to work. More dangerous yet than work itself is the low wage level. We have seen that the laws of industry constantly reduce wages and that the laborer's return becomes smaller with growing mechanization. Poor wages reduce the level of nutrition and thus also the working power. . . . When that happens the worker is caught in a vicious cycle of poverty and doom from which there is no escape. . . . The pleasure of work, which should lift him up, instead destroys him, and the wage level can consequently not be maintained because it corresponds to the amount and quality of performance. . . . What is going to happen if his family expenses increase and therefore a greater effort is required just when his earning power begins to decrease? The answer is simple: he is lost. We need courage to admit this tragic prospect which is pending over all members of a whole class of society as soon as their precarious existence is affected by the slightest misfortune. . . .

It is almost impossible to run a household satisfactorily if security of income and outlook for improvement are lacking. What is the situation of the industrial worker in this respect? The answer is clear: his income is not secure; any recession, any misfortune of his master, or even his master's whim can deprive him of his job. The worker's existence is threatened by any accidents which may occur to him; his small belongings do not contribute to his comfort but serve merely as a reserve to be sold or pawned if the need arises; and finally, instead of being able to expect an improvement of his condition, he has to rely on charity to protect him against starvation in old age. Is it possible to maintain a well-organized and efficient household under these conditions? Certainly not. Complete disorganization is inevitable under such circumstances. . . . There is no escape from this, and all members of the family will, under such circumstances, become absolutely indifferent toward the goods and benefits which family life is supposed to provide for all men. . . . The circle is closed. Nothing of value grows in this atmosphere. Misery and poverty are at home here and reproduce themselves through the processes which hasten the dissolution of the family.

It is at this point that the concept of pauperism derives its full meaning. It is not only the poverty of part of the laboring class, not only impoverishment which hits large sections of the population through industrial changes, but it is the poverty reproduced by industrial conditions and transmitted from generation to generation within the family which characterizes industrial pauperism.

The great differences between mere poverty and pauperism can be clearly seen. Lack of work and income result in poverty, but pauperism is brought about by work and wages in industrial society. Poverty can be coped with through charity; in order to fight pauperism the whole industrial working- and wage-system has to be changed. 'Poverty has raised the question of which institutions should collect the necessary funds to support the poor from those who are better off, and how such support may best be distributed among the poor; pauperism cannot be understood if it is not analyzed in the context of the social pattern. Any concern about it leads directly to research concerning the social order and its contradictions; it leads to the conclusion that only through far-reaching changes in society can pauperism be eliminated. The struggle against pauperism, which is a by-product of industrial development, is directed against conditions of work and of wages; attempts to change these conditions have been unsuccessful thus far. It is pauperism that has led practical people, in spite of their dislike of abstract problems, and the working class, in spite of their inability to really understand them, to adopt the ideas of socialism. . . .

A glance at Great Britain, the leading power in industrial development, may well suggest the answer to the question of whether pauperism is a danger to the social order; the almost unlimited amount of capital available there has had no effect in eliminating pauperism or even in controlling it. . . . Social investigations in many areas have shown that the price for work, the wage, remains by necessity on the level of subsistence; in view of this, the plea for saving, for domesticity and order sounds almost like mockery. . . . There is no doubt that industrial society consumes people, that it consumes the working population for the benefit of capital. . . . By destroying the vitality of the individual, by debilitating whole generations, by dissolving families, demoralization and destruction of the will to work seriously endanger the general conditions of civilized society.

Now . . . we may raise the question as to whether the above adequately describes the contemporary phenomenon of the proletariat. The answer is no. There is still one factor to be considered which binds all other factors together and facilitates their influence. The powerful social movement of our time can only be understood in its full impact when this particular element is taken into account. . . .

Conclusion: The Proletariat Proper

Any part of society whose members live under the same conditions originally appears as just an aggregate of individuals. . . . But the community of living and suffering in which the individual exists does not permit such an aggregate to remain merely a number of isolated individuals. A common way of looking at human problems spontaneously develops, and this is followed by the development of common goals. These common goals become all the more specific and powerful the greater becomes the contrast in living conditions in comparison to other parts of society.

The process is precipitated by an idea pertaining to the major social conditions which dominate people's lives. . . . This idea will become the expression of common experiences; it will appear as a light suddenly illuminating the whole problem and position of the proletariat and, as a consequence, the affected part of society will become a self-confident entity with an initiative of its own, . . . attempting to safeguard its interests within the framework of the social order.

Only after this has happened has the personal element of self-awareness, which eventually leads to the recognition of common aspirations, become established in the particular part of society which until then was only determined by the objective laws of the economy. Only at this stage does the social class or the social estate become a social power. This process occurs within the ruling class of society almost unnoticeably. No incentive provided by research, no common stimulus is necessary because the continuously present self-interest provides the necessary daily lesson, clearly illustrating the situation. But the dependent class needs a theoretical framework and a systematic approach to clarify its problem. The appearance of the new social power begins only with the appearance of such social systems. . . .

At the same time when, with the help of machines and the subsequent division of labor, industry and wealth rose to previously unknown heights, a reinterpretation of the nature of value, of labor and of wealth was undertaken. The effect on the history of ideas caused by this new interpretation is comparable to the influence of Rousseau in the area of political philosophy. Until then wealth had been explained in terms of money by the mercantilistic system or in terms of land by the physiocrats. The significance of these two systems by no means pertained only to economic but just as much to social phenomena. If their interpretation was correct, the owner was the possessor of all values and all wealth and therefore was the source of his own social prestige. The laborer, particularly the industrial worker, had no important place in society. . . . The impetus to make the laborer aware of his own conditions came from Adam Smith. The core of the famous opus of this great man is the sentence which states that in the economy labor is the productive element and therefore labor should be the ruling element. The first argument in support of this truly remarkable principle was that all value is derived from labor, that the relationship of the values of commodities is essentially determined by the amount of labor invested, and that goods may be used accordingly for exchange on the basis of their labor value. Wealth is wealth of labor; the more a nation works the higher its standards of wealth; the nation which receives raw materials from other nations and returns them after processing, then, has to be the wealthiest one. The laws of labor determine the distribution of goods. The producer will always rule over the consumer, and poverty will always be the companion of a life without work. The second argument, based on the first, states that the level of productivity is dependent upon the division of labor. . . . Thus one discovered with surprise that the movement and development of the growing industrial life of Great Britain was based on very definite and simple principles; the striking coincidence of theory and practice resulted in a quick and general acceptance of these principles. . . .

But if labor is really the source of all value and by its very nature the dominating force in society, is the relationship between capital and labor nevertheless reasonable? Is capital entitled to be the dominant power in society? If not, will labor necessarily be victorious over capital? Is labor entitled to gain monopoly of power and determine what the true social interests are? What will happen to the economy then? All these questions were apparently of such immediate importance that Adam Smith had to face them; although he did not integrate them into a system, he nevertheless approached the crucial labor problems in this area. . . . In the masterful sketch of castes and classes, the laboring class, although the interest of the laborer "is strictly connected with that of society" (B. I. Ch. XI.), is the class which gains the least by social progress and which has no voice in the process of industrial society although it suffers from its consequences more than any other class. He even states literally: "Civil government so far as it is organized for the security of property, is in reality instituted for the defense of the rich against the poor or for those who have some property against those who have none at all" (Book V Ch. I). . . .

Adam Smith's principles quickly became the common property of all classes. It was inevitable that the laboring class should begin to use them in order to comprehend its own condition of life. But a striking contradicton came to the surface at this point. If it could not be denied that labor and the division of labor were the sources of Great Britain's wealth, it also could not be disregarded that this very labor condemned the laboring class to remain without property; it became clear that the amount of property of the wealthy tended to grow to the extent that the wages of those who labored to produce this wealth were kept low. The laboring class was aware of this contradiction; for the first time it realized that it seemed to produce the value of all property through labor alone, and that this very function that it performed was the explanation of its limited share of the total product. The very same principle which regulated the distribution of goods and provided the well-being of the owners also excluded the non-owners from the enjoyment of the fruits of labor. The principle which regulated the social order was based on the complete separation of the two main classes. In view of such a contradiction, the laboring class was confronted with the alternative of either bearing its unalterable lot in silence or—instead of attacking the owner—attacking ownership itself, the very basis of the present community. The working class began to search for a new order of human society on the basis of a new principle for the distribution of goods. . . . The laboring class conceived clearly that the principle of abstract equality of all people was generally accepted but that the laws which determine the distribution of goods prohibited a concrete realization of this principle. The opposition against the system of distribution, the merely negative struggle against the existing social order, now acquired a positive content. . . . There were other factors than mere economic relationships which made the worker aware of the elements determining his unfortunate position. Industry had immeasurably enriched the big cities and at the same time had concentrated large numbers of industrial workers. . . . The exposition of the greatest wealth and refinement, apparently so close and yet unattainable, extravagances side by side with want, accumulation of possessions next to poverty, instigated the appetite of the proletarian and made his lot appear to be one of extreme deprivation. . . . The working class ultimately realized what the causes of its misery were; a common feeling of despair and, simultaneously, of hope for a change for the better, awakened the will to strive for it. Interpretations of working conditions by labor itself vary greatly. . . . However, what is common to all is the socially significant fact that they had begun to conceive of themselves as an independent class of society suppressed by capital, although entitled as workers and as individuals to social equality. This attitude puts the worker into sharp and growing opposition to the property-owning class; it also motivates him to think seriously about the means of changing his condition. . . . The awareness of the social antagonism has thus formed industrial workers into the proletariat of the present.

. . . To illustrate the point that not only socialists and communists recognize very clearly the relationship of contemporary industry to the concepts of liberty and equality, and particularly as related to the working class, we quote here one of the many statements of modern French literature before the Revolution of 1848. The *Encyclopédie Nouvelle*, written for popular consumption yet containing many excellent articles, states in an article *"Bourgeoisie"* by L. Reybaud: "Why are not all citizens personally free? Because there are many who, driven by hunger, are forced to sell themselves at the first opportunity. They lead a wretched life . . . and are exposed until they die to a thousand afflictions and to excessive labor. But conditions are such that if they would try to escape, misery . . . would force them to come back. . . . These mute and unhappy pariahs suffer on their long journey with us, because their only choice is one between suffering and dying, and it is a man's instinct not to die. They continue to live, it is true, but at the risk of starvation like slaves who only respond to the threat of the whip. These people, I have to state it again, are no free citizens." They are not free, they are not equal, because they possess no capital, only labor, . . . and yet freedom and equality is the motto of recent French history. . . .

During a period of about fifty years, the second main element of industrial society, labor, has established itself independently as a class in distinct and unalterable contrast to the first element, capital. The industrial society, until then only an abstract concept, has established its social order. The general principle that in any society owners are juxtaposed against non-owners has now become an established fact in industrial society, where capital and labor face each other as capitalists and workers. . . . If the social life and the elements of society determine the state and the history of the people, it will soon become evident that this antagonism between capitalists and the proletariat is the essential factor in the coming history of Europe, which is based on an acquisitive society. . . .

THE SOCIAL MOVEMENT OF THE LOWER CLASS

The Proletariat and The Negation of Personal Property and of the Family.

. . . The history of industrial society illustrates that even this type of society, in spite of its adherence to the principle of equality before the law and freedom of acquisition, nevertheless results in the dependence of those who do not own capital upon capital owners, and in the lack of opportunity for the former of developing their capacities to the fullest. Yet as compared with other social orders, industrial society is the one most strongly committed to liberty and equality—it depends upon them, advocates them constantly, defends them and accepts them. We have shown how inequality and dependence nevertheless grow. What is the consequence of this contridiction?

If freedom and equality are acknowldeged in principle and yet cannot be realized in this society, . . . they have to establish their validity in a different context and with reference to a different and not yet tested principle. . . .

What is the new and final testing ground for these ideas? The answer is obvious. Capital rules in industrial society. Capital makes one group free and happy, the other group dependent and miserable. Capital is an element of material development, yet it is not available to all like light and air. But is it capital as such which brings about the contradiction? Certainly not; capital, which is the end product of persistent and rational efforts, is at the same time an indispensable prerequisite of industrial growth. Nobody will deny that capital accumulation is necessary for the growth of the wealth of mankind which, in turn, is the prerequisite for a personal development. Nobody will deny that capital is the product of labor. . . . Capital as such is not an adversary but a prerequisite of real freedom. . . . Therefore, not capital as such, but only the form in which capital grows and is used, can be held responsible for the seeds of dependence. . . . Under what forms does capital appear? What is it that makes capital as such a capital good? . . . Which quality of capital hampers the movement toward freedom? . . . It is doubtlessly the law of personal property. This is the factor which identifies capital with the life, the personality, and the action of single individuals who are independent of the human community and not responsible to it. This is the factor which puts capital out of reach for everybody else, because the specific capital is inviolable and cannot be disposed of without the consent of its sovereign owner. . . .

This is the first great question which industrial society raises with reference to the basic order of society. . . . But it is not the only one. Is it only the institution of private property which establishes the barrier against the acquisition of capital by individual labor? What is it that makes dependence due to the lack of capital a permanent condition reaching beyond the life of the individual? What is it that gives to capital owners power to extend their rule beyond the life of those who first acquire it? What is it that gives permanent status to those who lack capital and wrestle in vain with their condition of dependence as well as to those who own capital without having to work? It is the family, with its inheritance laws and its educational function, which establishes a system of super- and subordination, which grants the pleasures of life as well as endless misery, which fosters personal growth and demoralization for the individual within the framework of specific social groups. While personal property gives status to the individual and reverses the original function of capital, family and family law transform it into a permanent universal condition, into the positive order of society.

Let us not be deceived. . . . Any persistent pursuit of the idea of liberty and equality will always lead to the conclusion that the true opponent of these ideas is not the constitution and not social privileges but property rights and the family. If these ideas are vigorous and strong, the insoluble contradiction between liberty, the realization of the highest human aspirations, on the one hand, and property and family rights on the other, will lead to the decisive question of whether the supporters of liberty want to suppress liberty in favor of these institutions or want to abolish the institutions in order to save liberty. Once the idea of freedom has been clearly conceived in the minds of its apostles, they will necessarily come to the conclusion that property rights and the family have to be sacrificed in order to attain freedom. This is not an arbitrary judgment, nor is it a mere ideology or a mistaken conclusion. There simply is no compromise solution possible. . . . The utopians, from Plato up to those of the last century, and the socialists and communists of today with their utopia, as well as the philosophy of law from Aristotle until the present, provide historical evidence and logical proof for this proposition. At this point, the ancient concepts of liberty and equality have reached an impasse, and an altogether new movement in a new area begins. . . .

What are these two concepts of property and the family? . . . Have they fulfilled their function if they have rendered the individual either independent and happy or dependent and poor? Quite to the contrary. The theory of society shows that any social order rests on the coexistence of ownership and non-ownership, that the antagonism between classes results from owning and non-owning, and that the internal stratification of these classes is determined by the amount and the quality of their property. The analysis of industrial society shows that capital is nothing but a specific kind of property and that capital owners, therefore, represent a specific type of ruling class. What is it, then, that requires a justification of property and the family? What makes the realization of the idea of freedom, which requires the abolition of property and the family, impossible? A principle is clearly involved here on which any social order depends. . . . To abandon it would mean the dissolution of what we call society. . . . This consequence is neither arbitrary nor accidental but necessary and inevitable. What is this principle of society? Society was and always will be the restriction of freedom, [Unfreiheit]. It will enforce the subordination and the dependence of one individual upon other individuals; in all its forms and in all its consequences society is built on the restraint of freedom, which is enforced by the cleavage between owners and non-owners.

Therefore, if one aspires to the realization of complete liberty, one must abolish private property and society in order to abolish social dependence; a completely different order of human relationships then becomes necessary; whether one searches for the Republic and for truth merely in the unknown sphere beyond our reach, as Plato did, whether one places it in the realm of the Gods, as did Rousseau, or in the never-discovered countries of this world, as More did, the institutions of private property and the family will not be found there. This is the necessary, though only negative, content of all systems projecting the idea of liberty and equality in whatever form—whether logically derived or imaginatively conceived—as a fully developed system onto human society. I want to mention here a phenomenon which is very closely related to the above subject matter and yet differing from it in form. This is the phenomenon of utopia. The utopia, of which Plato's Republic is the first, gives a picture of the human community living in freedom and happiness without private property and without the family, and consequently not living in society. However, none of these utopias has ever exerted any practical influence. Even socialism, which is most closely related to them through the two dominant doctrines it represents, does not show the slightest trace of a relationship, much less an influence of utopianism. Even though the utopias have been preserved and often reinvented throughout the centuries as the lonely guideposts on the road to the concept of freedom, they are without immediate interest in relation to the history of society. We shall bypass them here in order not to blur the original picture of French and British Socialism. . . . The social movement which we are analyzing has no relationship to these utopian systems. Even the works by Morelly, which have been considered as belonging to the communist predecessors of the contemporary French theories, belong to this group; Morelly also was without any practical influence. Therefore, it is important to avoid keeping these two sets of ideas too close to each other, because one easily makes the mistake, as Reybaud did, though perhaps unintentionally, of disregarding, because of the practical insignificance of the utopians, the great importance of the socialists. . . . .

We have traced the rise of the proletariat of present-day society from the propertyless class. The proletariat is the dependent class, not only factually but also in principle, because it cannot acquire capital. Is capital as such or labor as such responsible for this development? They are not. The cause lies in the fact that capital always exists as private property only. What are the roots of dependence and misery of the proletariat in industrial society? It is not industry, nor capital as such, but the institution of personal and hereditary property which leads to domination and subjugation. Once this truth has been understood, it gains a strong foothold in the minds of the proletarians; it becomes the center of their thoughts and ambitions. The antagonism against property and the family becomes rooted in the industrial proletariat. The proletariat becomes a powerful class ready to act.

A consistent interpretation of abstract equality and liberty necessarily leads to doubt as to the value of these basic social institutions and to the attempt to abolish them. The proletariat accepts these thoughts and is willing to attack both property rights and the family; this is an inevitable and necessary historical development. It is also the basic starting point of social antagonism in industrial society. Since it will necessarily result in the emergence of a proletariat, this proletariat, in the course of time, will eventually demand, as a consequence of the principle of liberty and equality, the negation of property rights as well as of the family.

This is the great challenge with which the new industrial society of France was confronted by the July Revolution. Never before has society produced a more ominous criticism or a more powerful enemy of the social order. And let us not deceive ourselves; it is not only France which finds herself in this serious condition; any industrial society will necessarily have to cope with it. . . .

These ideas develop when capital ownership has reached such proportions that mere labor is unable to acquire capital. The laboring class develops into an estate, and the state controlled by capital is no longer concerned about the well-being of this estate. The conditions of the proletariat become hopeless because the proletariat lacks means of its own—or assistance from the state—to free itself. It is at this point that the ideas of liberty and equality, which remain the principles of industrial society, necessarily turn against the basis of society, against property rights and the family; the time has come when the lower class of society begins the struggle against the ruling class by attacking those two pillars of its rule, by negating property and the family.

This, then, is the beginning of the social movement in industrial society, the intellectual content of the proletarian movement against the existing order. . . . The downright antagonism in industrial society is not a consequence of the existence of a laboring class which does not own capital, but rather the consequence of the fact that this class has developed into an hereditary estate. As long as dependence of labor upon capital has not become hereditary, the struggle, although perhaps lively in the realm of ideas, does not yet exist in society. This is the great challenge to industrial society and the power of its state. . . . It is certainly true that North America, although it has an industrial society, is not as yet confronted with a social struggle, because workers there still have the opportunity to become capitalists; . . . it is also certain that the proletariat in Europe, and particularly in France since the July Revolution, has become aware of the fact that this opportunity does not exist there any longer and that there the proletariat has become an estate. With the awareness of existing conditions the social struggle begins. The first symptom of this struggle is the negation of personal property and the family, a symptom which has made its appearance in a variety of forms since the July Revolution.

. . . Thus we are confronted not only with theories, nor with a predominantly political, but rather with a social, movement. This and nothing else explains the great importance of those theories and those revolts which have occurred for the past eight years or so also in Germany, where they have been regarded with seriousness and a certain amount of anxiety. Previously we had to state over and over again that those systems and the apparently nonsensical principles of socialism and communism, to which little attention has been paid, had to be interpreted as the most important historical facts of our time, as symptoms of a terrible sickness of the European world. Not having heeded the warning signal lights, one would be helplessly drawn into the social struggle. Nobody has any doubts about this now that the facts are known. The social contradiction has developed into a real social struggle; the time for con-- structed systems and theories is gone; for the time being, superior military strength has won the battle. But nobody need deceive himself; the settlement is only temporary. The spark glows under the ashes, and sooner or later the same struggle will break out again. Settlement of the surface has not solved the real issues; the proletariat still exists, it still clings to the main tenets of its dogma, and the problem is still essentially a practical one—namely, what does the proletariat conceive of as the realization of this principle, what does it expect from society, what kind of social order does it strive for?

Obviously, the negation of property rights and family is a powerful attack against tradition, but one cannot build a new society upon such principles. Something constructive has to follow. What is this positive content, or what is the social order which the proletariat, after the struggle with the property owners, wants to set up in the place of industrial society? This is the first logical question to ask. . . . And if that negation marks the beginning of a new social movement which will dissociate itself from the traditional interpretation of liberty and equality, of property and the state, then the positive content of the intellectual endeavors is clearly the first positive social movement emerging from industrial society. We shall call it by its proper name: i.e. socialism and communism.

Socialism and communism, therefore, are not only historical facts of an epoch which comes to its close; on the contrary, they have the same relation to the contemporary movement as, during the past century, Rousseau, Mably, Helvetius, Condorcet, Diderot and others had to the political Revolution of 1789. To the same extent as that Revolution deviated from the ideas of these men, the social Revolution of 1848-49 had to modify through compromise the ideas of the socialists and communists. But just as the Revolution of the last century received from the previously mentioned authors its philosophical and scientific background, its clarity of thought, its pungency of criticism, and the strength of its conviction, socialism and communism, too, influenced the events of recent years. Their significance will reach far beyond the period of the entangled present. This is why they are of practical as well as historical importance. An analysis of contemporary society will automatically refer to them as the roots of the social revolution. . . . With all their lack of reality and inconsistencies, they still belong to the history of the social movement to which they gave its first positive content. . . .

The Interpretations and Stages of the Social Movement

. . . Before the concept of society was even conceived, before the new society emerging from the ruins of the feudal order after the Revolution of the last century became even recognizable in its outlines, two men grew up in France who, for the first time in history, grasped with the assurance of strong conviction the importance of the contradiction which industrial society developed in the course of the next twenty years—the antagonism between the proletariat and the capitalists, between capital and labor. They wrestled with this contradiction, explored it, discovered its principle and, with great effort in the loneliness of their intellectual pursuits, built systems on the basis of this principle, systems which made their names famous but their lives rather unhappy. These two men, whom we might call socialists in the proper sense of the word, were Saint-Simon and Fourier. They are representatives of the social movement during its stage of theoretical and scientific analysis preceding its practical application. The value of their systems as solutions to the problems has no bearing on their significance. In all movements of similar nature the scientific period has the function of developing a popular awareness of the contradiction and the challenges to contemporary society. This is always accomplished by a theoretical system; . . . the principles of the systems of Saint-Simon and Fourier reflect the social contradiction of industrial society and suggest a solution through the abolition of this society. Saint-Simon and Fourier, appearing on the scene almost simultaneously and working in parallel fields, represent the first stage in the movement of society caused by external and internal separation of the proletariat from capital.

Misunderstood and not taken seriously, they completed their scientific analysis of social conditions while the proletariat, with a growing awareness of its dependency and growing pauperization, was developing gradually into a separate class of industrial society. We have shown that the principle of the state requires the state to lend support to such a class. We have also shown to what extent the upper class interferes with this task of the state. The first dawn of class-consciousness of the proletariat drove it to demand assistance from the state. But the constitutional state, controlled by the ruling class, rejected the demands of the proletariat. Consequently, the lower class turned away from the state. In order to improve its social position it began to conceive a new state order. This is the origin of the political stage within the social movement; its main manifestation is republicanism. This period lasted from 1830 to 1834, when the social movement gained the upper hand, a change indicated by the nature of things.

Political movements are always a consequence of the distribution of wealth and of the prevailing class system. Nobody is more aware of these conditions than those who suffer deprivations and are at the bottom of the social ladder. Wherever the political movement captures the imagination of the lower class, the latter will sooner or later turn against those social elements which hamper its class interests. The system of the distribution of goods as the basis of the political order becomes the center of intellectual and practical interest of the proletariat. And since, within the social order of industrial society, the proletariat necessarily turns against private property and the family, the proletariat finally comes to the conclusion that a new social order has to be established through the abolition of both. Thus the period of communism follows that of republicanism. It is the third link in the history of the intellectual efforts to cope with the contradiction in industrial society. . . .

The further socialism and communism penetrate, the more it becomes clear that an essential improvement in the situation of the lower classes is not possible, and that a realization of the ideas of socialism and communism is even more remote as long as supreme power in public affairs, the state, is exercised by those who have a decisive interest in maintaining the status quo of the social order. All those who want to cooperate for the improvement of the social conditions begin by first turning toward the state. The relationship between state constitution and social order prompts them to demand at least a constitutional change which would provide an organ for the new ideas which have developed in society. This trend marks the beginning of the last chapter in the intellectual effort of society, the reform movement. The circle of the social movement turns back again to the political elements, but it is now broader and more profound than pure republicanism. By including the program of social reform, it comes closest to dealing with the practical origin of the social contradiction. It embodies the seeds of transition from socialism to practical life. It is this train of thought which was responsible for the last Revolution.

These are the main directions in which the thoughts and demands of the industrial proletariat . . . moved. They are the positive results of the questioning of the value of property and the family which have provided the proletariat with an independent intellectual life— much more so than the purely negative earlier attitude. While the negative attitude made the proletariat aware of what it is now, these positive doctrines have helped the proletariat to learn what it may hope, demand, and try to accomplish. Only at this stage does the proletariat become a power, because only now does it acquire a purpose. . . .

All these schools of thought work in various ways toward the same end. From their vantage point, the gravity of the contemporary conditions of Europe, the significance of the antagonism of industrial society, and finally the magnitude of the last French Revolution, which came not altogether unexpectedly, become comprehensible. Now that the time for abstract systems and theories has passed, just as the time of Rousseau and Mably had passed in 1789, they are mere historical facts. At the same time, they remain the important guides for the future of the contemporary social order, the powerful monitors not to hesitate any longer but to work constructively toward the improvement of social conditions lest, otherwise, inevitable acts of brutality and violence destroy the most noble aspirations of men together with their divine impulse for freedom and for a truly beneficial development of mankind. . . .

Part Two, Chapter Two

SOCIALISM, COMMUNISM AND THE REPUBLICAN MOVEMENT

SOCIALISM

. . . All problems pertaining to socialism belong without any doubt to the field of the social sciences [Staatswissenschaft]. It is true that at first glance socialist theories appear to represent useless dreams of unscientific minds and that they seem to require our attention only as oddities and because of their practical relationship to the proletariat. However, it will not escape the more careful observer that the lasting influence they exert rests ultimately on the fact that they have added a new dimension to our knowledge of human life. . . .

If one discusses socialism as a scientific phenomenon, two different points of view have to be considered. . . . In the first place, socialism is a historical fact caused by and deriving significance from external circumstances; from this point of view socialism and its various manifestations belong to the field of history. The system devised by socialism is of secondary importance to history. The important point about socialism in this context is its influence on the conditions under which it developed. The historical place of socialism has to be sought in the history of society. This has not been done so far, and therefore the predominantly historical significance of socialism has either been overlooked, or, as in some cases, interpreted too narrowly or else overrated. It has been the purpose of our presentation to show the historical significance of socialism in the correct light and in its proper proportions. . . .

Secondly, socialism is a scientific system. The question can therefore be raised as to what its place is in the social sciences, to what branch of the social sciences it belongs. . . . Usually it is concerned with the problem of pauperization, mass poverty and the proletariat; it is generally regarded as a theory concerning the ways in which social conditions can be improved.

But if one looks closely at the historical significance of socialism, it becomes clear that these interpretations are not sufficient. For socialism does not grow out of the proletariat, it grows with it; it embraces not only the proletariat but the whole of society. Doubtlessly, socialism belongs to a different discipline. Only the most general principle of socialism will indicate what this discipline is.

We have stated the principle of socialism in the introductory chapter. Socialism, originating simultaneously with industrial labor, has been first to recognize and formulate the contradiction between the idea of personality and the rule of capital over labor. On the basis of this observation, socialism has established the principle that labor, as the free activity of the personality, ought to be free of the rule of capital and ought to be the determining factor in the distribution of goods. Since capital exists only in the form of private property and as such determines the economy of the country and the life of the family, socialism is necessarily committed to the view that labor should rule, not only over capital, but also over property and the family; it should rule in such a fashion that both, property and the family, would be abolished if they were opposed to the rule of labor over capital.

Since the whole order of the human community is based on property and the family, the whole order of human society would be dissolved if one acted in accordance with the two above propositions. And since all state constitutions are derived from the order of human society, the abolition of all hitherto existing forms of state would follow.

In this fashion the first principle of socialism has led to a negation, not only of capital in its present form, but also of society and of the state. Socialism had to replace them by something else. Socialism had to try to establish a new order of property and thus of society and of the state solely on the basis of labor. The systematic development of the idea of capital, of property and of the family, of society and the state under the rule of labor, is the goal of socialism. It is the great merit of socialism to have made us aware for the first time of the relationship of labor to the free personality and to have discovered the existence and the power of the social order over men, as well as the contradiction between the social order and the free personality. . . .

This, without any question, is the element in socialism which, aside from the historical importance of socialism, determines its position in the social sciences. . . . Socialism is, indeed, a part of the science of society, a part which has not yet found its proper place.

The very fact that socialism considers itself extraneous to the fundamental order of contemporary society makes it all the more aware of the necessity to justify its principles by bringing them in harmony with the loftiest human ideals. Man therefore turns away from his concern over mere social systems toward the realm of the divine and searches for the principle of what he wants to realize in this world, namely, the divine destiny of man. . . . The divine fulfillment of man's life is thus retraced to its loftiest beginning. This fulfillment consists not merely in the achievement of equality and liberty among men; it also means the establishment, through the rule of labor, of the kingdom of heaven on earth. As a consequence, the social order will save humanity and ascertain its happiness by means of labor. Thus, socialism turns from a mere science into a doctrine of the essence of deity and from that into a religion. This is why the various socialist systems usually become sects. . . .

If it is true that the greatest perfection of men through work is the highest goal of the divine destiny of mankind, then history up to the present must be the distinct, even though imperfect, manifestation of this destiny. . . . Socialism gives history a specific meaning; the more profoundly socialism dwells on its own principle the more confidently it strides into the unknown future of mankind. This is the beginning of the socialist philosophy of history. . . .

Man can comprehend the world only to the extent that it serves his destiny. As the awareness of his destiny increases, he begins to search for a confirmation of his awakening conviction outside of himself, in the realm of nature. Every ego gaining self-awareness, sees itself as a microcosm and is convinced that the center of the universe can be discovered at any one point. The idea that man's destiny lies in the enjoyment of material wealth may confine its manifestations to the organization of labor. If, however, this idea is explored more deeply, . . . one must attempt to cope with life on a universal scale and discover man's destiny as part of it. For the destiny of man appears to be directly given to and invested in man, as the will of the creator, as the law of God; it is to be realized in the existing world, which, created by the same God, consequently must have been created for man. . . .

Thus socialism becomes a philosophy of life, and there it takes its place among the great philosophies—a place of which it had so far been deprived, not due to the poverty of its basic ideas, but owing to the incongruity between its principle and reality, and partly also because of the lack of understanding and malicious misinterpretation. It is certainly worthwhile to study seriously the manifestations of socialism throughout history with Saint-Simon or with Fourier, who have attempted to formulate the laws of the productive forces of history. One must, in doing this, disregard the cumbersome details for the sake of gaining understanding of the general ideas of socialism. I mention the names of Saint-Simon and Fourier together because the same basic thought is expressed by both of them, although in each case different conclusions are reached. The question of the organization of industries is only one among many others with which they deal. It is easy to disregard the problems they raise, and even easier to attack or to ridicule them. Yet their systems reflect genuine progress; for the first time enjoyment of life has been accorded a definite, albeit too prominent, place in life. . . .

But the destiny [*Bestimmung*] of man, in the true sense of the word, embraces not only the benefits of the external world but also the highest potentialities of man's development in this world. It also refers to man as a moral being. For what is morality if not the fulfillment of human destiny as assigned by God? Whatever I do in harmony with my destiny I do in accordance with the will of God; there is no other moral principle beyond that one. Therefore, socialism—after having established its basic tenet—develops not only a philosophy of life [*Weltanschauung*] but also a hedonistic morality, the justification for the gratification of the flesh. The organization of industry which socialism demands is a demand not only on the basis of the laws of nature and history but a demand of practical ethics, the expression of God's will with regard to human action.

. . . If we try to summarize French philosophy of the last century, we can say that it is opposed to the notion of a higher destiny of man which cannot be realized in this world. This rejection of belief in God, in the state, and in the church is followed by the adoption of the idea of personal interest. While Voltaire was the main exponent of the negative side of this school of thought, Diderot is the philosopher of personal interest, and his greatest successor is Helvetius. The absolute Ego conceived by Descartes finds its place in the material world, while in Germany its realm is considered to be the realm of ideas. Diderot and Helvetius have a significance for France which is similar to that of Kant and Fichte for Germany. Personal interest provides the formula for the supreme justification of the Ego and its actions in the sphere of reality, in the confrontation with the historical Ego, the material, political, civil man. This is the idea which the last century has handed down to the present . . .

But where, if we look at France, do we find the application of the basic tenets of French thought to reality? . . . The answer to this question is obvious. It can be found only in what we have called socialism. We should not be disconcerted by the fact that the socialistic systems thus far have not encompassed the whole problem area open to them, nor that they have not probed into all the important questions or proved the assertions they have made. The main point is that these socialist systems represent for France . . . the point at which the perceptions of man's inner life and of nature merge into a practical system, the moment at which the understanding of being results in the law about what ought to be. Socialism has thus acquired a unique position in French philosophy. . . . Although claiming to present nothing but a social system, socialism has transcended far beyond the limits of the narrow field to which it had confined itself. . . .

What, then, is this society proper for which socialism had developed a set of interpretations? Society is not only a fact, not only a common way of living, like the state. Society is the order which assigns to the individual, according to a rigid law, his world destiny, the standard of perfection of his individual personality. . . . Socialism, by developing a philosophy of life on the principle of work, has for the first time set forth the demand to view the whole material world in relation to the destiny of the individual. Socialism has thus confirmed the truth that the society of men is not only a given order, but that, in the variety of its appearances and principles, it is the form in which the destiny of the external world manifests itself to serve the individual to reach his fulfillment. The specific social order is nothing but the specific stage which this individual development has reached. It is here that socialism has blazed the trail for the loftiest and most dignified interpretation of the natural world and its relationship to the idea of personality. . . .

COMMUNISM AND ITS RELATIONSHIP TO SOCIALISM

It is not unusual for communism to be interpreted as the essence of a number of systems which—having the same point of departure as socialism although reaching different theoretical conclusions—encompass the other half of the entirely doctrinaire movement in the development of the social contradiction of our time. This is an understandable interpretation, since communism is represented mostly by more or less elaborate theories with followers who set up schools of thought and engage in a purely scientific propaganda. In order to understand the essence of communism, one must search for a common denominator of the common principle of these systems. Many people believe that they understand the essential tenets of communism if they have grasped its main principle and its variations. . . . This opinion is the main reason for the many vague and erroneous notions about communism; if one wanted to understand how the phenomenon of communism occurred in the history of a nation, how it grew, spread and reached its present strength, one must above all guard against the interpretation of communism as a definite, clear and logical system. Even at present, communism, growing in strength and scope, has no specific doctrine; all the individual communistic trends and systems have little or no power at all over communism as a whole; communism has sometimes accepted, sometimes refuted them, has temporarily embraced them but again forgotten them without changing its character or its direction. This is precisely why communism is so much more important and more powerful than socialism. It cannot be denied that socialism is much superior as a system than anything communism has offered; socialism has had a deep influence on the various communistic systems, more than the communists ever like to acknowledge. Socialism is the scientific expression of the interpretation of the social movement by an individual, while communism is the response of a whole class, the expression of a whole social situation. Its specific doctrines, its pamphlets and other material it offers give but a superficial picture of communism. Its inner meaning cannot be understood like that of socialism—through one definite principle; communism can be understood only as part of the elements of industrial society and the inherent contradictions of this society.

Therefore, it is useless to attempt a doctrinaire definition of communism. Communism is a phenomenon and a trend in the contemporary world, which has first drawn attention to the contradictions within industrial society and which has made both major classes of this society aware of this contradiction. It has not developed logically but grown historically. Traditional history cannot explain communism; only the history of society can analyze its origin, nature and content. . . .

We have shown how the ideas of liberty and equality during the last hundred years have been accepted as the principles from which the social movement in France proceeded. . . . By the end of the Restoration, society apparently had reached its final goal, and liberty and equality had become the slogan of all classes. However, as soon as the alliance between the owning class and the proletariat had defeated the Restoration, it became evident that the emergence of industrial society growing out of the acquisitive society had again suspended liberty and equality by making it impossible for the industrial worker to acquire capital, which had become the prerequisite of liberty and equality.

This way of thinking had been accepted by the people ever since the Revolution, and liberty and equality had become the norm of all attitudes and the cause of all struggles. These two ideas have survived the subjugation of the working class by the capital owners; they prompt the workers to raise the question as to where—after so many victories of liberty—the enemy of liberty, the unconquerable germ of dependency, may possibly be located.

Since the people had overthrown the old regime in order to abolish dependency, it was only natural that they should look toward the new state authority to safeguard liberty. But for the people the new state remained essentially the same as before the July Revolution. Any changes which occurred did not affect the political position of the propertyless class, but only that of the owning class. The proletariat soon became disillusioned, and now the same antagonism which was formerly directed against pseudo-constitutionalism became directed against constitutionalism proper. This hatred became, with the support of political democracy, the fertile soil of republicanism and of the prolonged republican struggle, a struggle in which the Republic was finally defeated by constitutionalism.

After this defeat, . . . popular interest in political change slowed down; recognizing intuitively that constitutionalism was not a matter of principle but was rather a matter of secondary importance, the people now turned their attention toward the major antagonist in society. The social order also seems to be at first glance a mere fact; but it is easy to discover its dominant principle. It is the principle of the rule of the owners over the non-owners, enforced by the institution of the family and protected by the law and the power of the state. As soon as this is recognized by the class of non-owners, which is daily growing in numbers and importance, a complete change in the interpretation of public affairs suddenly takes place. A hatred against all property-owners develops, particularly against capitalists who live on unearned capital revenues. The question arises of whether a principle which tolerates the social subjugation of non-owners by the idle owners of money can be a just principle in relation to liberty and equality. This principle, the law of property and the preservation of the family, is increasingly being questioned by the non-owning class, the more quickly and radically the more they lack property and family life. The doubt about the value of these institutions soon results in an antagonism against these institutions and represents the spirit of this class. . . . It is this negation which makes the owning class aware of its social conditions and of the antagonism of the existing social order against the ideas of liberty and equality. This negation is the true and proper expression of the inner conditions which accompany the origin and the rule of industrial society; it is, so to speak, the light which makes these conditions visible; it gives rise to specific systems, more or less important and varying according to the basic interests of the individual author; however, the antagonism itself is indifferent to these systems; it persists in the pure negation of property and the institution of the family. It is therefore not in a position to explain what is supposed to happen if the institutions are abolished. After this it is hoped that a positive solution may be found in which the ideas of liberty and equality would be incorporated into a new system of property and labor relations. The longer industrial society persists, the clearer the position of the proletariat becomes. All individual systems and movements have essentially no other function for the masses of industrial workers than clearly to define their position. This is accepted by all communistic sects and all factions. It determines the general climate of popular opinion.

No specific system, no deep insight into its problems, no elaborate analysis is required in order to realize this. Any statement regarding the unjust position of the proletariat falls on the fertile soil of the sad and hopeless conditions of the proletariat, and simultaneously touches all the chords of its spiritual and material life. Any doubt in property and the family signifies to the worker an understanding of his misery; any demand for material independence and equality signifies sympathy with his hopes. The deep contradiction imbedded in industrial society has found its intellectual expression. The proletariat has found the definition of its position in the realm of ideas; these ideas have aligned the various social groups into the two great antagonistic camps.

This is the general trend of development of the proletarian consciousness. The awareness on the part of the proletariat of the contradiction between its position and the ideas of liberty and equality results in a negation of property and of the family; they become the great opponents of liberty and equality. All the systems, sects and movements which grow out of this awareness we shall designate by the term communism. It now becomes clear how wrong are those who interpret communism only as a specific system built on the principle of abolition of property and the family, and how deep is the error of those who want to fight communism with weapons appropriate to fight a wrong system. Neither logical refutation, nor a benevolent admonition, nor arrogant disregard will be of any help. Communism is, indeed, a historical fact of the greatest significance, a historical fact, however, exclusively for the history of society. Communism is the condition of which socialism is merely the symptom. It is nothing but a stage of intellectual development in the antagonism of the elements within industrial society which precedes the actual struggle. . . .

Let us not deceive ourselves. The great concern and interest which communism, even more so than socialism, has aroused also in Germany, even the fear which the concept of communism inspires, is a result of the growing understanding of the deeper meaning of communism, a meaning which transcends any individual communistic system. In fearing communism, its spread over the nations, its impending dangers, one is afraid not only of the dangers which a mistaken and ruinous doctrine may bring about; state and society are allied against communism not because they expect disturbances by the working class or even an occasional revolt. The true concern is the fact that communism, as the expression of proletarian class consciousness, may sharpen the opposition and the hatred between the two large classes of society and thus become the seed of a general European struggle within the very heart of society. Indeed, there can be no doubt that the intuition of the people has been right. If communism is really the terminal point which the development of the proletariat finally reaches, and if the proletariat necessarily grows out of the industrial society, . . . is it then possible to consider communism as an isolated French phenomenon? Is it not natural that it should spread over Germany and might spread ever further to the extent that the industrial order of society spreads? Is the incessant growth of communism a result of communistic propaganda?

Quite the contrary. Science must admit, without recoiling from the truth, that communism is a natural and inevitable phenomenon in any nation which has developed from a market society into an industrial society and which has given rise to a proletariat. There is no power in the world which can prevent the growth of communism. Communism is not only a fact but a necessary historical point of transition in the development of society. The specific systems which communism brings about are irrelevant, but communism itself as a stage of social development is inevitable. . . .

The following presentation of events is based on this point of view. . . . The communist systems are of secondary interest; they are only the sign posts in this area; what is essential is the attitude of the lower classes, which cannot be deduced theoretically but has to be studied empirically. . . . Therefore, we shall let . . . the course of events illustrate and explain the specific content of communism.

REPUBLICANISM 1830-1835

The Nature of Republicanism

. . . To the extent that the state constitution is a manifestation of the existing social order, the acceptance of a theory which aims at overthrowing the existing order is impossible, even if this theory is accepted by a considerable part of the population, unless this theory arises out of a corresponding antagonism in society. The same is true for the opposite case. Wherever there is social antagonism in a society, it is impossible to check the spread of such a theory. For this reason—which can only be discovered by the science of society—the hardest and most extensive measures applied against subversive theories and movements is either superfluous, as is illustrated by the history of the stable social order of England, or useless, as has been demonstrated by the historical example of France.

Therefore, if republicanism arises, spreads and gets a foothold among the masses of the people at any time or in any country, the first principle of political observation and historical analysis ought to be that as a political movement it is of minor significance. It is, however, all the more important as a symptom of the social movement. If one desires to suppress republicanism, one has to start out with changing social relations, instead of calling out the police. Republicanism has always been the precursor of the struggle of the numerically larger but socially suppressed class against the less numerous ruling class. With the exception of the last two years, this interpretation has never been more decisively confirmed than through the history of the French republican movement under the July monarchy.

Already during the Restoration, a lot of young men, particularly of the educated class, inspired by the struggle of the bourgeoisie against the reaction and unable to understand the specific nature of this struggle, had enthusiastically devoted themselves to this movement. But this movement, which had aimed predominantly to safeguard the influence of economic interests in politics, had rejected these young men, since they did not represent anything but their own rather confused opinions. . . . They conceived the idea of changing the order of the state exclusively on their own. . . . Commanding no public influence, partly as a result of their personality, partly as a result of their socio-economic condition, they could attain this purpose only by constituting themselves as a group whose power rested upon its secret aims and upon the complete obedience of its members. This is the origin of the first secret society in Paris, under the leadership of Bazard, who later became a Saint-Simonist, and of Flotard and Buchez, the founders of the group. This was the society of the Carbonari. It sounds paradoxical, yet is confirmed beyond all doubt by those who know, that this association, from the beginning to the end, never knew what it stood for. Its members had nothing in common except hatred against the Restoration; Louis Blanc is absolutely correct when he states: "Carbonarism in its organization is powerful and amazing, but its principle is childish. Its main supporters expressed their basic principle in the following statement: Power is not justice; the Bourbons have been re-established by foreigners; the Carbonari desire to reinstate the free exercise of the rights to which the French nation is entitled: to choose the government which it prefers." The association is based on as shaky a principle as "a conspiracy with a great deal of enthusiasm, but without any concept for the future, without any rational plan, a prey to any willful passion. The vaguer the formula the better it was adapted to the various manifestations of annoyance and hatred" [Louis Blanc, Histoire des dix ans I, 99]. At another point he adds: "There were among them Republicans, Orleanists, Bonapartists; some joined the conspiracy without any purpose but to conspire. The activities were as varied as the principles, and in the heart of the alliance there was at such a critical moment nothing but chaos."

And yet this movement had spread over all of France and beyond it. Outstanding men, such as Lafayette, participated in it and risked their lives for it. It was drowned in blood, and its followers died as if for a great cause. How was such a phenomenon possible?

We have shown how the inner struggle in France under the Restoration was led by factions of the acquisitive society against the reinstitution of feudal principles. Carbonarism, with all its devotion and confusion, had no specific role in this struggle. It obviously stood for something else, something that those other elements did not comprehend, did not perhaps even acknowledge. What was this third element which tried to assert itself emphatically although inarticulately beside those who fought for the rights of citizenship or for feudalism?

Until the July Revolution nobody had raised this question. Carbonism was forgotten. But its seeds had grown exuberantly.

The ordinances were issued, the battle began; within three days the fate of the Restoration was decided, and jubilantly France again raised the Tricolor over the Tuileries. Yes, the Tricolor was back again, the state belonged again to the people; they were free. The old injustices were destroyed. New laws had to be established. The message of the great victory had spread very quickly over all of France; people were prepared for new things to come; hopes went high; great memories were being revived. Apparently a new era had started.

Then, all of a sudden, only a few days later, before the people had recovered their senses and clear understanding, a second message arrived: The Duke of Orleans has been installed as hereditary king; he has sworn to uphold the Charter. The Revolution is thereby declared to be over.

How had this happened? Who has a right to stage a revolution? Who else but the people? And who had put an end to it? Were the people consulted? Were its representatives summoned? Did the people have a choice of drafting a new constitution? Did the necessary quorum of the Chamber of Deputies meet? Did all members present agree? And, above all, did those who agreed have a mandate to do so, and through the mandate a right to do it? Obviously not. Who, then, brought the revolution to a close? The people? No. Only the majority of a partly dissolved Chamber of Deputies, elected on the basis of a law which had been fought by the deputies themselves, without consultation with the people, without reference to the people and without a mandate from them. Was the election of Louis Philippe an act in accordance with the law of the land? Certainly not; it might have been an act of political wisdom, defendable or questionable as such, but it certainly was not a legal act.

Who had brought this off and who had secured a general acceptance of the new monarchy? It must have been a force outside the legal framework of the state, a power which had made the arbitrary decision to impose new laws upon the whole nation. What power could have dared to do that? Only that power which the Chamber of Deputies, during that August of 1830, represented by its very composition. . . . And what "power" was that?

One glance at the property qualifications for members of this Chamber which established the new monarchy answers this question. The voters were the small capitalists, and the elected were the big capitalists. The elected deputies represented, in fact, one specific social element, the main element of the acquisitive society: i. e. capital. It was capital or the capitalists who, without formal rights and without a mandate from the people, had reinstituted monarchy, had declared the revolution to be over and had determined the new constitution.

The capitalists had usurped the highest legislative power of the state in a decisive moment without consulting the people. The termination of the July Revolution through the old Charter and the setting up of the new monarchy were, indeed, acts by which the social class of capitalists, by taking possession of the government, established itself as the ruling class. The end of the July Revolution was followed by the establishment not only of the French state but also of French society; it suddenly taught the acquisitive society, as yet undivided in its elements, . . . that the capitalists were the ruling class. Thus the sudden transition from the preceding form of society to an industrial society was accomplished. A new form of subordination was established in place of the older one, which had not yet been completely abolished by the Revolution. This was the sweeping change involved in the apparently quiet and noncontroversial election of the new monarchy. The July Revolution, therefore, had not only destroyed the last vestiges of feudalism but had also established the rule of industrial society. . . . This is why the July Revolution was predominantly a social revolution.

Indeed, if capital now took the place of feudal monarchy, the ideas of liberty and equality, rekindled during the Restoration, soon had to take account of the new form of domination and to discover their new antagonist. . . . What would be the manifestation of this new antagonism between these ideas and the existing order? . . .

Since the new monarchy and the old Constitution had been reinstated by the representatives of capital, monarchy in particular was interpreted by the partisans of equality and liberty as the definite exponent of the rule of the capital-owning class over the rest of society—all the more so since it became increasingly more evident that the monarchy was the strongest pillar of the rule of that class. Indeed, the origin and growth of genuine constitutionalism proved that this interpretation was correct. Since the first days of the new monarchy the intuition of the people had been correct; the monarchy of the July Revolution presented for the people the permanent confirmation of the fact that this Revolution had established the domination of the ruling class of industrial society over the state.

The inevitable consequence of this insight was simple. The whole sector of the population which, for purely abstract or positive social reasons, represented the ideas of liberty and equality naturally turned against the institution, the monarchy, which it considered to be the expression and the stronghold of the most powerful adversary of those ideas. This sector of society was inevitably driven to fight the monarchy—not monarchy as such but that which it represented. From a logical as well as a democratic viewpoint, the ideas of liberty and equality after the July Revolution necessarily had to be opposed to the idea of monarchy. Thus the question arose as to whether monarchy was at all reconcilable with these ideas. And since the answer was in the negative, the republic appeared to be the only constitution appropriate to the principles of liberty and equality. For this reason republicanism after the July Revolution presents a very simple and natural phenomenon in the social movement of the French people. . . .

It ought to be clear by now that republicanism was not at all a mere theory; it gained acceptance, not only because the election of Louis Philippe was highly objectionable from a legal point of view and was accepted merely as an accomplished fact, but because republicanism was a part of the social reality of that time. It was the first and most vivid expression of the antagonism of the dependent against the ruling class in the new industrial society, the first and great slogan of the struggle of labor against capital. . . . Republicanism, no matter how one looks at it, is essentially negative; it is not yet anything except a rejection of monarchy; it knows what it does not want but it is very confused about its goals. Republicanism at this stage is only the expression of the antagonism of industrial society under a constitutional monarchy. Republicanism is as little aware as is society itself as to where the deeper roots of this antagonism are located, and therefore it cannot predict what will happen if it ever should be victorious. This is, on the one hand, clearly the strength of republicanism. Due to the vagueness of its goal, the two elements of republicanism, the democratic and the social, can still cooperate. On the other hand, this lack of awareness is also the weakness of republicanism, because vagueness deprives republicanism of the strength to act decisively at the proper moment and also of confidence, which is the final attribute of success even for moves which have been carefully prepared., Republicanism remained a pure negation of monarchy in the name of equality and liberty; it therefore had to come to an end before the specific character of the social movement could emerge.

. . . If we review the history of the first French Revolution, we also discover that pure republicanism preceded the theories of communism. The same phenomenon necessarily repeats itself. For republicanism is the political manifestation of the abstract ideas of liberty and equality; liberty and equality as practical issues arise only after those abstract ideas prove to be inadequate. The events of the years 1793 and 1795 repeat themselves in a new form; the eternal laws of the life of human society assert themselves. These laws are as eternal as the laws which control the atoms of material life and move the grains of sand and the solar systems.

The Struggles and the Defeat of Republicanism

After Louis Philippe had acceeded to the throne, Paris was by no means pacified. The Revolution had created considerable commotion among the population. State power, a little while ago still in the hands of the people, had not yet regained its balance. The army, the main support of the state, had not yet developed complete loyalty to the throne; it could not as yet be used to control the population. People were very restless; it was a period in which conditions were similar to those of 1791 and 1792. Two phenomena occurred again which we called to the attention of the reader earlier. Due to the lack of a completely independent state, the two main classes of society began to organize in two large bodies which, consciously or not, represented the inherent antagonism within society. They were the National Guard and the Clubs. Both of these reappeared immediately after the July Revolution.

One of the first administrative acts of the new government was the establishment of the National Guard, which spread over the whole of France at the beginning of the July monarchy. Its organization in Paris was pursued with particular zeal. Already on August 29th, 1830, the King was able to review a spectacular parade of the National Guard. The existing social order thus became armed and prepared for any eventuality. But at the same time Paris abounded with clubs and public speakers. All of them were opposed to the prevailing institutions. They aroused skepticism regarding the new monarchy and sowed the seeds of discord and opposition. . . . With the July Revolution, a large number of newspapers and pamphlets had appeared; they became the center of quarrels and fights, opposed the Chamber, attacked its position, its rights and its policy. They became the carriers and propagators of republican ideas. Soon enough the Chamber had to have a showdown with them. . . .

The struggle began on November 9th; . . . on that date the question of the republic was first raised; Guizot, indicating the trend of his future career, most decisively argued against the establishment of a republic in France. He stated: "France is not republican; one would have to distort one's convictions in order to introduce this form of government here." The ruling class accepted this declaration jubilantly; Guizot had dared publicly to challenge the republic; from then on he became the minister of the capitalists, all the more so since he himself was not economically motivated. The middle class, under Odilon Barrot, joined the right-of-center ruling class, since it had a chance to acquire capital also. The republicans felt distinctly for the first time that they were in the minority. The original separation of the various elements of the new society had taken place.

From now on the clubs increased their activities of agitation and propaganda for the republic; the bourgeoisie moved more distinctly into the opposition by supporting the existing Constitution. But the question remained uncertain whether the Chamber would establish the major republican institutions even if it were to reject the republican system as a whole. Only this question would, however, determine the future attitude of the republicans; the question was decided together with the question on the electoral reform.

It was imperative to revise the old electoral law of 1820. This law had made voting rights subject to high property qualifications; only the large capital owners were admitted to participation in politics. The industrial society had the power to modify property qualifications, but was unable to eliminate them because they corresponded to the very nature of industrial society. The republicans were very well aware of that. They knew that the dependence of the lower class could only be destroyed by extending its political rights, by putting the worker on a par with the capital owner. They knew that the reform law would establish the political equality of the masses, the first step toward the realization of the republic. If it was possible to accomplish a basic change in voting rights, there was hope of realizing the ideas of freedom and equality with the cooperation of the Chamber. If the old law remained in operation, capital would retain its power, the Chamber would be re-elected on the old basis without a revision in property qualifications; any hope of the establishing a republic with the cooperation of the existing organs of the state vanished. . . .

There was no question as to the decision. The representatives of capital considered themselves entitled to preferential representation. After violent debates which revealed the hopelessness of the situation for the republicans, the electoral law of March 9th, 1831 was passed. . . . The move to establish universal suffrage was completely defeated; the ruling class retained the exclusive constitutional right to participate in the decisions concerning the affairs of the state.

This was the crucial moment when republicanism had either to accept defeat or to transfer its struggle into another area. The clubs were still in existence; so was general participation in public affairs. But because of the Army and the National Guard there was no hope for immediate success through the use of arms. The Republican Party resorted to the last method of subversion by becoming an underground movement. . . . Well aware of the fact that splinter groups would weaken it, it attempted to concentrate its major strength in the "Société des Amis du Peuple," which grew in part out of the old Carbonarism. . . .

With the beginning of the year 1831 street fighting started. The republicans hoped in this way to gain the victory which was denied them by the electoral law of the Chamber. Toward the end of 1831 the first revolt broke out in Lyon. This much discussed revolt was neither republican nor socialistic; it was simply a result of a long dispute between masters and journeymen. But it was here that the laboring class became for the first time aware of the fact that its interests were closely interwoven with those of republicanism and that both had to struggle against a common enemy, the domination of the capitalists. . . . Indeed, this dispute established the bridge between democracy and the proletariat and the alliance of both for years to come. . . . The outcome of the dispute, of which Louis Blanc has given a detailed report (Vol. III., Ch. 2), which ended with the total rejection of the demands of the journeymen, contributed toward a more belligerent attitude of republicanism which was needed in order not to lose the powerful and important support of the workers. With the beginning of 1832, the leaders of the Republican Party stood up for their cause more openly. . . .

Side by side with the Société des Amis du Peuple there developed the "Gallic Society" and the "Société des Droits de l'Homme." They established contacts, but no other decisions were made except as is usual under such conditions—to be prepared. At this moment General Lamarque died. He had been one of the most distinguished leaders of the Republican Party; at his funeral the storm broke out. The government had been prepared; 24,000 men were ready for the struggle; they were supported by secret agents of the government in the clubs. The revolt collapsed. The republicans were dispersed and defeated, the rest, a handful of men, shot down near the cloister St. Méry. Such was the fate of the revolt of June 5th and 6th, 1832.

Republicanism had met a serious defeat. But the government did not limit itself to controlling the revolts of the streets. An investigation against the *Société des Amis du Peuple* was instigated. . . . The main purpose of this whole trial was to illustrate the criminal character of republicanism. This is the main reason why the trial is of historical interest. However, the memories of the Revolution were still much too vivid; the jury acquitted the defendants. This was a legal victory which very well compensated for the defeat of June 6th. Although the president of the jury had declared the society dissolved, republicanism again raised its head. A last showdown had to be attempted.

The year 1833 was approaching, the year of preparation for the last decision on the future of republicanism. The press of the party acted with ever growing recklessness. . . . The *Société des Droits de l'Homme* now became the center of republicanism. This society differed from all the others in one specific point. It was the first society which attempted to formulate a definite goal for its undertakings. It allied itself with the republicanism of the first Revolution and accepted as its program the Declaration of the Rights of Man by Robespierre. The declaration was published as its own manifesto. With the publication of this manifesto, the center of the new republicanism was established. . . . It was the turning point in the whole history of republicanism.

This declaration showed for the first time that two essentially different and incongruous elements existed within the republican movement. For the program of that society contained, in addition to proposals regarding the organization of the republic, a large number of social principles. It suggested an "emancipation of the working class through an improved system of distribution of labor, a fairer distribution of profit and the preparation of collectivization." The Rights of Man of Robespierre went even further; in Article 6 it had been suggested that "property be permitted only in those goods which were allotted in equal shares to all by the law; the state should take over the organization of labor and the distribution of commodities, and state power was supposed to be in the hands of the masses. There is no doubt that the members of the society did not clearly realize the consequences of these statements; but popular sentiment soon became aware of them. The republic of this republicanism embraced more than a plan for a specific structure of the state. . . . To be sure, the concept of communism or of socialism was not as yet known, but the first indications of these thoughts began to appear. The newspapers of the upper class exploited the weak points which republicanism had exposed. It became increasingly more obvious that the issue was not primarily one of a new form of the state but of a new form of society. Those who were doubtful on this question started to retreat. The inner strength of the society was broken before it even had an opportunity fully to emerge.

The Chamber recognized correctly that it had an advantage over republicanism, which had lost control over its own program. The government, however, tolerated further activities by the Society. But soon the first steps were taken: public sale of the newspapers was prohibited, and early in March, 1834, the Government introduced a law according to which secret societies were prohibited under the threat of punishment. This law aimed essentially at the *Société des Droits de l'Homme*. The law . . . was a declaration of war by the Chamber against republicanism in general. . . . As soon as the law was published the republicans took up arms for the last time. The struggle broke out simultaneously in Paris and Lyon. There has rarely been such a confusion, such a lack of control as at the outbreak of this struggle. The alliance lacked a leader, it lacked a plan, it lacked arms and munitions; it lacked, above all, already at this point, the support of the middle class. Republicanism was isolated. It fought bravely and long, but there was not the slightest hope for victory. The Government had been well prepared; it welcomed the attack as an opportunity to defeat its mortal enemy by one stroke. But most decisive was the position of the National Guard. It definitely sided with the Government and fought with great courage against an enemy which it suspected of being an enemy of property as well as of the Constitution. The republicans were defeated; they dispersed in all directions; the *Société des Droits de l'Homme* was dissolved, the prisoners condemned after a long and severe trial, and the power of republicanism was destroyed. At the same time, new elections took place. Republicanism failed completely. The Government identified itself closely with the ruling class. From now on, the industrial social order and constitutionalism seemed firmly established. . . . The September laws of 1835 were promulgated. They declared the public defense of republican theories and public assemblies a crime. . . .

We may now ask: Who, after all, won in this four-year battle; who was defeated, and what are the consequences of this victory and this defeat?

The Transition to the First Purely Social Movement—Communism

Glancing backwards over the development of French society during this period, one discovers that it was the July Revolution which had transformed the acquisitive society into industrial society. Furthermore, it becomes evident that in industrial society the opposition between the property owners and the propertyless is expressed in terms of the opposition between capital and labor, and that all dependency is in practice a consequence of the rule of capital. . . . The opposition which arose immediately against the July Revolution . . . was based on the abstract principle of liberty and equality, which viewed the republic as a form of government corresponding to this principle. This principle, which is limited to the political manifestations of equality and liberty, was indifferent to the distribution of property; it therefore had followers only in theory. The number of these followers was necessarily small and powerless against the prevailing law. If the republicans wanted to win they had to look for allies beyond the sphere of pure republicanism.

The July Revolution had seriously damaged the quickly advancing growth of industries. Many enterprises were destroyed, others were disrupted. Many laborers were, at least temporarily, unemployed—this in spite of the fact that the laborers in particular had participated decisively in the July Revolution. What was their reward for their struggle and their sacrifices? Did it result in giving them a politically significant role? An increase of their political liberty? No. Property qualifications, although reduced, were to them as prohibitive as before. The Chamber was not concerned with the lot of the laborers; they remained what they had been before, the rejected children of the nation.

But one thing had changed. Up to now during the Restoration they had had hope for an improvement of their conditions through a general change of circumstances. This change in circumstances had occurred, but their hopes were dashed; they had become so much the poorer for it.

The suffering laborers, . . . therefore, immediately turned against the status quo, just as they had done during the Restoration. But, isolated and unable to size up their own situation, they looked for leadership among the upper class. Here the republicans too stood alone. The community of interests was soon visualized, and by the end of 1830 the masses of the laboring class made common cause with the republicans. The opposition against the existing order contained now two different elements: the republicans represented the leadership and the intelligence; the workers represented the physical power. The masses were now united under the banner of republicanism.

On the surface, this republicanism was directed against the monarchy. However, the constitutional monarchy as established by the Revolution was essentially only the form of government through which industrial society ruled. The defense of monarchy meant the defense of the rule of capital in industrial society. With the defeat of republicanism . . . capital had gained a victory.

It was understandable that capital did not immediately identify its true antagonist. It assumed that it had to deal only with republicanism. It defended itself against republicanism and attacked it. The republicans, on the other hand, to hold their own, tied themselves closer to the working class, since they were the only reliable supporters they had. The laboring class, however, began to direct its demands for material improvement to the republicans. And while on the surface republic and monarchy seemed to be the sole antagonists, crucial changes took place internally which were to influence the future of France. For the first time since 1794 the problems of the labor movement and the republican system became fused; for the first time it became evident that something was happening in France which went way beyond mere republicanism. There was a vague awareness that the Republican Party contained two elements which, although united in their struggle against the outside world, were destined to fight for supremacy within their own ranks.

At first republicanism assumed that it would be able to exploit to its own advantage the demands of the laboring class without planning to meet them. The significance of this was not as yet understood. The republican leaders used the demands of the working class as a threat against the property-owning class; they blamed the Constitution for the misery of the laborers, and they promised everything to everybody in exchange for the establishment of a republican state government. But the power of the workers grew; every day they became more aware of their actual goals, and the republicans, almost without being aware of it, were slowly forced to transform themselves from representatives of republican principles into representatives of the workers and of their specific social interests. In order to retain the support of the workers, they had, already during the local disturbances in Paris in 1831, given them flags which carried the slogan: *"Du pain ou la mort."* During the revolt of Lyon the flags carried for the first time the well-known inscription *"Vivre en travaillant ou mourir en combattant."* When the defendants of the revolt of 1832 stood before the jury, Godefroy Cavaignac, the foremost speaker of the republicans, who had taken over their defense, went so far as to present republicanism as the general reflection of all those new institutions which were designed to change society rather than the state.

This speech (in part recorded by Louis Blanc Vol. III, Ch. 8) is a strange document. It illustrates how deeply Saint-Simonism had already penetrated. Cavaignac demanded the organization of science and the organization of labor; "With regard to work, we demand, that it should no longer be subordinated to the interests of the greedy or the idle. We demand that the worker be no longer exploited by the capitalists, that wages should not be the only compensation of the worker; and mainly that work more than anything else should be the title of the exercise of political rights, for the life of society is based on work and not on property." . . .

However, it could not escape some republicans that the alliance with the industrial working class had led them into a road whose end they could not envision. It was easy to formulate general phrases; it was quite difficult to decide on specific action; and it was altogether impossible to divert the thoughts of the workers from the direction into which they had decided to go. The leaders knew this perfectly well. At this point the relationship of the two elements had to be decided.

If it is true that social elements and social problems determine political conditions, the representatives of the latter have to subordinate themselves to those of the former. Once the social question had come into focus, republicanism, in order to remain the leader of the movement, had to subject its political to its social demands. Being the spokesman for a free constitution, it now had to become the champion of a free society. Neither the republican nor the democratic movement is able to evade this inevitable process. . . . As soon as the pure republicans perceived that their theories bore consequences which they were unable to control, they abandoned their theories. All distinguished members of the party withdrew; the middle class—in apprehension over its own condition, and in awareness of what would follow—also abandoned republicanism. Thus it happened that by 1834 republicanism was destroyed externally as well as internally. From that time on, democracy had to chose another champion. This was the great significance of the foregoing events. The attitude of the press reflected these important changes. A number of republican newspapers—especially the *"Populaire,"* by Cabet—closed down; others—such as the *"National"*—became organs of the parliamentary opposition; liberal organs severed their loose ties with the republican cause. There was no longer a republican faction represented in the Chamber. Indeed, one was led to believe that industrial society was now completely in control.

But republicanism, so easily defeated and apparently completely destroyed, had left a heritage for which its most outstanding adherents had abandoned it: this was the growing labor movement. It is here that the secret societies had had an immense influence, not only because of the principles they propagated, but because of their public activities. . . . The rank and file of laborers, artisans, non-owners of any kind had been until then without a rallying point. They had not been able to exchange and influence each other's opinions or to estimate their own total number. The emissaries of the *Société des Droits de l'Homme* contacted these groups of people, rallied them, pointed out to them what were their rights and thus aroused in them by their speeches, newspapers and pamphlets, the awareness that the proletarians were a unit in society, physically powerful, suffering, and yet a social entity with just claims. However, it was not only class consciousness which was thus awakened in the worker by republicanism. Constitutional monarchy was, after all, the legal form of government. If the republic was to overthrow this government, a principle had to be found which would establish that the existing law was in itself an injustice and that it was right to revolt against it. Thus republicanism was compelled to undermine the established law in the eyes of the proletariat. This was the second important effect of the secret societies. Wherever they penetrated they aroused hatred against the ruling authorities, contempt for the law and dissatisfaction with the prevailing conditions. This hatred and dissatisfaction coalesced with the growth of awareness of the specific conditions of the laboring class. The defeat of republicanism resulted in creating a spirit among the laboring class which shaped the proletariat into the present teeming and powerful social class which is capable of interpreting its own social conditions.

This is the origin of the proletariat in France. The antagonism in industrial society which is theoretically represented by labor and capital was now incorporated in a specific body. Society itself was split; two opposing elements confronted each other; the dominant social problem of the present social order, the relationship of capital and labor now determining the line of development for the individual, had crystallized into a specific social phenomenon and defined its basic interest spheres. What republicanism had only indicated and initiated had come to fruition after its downfall. It was the beginning of the great struggle within the new social order.

We know that this struggle had frequently been predicted and that it finally broke out in 1848. During the intermediate years the proletariat, under the influence of changing theories and movements, was becoming aware of the major factor which determined its fate: the question of private property. The common expression of the interpretation of this question and of the answer to this question for the proletariat is communism. Therefore, with the defeat of republicanism, the history of communism begins as the history of the social consciousness of the proletariat.

The Two Principles of Communism Since 1835

At first glance, it seems that nothing is simpler to understand than the main principle of communism. It includes the abolition of private property and of the family and their replacement with institutions based on collective principles. But the abolition of property and of the family affects major spheres of human existence; their abolition would be contrary to human history, contrary to human hopes and actions. It would inevitably lead to a reconsideration of basic tenets of the existing order. Even the most radical thinker, in order to destroy everything on which life and the order of human society rests, has to have a firm faith in principles which would justify such a revolutionary change.

There are two conceivable principles on the basis of which property and the family may be rejected. Both are contained in communism, but each has been differently interpreted and has led to the construction of a different system.

The first principle is based on the conviction that the happiness of man is the will of God, and that the supreme confirmation of this will is embodied in Christianity. Whatever is in contradiction to the happiness of man in this world is against the will of God and the Christian creed. It is true that law can be enforced, but there is a power superior to justice, the power of love. If the very needs of human life demand the abandonment of laws, love commands such an abandonment. And if the existing order of society illustrates that the prevailing law—the law of private property and family law—does not safeguard happiness, not even the hope for happiness, love, which is the expression of man's divine nature, must replace law; love must demand in the name of God and religion the establishment of conditions favorable to the happiness of man even against the existing law. It is not difficult to find support for this interpretation in the documents of the Christian creed; it is even less difficult to arouse emotions by them. Thus the first peculiar type of communism develops; it is based on the principle of the Christian religion. Religious communism aims to abolish the right of property and the family in the name of the religion of love; it desires to replace these rights by the community of those equal before God and chosen for supreme happiness.

The second principle is of secular origin. What constitutes law? Is it power? Is it the fact that it exists? The answer is no. Man is meant to be free and equal; inequality and dependence can never be derived from this concept of man. If inequality and dependence exist, they exist by way of external forces which can never be "right". What is it that fosters the greatest inequality and misfortune? Shall the laws of private property and the family determine what is right? If so, they both would be in direct contradiction to the destiny of man in this world. They may be facts established by power, but they can never be considered to be just. If our rights do not correspond to our potentials of development, our whole social existence becomes senseless; if they are in harmony, the laws of property and the family must be subordinate to the individual, whose life is meant to be free and happy; those who want to abolish the family and private property in order to allow man to fulfill the purpose of his existence are right. This is the second trend of thought in communism. The destruction of these two institutions is demanded in the name of man's worldly destiny. This is the basic tenet of materialistic communism.

These two major trends determine and guide the growth of communism in France; they are the keynote of the whole communist movement and only through them does communism become a consistent theory. One should not expect that it is possible to separate the two systematically and historically; they run parallel to each other and are correlated with each other; the systems which they create are mainly embodiments of viewpoints on the basis of which the inner development of the proletariat is interpreted. But they are the substance of the history of the proletariat since 1835. One is justified in saying that until 1843 communism had reflected the hidden processes which were undermining the order of industrial society since 1835.

THE REFORM MOVEMENT SINCE 1841

It is not the task of the social sciences or of history to criticize the various lines of thought among the adherents of communism; whether their ideas happen to be true or false is not, indeed, of any importance. But in their totality these ideas are a manifestation of the opposition of the dependent against the ruling class in industrial society; they symbolize the struggle of labor against capital, and it is through them that the proletariat has become aware of its social position, its conditions and its future. It is for this reason and not through its individual representatives that communism is a highly important historical movement. Communism is for the proletariat what socialism had been for the intelligentsia, and it is from this fact that communism derived its vital power. The growing significance of communism compelled those who believed in democracy to reconsider communism again. Thus communism has given rise to the most recent social trend—the Reform Movement—which led to the threshold of the February Revolution.

General Character of the Reform Movement

While communism was penetrating deeper and deeper into the increasingly independent working class, transforming it into a proletariat in the proper sense of the word, a similar movement developed in a related field. It is true that the revolt in May 1839 and its direct consequences, as well as the repeated attempted assassinations, had brought about an alienation between the liberal bourgeoisie and the lower classes. But radical progressives within the upper classes felt the need to approach the lower class. At the same time, the persistent unrest of the latter had become a matter of concern even to the complacent. It became quite obvious that the conditions of the proletariat were the main cause of all public disturbances. Only complete despair and unrelenting hatred could explain the willingness of the masses to embrace the most desperate and nonsensical ventures and theories and to support the ever-emerging communist associations and small local papers with their popular appeal. . . . To be sure, at the moment, the bourgeoisie ruled alone; but another revolution was very well possible. Who would be victorious if the masses, which until now had fought side by side with the bourgeoisie, would turn against it? Without question, the proletariat had constituted itself as an independent social element; its interpretation of the social conditions acquired an increasingly more serious character.

It might be possible to suppress the symptoms by control of the press and the persecution of the communist societies by repressive legislation. But only the simple-minded could assume that the evil would be eliminated in this fashion. There was only one possible way of action left: the progressive party of the ruling class had to approach the proletarian movement, perhaps even to attempt to obtain control over it, lest the latter attack the existing social order.

This trend was met halfway by a development within the proletariat. The more reasonable among the workers who cared to inform themselves about general conditions had to realize that, however great the necessity for a basic change in society, an improvement was hardly—if at all— possible without the consent and the cooperation of capital and of the ruling class. However, such consent and cooperation were conceivable only under one condition: the proletariat had to give up any attempt at a revolution by force and had to accept gradual changes in the existing order. This was a step toward reconciliation and agreement, and while communism proper, on the one hand, was developing into a power of growing importance, one could, on the other hand, observe a growing rapprochement of the two social classes. Beneficial results might have ensued and disastrous events might have been avoided if a new political movement had not appeared on the scene at this time. . . .

We have shown that, since 1835, pure republicanism in France had been utterly defeated. Republicanism no longer had any followers, neither in the population at large, nor in the Chamber, nor the press. Only after this happened was it possible for constitutionalism to grow undisturbed. A reasonable and sincere government could have secured the well-being of France for a long period to come. But Louis Philippe's unfortunate ambition, which aimed at establishing a so-called "personal government" and at reviving "pseudo-constitutionalism," proved to the bourgeoisie that its rule could be preserved only at the price of perpetual vigilance and of constant struggle with that government. This struggle, which continued for years, gave rise to a great bitterness toward the government which was in contradiction to the social order. It thus paved the way for a revolution more effectively than did any secret society and theory. Nevertheless, the bourgeoisie remained opposed to any revolution. A revolution would have meant, in the first place, an attack on constitutionalism, which represented the well-established form of government, and, secondly, an instigation of the lower class, which was basically antagonistic to the bourgeoisie. Thus there was only one way open for the opposition to take, . . . namely, an electoral reform. The opposition of the bourgeoisie against pseudo-constitutionalism had now thrown its support to the movement of electoral reform. . . .

Internal as well as external reasons prohibited the opposition to treat the masses, which it needed to support the movement, as a mere tool. The opposition within the bourgeoisie had to take into consideration the ideas and demands of the proletariat. In order to gain the support of the proletariat, the opposition had to promise in turn to support the demands of the proletariat; in brief, it had to offer the proletariat political rights. . . . This had a twofold consequence of major importance for the history of French society. First, the extreme opposition was now compelled to join forces with the social movement. From this point on, the social movement ceased to be merely a proletarian movement. . . . Secondly, the exclusively social ideas of the proletariat were merged with the elements of contemporary political interest. Instead of presenting a political utopia, as they had done up to this time, they now tended to suggest practical political goals. . . . The members of the proletariat began to consider the right to participate in political decisions as a right due them before reaching a level of education and a standard of living which would entitle them to such privileges. . . . Instead of gaining political rights on the basis of social development, they claimed them in the name of an abstract concept of liberty and equality, and they did so in order to raise their living standard so as to make them roughly equal to the ruling class. Such were the general and not yet clearly defined origins of social democracy. . . . There was only one way to avoid the danger and the difficulties that social democracy presented. The bourgeoisie should have used its constitutional power to foster the interests of the lower class as much as its own; instead it had used this power exclusively to favor its own interests. This fact formed—as a logical countermovement—the basis for social democracy. . . .

Thus a twofold development took place in France after 1840. Due to the nature of social conditions, this development gave the impression of constituting a single movement. On the one hand there was the political reform movement whose most radical wing favored the ideas of social democracy which provided the transition to the events of 1848 and 1849; on the other hand was the social reform movement which, based on a scientific approach and deriving its support from the proletariat, touched in its extreme upon communism. Both wanted to preserve the existing order, and both were striving for a change of conditions within that order. Communism as well as social democracy, however, aimed at something altogether new—they wanted to establish an entirely new order. Both the political and the social reform movement, were, in fact and in principle, transitory phenomena. . . . They did not offer to introduce a new system but only plans and suggestions for specific changes; they prepared but did not create a new order. They left socialism and communism undisturbed to pursue their own goals. Neither did they condemn the existing constitution. To interpret the reform movement as a third period in the social development of France does not mean that the movements of republicanism, socialism and communism have ceased; they continue as manifestations of the great political and social trends in the nation's life and in society; they have entered a new phase, because they now appear in a new form side by side with the old ones, both preparing and instigating in their own fashion the powerful events of the subsequent years. . . .

The Social Reformers

No matter how strong a stand public opinion had taken against any movement of the proletariat, no matter how devastatingly all communist and socialist theories had been ridiculed or condemned or simply ignored, one could not, after all, possibly misinterpret the deeper significance of these views. . . . The more scientific attitude of socialism compelled the adherents of this movement to consult in turn their own science as to the causes of the social evils and the possible remedies. The daily contact with disturbances made it impossible for them to deceive themselves about the nature of the events. Thus, there developed, mainly after the defeat of republicanism, a trend in the social sciences which we shall call the social trend. It originated in France toward the end of the 18th century and has continued to grow ever since. . . . We wish to call attention to those who had prepared the ground for a closer relationship between the social movement and the strictly scientific approach to social problems.

. . . 1841, Louis Reybaud published a book under the well-known title: *Etudes sur les réformateurs contemporains*. This publication created a sensation. . . . It was the first work in which the socialistic schools of thought of Saint-Simon and of Fourier were both interpreted as a symptom of a deep contradiction within society and as an attempt to find a solution to a vital but not yet clearly conceived problem of the nation. One may well claim that this book, contrary to the intention of its author, raised socialism from its merely utopian stage to a real force in public affairs. The book attracted attention mainly because for the first time it criticized the utopian systems scientifically and systematically. Reybaud, therefore, was the first to call attention to the existence of a profound social movement. . . . Through his clear and intelligent analysis he brought the thoughts of the socialists within the reach of a wider public. . . . Reybaud is the leading French scholar concerned with the historical presentation of the socialist theory and the socialist movement. While he summed up the facts of the intellectual life, a number of other authors concentrated on the analysis of actual social conditions. The most important among them is, no doubt, Villermé with his book: *Tableau de l'état physique et moral des ouvriers employés dans les manufactures de coton, de laine, et de soie*, in which he, for the first time, offered the first detailed description of the intolerable living conditions of the working class. It was the first study which analyzed the misery of the lower classes in terms of statistics, and which, at the same time pointed with gravity and sympathy to the dangers which were bound to arise from these conditions for the whole of society. . . . Villermé's work was all the more influential because it did not discuss communist and socialist projects but simply documented, through specific facts, the general and growing deprivation of the proletariat. . . . At the same time, two other authors, Blanqui and Villeneuve-Bargemont, . . . came, even though starting out from different premises, to the same conclusion that in the contemporary industrial system the position of the laborer—a slave of his basic needs —was hopeless and desperate, and that any germ of liberty was inevitably killed through the laborer's dependence on the factory owner. These authors, too, demanded improvements and anticipated grave results for the future unless state and society took the misery and the needs of this class to heart. . . .

All these publications had one thing in common. They showed the sufferings of the working class, the significance of this class, and the danger it presented, but they had neither a plan nor a theory which would offer a solution to these problems. It is their merit to have called to the attention of thoughtful people the growing contradiction inherent in industrial society. . . . While they looked from the outside into the intricacies of these conditions in order to impress upon the prevailing powers the need for reform, important spokesmen of the proletariat, at the same time, though living under conditions almost past endurance, suggested a sensible reform to alleviate the conditions of the working class in order to forestall the approaching conflict. The laborers of France's big cities were almost constantly in touch with the usually highly educated republicans and democrats. They frequently participated in the meeting of secret societies, became acquainted with the vast literature on public issues, and consequently became accustomed to thinking independently and to participating in discussions. It is not surprising, therefore, that the working class produced a number of authors whose main interest was, of course, to discuss their own living conditions. The two main representatives of this group in the beginning of the reform period were Charles Noiret with his *Lettres aux ouvriers,* published in 1840 and 1841, and Adolph Boyer with his pamphlet *De l'état des ouvriers et de son amélioration par l'organisation du travail* (1841). While Noiret emphasized primarily his strong opposition to the prevailing exploitation of the workers and the masses through the wealthy and the educated, Boyer shows a deeper insight into the situation of the laboring class. He shows the isolated position of the worker when confronting the factory owner; how the employment books (*livrets*), the competition, the factory courts, the employment offices, the rates of pay, are all aimed at controlling the worker; how even institutions such as hospitals, savings banks, and others are of no real value; and how the beginnings of self-help projects through the workers' associations are partially hampered by the law and partially corrupt. He tries to call attention to the practical conditions, advocating improved rates of pay, fair factory courts, and associations among workers, so that work, instead of being a curse, could become a pleasure. His work program suggests a reform of existing conditions. The little brochure is one of the best published in this field at that time. . . . Richer in ideas but much less practical and closer to the socialist school of thought was Flora Tristan, who published several works which are all, more or less, concerned with improvement of the conditions of the working class. . . . Her specific plan is described in the *Union ouvrière* (3rd edition, 1845). She advocates the organization of the working class into a comprehensive union which would choose its own representative (*défenseur*), who would defend the interests of the working class and be paid by the union. . . . Through this union the working class would gain the "right to own property acquired through work," the "universal right to work" and the right to "moral, intellectual and professional instruction". . . . The major goal of this working men's organization should be the building of a labor union palace (*"Palais de l'union ouvrière"*) which shall be erected in each *département* by voluntary contributions. The concept of these workers palaces is definitely taken from Fourier's *Phalanstère;* old people, the ill and feeble, and those injured while working are to be admitted there; at the same time, it is to provide a shelter for working men's children, who are to be taught various practical skills. Flora Tristan gave special attention . . . to working class women, whose condition she considered to be the cause for much of the misfortune and on whose help she counted in the program of self-help. She was the only person who had the courage to confess to the workers that "ordinary women are in general brutal, wicked and sometimes heartless" and who stated with concern that "one has to admit that there are very few workers' households where happiness prevails." . . . But she also knew that this maliciousness and crudeness is not in the nature of these women but is a consequence of the sad conditions and the daily struggle with poverty. . . . Here she touched upon a central problem of the condition of a whole class of society. Her style is clear and lucid, although she lacked any knowledge of economics; but she showed an awareness, more than any of the other like-minded authors, that the working class is an entity and that in order to improve conditions it must recognize itself as such and strive to achieve a solidarity which would help it to move towards a common goal.

One other publication has affected the class-consciousness and the growth of ideas in the working class more than all these separate pamphlets. This was the newspaper *L'Atelier* (*Journal des intérèts moraux et matériels des ouvriers*) whose motto was: "Whoever does not want to work, should not be allowed to eat." The *Atelier* began publication in 1840. Since 1840 it attempted to lead all reform movements and first offered cooperation to political reformers for common action toward the improvement of the living conditions of the lower classes. Its principle was that "one has to be a worker in order to understand the conditions of labor." . . . The aims of the newspaper are summed up as follows: "The sponsoring committee acknowledges the fact that future improvements have to be based on the moral principle reflected by the motto of our forefathers: 'liberty, equality, fraternity, unity' from which springs the political principle of popular sovereignty and the industrial principle of social solidarity (*Gesellschaftung*). Our newspaper will support electoral reform as the only way to establish a popular government, and industrial collectivism as the only means for a fair distribution of the products of labor. It is a peaceful crusade which we open against political and industrial privileges." However, the *Atelier* states that it is definitely opposed to communism, it favors a legal and gradual reform. . . . For "equality is distinctly not absolute." "There are always some inferior people"; equality is realized if "all roads are open. to everybody so that each one attains the position corresponding to his contribution to society." To achieve this, the laborers must unite so as to enforce the electoral reform and on the basis of the new system of representation initiate industrial reform. Thus the outlines of approaching events were already discernible on the horizon of time, but only a few observed them and evaluated them correctly. There is also an appeal to the worker that devotion be the basis of morals and unity. Thus the *Atelier* turned seriously against communism and even attempted to make converts in favor of reform; it thereby exposed itself to bitter attacks from the communists, particularly from Cabet. . . .

Alongside these, other movements developed among the proletariat which, starting out from a similar basis, did not identify themselves entirely with any of the others. . . . Of importance particularly is one manifesto which undoubtedly came from a reform party; it was published on March 3, 1842 and shows that the authors are familiar with and appreciate the various activities of the proletariat. . . . But none of these attempts satisfies them; some want too much, some not enough; but they themselves, just like those whose vagueness they criticize, do not come to any specific conclusions. They too start out with the principle of equality, the eternally recurring concept; they want "to preach the exercise of fraternity to the citizens as the first task," to further "ethics as the only source of happiness" and "rationalism, which is the belief based on empirical evidence and reason." From there they come to the conclusion that "inequality of conditions, whatever its form, is a constant source of misfortune and degradation which cannot be alleviated by equal political rights alone," that "the realization of the doctrine of equality is based on the community of work," as well as "on equal rights in the use of common production distributed by a prudent and circumspect organization, on the community of education and the modification of the family in order to undermine the caste-spirit, though, of course, without promiscuity and without disregard of paternity."

We do not put too much emphasis on these sporadic publications stating general and rather vague principles which are neither new nor fully developed. But these publications demonstrate that there were trends in the large and rather diffused circle of reformers not unlike those in the socialist movement; they were associations and alliances designed for information and discussion rather than action. And no matter what was their original purpose, they all contributed to making the working class aware of its conditions and goals and to shaping it. . . into a compact, class-conscious, active proletariat.

These are the diverse views expressed during the epoch which we call that of the social reform movement. At the extreme, almost verging on communism are authors like Villegardelle, . . . Cherbuliez, Celliez and others who are of no specific importance except that their work reflects the social contradictions. Among them we find *"Esclavage du Riche"* by A. Hubert, 1845, a member of the radical group, distinguished by precision and clarity but representing essentially only a negative view of the rule of capital. He interprets freedom simply as the reversal of the present power constellation, namely, the rule of labor over capital, without presenting a specific plan for this turnover. These authors represent the transition from reform movements to the doctrinaire form of materialistic communism, while the magazine *Atelier* represents the transition to the political opposition.

All these views existed side by side without being integrated into one theory, such as those of the communist and socialist schools of thought. At a first glance at their content, one recognizes that they do not lend themselves to being coordinated. They do not grow out of a common principle nor out of a common approach; they are concerned with different sectors of society and with the different functions and interests of these sectors. On the surface, they are, therefore, definitely less important than socialism and communism. But their influence upon the inner life of the proletariat is all the greater because they are versatile, influencing different people in different ways, yet clearly showing the deep contradiction in the heart of society, the great cleavage of the two elements of industrialism and the antagonism between them. Their true significance lies in their explanation of the grave problems of our present society. However, they lacked a central focus, which developed only after the new point of view severed itself from pure republicanism, constituted itself independently, and turned its interests toward the social order. With its appearance begins the last phase of the period immediately preceding the February Revolution. . . .

The Political Reform Movement and the Beginning of Social Democracy.

. . . Already during 1841, Ledru-Rollin approached his constituency . . . with an electoral speech which went far beyond the limits of a mere parliamentary opposition. The principle on which he based his program was new for that time. He dared to state that political questions were no longer an end in themselves for a given political movement but only the road to social improvement for the betterment of the lower classes. . . .

Indeed, this speech was a great event. For it was the first time that a man who was a candidate for the Chamber, which was controlled by capital, frankly admitted to the voters, who were, as a consequence of the election law, anything but proletarians, that he considered it the true mission of the representatives . . . to use their power in favor of the interests of the laborers. It was the first time that the opposition was expected to go beyond the sphere of mere politics and vote for or against the social interpretation of the idea of the state. It was an audacious step, and a profound change of public opinion had to precede it in order that such a step could be taken with some hope for success. His specific suggestions were of no importance; the decisive point was that he had put the question of social contrasts into the foreground and asked for his mandate in the name of this social antagonism.

He was elected. . . . With Ledru-Rollin the social question became an issue in the Chamber. He was, of course, not only alone but completely isolated in the Chamber; he had no followers and no opportunity to act, and yet his reckless performance was of the utmost significance. From now on it became possible to raise the social question in the Chamber of Deputies. . . . There was now a political party representing it. The lower class was represented side by side with the upper class, and the difference henceforth was merely one of degree. This development signalled a tremendous gain for the lower class; it aroused great hopes and gave it new energy and new impetus, and in a way it changed the features of the whole movement.

Until then the complete hopelessness with regard to political equality had forced those who were concerned with social conditions into abstract speculations. The successes of the different systems and theories of socialism and communism originated partly from the fact that they alone expressed ideas concerning the contradiction of society. But now the adherents of socialism and communism began to identify themselves with a political party. A large number now disregarded the abstract speculations and turned again toward politics. Although what was demanded was predominantly a political reform, the main reason for this demand was the hope for a subsequent social reform. . . . The politico-social reform movement quickly won over all those who, without having had a clear concept of another social system, had felt that the future would be dominated by social issues and recognized that these issues should not be left to the decision of the brutal force of the masses but should be taken care of by the state.

At the same time, the system of "personal government," as pseudo-constitutionalism was called, grew step by step. The Chamber of Deputies became more and more corrupt, and informed people began to doubt that such a government could survive for long. This despair over existing condition, although first directed against the government, was bound finally to turn against society, whose principle had made such obvious corruption in public affairs possible. The exclusive rule of moneyed power and material interests led the people and the state day by day closer to the brink of ruin. This had to be stopped. There was only one way to do this. It was necessary to change the law which had guaranteed exclusive power over the state to capital and its interests. This law was the election law. The electoral reform was an inevitable consequence of the rigid and corrupt management of public affairs; however, it was simultaneously directed toward a reorganization of the social rule of capital and thus toward a transformation of industrial society itself—a fact which at first was not recognized but which became clear in 1848. . . . The electoral reform was not exclusively a political problem; it was rather an incarnation of the problem of the social order; it confronted the state with the contemporary social issue which now developed its full impact.

. . . Clearly, there were enough groups which could form a strong party—side by side with the conservatives and the abstract liberals—committed to political equality as a means of changing social conditions.

This party was the intermittent link between communists and socialists on the one hand and the republicans on the other; it became the center of the social reform movement; it united all those who accepted the necessary premises of a basic external and internal reorganization of the state and society. Celliez has expressed this very well in saying: "Socialists as well as revolutionaries have understood that the social revolution cannot be enacted without a political revolution nor can the political revolution take place without social revolution." This in fact was the basic tenet of the new party, and it was precisely the undetermined generality of this principle which made possible the great variety among its members.

At this time a new phenomenon gained attention in France—the concept of democracy. Although the terms had existed before, it had never had a specific meaning. Democracy is essentially different from republicanism; . . . republicanism stands for the principle of equality, which is, however, not contradictory to actual inequality. Republicanism aims at safeguarding by law the right for everybody to attain the highest position in society as well as in the state; but that is all; whether and to what extent the individual is successful is of no concern to it. Republicanism accepts society with all its social differences as it develops through its own forces under the rule of legal equality; republicanism does not expect the state to go beyond the realization of abstract equality, the abolition of privileges, and the provision of equal chances for the acquisition of property. For democracy, however, the political rights are not the end but the means and the symbol of its principles. Democracy aims to achieve equality by political means; universal suffrage and equal representation are considered to be the proper means by which the state will eliminate all practical inequality. Since inequality affects the lower class, the essential feature of democracy is the use of popular authority in order to raise the status of the lower class. With democracy the republican idea of legal equality is transformed into the idea of social equality. Wherever the democratic movements develops, the social issue becomes the main content of all political controversy. Once this development has taken place, a return to abstract, pure republicanism is practically impossible. Therefore, wherever democratic ideology develops in an industrial society it will be the corresponding political manifestation of the antagonism of the working class toward capital; through democracy the very nature of that society, originally envisioned by socialism and communism, reveals itself. It is therefore natural that these latter movements recede into the background as soon as democracy asserts itself. This is what happened in France during the period under discussion, and the closer the situation came to a showdown the more the democratic ideology gained over the socialist and communist movement.

The organ of the thus developed democracy was the *Réforme*, which was founded in 1843. This magazine took the position that though inequality of ability and of occupations are the basis of society, superior talents account for greater obligations to society but not greater privileges. This is the basic principle of practical equality which can be established by collectivization. In order to accomplish this, workers' associations should be organized so that wage earners can become free laborers. It is the task of the state to do that. As long as the old electroral law exists, the government will not accomplish this task. What is most needed, therefore, is an electoral reform to lay the foundation for a new social order.

Next to Ledru-Rollin, the main correspondents for the *Réforme* were Godefroy Cavaignac, who had been an active socialist and Dupoty, former owner of the *Journal du Peuple*, which had been predominantly republican; Louis Blanc was another correspondent, and Georges Sand contributed feature stories. The well edited newspaper received the greatest attention. It avoided supporting specific social theories but strongly favored the interest of the workers, initiated workers' petitions, discussions and alliances. It would have outstripped the *National* except for the fact that the policy of Louis Philippe and Guizot called public attention again to the throne and provided new support for republicanism among the upper classes, which made good the losses of republicanism among the lower class.

Ever since the appearance of the *Réforme* and the idea of democracy, concern over social issues was voiced also in other papers. Perhaps it is of interest to restate the program of the *Réforme*, a program now completely forgotten. . . . Regarding the social issues it states: "While on the one hand political freedom is slowly destroyed, on the other hand the social question grows in importance and affects the government, the state and society. Our principles according to which we are going to take a stand regarding these problems are: All men are brothers. Where there is no equality, liberty is a farce. It is true that society requires differentiation of ability, but superior abilities are no basis for privileges; they only impose greater obligations. Such is the principle of equality; its appropriate form is the Association, the purpose of which is to satisfy the intellectual, moral and material needs of all through the exercise of different faculties and through cooperation.

"The laborers have been slaves, they have been serfs, they are now wage earners; one should attempt to raise them to the status of Associates. This can only be accomplished through the efforts of a democratic government. The principles of democratic governments are popular sovereignty and universal suffrage, the task of democratic governments is the realization of liberty, equality and fraternity.

"In a properly constructed democracy those who rule are the authorized agents of the people, they must be held responsible and they are subject to dismissal. Public functions are not distinctions, and should not constitute privileges; they are obligations. Since all citizens have equal rights to participate in the nomination of representatives and in law making, public functions should be paid for, since otherwise equality becomes illusory. . . .

"Freedom of the press has to be upheld and sanctioned as a guarantee against possible errors of the majority and as a necessary tool for intellectual progress.

"Education ought to be equal for all citizens, it ought to be public and free, the state should be responsible for it. Every citizen has to undergo military training. Nobody is allowed to buy himself an exemption from the duty to defend the nation.

"The state should take the initiative in starting industrial reform which would lead to an organization of work by which the laborer would be raised to the status of Associates. The laborer has the same claim to protection by the state as does the soldier. To the strong and healthy citizens the state owes work, to the old and feeble citizen it owes assistance and protection.". . .

With this program the social issues had found expression as well as acceptance. A vast unexplored field of action had thereby been opened. A steadily growing interest in the conditions of the working class testified to its growing power. It would be wrong to expect that definite social systems were advocated, but wherever formerly one was used to dealing with only a simple opposition within the Cabinet, one now found a no less determined opposition against the rule of capital and a steady reference to the labor problem. . . .

This is, briefly, the history of French society since the July Revolution; the most important part of which, the history of the proletariat and of its growing class-consciousness, was until now buried under the development of political affairs. . . . Of greatest historical value is the general fact . . . that the acquisitive society has necessarily to develop into an industrial society under the rule of capital and the political and social control of the workers who, though free, have no capital; it is this contradiction which transforms the class of laborers into the proletariat, and a social revolution will necessarily ensue unless the capital-owning class seriously supports social reform. . . .

Part Three

The Monarchy, the Republic and the Sovereignty of French Society since the February Revolution, 1848

Part Three, Chapter One

THE JULY MONARCHY, ITS STRUGGLE WITH INDUSTRIAL SOCIETY AND ITS DOWNFALL

Monarchy and the Ruling Class.

If monarchy represents the idea of the independent state, its autonomous action, in order to correspond to that idea, is only possible if the monarchy carries out the principle of the state in relation to society. The principle of the state is the principle of freedom, according to which each member of society should be able to reach the highest degree of personal development. The principle of society, on the other hand, is the principle of social dependence, according to which the individual is thrown back upon himself and his property.

We have shown how the principle of society gains the upper hand and even dominates the constitution and administration. The subjected have no other choice . . . but to seek support from the state which, by its very definition, ought not to be controlled by any social interests. This is the idea of the independent state. Its representative is the king. From here it naturally follows that the subjected part of society turns, in part intuitively and in part consciously, toward monarchy as its natural protector.

Since, on the other hand, monarchy as a symbol of the state encompasses the total idea of the state only by raising the hitherto subjected, poor and destitute class out of its misery, it is only natural that monarchy . . . should use its power to assure the welfare of those classes which have no means of bettering themselves and who therefore have become more and more dependent on those who possess these means.

The ruling class, in accordance with its interest, wishes to keep, more or less consciously, the lower class in a continuous state of dependence by all available means. For this purpose it intends to use its social position as well as its share in the power of the state, which it has in turn gained through this social position. . . . The lower class has no control over the state or over society to improve its lot and to gain its freedom. There is only one single institution which, standing above all social interests, has no other task than that of developing all elements of public welfare. This organ of the state is the monarchy.

Because of the nature of the class antagonism in society, monarchy is not merely a static representation of the idea of the state without any self-propelling force. We have shown that monarchy is an independent living entity, with a personality of its own, deciding and acting. . . . It is the purpose of monarchy to oppose the will and the natural tendencies of the ruling class, in order to support the lower class, which has so far been socially and politically subjected, and that it use the supreme power of the state to this effect. . . . On this basis monarchy under an intelligent ruler will not only gain the general support of the heretofore subjected class of society; it will also create in the minds of the members of the class an image of monarchy in which the whole future and well-being of the state, the love and trust of the people, will be safeguarded. . . . It will even identify the throne with the idea of freedom and give to it the strongest support. For true freedom is one which is shared between the privileged class and the lower class, by providing the latter with the opportunity for this freedom. . . .

But the upper class will also be grateful to the monarchy for using its power not only in favor of particular interests but in favor of the interests of all the people. For monarchy will not only eliminate the power struggle among the different factions of the upper class but will also make it easier to convince the upper class that it is in its own interest to alleviate the position of the lower class, which is usually a necessity and always to the advantage of the whole society. Finally, the monarchy will gain, in addition to its political power, an immense social power. It is an unquestionable fact that the monarchy is never more powerful than when the population at large supports it. . . . The true, the most powerful and lasting, the most beloved, monarchy is the monarchy of social reform. . . .

. . . Monarchy, as a representative of the pure idea of the state, stands above the classes of society and their antagonism. As a personal agent of the state, it necessarily attempts to intervene autonomously in the movement of the state. The ruling class opposes this and wants to control the state for its own ends. The struggle which develops between this class and the monarchy may remain undecided for a while, and success may vary; in this struggle monarchy will always be defeated in the end, either by being destroyed or by being transformed into a manipulated representative of the state. Otherwise, monarchy has to destroy the social order by unethical methods, which would lead to the slow decay of morality and freedom as well as of society and the state. In this struggle monarchy can preserve its independence and its position only by placing itself, in the name of public welfare and freedom, at the head of the social reform movement. . . . In the future, monarchy will either become an empty phrase, or it will degenerate into despotism, or be replaced by republics, unless it shows the high moral courage to become a monarchy of social reform. . . .

Now, on the basis of these principles, we can proceed to trace the fate of the last monarchy in France . . . and to describe it—not only in its growth and struggle but also in its defeat—as a consistent whole.

The Position of the July Monarchy in French Society

. . . In some countries, for instance in England, the third estate triumphed simultaneously over the aristocracy and monarchy and from then on became the ruling element in state and society, so that the monarchy, losing its autonomy, subjected itself unconditionally to the third estate, represented in parliament. In other countries, for instance in Prussia, the monarchy itself broke the rule of the estates and subjected the aristocracy to itself without producing a ruling class of industrialists. It gained sovereignty with the establishment of a bureaucracy. In still other countries, for instance Austria, the same thing happened but lasted for a short time only; the aristocracy reunited with the monarchy to establish an absolute monarchy, while the aristocracy retained an absolute rule in society. Finally, in France, . . . the Revolution was simultaneously directed against privileges and the monarchy, and a new order of things started with it. All over Europe this has resulted partly in a decisive victory of the third estate and partly in gaining equality with the aristocracy; the position of the monarchy in this new order of society is determined by the respective constitutions. Europe is now divided into two large parts; monarchy has an altogether different significance in the West from that which it has in the East. In Western Europe, the domination of industial society fosters the rule of capital over labor; in Eastern Europe capital and labor are both controlled by the aristocracy. . . .

Yet there remained one other constellation of the elements. . . . As has been shown before, in France as well as in England industrial society dominated the state. However, in England this domination was so secure that the monarchy did not even make an attempt to free itself from it. But monarchy as a living organism has to be autonomous; the domination by the bourgeoisie was contrary to its nature. Was it possible for monarchy to fight for the control of the state with the bourgeoisie? What would be the course and the consequence of such a struggle, and what would happen when the fully developed industrial society—in which the stage of class antagonism had already been reached—overwhelmed the monarchy?

Obviously this question was of the greatest importance. For all over Europe estate society had been destroyed, and nobody could doubt that industrial society would replace it with the rule of capital. But in the period of transition, during the 18th century, monarchy had gained considerable strength; it was certain that monarchy would not yield its acquired sovereign position, least of all to capital. The situation in continental Europe was more or less similar to that in France, and the same question arose everywhere. It was necessary to find an answer to this question.

The answer was provided by the July Monarchy. . . . The following analysis will present the history of the July Monarchy from this point of view. . . .

The Concept of Legitimacy and of Personal Government in the July Monarchy

According to all the information we have about the July revolution and the ascendancy of Louis Philippe to the throne, it is undoubtedly true that he, as the Duke of Orléans, had neither the intention nor the hope of succeeding the last Bourbon. . . . His accession to the throne was to him an unexpected event, not the success of a long struggle. . . .

It was clear that if the ruling class had at this moment established a state in which power was equally shared by both social classes, the propertyless class of society would not only have suddenly gained political power by virtue of its physical force, but the property owning and ruling class would no longer have remained the ruling class. This would have presented—aside from practical considerations—a contradiction to the innermost nature of industrial society. Such a contradiction had to be avoided at any price. There was only one way to avoid it.

It was necessary to establish a power which would stand as an altogether independent element of the state above the restless lower class. Consequently, it was also necessary to put this same power above the ruling class. However, by establishing a monarchy and keeping legal control over the constitution and administration in its own hands, the ruling class remained strong enough to protect itself . . . against the lower class and to maintain the control of the state. The new form of state, therefore, had to be a monarchy. Intuitively the ruling class turned toward monarchy. While others at the *Hôtel de Ville* indulged in sentiments of victory and hope, while the Chamber of Deputies was only slowly coming to terms with the situation, the important bankers were deciding the future of France at the *Hôtel Lafitte*. The signal was given from this banking house. It was received jubilantly by the Chamber of Deputies, and the new monarchy was established before the people had even recovered their senses. Through the monarchy the position of the ruling class against that of the dependent class was firmly established. But there was one problem that had not been considered, and even if it had been considered, nothing could have been done about it. That was the problem of the relationship of this monarchy to the ruling class. . . .

The ruling class of France held the opinion, still prevalent today, that the state was an institution of expediency and of practical necessity. It did not regard the new monarchy as necessary, but it decided to reinstitute it for its own purposes. It transformed monarchy, which by its very nature is autonomous, into a dependent institution. It instituted monarchy as a means of achieving its next urgent purpose. . . . It assumed that it would be able to create a monarchy, while in reality it could only control it. . . . Perhaps the ruling class could not have acted differently in that moment of danger, but by acting in this fashion it created a monarchy which, in name, power and external position, stood in direct contradiction to the true spirit of monarchy. . . .

As soon as Louis Philippe had become king, an uncertainty with regard to the traditional opinions of the ruling class began to spread among its own members. People began to watch the behavior of the monarch carefully; they enjoyed his bourgeois manners, they criticized vigorously any inclination which seemed to indicate a deviation from bourgeois values. The fact that he shook hands with the people, that he received deputies of the people with informality unusual among kings, that the ministers met him in shirt sleeves,—all these and other tales, had, in spite of their insignificance, a deeper meaning. They represented the early realization of the unity of the yet incompletely fused but externally closely interwoven elements.

Louis Philippe, on the other hand, exhibited an extraordinary intelligence. He had not as yet developed any interest other than that of the ruling class, nor did he command the support of any other group. He obliged members of that class by being personally amiable and showing an understanding of the wishes of the bourgeoisie in the Chamber. Yet he and the ruling class both had their enemies; these were the masses of the people and the party of the legitimists. The ruling class most feared the former, the king feared the latter. But soon it became evident that these enemies were not strong enough to become dangerous to the new bourgeois monarchy. . . . Since the beginning of 1831, the new monarchy, as well as the social domination of the capitalists, were externally secured.

If there was any contradiction in the position of the July Kingdom, it was now the time for it to become evident, because from now on the monarchy and the ruling class confronted each other alone.

This contradiction did become acute through one element of European political life whose significance the ruling class had not properly appreciated. This element was the legitimacy of the monarchy.

Since the time when the term *"legitimité"* had first been used at the Congress of Vienna, it had been interpreted in diverse ways. Usually it was intended to designate a certain, not clearly defined complex of princely rights. Actually legitimacy is nothing else but the essence of true monarchy, which makes it the absolute prerequisite of any constitution. In this sense the princes of Europe called themselves the legitimate rulers. The same idea is expressed by the phrase "by the Grace of God", which had originated in Europe at the same time that the principalities were becoming aware of the importance of their position. . . . But since the crowns had been distributed through the victory of the armies, particularly by Napoleon, legitimacy, as a claim of the princes to the throne by birth right, found its opponent in the princes whom the Revolution had raised to the throne. Only by contrast to the revolutionary monarchs did the old principalities gain a clear concept of legitimacy. It became a power ever afterwards. . . .

Compared with this, the monarchy of Louis Philippe was altogether different. Not only had he been elected by the people—he was the only and the first king who had not received the crown by the "grace of God"; he also was a mere tool in the hands of the ruling class. The crown had become a bourgeois institution. Louis Philippe stood outside the sphere of the old legitimacy; his monarchy was a constant living contradiction of the latter. . . . According to its own principle, therefore, the July Monarchy, as such, had the whole system of legitimate kingdoms in Europe as opponents.

Louis Philippe was well aware of this. He knew that his royalty was incomplete and that his dynasty, therefore, had no support outside of France, that beyond the French frontiers his downfall would be received with pleasure, perhaps even actively furthered. He hoped to survive with the help of his army and by his shrewdness, but only royal legitimacy could protect his children in the future. He had to gain legitimacy at any price.

Since he could not deny that his dynasty was established by the people, he had to attack the domination of the monarchy by the bourgeoisie . . . He either had to give up hope of being regarded as a legitimate king by other European monarchs, or else he had to destroy constitutionalism —the legal dependence of the monarchy upon the constitution—which was the result of the Revolution. . . .

The accession to the throne of Louis Philippe had illustrated that the ruling class of industrial society may be able to change the dynasty but not the substance of monarchy. The rule of Louis Philippe, the manifestation of the contradiction between both elements, was found to provide an answer to the question of whether the power of monarchy was sufficient to subjugate the ruling class of industrial society through a royal government.

Ever since Louis Philippe came to the throne Europe had viewed France with suspense. Nobody was able to account clearly for what was going on, but nobody could overlook the fact that not only a French question but a question of universal and historic significance was about to be decided. . . .

We have pointed out that with the advent of industry the industrial order of society developed also in other parts of Europe; with it developed the ruling class of capitalists which, by its very nature, also strove, under the general slogan of liberty, to control the state. In all of Europe the legitimate monarchs were opposed to these endeavors. In all of Europe the antagonism grew under different names and in different forms, but the only clear manifestation of it was provided by France and the July Kingdom.

If . . . monarchy in France were to be victorious, the major representative of industrial society in Europe would be subjugated. If, however, this society was to be victorious, the old system of legitimacy would be under attack in all of Europe. This was the crucial issue in public affairs of the past eighteen years. . . .

The Development of the Principle of Personal Government

. . . At the moment of his ascension to the throne, Louis Philippe made his decision with regard to the preceding alternatives. He was determined to break the political domination of industrial society for the sake of gaining a position of legitimacy.

Wherever monarchy lacks historical legitimacy, it can acquire it only by independent action and by establishing its supreme power over the whole state. . . . To accomplish this it must destroy, by whatever means possible, the power of the ruling class of society; it must do so all the more effectively . . . the stronger the position of the ruling class is. It must always let the king act as a free and independent agent, rather than delegating power to officials who are more or less controlled by the elements of society. The independent and personal manifestation of the royal will, the royal action, is always the beginning of the struggle between monarchy and society. . . .

When Louis Philippe began the struggle against the ruling class, he had to make personal government the leading principle of his whole state administration. The whole government of Louis Philippe, is, indeed, expressed through this principle. . . .

But the real power of society, the legal recognition of society by the Charter and the representation of the ruling class in the Chamber of Deputies, stood in opposition to this simple principle. Confronted with that, a mere principle could accomplish but little. . . . The ruling class of society controlled the state in two ways; first, by the representative organ, the Chamber of Deputies, and second, by the fact that it attempted to control the ministers through the Chamber, and the government through the ministers. If the personal government wanted to subject industrial society and break constitutionalism, it first had to break the power of the Chamber, for if it could not dissolve the Chamber it could only rule by making the majority subservient to the ministers nominated by the king, instead of allowing them to be servants of the majority. . . .

This principle can be put into practice in either of two ways, by simple or indirect purchase of votes or by filling the Chamber with persons who are dependent on personal government; for this purpose, officials, particularly those who can be dismissed or removed, are especially suitable. The first principle was the one which Louis Philippe applied with great circumspection and also with great consistency. However, he could lend a point to this only if at the same time the second principle was pursued with endurance. . . . Even though the above principle subjugates the Chamber to personal government, this could not guarantee the successful control of all subsequent elections. To accomplish the latter purpose another road had to be taken, a road which is indicated by the order and the antagonism of industrial society.

The faster the domination of capital grows, the faster the proletariat becomes consciously opposed to it. This proletariat is, though in a different way, just as determined an enemy of the political rule of capital as is the monarchy. The latter struggles only against the political power of the capital-owning class, while the proletariat opposes the factor that determines its existence, namely, private property. The proletariat hates capital, but capital fears the proletariat. This antagonism between the two elements of industrial society manifests itself in a peculiar way which characterizes the whole life of this society. Every enterprise, involving as it does the cooperation of capital and labor, rests on the subjugation of labor to capital. If this relationship is disturbed, if capital is left without labor or if labor refuses to serve capital, no enterprise can endure. As soon as this relationship is undermined, industry itself becomes threatened. Since the proletariat desires to abolish this subjugation, the principle that dominates its life is decisively opposed to the industrial order of society. In order to survive, the industrial order must enforce the subjugation of labor to capital by external means. For this purpose it has to set up a law which regulates the relationship of capital and labor in such a way that the laborers are compelled to work in the factories, . . . that they work under the direction of the employer who himself cannot be easily controlled. This is accomplished by prohibiting labor unions and strikes, by introducing work books, factory regulations and factory courts. These are the social rights of industrial society. The ruling class . . . has to legitimize its domination and has to maintain it, if need be, even by force, because the opposition of the lower class constantly threatens it. This subjugation of labor to capital—which corresponds to the nature of industry—becomes legal, and henceforth it is considered to be the established order of society.

What is the attitude of constitutionalism and of monarchy toward this concept of "order"? Obviously the actual power of the ruling class in this order consists not so much in its material privileges as in the fact that this power is acknowledged by the state as a social right. As long as monarchy exists the state is independent of the ruling class. The state may oppose these legal claims; the state may offer assistance to the lower class and, by doing so, gain more power than if it tolerated the domination of the ruling class, which always aims at controlling the state. If this were to happen, the ruling class would not only surrender its political rule to the monarchy but would also surrender its social domination over the lower class. This possibility is dangerous to the rule of capital. Where its domination is not yet completely secured, as it is in England, prudence dictates to the ruling class that it ought to avoid making an enemy of the monarchy by too great restrictions. The ruling class, therefore, has to give in to the monarchy, that is to say, it has to strengthen the monarchy in the interest of order by granting more power to the royal government than its own principle and its secret wishes would warrant.

This is the first principle of constitutionalism, a principle which can be derived from the antagonism of the social classes.

But since this antagonism nevertheless continues to exist, and since industrial growth leads to a decrease in the number of ruling capitalists and to an increase in the number of propertyless workers, it follows that the practical danger to that order is not yet eliminated. For this danger consists in the potential revolt of the working class against the owners. The seriousness of such revolts . . . lies in the fact that the social rights of the capitalists must gradually appear as an injustice to the proletariat, and that the whole relationship of subordination of labor to capital could thereby be shaken. Wherever this happens, an attack of the united proletariat against the rule of capital is inevitable. . . . The ruling class must prevent this danger at any price. . . .

However, the prevention of such a general movement can only be accomplished by the state. . . . If industrial society restricts too much the power of the state, as represented by the monarchy, it also reduces the means of keeping the working class in check and of upholding the social rights of industry. From here there follows the second principle of constitutionalism, which is in the interest of the ruling class: not only should a rapprochement of monarchy and the lower classes be avoided by too fierce attacks on the former, but monarchy ought to be strengthened so as to be able to guarantee the established order through its strength. . . .

In this fashion there develops, in the political and social life of the nation, a constellation of forces which has been of extraordinary significance in the recent history of Europe. . . . As a consequence of this schism in industrial society, monarchy has been identified with the task of preserving the social order. In accordance with this interpretation —the meaning of which ought to be clear by now—the ruling class of industrial society is allied with the monarchy. As far as the former is concerned, it is then easily possible to exert an influence on the voters who belong to the ruling class so that a Chamber is elected which, though not altogether dependent on the government, still upholds the principle that the ruling class should never seriously infringe upon the autonomy of the government because of the threat to the social order. . . .

Louis Philippe wanted to gain legitimacy through the system of personal government. . . . He found a strong Chamber, a nation which was definitely in favor of constitutionalism, but also a ruling class of capitalists threatened by the proletariat in its pursuit of wealth and luxury. His road was clearly circumscribed. Either he had to accept the position of a genuinely constitutional monarchy and, in order to protect himself and his throne against society, to slowly establish a monarchy of social reform, abandoning the claims of legitimacy, or he had to subject the Chamber to his personal interests and the voters to the fear of social unrest. . . .

According to the unanimous opinion of even the most discreet authors, corruption since 1830 had reached an almost incredible scope in France. . . . At the same time, the danger of social revolt was being ruthlessly exploited. . . . Communism was allowed to grow in order to make use of its downfall as a weapon against those in whose interest it was destroyed. Social discord was sowed to gain social subservience. If the proletariat was attacked, the ruling class always had to sacrifice a political right in order to preserve a social right. The monarchy was actually supported by the majority of the Chamber and ultimately also by the majority of the voters. Since 1841, the King's goal—namely personal government in combination with a Chamber which ruled according to the law but which in reality was completely dominated by the King—seemed to be definitely accomplished. Louis Philippe was now admired as the most clever prince in Europe. It was hard to describe clearly what he had done. Sometimes he was seen as the man who had tamed the Revolution; sometimes as the one who had rebuilt the monarchy and the throne on a secure basis; sometimes as the shrewd tamer of the most restless and most powerful nation of the world; or it was felt that he had solved a problem upon which the stability of all constitutional monarchies depended. For a whole decade he was praised and imitated as the model for all wise princes. The essence of these rather vague perceptions was that actually, through Louis Philippe, monarchy seemed to have found a method of systematically undermining the principle of the rule of industrial society over the state and of recovering and securing self-government for the monarchy in relation to its organ, the elected legislature. Through him industrial society appeared to be defeated by the monarchy, which seemed finally to have solved its task. . . .

Louis Philippe's Struggle with Industrial Society

When Louis Philippe ascended the throne, he had neither popular support nor the support of a single party in the whole country. For the monarchy had been only a means to reach a specific end of the ruling class; one could respect it for the purpose it had served, but one could not love it. The strength of Louis Philippe at that time was based merely on the fact that the strength of the competing political factions—the financiers favored by the owners and the republicans favored by the masses—was almost equally distributed.

The real power was undoubtedly on the side of the financiers. They had subjugated the Chamber through the voting system and the high property qualifications; they had subjugated monarchy by enthroning the king, and they had gained control over public law through the Charter. Louis Philippe could not possibly think of waging an open battle with them. It was also impossible for him to ally himself with republicanism, for the republicans were shortsighted enough to consider the abolition of monarchy as their most important task and as the fulfillment of the highest ideal of liberty. While the property-owning class was the controlling power of the monarchy, republicanism was its deadly enemy. Such was the situation at the beginning of the July Monarchy; . . . What could the king do to raise himself above both antagonists? . . . Since the money rulers had delegated the power to the ministers, they also held the ministers responsible for carrying out their plans. But in spite of all their power, the ministers were not able to establish the inner equilibrium of society. It was not their fault, but they had to take the blame. When in 1834 the great revolt broke out, . . . the question was naturally raised of whether it might be in the interest of the property-owning class to invest more power in the monarchy, and therewith gain safety, rather than keep the power and endanger capital and industry through the increasing internal unrest.

The great significance of this question will have become clear by now. It implied, in fact, the political resignation of the ruling class. Louis Philippe had, very intelligently, restrained himself up to this moment. He could not have obtained the longed-for power by violence; he had to wait until this power came to him. The monarchy which the republicans had attacked so furiously appeared in an altogether new light to those who themselves could have become dangerous to the monarchy. . . . The monarchy was in charge of the state; it had no other task but to secure order—why not transfer power to the monarchy so that it could rule in the interest of the ruling class? The question contained its own answer. The property-owning class gave up the desire to rule the state by itself. Thus the task of ruling fell to the king almost without his having taken a hand in the matter. The more the property-owning class had lost confidence in itself, the greater was the confidence it placed in the king. The ruling class wanted to elevate the king to the role of the representative of "order"; the king quickly accepted the duty of protecting this order. In this way . . . monarchy came to be identified with the concept of order. And even if it may sound paradoxical, it is, nevertheless, true that republicanism had changed constitutional monarchy to a form of personal government.

This was the course of events during the first stage of the conflict between the monarchy and the ruling class; the sovereignty of the ruling class was broken, and personal government had for the first time been firmly established and accepted by the people. The natural consequences of this development became immediately evident. The voters who came from the ruling class favored the monarchy. Immediately after the great revolt of April 1834, in which republicanism had been decisively defeated, the Chamber had to be re-elected. The elections took place in June, and the republican element was altogether defeated. At the same time, the Chamber transferred to the monarchy the power to persecute republicanism. The monarchy exercised this power to its fullest extent and to its own advantage. During that year the foundation of the rule of the new monarchy was established. Was the personal government now secure after so brilliant a victory? . . . Had the property-owning class endowed the monarchy with its power for the sake of monarchy? Did the property-owning class now view the monarchy as legitimate—that is to say, as an unqualified and unquestionable prerequisite of any constitution, as an end rather than a means?

It did not. The monarchy was actually, even at this point, nothing but a tool of the ruling class. It was, it is true, the only and inevitable means used by the ruling class, but it was not yet anything else. It was accepted as the necessary prerequisite of the social order but not yet as the necessary prerequisite of the state constitution. . . . Here was another more difficult task to solve. Louis Philippe took on the risk of solving it. At this point begins the most brilliant period of his government, the period of the battle for the idea of monarchy. It extends from 1835 to 1841. . . .

In June, 1834, the ruling class had, indeed, voted in support of the government. But it had voted under the impact of the danger brought about by the revolt of Paris and Lyon. After five years, new elections were to take place. If the king meanwhile succeeded in stabilizing the situation, was it then not easily possible that the necessity of an autonomous monarchy might become subordinate to the demand for parliamentary control? . . . This was the first question which the monarchy had to ask itself. . . . This question will be put to every monarchy which struggles with industrial society for the right of government. Louis Philippe's claim to fame consists precisely in the fact that, with regard to the institution of the monarchy, he used primarily those means which are natural and correct for the principle of personal government. In this respect he has become the preceptor of Europe.

The great majority of those who belong to the property-owning class in industrial society will always be first and foremost engaged in the economic administration of their property. It takes a great deal for a person to step out of this sphere into public life. . . . There are only two forces which prevent the individual from being lost in political apathy: the associations and the press.

Let us consider the French press of the period and Louis Philippe's task concerning it. The character of the French press until 1834 had been clear cut. The property-owning class still believed itself to be capable of ruling alone. When it discovered the autocratic tendencies of the monarchy, it went into opposition. But monarchy was the legal basis of the Constitution. The opposition to the personal government of the king appeared to a large part of the population as an opposition against monarchy itself and thus as an attack on the Constitution. Thus the point was reached where the conservative opposition press joined hands with the press of the social movement. The combined power of these was great. The revolts of the past years and, in general, the disbelief in the right of monarchy had grown out of it. As long as this alliance lasted, monarchy could not gain a majority in the Chamber. It was of decisive importance for the monarchy to break this alliance.

In order to do so, it was necessary to interfere with the law. It was necessary to draw the dividing line for the discussion of the Constitution in such a way that the opposition press had either to give up its opposition to the Constitution and join the merely parliamentary party opposition or to declare war on legality as such. The method chosen to accomplish this was to present the monarchy as the true and legally unassailable center of the Constitution. The plan for this had been developed by the throne considerably earlier. With the impression of the last revolt still fresh in the mind of the people, and with a Chamber definitely opposed to any republicanism, it was considered justifiable to execute this plan. The blow had to be decisive. This was the origin of the famous September laws of 1835. . . . The spirit and the substance of the first and most important press law consisted in the fact . . . that it prohibited any attack directed against the monarchy as the basis of the Constitution. It accomplished this by declaring the doctrines and opinions opposing the monarchy a crime. . . .

The Chamber approved the law on August 29th; it was promulgated on September 9th. The monarchy had gained a very great victory. There can be no doubt about the significance of these press laws. They were not general laws concerning the press; they imbedded in the law the principle that from now on monarchy was legitimate, i.e. that it was the absolute, unquestionable prerequisite of the Constitution. . . . The first objective was thereby attained. The ruling class had abandoned the principle that the monarchy was an institution among others; it unquestioningly accepted monarchy out of fear of the lower classes; the personal government of the monarch was thereby legally recognized.

The former alliance between the opposition and democracy was now split. The opposition press joined the press of the existing order and became a party press. The democratic press, on the other hand, became isolated. . . . In consequence of the law, the former elements in the Chamber now formed two large ruling factions, the *"parti de la cour"* and the *"parti parlementaire"*; the former held the power, the latter aspired to it. The relationship of these two parties was from now on determined by their size. And as soon as the importance of numbers had replaced the former antagonism of principles, the function of the monarchy as regards its domination over the Chamber became very simple. The monarchy had merely to gain the support of the individuals in order to control the whole. Graft was used, and by means of suppression of the free press and of bribing individual representatives, the monarchy slowly and systematically began to replace true constitutionalism by personal government. This is the sequence of events during the second stage in the peculiar struggle between the ruling class and the autonomous monarchy. The third stage was yet to come. . . .

The more the danger of new revolts became removed, the more clearly the ruling class came to understand that, in fact, it had installed its political opponent, the monarchy, as its ruler in order to control its social opponent, the dominated class. But the eternal laws of society asserted themselves. The ruling class recovered its senses. It desired to preserve the monarchy just as before, but it desired to subject the authority of the state in the name of monarchy to its own rule by purely constitutional means. If they were to succeed, the king would again lose the prize of his victory of 1835; like the King of England he would become prince without any personal power and without even a legitimate claim to power. The pressure of the ruling class against the personal government grew, the antagonism increased. Nobody has characterized this conflict better than Thiers in his famous statement: *"Le Roi règne, mais il ne gouverne pas."* That was what the ruling class, represented by the *parti parlementaire*, wanted. The King resisted with all means at his disposal. And now the last phase of this memorable struggle began. . . .

Since the conservative party was in the majority, the opposition was completely excluded from the administration; the only way to participate in the government was by gaining the majority, and this the opposition could not achieve. Therefore, the opposition turned away from the existing political system and began to doubt the justice of a Constitution by which it was completely excluded from the administration. Thus the ground was prepared for an alliance between the opposition and the democratic party; combined, they mustered considerable power.

But at the same time the proletariat had come into existence, and the socialist press was an indication that it had become powerful and was alive to its interests. No matter how great the distaste of the opposition toward the monarchy was, the fear of the social movement was naturally much stronger. The opposition, therefore, had the difficult task of separating the democratic from the socialist element and of proposing a Constitution which would destroy the domination of the monarchy over the ruling class without bringing the propertyless class any closer to power. . . .

The method of accomplishing this was electoral reform. It was designed to allow the bulk of property owners to participate in voting by lowering the voting requirements. . . . This would have made bribery of the elective body impossible, and bribery of the individual representatives difficult or useless. The preservation of property requirements would have excluded the non-owning class from politics, and the Chamber, based on low property requirements, would have replaced the personal government of the king by the government of the ruling class.

It was natural that this idea . . . was taken up eagerly by the owning class, whose political power had been dwindling. It was equally natural that the monarchy should declare itself vigorously against it. . . . And victory seemed to be easy enough for it.

In the first place, the Chamber would have to enact the new electoral law. But the majority of this Chamber was loyal to the Cabinet, which was in the service of the Court. It was clear to everybody that the enactment of a reform law under these circumstances was out of the question. Such a reform would have subordinated the individual interests of the members of the Chamber to general social interests. The Chamber would have to sacrifice its own interests; it was, therefore, understandably against any reform. . . . However, in a certain sense, another factor was still more decisive in this issue. The democratic party had seen the social party developing and growing side by side with itself. A large part of the democratic party went over to the social party, convinced of the weakness of political democracy. This half democratic, half socialist-minded party joined the reform movement in full strength. This fact called the attention of a part of the property-owning class to the deeper significance of this movement. It was recognized that behind the idea of an electoral reform there was another, much more powerful idea; . . . this was the principle of bringing the heretofore subjugated class of society one step closer to political power. . . . The opposition proper wanted to reduce the property requirements for voting, but the social party, together with the democrats, proposed already at that time to eliminate property requirements altogether. This aroused the concern of the opposition proper. . . . There is no doubt that participation of the multitude in politics would have resulted in an attempt to improve the conditions of the working class through state action. It would have carried the doubt in the right of personal property out of the general consciousness of the people straight into the representative legislature; it would attack the institution of personal property itself or at least its present distribution; it would take the power of the state away from the property owners and thereby force the state to participate in the controversy of society. . . .

These were the reflections which the entry of the social party into the reform movement aroused in the minds of the property owners. . . . These considerations cost the movement some of its support; but the loss was made good by gains in other quarters. The government understood this very well and had no difficulty in restoring an equilibrium in the ruling class by installing the fear of social reform, which was closely connected with political reform. It based its hope on such an equilibrium and in fact apparently succeeded in controlling the reform movement.

This was, generally speaking, the state of affairs as the year 1848 was approaching. Had Louis Philippe not been definitely victorious? Was he not finally the personal ruler of the state? Had he not paralyzed the ruling class, defeated constitutionalism, and raised the throne above the Chamber? In short, had not monarchy really subdued society?

This is how things looked. Even reasonable statesmen believed this to be the case. And yet, it took only one single night to prove the unalterable truth that, wherever social classes have fully developed, the security and even the existence of personal government depends on the destruction of the ruling class, that, however, no monarchy is able to exclude a mature ruling class from sharing in the authority of the state and to invalidate the laws which determine the relationship between society and the state.

The Downfall of the Monarchy

Few princes may have looked with such pride on the achievements of their governments as Louis Philippe at the end of 1847. The admiration of Europe was paralleled only by the secret gratitude of the European princes. Three of his children were, or were expected to become, reigning princes outside of France. His army was the best in Europe, his own sons had gained fame through the army. The country flourished, trade and commerce grew; the King himself still had enough enemies, but he was entitled to believe that he had no longer any major opponent. The majority of the nation looked at the king as the stronghold of order, and at monarchy as the prerequisite of the constitution. He had either bought, subjected, or suppressed all the parties. The Chamber obeyed his Cabinet, and already two charming grandchildren stood beside the throne, heirs of the tremendous victories which the father of the dynasty had won over all its enemies. . . . What more could a monarchy want after such successes?

And yet in the background something permeated this whole magnificent edifice of human intelligence and power with a secret and constantly growing disharmony. Whoever looked more closely at this whole organism, which the monarchy had extended over the whole country by the principle of personal government, was overcome by a feeling of danger, not a distant and unpredictable one, but a close and immediate danger. . . .

Indeed, the organism of government presented a strange picture. Every part of the whole was perfectly coordinated, neither the firm basis nor the execution of details could be found lacking; it was impossible to recognize in any part the instability of the whole. Although the uncertainty of the existing system could be definitely felt, it had not yet clearly manifested itself. All those who talked or wrote about it attacked one or the other part to prove the untenability of the whole; but nobody had yet been able to point out the truly sore point of the system, and therefore nobody had the full support of public opinion and the power deriving from it. Nobody knew what to do, because everybody searched for the dangers in details. Nobody could extract true reforms from the monarchy, because only a systematic force is capable of counteracting the system. And yet everybody stated quite frankly that this condition would not survive its royal founder, although nobody knew what should follow.

Those who meditate upon human conditions are not as yet used to tracing the conditions and the changes of the public life to their actual and dominant elements, the basis of society and the inherent contradictions of society. . . . The single events out of which the history of that period was composed do not present the whole history of that period. All opposition of the Chamber, all the brilliant public speeches of men, all the activities of the newspapers, all agitations, electoral contests, pamphlets, crimes, legal procedures and even revolts are merely indications and symptoms of the actual changes and the actual character of the basic elements of this historical period. . . . We have offered the thesis that all changes in the state are determined by society. If this is true, no explanation which disregards the role played by society will suffice. . . .

The fully emerged ruling class of society has to take possession of the state, not because it considers this useful and clever, not because it desires it or because it is easy to do so, but because it is forced to do so by its very nature. . . . Wherever a ruling social class exists and yet the state fails to acknowledge it—regardless whether through conquest, military despotism, or the government of the king—a struggle between the two will inevitably follow. And this struggle will end either with the destruction of the existing social order or with the defeat of the existing governmental power. No other outcome is possible.

Out of the acquisitive society, in which the rule of a definite class was not yet established, emerged industrial society, with the rule of capital. It had emerged in France after the downfall of Napoleon. The quiescence which prevailed in France throughout the reign of Louis Philippe had particularly accelerated the growth of capital domination. . . . The class of property owners was separated from the propertyless class and recognized itself as a unit. This class, however, was prevented from exercising its rule in the Chamber, partly through the high property requirements, partly through the pseudo-majority which controlled the Chamber. Instead of the interest of the property-owning class, the personal interests of the deputies dominated the Chamber. The Chamber was in absolute contradiction to the principle of society according to which the interests of the whole ruling class have to dominate the state.

The ruling class could not endure this contradiction. It tried to recapture the Chamber. However, at this point, not the Constitution but the monarchy interfered. It had been the monarchy which, by its action, had subjugated the interests of the ruling class to the private interests of the deputies. By relying on the majority of the individual votes which had been bought, the monarchy had identified itself with a principle according to which the power of the Chamber, and thereby the power of the ruling class, had to be abolished in favor of personal government. Therefore, it was natural that the contradiction in the relationship of the ruling class to the state was transferred to the monarchy. If monarchy prevailed, the ruling class could not fulfill its destiny.

To cope with this situation, the monarchy had either simply to yield or else to destroy the ruling class. If it should avoid both alternatives, its own downfall would be inevitable. . . . What did the July Monarchy, which wanted to rule over the ruling class of society, do? . . .

Louis Philippe did not want to give in; he wanted to continue to rule. . . . His idea was not so much to control the ruling class as such but rather the individual representatives, which he proceeded to bribe. If it was possible to do so continuously, pseudo-constitutionalism would be secured by a pseudo-majority of individual votes, and thereby personal government would also be secured. . . .

The acquisitive, and—even more so—the industrial society cannot endure bribery in the long run, because the tax-paying property in those societies is independent. And since in France, under Louis Philippe, the latter was in the process of being fully developed, the system of corruption by which he wanted to subject the voters and the representatives to personal government, presented an inner insoluble contradiction. There was no doubt that the whole system, in spite of its technical perfection, was doomed. . . .

But the government of Louis Philippe presented another contradiction in its relationship to society. If he wanted to subjugate the ruling class, he had to slow down its growth and prevent the spread of intellectual life and the cohesion of the whole class. But Louis Philippe felt that he would gain the gratitude of the ruling class if he would foster its interests in this respect; instead of abstaining from doing so, as would have been in his own fundamental interests, he followed his more direct apparent interest. He organized large industrial exhibitions and, by means of these as well as by the promotion of industry in general, fostered the growth of the power of free property which alone would be able to oppose his personal government. He issued the well-known law of 1833 concerning primary education, which provided that every community was obligated to have at least one school and that all teachers were to be supervised and examined by the University. By thus laying the groundwork for public education, he promoted intellectual and moral values in the state . . . and prevented their decay. Through the spread of education the property owners became stronger and the propertyless became better equipped for the acquisition of property and thereby more eager to gain freedom. It was an excellent law, but it was definitely against the interest of personal government. . . . Thus the true contradiction of this most peculiar of all monarchical governments developed. . . . The July Monarchy, through the systematic corruption of the Chamber, was bound to reach the point where the ruling, and not completely subjugated, class of industrial society, according to the laws governing industrial society, would take up arms against the personal government. . . .

One problem remained and has to be mentioned here. We have indicated the danger which threatened the ruling class through the social movement. We have shown that the monarchy was the only power able to prevent the struggle of the social classes. Was it possible that the ruling class, in view of this danger, would dethrone the protecting monarchy in order to establish a state which would then be attacked by the propertyless class with just as much antagonism as the former was now harboring against the monarchy? And was the monarchy not perhaps safe due to this fear of the ruling class, safe from political revolution because of the greater fear of a social revolution? . . .

It is an imperative need of the property-owning class to be rulers of the state. And even though the danger of social struggles delays for some time the outbreak of the political struggle, the moment inevitably —though often unexpectedly—approaches when that class rises against the estranged government, even if it has to pay for the victory, or merely for the struggle, by its own downfall. It simply has no other choice. . . .

The personal government of the King was based on this tremendous contradiction. This contradiction was so great that the King, the Court, and the Cabinet were constantly and profoundly aware of it. It is wrong to assume that Louis Philippe was unaware of the most critical danger to his crown. . . . With open eyes he saw the tensions growing daily between his government and the property-owning class. He expected the approaching revolution, he reckoned with it, he moved towards it. He knew that he would be attacked by democracy at the decisive moment and, at best, be deserted by the property owners. He understood very well that the Chamber, which he had made powerless against himself, would not be powerful enough to support him. He knew perfectly well of the tremendous powers of the Parisian people once they take up their arms. And therefore, systematically, as he did everything, he prepared for the struggle systematically. He reorganized the Parisian National Guard by splitting it up. He surrounded Paris with bastilles, he built strategically distributed barracks in the city, he maintained a strong garrison, he had his sons serving in the army, he filled all posts with loyal generals, he persecuted all democratic movements; and in this way he prepared the monarchy for military resistance against the attack which was bound to grow out of the social contradiction. . . .

And then, all of a sudden, in a single night, without any great effort, without preparations, yes, almost like a miracle—the outbreak occured with the participants not yet clearly aware of the purpose of this struggle. Paris revolted; and the work of eighteen years, the delicate building of human cleverness, was caught by a whirlwind and blown away without leaving a single trace. . . .

The February Revolution is the most significant event in the whole history of modern Europe. It proved with elemental power that neither the highest form of monarchy nor the greatest danger of the social revolution will prevent the property-owning class of industrial society from destroying any personal government which does not respect the principle of popular representation.

Part Three, Chapter Two

THE REPUBLIC AND THE SOVEREIGNTY OF SOCIETY

The Revolution of February, 1848

If one studies the history of this revolution from its early beginnings, . . . one discovers that, considered as a single event, it had three very definite, essentially different phases. The difference among these phases is not superficial. It is deeply embedded in the conditions of French history. . . . The monarchy was well aware of being the object of increasing antagonism on the part of the ruling class and its interests. But this time it was determined to dare the utmost. This led to the decisive struggle, which was partly provoked by the monarchy itself. It was only natural that the organ threatened directly was the first to take a stand against the monarchy in this struggle. This was . . . the minority of the Chamber. The minority knew very well that according to the letter of the law it had to submit to the absolutist majority; it knew that, as long as the mode of election remained unchanged, a victory over the majority was hardly—if at all—possible. The minority, therefore, wanted an electoral reform. But there was no way of obtaining it by the usual procedure. In order to increase its influence in the Chamber, the minority had to demonstrate to the King and to the country the support it commanded outside the Chamber among the population at large. Only thus could it again lend emphasis to its position in the Chamber. The minority was hopeful that through an impressive and lasting display of its strength it might gain a victory over the majority and its system by means of the electoral reform without having to take recourse to other measures.

With this aim in view it proceeded systematically though cautiously. . . . Since early 1847 members of the party had held—after the model of the British—large banquets in all parts of France, whose objective was the discussion of electoral reform. These banquets were neither popular assemblies nor clubs; even the form these meetings took indicated that the minority did not represent the masses but merely the property-owning class. Only the well-to-do had admission, because only they could afford to pay the price. The banquets therefore were not principally but factually a protest of the property-owning class against their exclusion from political power by the personal government of the King. They were not intended and were not supposed to represent both classes of the industrial society; they were supposed to demonstrate to the government that the property-owning class was represented by the minority in the Chamber, that this position was contrary to public opinion, and that this class was no longer willing to tolerate it. In fact, the reform-banquets did succeed in showing all this; they were a perfectly legal but determined declaration of war of the ruling class against personal government.

Unanimously supported by the ruling class, the constitutional minority entered the Chamber in 1848. Its representatives were determined to oust the Cabinet of Guizot, the representative of personal government, and to replace it by a parliamentary government. The government knew this; instead of avoiding the inevitable showdown it chose to face it. The King declared himself in his speech from the throne, just as Charles I had done, against the efforts of the minority, particularly against the agitation of the reform-banquets, which had been organized to strengthen the opposition. . . . This involved not only a condemnation of the minority itself, but also of its attempts to establish a constitutional government by gaining a majority through an electoral reform. It was a declaration of war by the monarchy against the ruling class of society and its representatives. . . . Thus began the first period of the Revolution, the struggle of the minority of the Chamber against the Cabinet. After the debate was opened, the main leaders of the opposition came into the foreground. With a display of great intellectual effort they raised their voice against the existing system of government. One brilliant and powerful attack followed the other. . . . Lamartine deplored and predicted . . . a settlement by violent revolutionary means; . . . Ledru-Rollin threatened and goaded, fighting disdainfully and yet furiously against a majority which he knew would never yield. . . . These are the most powerful and striking illustrations of the conditions prevailing in Europe and in France before the Revolution; they survive as monuments of that period during which the monarchy wanted to sacrifice the liberty of Europe in order to preserve the dynasty; . . . the speeches showed that the public funds were exhausted, that the principles of administrative procedures were disregarded, and that the elements of freedom were destroyed and banned in order to tie the people to the majority of the Chamber, subservient to the personal government. It is understandable that the powerful storm which destroyed the monarchy also obliterated the memory of this grandiose parliamentary battle, which did not yet want to attack the monarchy as an institution. But the historiography of future generations will reconsider this period in order to evaluate what the July Monarchy had dared and tolerated to transform the constitutional government into a legitimate personal rule which stood in contradiction to the spirit of the nation.

The Cabinet of Guizot kept silent in the face of these powerful attacks. . . . Guizot knew that the aim of the unified opposition was to gain a few votes from the bribed majority; he knew that the opposition would not succeed, . . . and he assumed that it would stop there. He was right insofar as the parliamentary opposition was concerned. The rebuttal to the debate was accepted without discussion; this rebuttal repeated, almost verbatim, the arguments of the King. It condemned the reform movement, and with it the minority, and with the minority the whole concept of a parliamentary government, the constitutional rule of the property-owning class. . . . The majority was victorious, the Cabinet was saved, the opposition . . . accepted defeat. The other members of the Chamber, the majority of the Cabinet, had dissociated themselves definitely from the majority of the ruling social class, and pseudo-constitutionalism became the acknowledged principle of government.

At this instant the Chamber withdrew from the battle; the Chamber was no longer of importance. . . . The first period of the Revolution was over. Now began the second stage, during which the parliamentary representatives were no longer the main actors. The actors were now that part of the nation who had attended the reform-banquets; they now confronted the King directly, without a political intermediary. They were the property-owning class, who now had to step in to demand participation in government which the minority had failed to obtain. . . . The address of the majority had been accepted on February 14th. There was much excitement; the Deputies of the Left did not know any more what to do. This was the time when the so-called bourgeoisie itself had to appear on the scene. Secretary Duchatel had stated that he was going to suppress the banquets by applying a law of 1790. To prohibit the banquets was to take away from the property-owning class the organ through which it had so far succeeded in upholding the opposition in the Chamber against the absolute monarchy but through which—after the defeat of the minority—it now needed to express its views independently. The Cabinet of the Government, by planning to prohibit the banquets, went now into direct opposition to the ruling class of society; thus began the second phase of the battle. . . . As an answer to the declaration of the Secretary, the 12th *arondissement* of Paris arranged a spectacular reform-banquet; 92 Deputies of the Left stated that they would participate, as did 3 Peers; . . . the Left of the Chamber thus rejoined the ruling class, . . . the bourgeoisie felt that they could not yield any further without submitting to the autocratic monarchy. About 10,000 members of the National Gaurd, interpreting the situation . . . correctly, joined and offered their support to the banquet. . . . The two great elements which were to compete for the power of the state, the monarchy and the ruling class, stood ready, facing each other. Nobody spoke about the Chamber any more.

What followed, on February 21st, is of particular importance, because it illustrates clearly the profound ignorance of the King, as well as of the leaders of the opposition, with regard to the nature and dynamics of contemporary society. The monarchy assumed that it had merely to deal with the leaders of the opposition in the Chamber and that the approaching rebellion would collapse with their resignation. The government therefore displayed its apparently enormous strength before the eyes of Odilon Barrot, the leader of the opposition. . . . It demonstrated that he was legally in the wrong in resisting the decisions of the legally ruling majority of the Chamber, and that, by continuing his resistance, he would plunge the country into a revolution beyond control. The Government persuaded him that it was capable of defeating the rebellion with one big stroke and then, after the victory, . . . it would destroy the remnants of still existing rights. Odilon Barrot lost courage. He, for his part, also assumed that the whole movement depended on the Deputies. He had not understood that these deputies were never of any significance by themselves and that all parliamentary activities were nothing else but an expression of the demands which the ruling class, according to its nature, had to raise. He therefore could not see that this class had to take up the battle by itself, regardless of the position of the deputies, and that this was not a continuation of the parliamentary quarrel but an inevitable struggle imposed by the laws of society. Odilon Barrot and four-fifths of the deputies withdrew from the banquet; as late as the 21st an order was issued to cancel the banquet. The Government believed that it had finally won a decisive victory.

And yet the street fighting began on February 22nd; . . . the whole city of Paris arose, the National Guard took up its arms, Government troops filled the streets and public squares; . . . the next day the decisive battle became inevitable. . . . The ruling class felt that this battle was fought for its rights against the pseudo-constitutionality of the monarchy. On the 23rd, the whole National Guard was under arms; one legion after the other joined the insurrection. The slogan of the revolutionaries was: "Long live the Reform! Down with Guizot!" That was the essence of the struggle as understood by the bourgeoisie proper; monarchy and the Charter were left untouched; a government was wanted which, under the protection of the monarchy, would accept the rule of the property-owning class. The Army wavered; it did not attack the National Guard. . . . The King, still stubborn and incredulous, finally recognized that he had to give in. Guizot was dismissed; the King considered appointing somebody else. He did not yet understand what had happened; he assumed that a change of Cabinets would be satisfactory. On the evening of February 23rd, the ruling class had definitely gained the upper hand. The main demand was the one for reform. The King had not yielded on this point; it would have destroyed his whole system. He rather wanted to take the utmost risks. But at this point it was already clear that the victorious bourgeoisie would wrest the reform law from the King. . . .

At 10 o'clock at night, a new column of workers and members of the National Guard . . . ran into the famous battalion of the 14th regiment, which fired a volley of shots and thus renewed the already abating battle. It is easily possible that misfortune or misinformation caused such a turn of events. But in this instance it was apt to be decisive. The King, when he ascended the throne, had confirmed the sacredness of the Charter by oath; he had used the eighteen years of his rule to destroy it. Who could assure the people that his present royal promise would not be just as invalid? Peace depended upon trust in the king; the only basis for the monarchy, after the victory of the bourgeoisie, was one of faith in the royal word. Never had distrust against a king been more justified than in this instance. At the moment when he was defeated and ready to give in, how could he have murdered the harmless population of the capital? If such was the case, if royal promises could not be trusted at all any more, if the people were betrayed, then there was no other way out except to destroy the incorrigible monarchy itself. Thus the shooting echoed in the hearts of the Parisians. At this moment, the second period of the struggle came to a close with the victory of the ruling class; the ruling class had lost confidence in the monarchy; . . . the struggle for reform receded, . . . and on February 24th the amorphous masses of the people began to attack the monarchy, and with it the rule of large capital over the other classes, as well as the existing order of society.

This was the third day of that remarkable Revolution. The second important element of industrial society, labor, stepped into the foreground. Labor was aware of the fact that the exclusive rule of capital was destroyed through the monarchy, that, on the other hand, capital desired above all to regain through a revolution its own ruling position under the monarchy. It understood that monarchy without a constitution would suppress both classes of society; it also understood that a constitutional monarchy, obeying the ruling and property-owning class, at least had to further suppress the subjected laboring class. Labor, therefore, arrived at the conclusion that monarchy is under any condition an antagonist of the working class. It realized that monarchy would become stronger than society as a whole by the defeat of the ruling class; therefore it aligned itself with the ruling class. But it knew just as well that through the defeat of monarchy by the ruling class the rule of the latter would be infinitely strengthened. Therefore, labor did not want to stop the revolution at this victory of the bourgeoisie. As long as the first part of the battle was being fought it restrained itself; but when, after February 24th, the second part began, labor came into the foreground; and as soon as that happened, the issue was no longer restricted to the struggle between genuine constitutionalism versus pseudo-constitutionalism, but became a struggle of monarchy versus the abolition of monarchy.

One question arises here which we still have to explore: If monarchy is the most natural and the simplest basic form of government for industrial society, how did it happen that during the revolution the victorious bourgeoisie abandoned the monarchy under attack by the proletariat at a moment when it could have obtained from it anything it asked? . . . The answer to this question is given by the history of the French monarchy itself. Ever so often since 1789, the ruling class had attempted to lay the foundation for a constitutional monarchy similar to the British. The ruling class had been deceived so often that it finally identified monarchy with political repression. . . . Through the reign of Louis-Philippe, confidence, not only in the king but also in monarchy as such, had been undermined. . . . This is why the ruling class could not defend the monarchy when it was attacked by the laboring class. . . . The ruling class did not want to destroy the monarchy, but the lack of trust resulted in a lack of determination at a moment when only trust could have saved it. . . . Thus complete confusion followed on February 24th, when the ruling class was overpowered by the proletariat and the Chamber of Deputies by the *Hôtel de Ville.* The monarchy collapsed not because its enemies were all-powerful, but because its natural friends had been completely alienated. . . .

Thus the February Revolution came to a close. It ended with the abolition of the monarchy. However, this was, in fact, only a negative result. With it the basic form of the old Constitution was destroyed, but a new one was not yet put into effect. It was the end of past history but not yet the beginning of a new era. . . . What was going to happen after the power of the state, through the abolition of monarchy, had fallen back into the hands of the people? . . .

The Sovereignty of Society

Popular sovereignty, prescribed by political democracy and realized by the ideal republic, identifies the state with the aggregate of its members. . . . The will of the state is the joint will of all individuals, and each of their wills is an independent will. Under popular sovereignty the reasons for the will of the state are therefore the same as those of the individuals; these are based on the assumption that the individual believes he is furthering his own well-being by realizing his own will. Therefore, we call these reasons his interest. . . . In a state based on popular sovereignty, the unity of the joint will is secured only through the identity of the interests of all individuals. If individuals or whole segments of the population have differing and opposing interests which can be realized by the will of the state, the inner unity of the will of the state will necessarily be destroyed. Popular sovereignty, therefore, begins to develop an inner contradiction. As long as the differentiation of interests remains casual and transitory, the disruption of the will of the state is merely temporary. . . . If contradictory interests did not exist within the community, popular sovereignty might be realized, without danger, by the ideal republic and democracy.

The science of society shows that property is the material basis of personal development. Preservation and the growth of property not only correspond to the material interests of men, but are also required for the development of the human personality. Property appears to be only the pursuit of material goods but actually is also the pursuit of personal interests; the interests of property become the truly justified interest also of those who are free and independent. This interest demands that the labor of others be utilized for the increase of private property of the ruling class. But the work of one individual for the growth of property of another individual means dependence. Thus it appears that the personal interest of those who own property must necessarily entail the dependence of the laborers. The laborer, on his part also free to pursue his aspirations, demands not only that this dependence be allayed, but that he too receive a share of property as large as possible, because such property is the prerequisite of his personal fulfillment. . . . Hence there are in each state two sets of interests mutually exclusive, although both are a logical consequence of the inner nature of the personality. . . . Since the highest evolution of the state depends upon the growth of all individuals, the high value of property is a decisive reason why the state must preserve and foster the growth of property of those who already own it, and at the same time foster the acquisition of property by those who do not own it. These two interests are not extraneous to the state but inherent in the community, and are inseparable from the concept of the state. The absolute contradiction reflected by these two interests is the germ of disruption of the will of the state. . . .

As soon as one conceives that the state based on popular sovereignty . . . has a will and is capable of acting, the unity collapses and dissolves into its opposing elements. The concept of "the people" does not suffice to explain or to solve the growing contradiction: what really emerges from the antagonism between owners and non-owners . . . and what wields control over the state is the order of society and the conflict of its interests, which always have and always will dominate the state. . . .

If we assume that the state, embodied in the monarchy, loses its own representative—just as it did in France through the February Revolution—and that the power of the state or sovereignty reverts to the community, what consequence will this have? Is—as constitutions state and as the popular saying goes—popular sovereignty thereby established? It is indeed established, but only as a principle. It expresses the fact that the community is the only sovereign. In reality, however, in any positive action of the state, the will of the state is determined by those forces which have created the inevitable opposition of interests, the order of society. It is this social order which rules under popular sovereignty. The life of any republic is determined by the following rule: as soon as popular sovereignty is accepted as a principle in a country without a monarchy, the sovereignty of society becomes the true basis of state order. . . .

The science of society, of its elements and laws, gains more practical significance the closer a nation moves—be it through inner conviction or through circumstances—toward the abolition of monarchy. Only this science can then explain the forms which the state may develop; only this science can discover and predict the dangers which the abolition of monarchy brings about; only this science will enable us to understand the importance of governmental laws and governmental measures, the significance of the popular excitement and the struggles which necessarily follow the abolition of monarchy.

If it is true that the social order always controls the state—inasmuch as the ruling class of society gains control of the state by the constitution and the administration, while the dependent class is excluded from power—it may be asked in which respect the rule of society in the republic differs from that in the monarchy, and whether the position of the social elements is different under these two systems of government. . . .

After the monarchy is overthrown and the people as a whole gain sovereignty, the ruling class of society—according to the laws of society

—takes political power into its hands. No constitution, not even universal suffrage, can change this inevitable consequence. . . . Since what we want is determined by our interests, and since those who own property have an interest in the preservation and growth of property rights, it follows that through the subjugation of the state by the ruling class the interests of property become the principle of the state represented by this class. The sovereignty of society—which is the true meaning of the term popular sovereignty—manifests itself as the sovereignty of the property-owning class over the propertyless class. The republic, therefore, necessarily represents the domination of the interests of the property owners over the interests of the propertyless. . . . This rule of the interests of property owners—set in action by popular sovereignty—is in direct contradiction to the idea of the state, . . . because the interests of the propertyless class become suppressed not only in fact but also by law; the lower class is no longer protected by monarchy, and is too weak to build up any resistance by itself.

The inherent aspirations of the individual toward freedom in the state as well as in society assert themselves the more as the subjugated class is further removed from its potentialities through the rule of the upper class. The contradiction inherent in the concept of the state develops into an open antagonism in the life of the people. Both classes become more aware of it; hatred and scorn grow on one side, arrogance and fear on the other. The rule of the property-owning class creates the hostile opposition of the two social elements of the state, each of which wants to gain control over the government.

The conflict usually results in the definite rule of one class over the other, after a series of revolutions which, as the science of society shows, are violent attempts on the part of the lower class to gain control over the state. During these revolutions, sometimes the one, sometimes the other class is victorious. But since the exclusive rule of one class is in contradiction to the idea of the state, . . . the existence of the state is threatened in either case.

If popular sovereignty can be interpreted as the rule of society over the state, this sovereignty necessarily results in a continuous battle between the social classes and their opposing interests. The final victory of one class over the other . . . inevitably leads to the ruin of the nation and the state. . . . Does this not suggest . . . that any form of government is irreconcilable with universal freedom? Proudhon, after many doubts, reached this conclusion. Plato had drawn a picture of the Republic as an image of an idea to which there was no counterpart in reality; Thomas More transplanted it to Utopia, and Rousseau, who considered political democracy just as impossible as monarchy, stated that the Republic was possible only among the Gods. As long as the existence of the state was an unchallenged fact, these opinions could be quietly ignored. But now the nations begin to doubt, to investigate and to reconsider the situation. Can the social sciences offer them only this deplorable answer? Is there no solution and reconciliation for this apparently total contradiction? There is such a solution. But one has to have the courage to search for it by an analysis of this contradiction.

The Elements of Ownership and the Law Resulting from their Relationship

Up to now we have interpreted the concept of ownership in a general way as the basis of the order of society and the state. From this . . . concept we arrived at an apparently absolute contradiction. We have characterized the absolute antagonism between the classes under a sovereign society as the beginning of the decline. . . . The possibility of realizing popular sovereignty depends upon the possibility of eliminating the antagonism between the classes . . . by developing opportunities making it possible to rise from the status of the propertyless to that of property owner.

Thus the question arises whether the inner nature of ownership and the distribution of property, which controls everything, offer such a solution. Unless they do, the above contradiction is insoluble and all historical developments come to a permanent stagnation or a quick dissolution.

A closer examination of the concept of ownership reveals that it is composed of several elements. In a narrow sense, ownership means the possession of tangible goods which we call property; however, these are the result of labor; this is the second element in the concept of ownership: possessions cannot be acquired except by labor. Acquisition, or ownership through labor, represents the third element in the concept of ownership. . . . The concept of ownership, therefore, is composed of the elements of property, labor and acquisition. These three elements have a definite interrelationship. According to the concept of ownership, neither one is conceivable without the other two; there can be no property without labor and acquisition, no labor without acquisition and property, no acquisition without property and labor. The concept of ownership in a society in which it is generally accepted requires that property cannot persist without labor and acquisition, and labor not without acquisition and property. As long as property depends upon labor and acquisition, and as long as working people gain property through acquisition, the economy corresponds to the concept of ownership, and society, ruled by property-owners, includes two classes: those who come to work and gain acquisition through their property and those who gain property through work and acquisition.

But it is possible for men to disrupt this natural relationship. Since property is not only an economic concept but also a legal one, each individual owner may keep his property for himself or consume it without using it for work and acquisition. Secondly, the whole class of property owners can introduce laws and establish institutions which will obstruct the acquisition of property; it can eliminate the process of labor as a means of acquiring property. The property-owning class has the power, because property, as a prerequisite of labor and acquisition, is the most powerful of the three elements in the concept of ownership and rules over the other two. The property-owning class wants to do so because everybody prefers unearned and secure income to the uncertainty of acquisition; it carries this out by separating property from acquisition.

Thus a contradiction develops between the economic order and the concept of ownership, which presupposes that the acquisition of property through work is the basis for the growth of the individual personality. This contradiction cannot persist. The complete separation of property from acquisitive labor has to be overcome and replaced by a reciprocal relationship, if it is true that the idea of personality grows out of the various elements of ownership and if world history is the history of this development. This, however, cannot happen suddenly or by mere chance. On the contrary, a continuous and organic progress has to take place, unfolding the gradual harmony of both. . . .

The stages of development in the relationship between property and acquisitive labor are not only equivalent to specific periods in the economic history of a nation, but also equivalent to specific periods in the history of society and of the state. Each of these stages has its characteristic quality, which is determined by the peculiar relationship between property and acquisitive labor. . . .

And now let us return to France. What happened after the proclamation of the Republic in 1848? A constitution was created whose stability and duration, indeed, depended upon the relationship that prevailed at that time between property and acquisitive labor in French society. . . . This particular French Republic differed from all previous Republics to the extent that this relationship had changed. . . .

The Republic of the Industrial Society

a) The Republic of Industrial Ownership

. . . The progress which separates industrial from estate society rests upon the fact that industrial society establishes, as an unconditional principle, the equality of all in terms of equal rights to any acquisition. . . . In principle, all kinds of property can be acquired; equality implies equal possibilities for everybody to attain any kind and any amount of property and thereby also the achievement of the corresponding social status. The social order determines public law by making social equality, which is the accepted principle of that order, into a principle of the industrial republic. The social maxim which any industrial society presupposes—namely, the equality of all with regard to acquisition—determines the supreme political principle of all constitutions of sovereign industrial societies: that the power of the state rests with the general public or that sovereignty is vested in the people at large. . . If this be true, how is it possible that the real constitution of the industrial republic is, in spite of this principle, no more able to guarantee freedom than is the feudal republic or the republic of estates? . . . Here it becomes of practical importance that the abstract concept of popular sovereignty in reality leads to the rule of society. . . . The state, in the process of choosing and acting, has to have a goal. Its intention, determined by the will of all individuals, corresponds to the interests of the individuals. The theory of society demonstrates that when acquisition and property are free the interests of capital become all the more opposed to the interests of labor. As soon as the state based on the community of men becomes active, it is motivated by the necessarily and universally contradictory interests of the property owners on the one hand and of the propertyless class on the other. . . . Thus, through the antagonism of capital and labor, two different concepts of the republic develop in industrial society.

The interests of the owners demand of the constitution that some property qualifications be set as a prerequisite of political rights. Only an inferior interpretation would identify this interest of ownership with the selfish interest of the individual owners, as if the situation could be changed merely by good intentions or be upheld only by their maliciousness. On the contrary, the very nature of ownership makes this demand necessary. It is a necessary requirement, because only ownership can safeguard the growth of the individual personality; . . . in addition, the state is dependent upon the financial contributions of the property owners, and it is necessary to avoid the danger that people who have not contributed to the treasury of the state dispose of its funds. It is, therefore, necessary for property owners to demand that only they themselves be entitled to participation in the affairs of state. . . . This is achieved by making property ownership a prerequisite for the right to vote. Regardless of the amount of property required and the method by which it is determined, property qualifications are always the basis of every constitution, as demanded by the ruling class in the industrial republic in accordance with the interest of the ruling class.

The second principle of this class is the establishment of an organ which represents the idea of the state as an independent institution, standing above society and free of class control. This demand is also part of the nature of industrial ownership. . . . Industrial property differs from feudal property because it is the basis of acquisition rather than the source of income. . . . It does not make any difference whether industrial property is landed property or capital. Landed property becomes a form of industrial property as soon as it is no longer used exclusively for the support of the family but for acquisition. The symptom of transition in the use of land from the household economy of the landlords in a feudal society to industrial farming is the investment of capital in land for the improvement of agriculture; as soon as the landlord borrows money for investment, his property enters the sphere of the industrial economy and becomes subject to its laws. The theory and history of agriculture demonstrate that at this point a new type of enterprise emerges, which represents new interests and a new interpretation of ownership. . . . The class of landowners no longer differs from that of capital owners, as was the case in feudal society; both now have the same interests, the interests of the acquisitive capital. This acquisitive capital—or acquired property—requires a new interpretation of the idea of the state. Acquisition through capital presupposes security and peace for a smooth functioning of industry. . . . Law and order are mainly threatened by the working class, which wrestles with the ruling class for control of the state. If the ruling class is in control and has to defend itself against the pressures of the working class, an important part of its strength is thus taken up; this disturbs the regularity of work and thus harms the interest of the ruling class more than the benefits it derives from sovereign rights. Therefore, the ruling class in industrial society prefers a monarchy, though only under specific conditions. In the absence of a monarch, the personal idea of the state is represented by an elected president and his ministers.

I have to add here a few remarks about the presidency. . . . Most people consider the institution and the prerogatives of the presidency—as it exists, for instance, in France and in the United States— as the natural and quasi-perfect form of the state inseparable from the concept of the republic. But a glance at the republics of antiquity, where free labor did not exist, or at the republics of the Middle Ages, even including the free cities, shows us that the presidency is something altogether new and a characteristic of our own time. It is not identical with the Archons, or with the Consuls, or the feudal lords or the Lord Mayors of the cities; it came into being only in industrial society and with its sovereignty. This shows clearly that the institution of the presidency is conditioned by the structure of society, that it is a form of government not theoretically invented but appropriate and ever-recurring under specific social circumstances. The institution of the presidency belongs to the rule of industrial society as its specific form of government. This institution contains two elements which clearly indicate the source of sovereignty. In the first place, the president is elected by the people; this election is the most general manifestation of the principle of the industrial republic based on popular sovereignty, since by the very act of the election the will of the people bestows upon the president the right to represent the state. It is appropriate to a republic that this election should be a popular election and not an indirect election, for reasons not so much of prudence but of principle. The constitution of every industrial republic demands the election of the president by popular vote. This fact distinguishes the presidency from the highest offices of other types of republics. Secondly, the supreme power of the state is concentrated in one person. This ties it to the Germanic monarchy, . . . which it resembles closely except for the hereditary nature of the latter and for the outward symbols. But at the same time, the president, who is not responsible to anybody, represents the state, which is more powerful than the property-owning class as well as the propertyless class and thus satisfies the previously-mentioned need of the ruling class, by embodying the idea of the independent state. In this fashion the presidency grows out of the social order of the industrial society as its corresponding form of government, and this is exactly how it came into existence in France.

The third principle of the republic of industrial ownership is the accountability of the ministers. There is only one specific point which has to be mentioned with regard to the accountability of ministers in the industrial republic. This is that ministerial responsibility is not so much a legal responsibility as it is a responsibility toward the majority in the legislatures. It is obvious that such accountability is requested by the ruling class particularly if the rule of the upper class is secured through property qualifications. The peculiarity of this responsibility in the industrial republic is that it is a responsibility toward the legislature. The people at large—in spite of their sovereignty—are denied the right to control the ministers by any other institution except the legislature. . . . The control of the legislature over the cabinet is indeed nothing but the rule of the majority interests, always exercised by the owning class, over the government. . . .

. . . The administration in the industrial republic also has its characteristic and solid principles, given the circumstances of industrial property. . . . Through the principle of free competition on the one hand, and that of personal status based on acquisitive success on the other, . . . acquisition becomes the vital principle of industrial society. The theory of the industrial enterprise exemplifies the principle that the accumulation of capital depends mainly upon labor, which is specialized for reasons of productivity and integrated in the individual enterprise. The prerequisite of entrepreneurial success is, therefore, a steady labor force. Much can be done by the owners themselves to secure such stable conditions of production, but not everything. The entrepreneurs dispose of sufficient means to make the individual laborer dependent and to keep him on the job, but they are powerless against the whole laboring class. It is of great importance for their success that the working class should be prohibited from acting as a body. The entrepreneurs can attain this object only by inducing the state to prohibit by force and legislation the formation of an organization of the working class. The relationship of the working class to the entrepreneurial class . . . can only be a rigid subordination of all industrial workers to the requirements of industrial acquisition. The appearance of a unified working class in opposition to the entrepreneurs obviously represents a disturbance of the industrial order. The entrepreneurial class, therefore, demands that the state stabilize the relationship of the classes in opposition to the interest of the laborers. This is the "order" of the industrial republic, which also prevails in a monarchy, though not in the same fashion. . . . This "order" can only develop under an economic system of acquisitive property. It demands not only the submission of the propertyless class, as in the estate society, but also a provision of industrial labor for industrial acquisition. . . .

The second demand of the property-owning class . . . is hard to specify.

It does not have any direct relationship to either class but demands that the state use its power to promote private enterprise and acquisition by all available means and through all existing institutions. This demand . . . may touch the dependent class to some extent, but never exclusively. We might only mention . . . the problem of free trade versus protectionism, where the interests of industry and trade differ, and the problem of tax distribution. . . .

These are the outlines of the republic established in the sovereign industrial society by the ruling class. If we recall the constitution of this society under the monarchy, it becomes clear that the difference between this type of republic and a truly constitutional monarchy is a minor one in terms of the constitution and the state administration. The demands of the ruling class in a monarchy are exactly the same. . . . After the industrial society has developed and has been officially acknowledged by the monarch by the granting of a constitution, a firm alliance between the monarch and the ruling class will develop and persist as long as the king is willing to accept the majority rule in the legislature. If the monarchy is destroyed in an industrial society, it is safe to assume that it is the fault of the monarchy, because it was unwilling to subject the crown to the rule of the majority of the legislature. England is the great example of the first type of monarchy; the Republic of France is the great example of a state in which power is vested in the property-owning class and the state is governed according to its demands.

b) The Republic of Industrial Non-ownership

. . . The dependent class, well aware of the fact that the fulfillment and the possibility of personal development and of true equality with the property-owning class cannot be secured by the empty acknowledgment of the general principle of human equality and popular sovereignty, . . . has its own specific and special interests. The working class knows how difficult—in fact, how impossible—it is to raise its status only by its own resources. No matter how it interprets this advancement, it will always assume that the best method for attaining its goal is to control the state. However, the law according to which political power is distributed makes the given differentiation in property rights of individuals as well as classes the determining factor of participation in the affairs of the state. The working class does not own such property, nor does it have any chance of acquiring it as long as industrial society prevails. What, then, remains to be done? In order to control the state, the propertyless class demands first, disregard of inequalities based on prop-

erty, with a view of gaining control over the state without owning property, and second that the major function of the state should be to
use state funds in order to raise the standard of living of the lower class
and thus to enable the laborers to acquire property. . . . The demands of
political democracy coincide with the demands of the dependent class
under the rule of industrial society. . . . Since those who do not own
property have little or no prospect of gaining property, they must reject
property qualifications as the condition of constitutional rights and pro-
pose that all individuals, regardless of their social position, be given equal
political rights. This is the principle of universal suffrage. . . . This principle is, in its essence, merely a negation: the denial of property rights
to interfere with political equality; it is the only way by which the
dependent class may hope to control the state. Because it is mainly a
negation, it is rarely or never used in order to promote the interests of
the propertyless class, but rather as a principle of democracy and thus
as a positive measure. Only if the nature of society is understood does
the double meaning of this principle become apparent

The second principle advanced by the interests of the working class
is the principle of direct control of the highest state organs. For the propertyless, the control of the state is only a means to an end. The purpose of
using the power of the state to put the dependent class on a par with the
ruling class is one of the functions of the state in general. But since the
state has to accept and respect the property rights of the property owners as well as the needs of the propertyless, the task of improving the lot
of these will, for the free and independent state, be only second to the
task of preserving property rights. . . . Thus the state, in accordance with
its nature, confronts the propertyless class independently, pursues its own
ends, and does not always consider specific class interests as generally
valid. Proudhon, in stating that every government is basically conservative, was the first to sense, although he did not grasp the full meaning of
his statement, that every form of state contains elements which make it
impossible for the state to submit itself under all circumstances to the
demands of absolute democracy or of the dependent class. . . . This is
why the demand is made in the interest of the propertyless class that the
independence of the all-powerful state be curtailed. To attain this end, a
state in which power is not concentrated in the hands of one man and
in which the area of personal decisions is restricted is definitely preferable. The dependent class does not favor a president, least of all a president who is independent. It prefers an elected and controllable committee as executive and administrative organ of the state. All decisions are
to be made by the legislature, while the committee would only be in

charge of the executive function. This is, indeed, a wholly democratic principle in appearance; as to its practicability, the lack of personal independence reduces the all-powerful state to an exponent of the numerical relationship between the two classes. . . . The attacks of the dependent class on the presidency become all the more powerful the greater the difficulties become of acquiring property by mere labor. . . .

Thirdly, the accountability of the cabinet acquires a specific meaning. If the state is represented by an independent organ, it has to have the right to nominate the ministers, since they represent the executing will of the state in the various areas of public life. But if one presupposes a direct dependence of the state upon the will of the people—as the specific interest of the dependent class demands—the cabinet should be nominated by representatives of the people. This is the final consequence of the concept of popular sovereignty. By eliminating the last support for the independence of the state, the power of the state is relegated to the population at large. . . . As long as one assumes, although erroneously, that "the people" are an entity within the state, such a demand makes sense. But as soon as we become aware of the fact that what is generally understood by "the people" is in reality an organized and divided society, the idea of reverting the power of the state to the people implies a dissolution of the state into the antagonism of society. Whenever the nomination of the cabinet would be made by representatives of the people, the struggle between the classes of society would break out. The personal independence of the state, which implies a consideration of the interests of both classes, would be replaced by making the decisions of the state dependent upon the number of votes—a quantitative value. The order of the state would thereby be destroyed and the road open to dictatorship, which frequently follows under such circumstances. Every state in which the holder of supreme power is deprived of the right to nominate the cabinet and the highest state officials contains the germ for an open struggle between the social classes. . . .

These are the basic features of the constitution favored by the interests of the propertyless class and by labor. This constitution differs sharply from the constitution supported by the property-owning class in the industrial republic. The administration, as conceived by the dependent class, shows an even greater contrast. . . .

Labor without capital can accumulate property only through a very slow accumulation of the daily surplus over consumption. Clearly, the lower class wants to earn and save such a surplus. But the state constantly preempts it through taxation. Through taxes, the state constantly interferes with the budgeting of the worker. Taxation affects the budget of the entrepreneur much less, since even the minimum of taxation takes a greater proportion from the laborer's savings than do high taxes from the surplus capital of the entrepreneur. The first demand of the propertyless class with regard to state administration is, therefore, a system of taxation which does not affect the accumulation of savings. This demand of the propertyless class has not yet found a systematic presentation. . . . Generally speaking, this class demands a fairer tax distribution; but with every step toward a deeper understanding of the relationship among labor, acquisition and property, the demand for progressive taxation will soon be made by the worker.

The second great demand of the working class is for an adequate general education at public expense. This is basically a demand, particularly in connection with progressive taxation, for a right to intellectual development which is paid for by contributions of the upper class raised by the state. It is a generally acknowledged demand, growing out of the interests of the propertyless class; the more their cultural level improves, the more determination they show in insisting on this right.

The third demand can only be described in a general way. The taxation program, as the idea of progressive taxation indicates, is primarily a merely corrective measure concerning the relationship of labor and property, because it aims only at prohibiting the state from eating away the small savings of the workers. Free education, it is true, represents a constructive use of state funds for the acquisition of goods, though only intangible ones. The third demand may consequently be summarized by the question of whether it is possible and desirable for the state to use its funds to promote the acquisition of property through work, and if so, in which way this should be done. This does not refer to the mere support of those unable to work or the unemployed. The dependent class—according to the concept of ownership—wants not only property but the right to acquire it; it wants the state to provide a way of acquiring property through work. Whoever interprets the above question as a claim for public support and perceives the dependent class as merely begging for support, not only misinterprets the true meaning of this demand but reaffirms the difference between the property owners and the propertyless, by eliminating the possibility of acquisition through public support as a connecting link between labor and property. . . .

But what labor without capital actually wants is state aid for work which, without this assistance, cannot result in the acquisition of property. This can take various forms. The two main systems are those of organization of labor and of organization of credit. Regardless of their feasibility, it is obvious that the interests of the dependent class demand that public funds be used for the establishment of some such system or of taking some such measures. Hence this is the third, positive and practical demand which the non-owning class would make on the state administration which it controlled.

To sum up the main content of our analysis: the republic of the industrial society, for the first time in the history of all republics, conceives of popular sovereignty as a basic principle of government. This republic, therefore, appears at first glance as the true realization of freedom. But as soon as it shifts from the abstract concept of popular sovereignty to practical political action, the sovereignty of society becomes apparent—and thereby also the antagonism within industrial society expressed in the opposition of two essentially different republics which the two main classes of this society want to see realized. The substance of this opposition is the antagonism between the classes; its deeper source lies in the relationship of the state to the three elements of ownership: labor, acquisition and property. Thus, the abstract concept of popular sovereignty dissolves. . . .

European society . . . is an industrial society and is becoming more so every day. Every republic which may emerge will not be a realization of an abstract popular sovereignty but an industrial republic with its corresponding great principles, but also with its great dangers and antagonisms.

The Antagonism of the two Republics and the End of the Sovereignty of Industrial Society through Civil War

In a letter of Leroux to Cabet (see supplement to Stein: "Der Sozialismus und Kommunismus in Frankreich" [Second Edition, 1848, p. 34]) we find the following passage: "Oh, how menacing is the future because there are two republics at present". These few words have important implications. France had abolished the monarchy at a time when industrial society, with its control of capital over acquisition, had been fully developed. Already under the monarchy the two classes stood strictly in opposition to each other; when the monarchy fell they developed, after uniting their forces briefly against the common enemy, a fierce hostility towards each other; and it is here that the double form of the republic became an established fact. . . . A new constitution had to be drafted, but there is no constitution which does not give over the control of the state to either one of the two classes. . . . The property-owning class feared, and the dependent class hoped that the power of the state would be subjected to the social interest of the propertyless class through introduction of universal suffrage. . . . The development of a new state— as in the case of Germany in 1848—is endangered and even brought to nought if it coincides with the struggle for universal suffrage. . . . To raise this demand at a moment when Germany desired to become an empire destroyed this empire, because this demand identified the origins of the empire with social antagonism. . . . The same demand brought the already existing state of France to the brink of disaster.

This is the moment at which the two republics of the property-owning and the propertyless class, potentially existing in industrial society, are separated in reality. Universal suffrage produces the cleavage between them. . . .

Since in industrial society the interest of ownership is definitely opposed to the interests of the propertyless—the former requiring dependence, the latter independence of labor—the opposition of these interests results in an antagonism over whether the rule of ownership, through property requirements, or the rule of non-ownership, through universal suffrage, would be established. . . . The antagonism soon develops into a dogmatic and systematic struggle. . . .

The property-owning class feels and knows that the realization of the idea of the free human personality is contingent upon property; that the best abilities are usually found in the property-owning class; that the destruction of ownership leads to a destruction of acquisition. It also knows that even if ownership were to be temporarily abolished it would soon reappear in full force. It demands, therefore, in the name of the higher nature of ownership, that it should not be controlled by the non-owning class through the constitution. It knows furthermore that the basis of correct state administration is an understanding and an acceptance of capital, its necessity, its demands and its operation, and . . . that without such attitude the whole organism of industrial acquisition, . . . the wealth of human society, would be undermined and destroyed. Finally it knows that the attack on capital and the rule of capital is concurrent with an attack on property and the right of inheritance and that, indeed, the interests of property and the family identify themselves with the interests of capital. If the possession of material goods provides the basis for the highest personal development, the property-owning class necessarily has to demand, in the name of this truth, that also in the administration it should not be sacrificed to the interest of the propertyless, . . . and that the republic ought to exist for the interest of property reinforced by both the constitution and the state administration. There is no other way open to the property-owning class than to fight for the establishment of the first of the two republics at all costs.

The propertyless class, on the other hand, feels and knows that the pure concept of personality requires the free self-determination of all human beings, independent of external and accidental circumstances. It is convinced that only the free growth of the personality will guarantee the rule of ability in all important respects. It therefore demands, in the name of the supreme concept of the personality, a constitution in which . . . ownership is no longer a prerequisite for the highest manifestation of the personality.

The propertyless class is also acutely aware of the importance and power of property. But precisely because property affords the highest form of expression of the true personality, it demands that state administration endeavor to help the propertyless to become property owners. Because ownership of material goods is the basis of the highest personal development, and because it is denied to a whole class, which also lacks freedom for this very reason, the dependent class has to demand, in the name of true freedom, that the administration promote the interests of the propertyless. . . . There is no other way open for this class but to fight for the second of the two republics.

Since, after the abolition of monarchy, state sovereignty is invested in the two classes of society, both classes have an equal right to power within the state. However, their points of view concerning what they want of the government are mutually exclusive. What follows? Both of these classes consider their rights supreme because they are based on the concept of personality and freedom; and neither of these classes wants to subject its right to the rights of the other. Popular sovereignty becomes only an empty phrase for whichever class is excluded from power, but . . . it can be interpreted differently by the two classes, thereby bestowing equal rights upon both classes to bolster their claims against each other. Both classes—like two states within a state—confront each other, irreconciled and irreconcilable, driven to subjugate each other, and yet so closely linked with each other, and thoroughly interwoven, that they . . . are unable to separate and exist by themselves for the sake of peace. It is the absolute and incarnate social contradiction.

What are the consequences of this terrible fact? . . . Nothing more than that the social classes take up arms and fight a mortal war to secure the victory of one republic over the other, . . . although they must be aware of the fact that victory cannot be beneficient or lasting because it does not solve the inner contradiction. . . . Victory as well as defeat is hopeless and disconcerting for the individual and for the community. . . . What one class wants to protect and the other wants to acquire—property and well-being—are destroyed, not to mention the complete destruction of true freedom wherever the sword rules. . . . If an industrial society wants to establish a republic, the antagonism of the two social classes, necessarily leads to civil war, followed not by peace but by disaster. . . . The antagonism in industrial society stems from the fact that the specific attributes of property make it impossible for labor to acquire it. Such is the basic nature of industrial society. As long as it persists, it is impossible to bridge the opposition and master the dangers of the industrial republic.

But is it conceivable that this relationship can be changed? Obviously this can be done only by utilizing the acquisitions which property yields and retains from labor, to support labor . . . in the process of acquisition. But such use of acquisitions . . . can only be made voluntarily by the property owners. Every will is determined by an interest. The property owner will give up some of the acquisition of his property to labor only if there is an interest more powerful than his interest in acquisition. If such an interest can be found, society has also found a common ground, in spite of the cleavage between propertyless and property owners; only then will society be able to accept the superior position of the state, because only then will both have a common interest. Social peace and the existence of the republic depend upon the possibility of discovering and establishing a common basis of interest. . . .

Society and the Republic of Mutual Interest

. . . Industrial society is no more the last form of human society than the industrial republic is the highest manifestation of political freedom. Both have to perish through their inherent contradictions. Since these contradictions are the consequences of freedom, new social forms will develop out of them. What kind of society and state will succeed the industrial order of the human community? The few things which we will have to say now constitute perhaps the most important part of our whole work. By pointing out the next higher stage of development, the goal is set for which we ought to strive. It allows us to hope for the final solution of the apparently desperate conditions, and to preserve our courage in the struggle for improvement through confidence in the future. It also serves as an indicator of the directions in which we should move. . . .

Let us first return to the question of where the contradiction in industrial society is located. . . . The natural interest of capital owners is to avoid any reduction of capital earnings, even at the expense of the earnings of labor. Any administrative or legal interfering with these earnings is likely to drive capital away from industrial enterprise. . . . Any further social growth going beyond industrial society must be based on the acceptance and the expansion of capital earnings. This simple principle explains why nearly the whole industrial society, necessarily always the property-owning class to which also belong the small proprietors, are definitely opposed to all ideas of social democracy which aim at a reduction of capital gain, on the assumption that labor would profit by such an action. . . . The property-owning class knows very well that to deprive capital of profits is to destroy capital, and with the destruction of capital . . . the opportunity for work. It is, furthermore, aware of the fact that . . . even if labor were to acquire capital the conditions of industrial society . . . would remain the same. . . . Capital earnings are the presupposition of all future growth, which should therefore not be tampered with. . . . It cannot be denied that progress in human affairs will never be attained by a destruction of existing conditions, but only by improving them.

What is the source of the earning power of capital? Is it independent, or is it not, rather, produced through the process of labor? The latter is certainly the case, and therefore capital increases with the quality and quantity of labor. . . . Not only does a better quality of goods produced by qualified labor yield higher prices and a greater turnover; even the production of other goods increases, . . . and thereby more goods become available to the not so well-to-do. In this instance also, capital and labor are closely correlated with each other. Since capital earnings are dependent on the quality of labor, it is in the highest interests of capital to contribute to a higher quality of labor. Excellent quality of work coincides with the highest rate of capital profit, . . . and the conditions which lead to an improvement of labor are identical with those which promote the growth of capital earnings.

What are the conditions under which free labor attains its highest standard? Two conditions are of essential importance. First, the educational level of the laborers, which changes the worker from a tool to an intelligent and responsible human being doing his work with precision, regularity, and care, while at the same time nourishing his mind and strengthening his self-confidence. . . . Only education, which raises the worker from his inferior position through the acquisition of what is nobody's exclusive domain, . . . the possession of intellectual goods, can restore social equality and the moral dignity of work. . . . Secondly, the worker should be granted the opportunity of acquiring capital, even though only in small amounts. This demand grows out of the concept of ownership, which embodies the interrelationship of labor, acquisition, and property. . . . There are many conceivable ways to arrange for a small surplus which can be earned through labor, and to raise the worker gradually to the status of property-owner. . . . This is of minor importance. The important point is to acknowledge, as the principle of social reform, that labor should have a chance to acquire capital.

Education and the opportunity of acquiring a small amount of property are the two conditions through which labor attains its highest level of development; they are, at the same time, the presupposition of the highest rate of earnings for capital. The interest of the property-owning class in industrial society lies in high capital earnings through labor; the interest of the non-owning class is in the acquisition of a higher education and of capital. The interests of both classes are really identical; one presupposes the other. In fact, a mutuality and solidarity of interests exists.

How is it possible then that an antagonism of the interests of the two classes has developed in spite of the mutual interest? And how can this antagonism be overcome? . . .

Since the amount of capital determines the social position of the property owner in industrial society, every property owner uses whatever method is available to him to increase the amount of his capital for reasons of personal interest. He first reduces the wages paid to labor. Therewith he promotes his personal interest, but he also separates labor from capital and makes labor dependent. In this way develops that antagonism which destroys the natural relationship between labor and ownership. . . . The general interest of capital acquisition is dissolved into the separate interests of the individual capital owners who, disregarding the true interests of capital acquisition in general, forces labor into a relationship of dependency for the sake of their own individual interests. The solidarity of interests of capital as a whole is broken down to an infinite number of individual interests which are satisfied at the expense of labor. This is the source of the adversity. The worker, deprived of acquisition, is misled into believing that the nature of capital deprives him of property. He develops a hatred against capital, and the threat of this hatred unites the capital owners into a community of interests which, instead of reconciling the laborer by providing him with the opportunity of acquiring property, attempts to keep him in submission with all the power property rights can bestow. The cleavage between classes is thereby completed, and the natural social harmony is destroyed. To revive this harmony, the true solidarity of the property owners has to be restored; the general capital interest has to replace the interest of the single capital unit. . . .

The solution of the conflict growing out of the rule of industrial society is plain and natural. Guided by self-interest, which rules the order of human society, we pass through industrial society and reach a stage at which labor and capital coexist and cooperate through acquisition. . . . If capital provides education and acquisition for labor, it is in the interest of the laborer to preserve and foster capital acquisition which meets his demands. If labor cooperates and performs well, it is in the interest of the capitalists to provide the necessary conditions for such a performance. The antagonism is replaced by the mutuality of interests, and a new social order is thereby established.

. . . It is not our task to elaborate on the form of society based on mutual interests of labor and capital; unfortunately, this is a matter of the future. The present shows only its very first and uncertain beginnings. But I think it has become clear where the solution of all the struggles of the social order lies. . . . It does not lie in the elimination of capital, or the submission of capital to labor, or the destruction of competition, or in the restoration of free capital acquisition, or in the condemnation of industry. It is also not to be found in a sudden transformation leading to the control of labor over capital, to the community of property or a communistic labor organization; it does not at all entail the impossible elimination of class differences and their specific conditions or of differences among individuals; for these differences are a prerequisite of the complementary activities without which men would not be able to rise beyond the raw state of nature. The starting point simply lies in the relationship of the interests of capital and labor. Capital needs labor in order to gain large profits; labor has to support capital by a readiness to work diligently in order to gain the necessary means for education and acquisition. By their very nature, labor and capital are mutually dependent and therefore have a solidarity of interests. If this is disregarded, a struggle ensues between these two elements, . . . and this struggle is more costly than all the sacrifices of one class in favor of the other . . . . If both classes, and particularly the ruling class, accept this fact, if the latter pursues its interest not by submitting and exploiting the workers but by raising their standards and liberating them from their state of material dependency, then the awareness of mutual interests will lead to a harmony in economic life, and with it true freedom will be established.

. . . Suppose now that both classes of society recognize their common interest and attempt to attain this goal through common efforts: what are the conditions for success, and what are the roads open to them? . . . In order to secure a lasting peace, the dependent working class demands from the owning class action . . . which indicates serious and uncompromising intentions to assist labor. Is there any provision as to how this can be done without doubt as to the intentions of the ruling class? . . . We have shown that the ruling class necessarily dominates the state, no matter what the constitution. But the nature of the state demands that its power be applied for the benefit of all classes. . . . Only the use which the ruling class makes of its power within the state will prove whether or not it is willing to improve the conditions of labor and therewith acknowledge the mutuality of interests as the true principle of society. . . . For the dependent class the administration of the state, as carried out by the ruling class, will be the criterion by which to judge the social attitude of the latter. Here is the point where the concept of mutuality of interests takes on the practical form of political action. . . . The ruling class will be content only if it remains in complete control of the constitution. But in order to make this acceptable to the propertyless class, the administration must constantly strive to promote by all means at its disposal the essential interests of the laboring class: the right of each individual worker to acquire capital; that is to say, it has to be an administration of social reform.

We have come back to the same concept which presented itself at the close of the chapter on theory of society, the concept of social reform. But in this context, social reform, social progress and the growth of social independence are no longer abstract demands; they are, rather, . . . the basis of a truly free constitution, the final stage of a series of apparently insoluble contradictions. Now the following propositions on which the republic of mutual interest is truly based become clear.

If the dependent class attempts to gain power over the state on the basis of the abstract concepts of democratic equality, the property-owning class will, by the number of its votes, be its natural and irreconcilable enemy; the state will succumb to the power of arms, and the destruction of freedom will result.

If the ruling class uses its administrative power essentially in the interest of ownership, the dependent class will become its natural and irreconcilable enemy, and the social order will have to be based on sheer force.

If the dependent class has any doubts regarding administrative policy of the ruling class in the interests of the propertyless class, particularly the workers, it will immediately stand up for general suffrage as a constitutional norm to gain control of the state, in order to guarantee state support of its own interests.

If, however, the ruling class uses administrative power in favor of the propertyless class by improving the lot of the workers, providing free education and the opportunity of capital acquisition, the dependent class will become indifferent to the type of constitution, as long as its interest is furthered. Such an administration is equally possible under a monarchy, a dictatorship, an aristocracy, and a democracy, because the acquired property makes a state of dependence impracticable and the furtherance of acquisition becomes identical with the progress of liberty. . . . The transformation of democracy is already indicated in the new concept of "social democracy". . . .

The law according to which the distribution of goods controls society, and consequently the state, is the controlling factor in the life of Europe. This law has to follow its course. It has made labor free and confronted it with ownership; it now calls for a new principle of society, which consists in the acceptance of a mutually dependent relationship, leading to the well-being of all and to the sacrifice of the special interests of one in the interest of the other. It is impossible for society and the nations to continue to live without this principle, for they have already lived through the preliminary stages of antagonism. If there is any future for Europe, it rests with the ability of the people to accept this principle. If they do not show the resiliency, if labor and ownership remain in opposition, Europe, with all its treasures, will have reached the peak of its development with industrial society, and will then relapse, by a slow process of dissolution, into barbarism. Neither democratic principle nor political freedom, neither a strong monarchy nor a republic can protect it against decay. . . . If labor fights dogmatically against the profits of capital, and if capital makes it impossible for labor to acquire property, if neither one understands that their true interest is not mutually exclusive but mutually dependent, Europe will have proven to be incapable of outlasting the first two periods of the development of social independence. . . . Whether Europe will be able to preside over the beginning of a new era, whether it has the strength to sacrifice the special interests of both classes to the ideal of the common good, whether its destiny is not merely to hope for a great and harmonious future but to realize it, no human being can venture to predict. . . . But if Europe is destined for a great future, it will be only by following this road and accepting this principle.

In view of the decision with which contemporary society is faced, we shall describe one act of the great crisis, the history of France since 1848. . . . This period is more than merely a political crisis, it is the first phase of the new social order, not yet clearly understood but never-theless irrevocable. It is the first challenge to the ability of a European nation to enter the new era of social life, the first attempt to establish the rule of mutual interest in society. . . .

Part Three, Chapter Three

THE SOVEREIGNTY OF INDUSTRIAL SOCIETY IN FRANCE SINCE THE FEBRUARY REVOLUTION

Introduction

We left the French Revolution at the point where the monarchy had been abandoned by the ruling class and had been defeated by the propertyless class. The people had been victorious and had destroyed the traditional form of the state. . . . They could have tried again to change the dynasty and establish a new monarchy. However, not only the trust in the Orléans dynasty since 1830 and the trust in the Bourbons since 1815, but the trust in monarchy in general, had been destroyed. Monarchy had been discredited, not only among the adherents of democracy, not only intuitively among the members of the lower class, but also, as a result of the bitter experiences under Louis-Philippe, among the whole property-owning class. There were no adherents of monarchy anywhere; a change in dynasty was impossible.

The other alternative was the establishing of a dictatorship. But a dictatorship can be established only under specific historical conditions. A dictatorship cannot be instituted; it has to establish itself. For this a personality born for personal rule has to be available and has to be carried to supreme power through the course of events. This implies the dissolution of society into parties struggling with each other. There was no man in France whom the country wished to endow with unlimited power; society was still stable, a dictatorship was out of the question.

The only remaining alternative was the establishment of the republic. And without a special decree, without a struggle, almost without further consideration on the part of the classes and parties and their leaders, the republic appeared as the natural, simple and most appropriate form of state for France after the February Revolution. . . .

At first glance it was natural that, as in the past, the republic . . . was thought of only as a specific form of government. The only difference between this republic and the monarchy appeared to be the principle that supreme power was no longer vested in a single person with hereditary rights, but in the people. This changed only one thing in the whole state organism—namely, the organ which represents the personality of the idea of the state. But simultaneously it discarded something else, namely, the system of pseudo-constitutionalism. The leaders of all the parties were well satisfied with the first change, which brought them one great step closer to the power of the state; the second change was welcomed by the ruling class, which hoped to regain its natural power position within the state through the downfall of the old system. The most powerful people, as well as large sectors of the population, were therefore well satisfied with the change and readily accepted the republic. Never before had a political revolution proceeded so quickly, so quietly and so naturally.

But what was this republic? . . . When the Provisional Government proclaimed the republic most people still believed in popular sovereignty. The republic was the constitution of popular sovereignty. But popular sovereignty is not a fact, it is a principle. In reality . . . people live in a well-ordered society moving according to definite laws. The proclamation of the republic and of popular sovereignty was in reality nothing but the proclaimed sovereignty . . . of industrial society.

In industrial society, the capital-owning class rules over labor without capital, and a strong antagonism between the interests of both classes develops as a consequence of the generally accepted principle of liberty. This antagonism, which permeates the whole life of the people, is the actual constituent principle of the sovereignty of society. This antagonism cannot be dissolved, and leads of necessity to an attempt at a solution through force. But even this does not in fact constitute a final decision. Whatever the outcome, a violent solution will either result in the resurgence of the propertyless class with its old demands and contradictions, in case the ruling class is victorious; or, if the working class is victorious, industrial society itself will be destroyed. The knot will be cut without being unravelled. Thus, it becomes clear that with the rule of industrial society there develops a state of affairs whose inner contradictions cannot be dissolved by industrial society itself. It is true that there is a solution to this contradiction provided by the society of mutual interests, but the transition from industrial society to the society of mutual interests would require more than a few years. The substance of the events leading to the proclamation of the Republic in France after the fall of the monarchy was the following: Popular sovereignty immediately dissolved into the sovereignty of industrial society; and the two large classes of the society, under the name of capital and labor, began a struggle for control of the state; labor was defeated, but the exclusive rule of big capital was also broken. No final reconciliation of the social antagonism through a commonly accepted principle or a thorough-going reform was reached.

The Character of the Provisional Government.
Lamartine. The Basis of the Social Struggle.

. . . The King was expelled, the monarchy destroyed and the republic established, at least in fact. The feeling prevailed among the united population that the state had fallen into the hands of society and its interest groups, and that it was now of the greatest importance to create a state which would at least not be antagonistic to either of them. How could this be done? . . .

The ruling class, in order to gain control over the monarchy, had demanded an electoral reform. It could not retreat from this demand; but it was well aware that an electoral reform on a broad basis would threaten its ruling position. It furthermore anticipated that . . . con-siderable concessions would have to be made in the political as well as the social sphere. Unable to grant such concessions, since they would have been in direct conflict with its own interest, the ruling class could not help but wish that these would be granted by a government which although acknowledging political freedom on a broad basis wanted to uphold the existing social order. . . . The price for the preservation of this social order seemed to be the concession of full political rights to the workers. For the time being, everything seemed to depend on finding a government which . . . could establish and defend unrestricted political freedom on the basis of the existing social inequality.

The propertyless class knew equally well that it was as impossible for it to gain exclusive power as it was impossible for the owning class to retain it. What it was able to gain rested upon the following specific supposition: Since its social position did not provide any chance for the complete control of the state, it had to demand that the political right be given to each individual as such, irrespective of his position in society. This was the price for which the dependent class was willing to leave the social order intact, in the hope of gaining exclusive control of the government legally through universal suffrage and carrying out the desired social changes by the same means later on. Therefore, it had to be perfectly satisfied that a government was instituted which—disre-garding the social question—granted, through the establishment of com-plete political freedom the necessary conditions to gain control of the state and therewith to change society.

. . . The propertyless class was satisfied to obtain complete political equality, and the ruling class was willing to accept this equality. This was the point of common agreement. The former wanted political equality merely in order to change the social order by state action, and the latter was willing to grant it in order to stabilize the social order through these concessions. This was the point of disagreement. Was an enduring peace possible with these germs of future conflict? For the near future, everything depended upon finding a government which was definitely in favor of political freedom and definitely neutral with regard to the social issue. . . . Such a government was presented by the party which had fought, ever since 1834, exclusively for the democratic principle without regard for the social question. That was the party of the *National*. It was the party of the republic, disengaged from the struggle; it was the party of the doctrine of universal suffrage and popular sovereignty. This party was therefore the natural center of the various opposing groups, whose powers were more or less equal. It was put into power almost without asking for it, while each class excluded the other from the government through its respective opposition. This party immediately assumed leadership in public affairs, and was accepted by everybody without any objections.

The first act of the Provisional Government, which was dominated by the party of pure republicans, was the expression of their doctrines as well as of their specific position. It declared itself to be the authorized agent of all the people and repeated on every occasion that it was waiting only for the crystallization of the general will through the convocation of the constitutional assembly in order to return the mandate to the people. . . . Since the members of the Provisional Government were not familiar with the nature of society, they were unable to anticipate a series of disturbances which always follow a revolution. They all believed that it was most important to counter the turbulent excitement of the ordinary people with firmness, in order to avoid excesses and to preserve what they called "order". To this end they were willing to make some concessions to the lower classes; they considered these concessions partly as transitory, partly as insignificant; and some considered them as the lesser evil preferable to permanent disorder in public affairs. Such concessions included the admission of Louis Blanc, Flocon and Albert into the Provisional Government, as well as the first decree and measures pertaining to the conditions of the lower class. . . . More, they thought, could not and would not be demanded; once universal suffrage was accepted as the basis for the republic, the highest possible political standards would have been reached. If firmness was maintained during the initial period, the healing power of political freedom would prove its value and peace would be preserved. This is the way the Provisional Government interpreted its position; this was particularly the noble and honest, but unfortunately erroneous, idea which animated the head of the Provisional Government, the high-minded Lamartine.

The historical significance of an individual does not rest so much upon what he does and is, . . . but on the way in which he symbolizes the general opinion and hope in a decisive period and champions this cause with all his strength and conviction. Through the suppression of freedom the French people were, whatever their social position, conditioned to cherish the idea of freedom. It was not only the party of the *National* that believed in the supreme power of this idea; the better elements of all people had set their hearts on it; the more they became aware of the danger that social suppression might occur in a state form designed for freedom, the more closely these defenders of freedom drew together. Since they all lacked knowledge of the social movement, they were unable to understand what the people wanted beyond free self-government in the republic; what they did not understand they attributed to the misunderstanding on the part of others. . . . They realized vaguely that great dangers might develop if this agitation was not stopped at the proper time and by the right means. But they considered the danger to be over if they could illustrate to the lower class and impress upon them the importance of what had been attained, the value of political freedom, the folly, the danger, and the common disaster which would follow if one were to go further. They were willing to make sacrifices but could not understand how one could talk about a change in the social order, attack that order and work for changing it. Therefore, they were primarily searching for a man who, with the whole power of his personality, would fight the disorder among the lower classes in the name of political liberty, lead them back to the consideration of political problems, and force social antagonism into the background. This man should not lack sympathy with the lower classes; he should watch and be familiar with the social movement; yet he should have no true understanding of the social antagonism, in order to be able to stand above it in the name of freedom. This was the basic tenet of most of the reasonable and freedom-loving citizens of France after the Revolution had been victorious. They were looking for somebody who would represent this attitude, and were willing to give him almost unrestricted power and unlimited confidence in exchange for the great difficulties which his position would entail.

Lamartine was a man well fitted politically for the position; he was a good orator; his naivety with regard to the social question was well known; he had a brilliant name, and he was ambitious. Lamartine understood the Republic as a poet, understood public order as a citizen; but the social antagonism he did not understand at all. He never claimed to be an administrator, nor did he ever attempt to be one; there is not a single blemish to be found in his pure and selfless love of freedom; he struggled relentlessly for political freedom against its opponents from below and from above. More than once he had saved the endangered Republic through his oratory as with a shield and had placed himself between the excited classes, ready to die for the "order of liberty." It was he who embodied all impulses for a purely political liberty; therefore he became, from the very first days of the new government, the personal representative of all republican hopes held by those who regarded the republic as the ultimate goal of freedom. If he had known more about society or had believed less in the power of liberty, he would not have become the leader of France at this time. The very fact that he wanted the state to be the pure republic and society to represent nothing but the existing social order made him the rallying point of all better elements. In this sense he accomplished as much as he was able to with the members of the government and with the masses. As long as he remained in charge, hope prevailed that the February Revolution would not go beyond the limits set by political freedom; in other words, as long as this hope was alive, Lamartine remained the leader of France. Such is the position of this peculiar phenomenon; never did the social movement have a more suitable exponent as did the young Republic of France at this time; there never was a man, who like Lamartine, achieved prominence not so much because of his personal qualifications as because of the particular constellation of the existing social conditions.

It ought now to have become clear why the first disturbances of February and March, the closing in of the lower classes on the seat of the Provisional Government at the *Hôtel de Ville*, the excitement in the streets, the first indications of more serious clashes, meant very little to Lamartine and to all those who did not see anything but factions in the socialist and communist movement, which would disappear with the establishment of real political freedom. They all believed that, after a powerful revolution guided by a new and as yet unknown law, these disturbances would cease, that the revolutionary masses . . . would recede to their former position within the precisely and rigidly organized pattern of industrial society—under the condition, of course, that the newly established state, as a representative of "order under freedom," would remain in power. The more unlimited the power of the government the more inviolable did the social order appear to be.

Thus, under the Provisional Government, a situation had developed which astounded Europe. The same nation which had once established a republic through massacres, which had idolized Robespierre and which with Napoleon had spread the inner conflicts of France all over Europe, now accepted a republican government without the slightest agitation, without war, without threats, without blood; it submitted to a poet with the same obedience with which it had once submitted to Napoleon. And yet this change was quite natural; it was brought about by the awareness that the interest of all required obedience to the state, which alone was able to protect the existing order of society, while under the first Republic the interest of the emerging society required with equal intensity that the remains of the old state be destroyed at any price to give way to the new order.

But if the Provisional Government was so powerful, . . . how was it possible that, before a month had passed, the most serious agitations were threatening it from without and undermining it from within? This is a very important question, which provides the starting point for the history that follows. It is possible, and is usually still considered satisfactory, to explain this fact by simply enumerating generally known factors, the socialist and communist intrigues, the clubs, the mobs in the streets. One also can list the weakness of the government, the indifference of the middle class and the unemployment rate among the workers. But these are only external symptoms, consequence of a great movement which started with the Provisional Government and which, growing at a fast rate, finally carried away everything. Such a movement, which seizes all the elements of the existing order, has to be explained by these elements; and these elements resulted . . . from the relationship between the principle of the government and the social conditions in France.

The Provisional Government was essentially democratic. Political democracy, however, does not extend beyond the constitutional order. With reference to the constitution the democratic concept is clear and stable. . . . But the state, which is governed by a democratic government, is not only concerned with matters of constitutional rights. The state has to be administered; that is, it has to use the political power in order to achieve certain ends not mentioned in the constitution. If a state wishes to be strong, its administration has to be based on a solid and clear understanding of the needs of the people. What was the attitude of this democratic government with regard to these questions?

Obviously it had no established principle at all; it had no definite goal for the attainment of which it would use funds of the state. And yet it was called upon and had to administer. . . .

When the Provisional Government was proclaimed, both classes of industrial society were already definitely aligned against each other; both held distinct and clear views concerning the role of government. The Provisional Government did not have any principle; but, since it was a democratic government, it was also incapable of resisting the pressures of either the ruling or the dependent class. And since—unaware of the nature of society—it took neither a positive nor a negative stand, everything depended on which of the two classes exerted the greatest pressure on the government. The power of the state would go to the class which was most successful in this respect; its victory over the other class would thereby be established.

Since labor as well as capital knew very well what was in store for them if one was victorious over the other, they both exerted the greatest effort to subjugate the partially neutral, partially split government. The time to establish a definite system for the future social order had not yet arrived; there was still time to experiment once victory over the other class had been secured. What was certain was that victory of one class over the government, and therewith over the opposing class, could establish the norm for all administrative measures carried out in the interest of the owning class in one instance, and the realization of a socialist or communist system in the interest of labor in the other. . . . Both classes of industrial society were aware of the necessity of a decisive attempt to secure predominance, and as soon as the Provisional Government was in operation the first steps in this direction were taken. . . . Indeed, never before had the state been so powerless and society so powerful in France as during this period. . . .

The General Movements. The Press and the Clubs

If one reviews the time preceding the February Revolution, it cannot be denied that the masses of the propertyless workers, once dispersed, suppressed and lacking a class consciousness, . . . slowly began to develop a solidarity and to realize that their interests were opposed to those of the property owners. But all these efforts were as yet lacking a common purpose. On the one hand, the various sects and theories had split the masses into larger and smaller groups appearing as specific associations or schools; on the other hand, the whole non-owning class was so remote from the exercise of political power that even unity might have helped little and would probably only have provoked a stronger and more dangerous counter-pressure. The non-owning class was as yet an amorphous mass, and it had to undergo a great transformation to enable it to come forward as a united power.

After the fall of the monarchy, the democratic Republic, for reasons of principle as well as prudence, could not possibly refuse the lower class some share in the power of the state. . . . And so it happened that one of the main leaders of the opposing party, Ledru-Rollin, got a seat in the Provisional Government side by side with the strong democratic majority. He was the representative of the old and violent Republic but was really neither a socialist nor a communist. But next to him, in a secondary position, appeared the representatives of specific social ideas: Louis Blanc, Flocon, originally a laborer but now co-editor of the *National*, and Albert, a worker. But these men had no official sphere of activity. . . . Ledru-Rollin, however, was Minister of the Interior. . . . It was important to have a man in charge of affairs who could be depended upon for the defense of the young Republic against monarchistic attacks. Ledru-Rollin was such a man. The choice was accepted. . . . The Provisional Government considered itself and the existing order safer, the broader its representative basis was.

But the acceptance of these men had a completely different and unexpected result for the masses of the people. Until now excluded from all power, the lower class suddenly saw itself as an equal to the ruling elements in the highest political positions. . . . A tremendous step forward had been taken toward the great goal: the equalization of social conditions. Why not now consider the next step? But in order to take the next step, the lower class had first of all to overcome its internal disharmony and bickerings and to appear in opposition to the ruling class as a united front. To accomplish this it had to give up the sectarian hatred, the mutual calumnies, the intrigues of the secret alliances; it had to accept and support those men who worked in its interest in the new government. . . . Finally, it had to make every effort to keep the working class constantly alert, ready to fight in order to be able to take the initiative. In brief, the lower class had to establish itself as an independent power, fighting under a specific slogan in opposition to the bourgeoisie. . . .

As in any revolution, the two main factors promoting this development were the press and the clubs. . . . A vast number of publications, most of which are not even remembered by name today, flooded Paris and from there the whole of France. In general they were of little originality, mostly dull copies of newspapers of the first Revolution; only a very few were of a high quality. Nevertheless, edited by the main leaders of the movement, they had great influence; they shaped the opinion of the new followers of the movement; they instigated these followers; they sowed hatred and animosity; and, being available for sale at all street corners, they represented, for a certain period, the powerful press of the movement. Most of them had few or no subscribers; they depended on street sales, and the street sales depended in turn on publication of news, sensational cases and violence. The government had no power to counter the offense; the unlimited power of the monarchy over the press had given way to a complete lack of power of the republican government over the press.

More important than the press were the clubs; they had a peculiar character during this revolution. Most of them came into existence, as usual, without a specific organization, without a definite plan for their activity, without rules or a program. . . . They were attended by people from all social classes; but naturally the workers were in the majority, and they determined the type of lectures given. . . . The "Club for Human Rights" (*Club des Droits de l'Homme*) was of particular significance. The Provisional Government had immediately released all political prisoners, among them Blanqui and Barbès, neither of whom had given up his old ideas while in prison. . . . These main representatives of the ideas which had suffered continuous defeat but which were now generally accepted, were nevertheless excluded from all political activities. Thus they were immediately driven back into the movement; glorified martyrdom in the service of freedom seemed the only compensation for their suffering. They became the leaders of the "Club for Human Rights" and all the remaining old secret alliances joined them as experienced leaders. The club became powerful; it was the only club which was well organized and knew what it wanted. The rush to join was enormous; Blanqui and Barbès thus became leaders of the masses of the proletariat, which identified itself with them; and while Louis Blanc and Ledru-Rollin represented the movement within the government, Barbès and Blanqui were the leaders of the masses in the streets.

Notwithstanding the similarity of their positions. Barbès and Blanqui represented two very different types. Barbès, a man of means, had devoted himself to a fight for political democracy with great sincerity. He used to distribute his yearly income among the poor, and lived frugally himself. Having no ambition, he considered it his duty to live and fight for the lower classes. His attitude was that of a religious visionary. He did not advocate a specific social system, but he devoted himself with great warmth to any idea in favor of improving the lot of the lower classes. . . . His intellect was less powerful than his heart, a fact which strengthened rather than reduced his influence. He was not a public speaker, not a leader, not a sympathizer; but he was the favorite of the lower class. All this contributed . . . to making him a tool of cunning people who saw in him a powerful and useful ally, especially since they did not have to fear his ambition.

Blanqui, on the other hand, was a man of inordinate ambition, eager to satisfy this ambition at any price. He was forever driven by his thirst for influence, for fame, for a position which would inspire fear; but since all his efforts were centered around himself, they usually ended up in intrigues designed to enhance his frame. Once a ruthless conspirator, he had become a skillful leader of the people; he had studied human passions and human weaknesses, and unlike anybody else he could transpose the vague feelings of the masses into an idea, which, however, was usually intended as a tool for his own interest. . . . Blanqui was the brain of the masses, while Barbès reflected their heart. The alliance for human rights . . . submitted to both of them with the absolute obedience so characteristic of revolutional organizations. Whatever the leaders said or did was accepted at face value. And thus the basis was laid for a disciplined movement among the as yet unorganized masses. This helps to explain the terrifying events of May and June.

In a few days the elements of the streets had somehow become organized. The masses began to become a power. The government, which did not yet know to what extent it could rely on the other classes and on the army, felt that the masses might easily become dangerous to its position. The partly political, partly social party of the movement within the government, Ledru-Rollin, Louis Blanc, Albert and Flocon, on the other hand, recognized that the property-owning class mistrusted them and the monarchist hated them, and that in order to stay in power they had to look for support from the suppressed, and so far inarticulate, sector of the population. Therefore, they generally welcomed these movements. . . . Aware of the coming struggle, the whole population began to separate into two parties, held together through the government by their mutual antagonism. . . .

The First Laws and Measures of the Provisional Government.
The Proletariat Constitutes Itself.

Since 1830 it had become a common notion in the republican party that it had been the lower classes, preferably called "the people," who had made the Revolution but nevertheless had not derived the slightest benefit from this Revolution. This opinion was deeply engrained in the mind of the proletariat. It was quite natural that, after the second Revolution had succeeded through their forceful actions which led to the establishment of the Republic, these same people looked for the benefits it might bring them, and that the republicans, at the same time, wanted to do something for this class in order not to lose its support. This all seemed so plausible that nobody was surprised about either the demands or the compliance with them. But there was . . . a tremendous difference between this Revolution and all the preceding ones. It was not so much political power that was demanded; it was the use of state funds for the improvement of the conditions of a class which was unable to help itself. This was the true content and the true goal of this Revolution. In this sense it was a social revolution, and however little this could have been anticipated, the first measures taken by the government drove it into a direction which it was later unable to change. . . .

The Provisional Government had taken over a well-organized state. There was nothing new to be instituted. But people expect great and important measures from any revolutionary government. There was only one area of activities left to this government: the attempt to improve the condition of the lower class. From all the socialist, communist and social political factions and doctrines there were only a few statements left which the more reasonable people considered as the true content of the complaints of the laboring class. These concerned the too high taxation of products indispensable to the daily needs of the lower class, the hardship of working conditions, and the lack of support in case of emergency. All the burdens and all the privations had grown through the Revolution. Whoever interpreted the movement as predominantly political might have believed that the working class would be satisfied with a change of those conditions. Whoever interpreted it as a social revolution had to admit that in any case such change had to come forth. Everything indicated that the Provisional Government was forced to act.

Thus a series of decrees was published which have to be interpreted as the beginning of the movement which developed consequently. . . . First, the Provisional Government reduced the working day from 11 to 10 hours. The reduction of working hours had long been demanded, and the government considered it a great step forward. But it forgot that a shortening of hours implied a reduction in wages and that such a measure makes sense only when accompanied by a raise in wages.

As it was, the measure only disturbed the industrial order without bene-fitting either employers or employees. . . .

There were other decrees, which dealt with taxation. The government, under the pressure of the lower class, began to change the existing tax system. It abolished the tax on beverages, on meat, on bread, and finally also on salt. These decrees were received with cheers of welcome by the lower class. . . . The property-owning class did not voice any opinion about the abolition of these taxes, which was but a negative measure. But the government had to cover the deficits. Therefore, a tax of 1% was put on mortgages, and the tax on landed property . . . was raised. This positive side of the measure had already a totally different character. It was not only a relief for the workers but a bur-den on capital and ownership in favor of labor. It was reminiscent of the idea of progressive taxation; for the first time the government appeared to subordinate ownership to work. The ruling class took notice; . . . it grew suspicious of a danger threatening the stability of the status quo. The classes began to separate. But the antagonism between them had not yet found a specific expression outside of the various schools and sects.

At the same time, the government had to carry out a measure which it considered correct in principle though dangerous in its consequences. The old National Guard of Paris had to be reformed in accordance with the principles of universal suffrage. The government decreed that every adult and honorable Frenchman should be a member of the National Guard, and that the officers be newly elected by the newly formed squadrons. This decree corresponded to the changing situa-tion. However, by subjecting the masses to a strong discipline and apparently controlling them, the government also equipped them with weapons; the consequences seemed to be unpredictable; . . . nobody could be sure that the arms might not be used as weapons against ownership. The decree hit the property-owning class hardest. Up to now the National Guard had been considered as the armed organiza-tion of ownership against the dangers presented by the dependent class. This corresponded to the character of the National Guard and was a view fostered consistently by the King. When the February Revolution broke out, the property-owning class had considered the National Guard as the best safeguard against the mob, whose growth endeared the National Guard all the more to the ruling class. Now the old organiza-tion was destroyed, and nobody could foretell whether the newly recruited masses would gain the upper hand and succeed by their number as well as their voting rights in using the National Guard for their own purposes and as a basis of the rule of labor over capital. According to Emile Thomas in his *Histoires des Ateliers Nationaux,* the decree roughly doubled the total number of National Guard members. The reform of the National Guard alarmed the property-owning class considerably. . . . There was a growing concern about the immediate future.

However, all this could also be interpreted from the standpoint of political liberty. The government had not yet taken any steps acknowledging the existence of an independent, important and powerful new class. The first traces of a deeper antagonism could still be explained as transitory phenomena and the doctrines of socialists as mere utopia. But the government did not stop at this point. Two major measures were adopted which, after all these events, have to be considered as indications of the real state of affairs and the beginning of the class struggle: they were the *Ateliers Nationaux* and the Workers' Parliament of the Luxembourg.

The Ateliers Nationaux

. . . The lasting significance of this peculiar institution lies in its relationship to the development and constantly growing antagonism between the two classes. On February 25th, while disorder still prevailed, with the army still disorganized, the National Guard dispensed, the King still on French soil, the opinion of the provinces not yet known, the Provisional Government not yet generally accepted and residing without proper protection at the *Hôtel de Ville,* a relatively small but determined group of armed workingmen suddenly appeared before the *Hôtel de Ville.* The leader was a worker by the name of Marche, who, armed with his gun, invaded the conference room of the government and excitedly demanded in the name of the people the recognition of the right to work. . . . There seems to be some indication that he was an emissary of communist groups. The government listened silently; nobody answered; suddenly Louis Blanc got up, withdrew, talked privately with Marche, and consequently proposed the following decree: "The Provisional Government of the French Republic commits itself (*"s'engage"*) to guarantee to the worker his support (*"existence"*) through work. It commits itself to provide work for all citizens. It accepts the fact that the workers have to form associations in order to enjoy the legitimate benefit of their work." . . .

It is almost incomprehensible that reasonable men could issue such a decree. But the ruthless arrogance of Louis Blanc and the impending danger made such a step possible. The decree was issued and publicized. In his *Pages d'histoire de la Révolution* (p. 32) Louis Blanc states: "I knew very well how deeply the decree committed the government; I knew exactly that it could only be carried out by way of a social reform, the establishment of worker's associations as a principle and the elimination of the proletariat as a goal." This was what he considered to be "the actual value of the decree." Not much discussion followed on that turbulent day; other things were to be done and the matter was momentarily forgotten. But it began to spread through the country like the seeds of bitter fruit. For it was . . . the declaration that the Revolution was to be transformed from a political to a social revolution and that the government would take the lead in instituting social reform. All other governmental measures were now seen in a different light.

In the beginning little attention was paid to the decree. The diligent workers who were able to support themselves saw no great advantage in a right to work guaranteed by the government; the poor workers saw no advantage in the decree, since it implied the necessity to work. The property-owning class did not grasp its meaning, the more astute people believed that it was only a measure of appeasement. And since work was the determinant for governmental support, the decree could only gain practical importance if there was unemployment.

This, however, was precisely the case immediately after the Revolution. The shops closed and some thousands of workers were put on the streets without any means of support. They were the ones for whom the decree had apparently been issued. They approached the government in the name of this decree and demanded bread and work. Now the government had to go further. On February 26th the second decree was published, which established the *Ateliers Nationaux* . . . and authorized the Minister of Public Works to execute its provisions. . . .

As long as the number of unemployed did not exceed six or seven thousand, as was the case during the first few days, everything went smoothly: that many could be placed without trouble. But the number of unemployed grew rapidly. . . . There were two ways out of this difficulty: The government either had to provide more work or it had to support the unemployed. The former, as was demonstrated later, would have been useless, but the latter measure was dangerous. Nevertheless, the government decided in favor of the latter solution. . . . Every worker who was admitted to the public workshops received 2 francs per day, regardless of age and ability and regardless of the kind of work he performed. Whoever remained unemployed received

HISTORY OF THE SOCIAL MOVEMENT IN FRANCE

1½ francs per day from the Government. The laborers now, of course, told themselves that it was better to get 1½ francs daily without work than 2 francs for hard work. . . . The number of applicants for work began to increase to the extent that the availability of work decreased. And the government found itself in an absurd position. There was only one thing it could now do. Since it did not have the courage to discard the *Ateliers*, it had to supervise strictly the distribution of money and demand some kind of work in exchange for it.

Here begins another chapter in the history of the *Ateliers*. . . . The course of events was, briefly, the following. The government had the intention of centralizing public support and at the same time of removing it as far as possible from the city. For this purpose it called a young man by the name of Emil Thomas to the *Hôtel de Ville* on March 3rd. He explained the system according to which the government would have to proceed. . . A central office for the support of the workers had to be established, where every worker would receive a working book. . . . The Minister of Public Works had to inform the Director of the public workshops daily about the work in process and about the number of workers who could be placed. . . . Secondly, the office was to operate as an employment agency for private industry. . . . The Provisional Government accepted this project, a decree of March 6th appointed Emil Thomas as the Commissar of the government at the head of the national workshops. . . . Public support was also regulated and therewith temporarily connected with the new organization. But a new complication developed which Emil Thomas deplores seriously and for good reasons in his pamphlet: "*Histoire des Ateliers Nationaux.*" There was a shortage of work. The original plan could not take care of more than 1000 workers; but the number of applicants grew from day to day, all the more so as those who did not work also received money. By the middle of March there were 49,000 unemployed. Emil Thomas now approached the Administration of Bridges and Roads in order to find work for the unemployed. But either out of antagonism against the new institution or out of fear of getting poor quality of work this administration balked; in spite of considerable pressure it was impossible to make it respond by providing an adequate amount of work. This was the first great drawback which obstructed the functioning of public workshops. . . . Secondly, the absurdity of such newly created work, unconnected with the naturally developed volume of industrial production, became manifest immediately. For, obviously, workers of various skills applied for work, and people who were used to a specific kind of work. Suddenly they

were asked to do work for which only very few were suited. Some complained that they were unable . . . to work with pick and shovel all day long; others declared that they could not do the hard work because it would injure their hands and deprive them of future means of support; workers were sitting along the roads, reading, talking, loafing; nothing was being accomplished by these thousands of hands. Discouragement spread. People were defeated by the work they did not respect and which some of them were unable to endure; they were like a defeated army. At the same time, frauds of all kinds could not be avoided. Many got their payments in the morning and then worked somewhere else; others managed to get paid twice; the money was squandered; work, in general, became discredited. And then even the workers who had their regular jobs in private industry began to give up their hard-earned income in order to get easy money in the public workshops. Private industry, already depressed by the general circumstances, suffered more and more. Masters and factory owners turned in vain to the workshops to find workers; either the workers did not care to return to the city and to hard work, or the offices, snowed under with work, were unable to cope with the situation. Conditions grew worse from day to day. Already on March 1st, Emil Thomas, in a report to the Minister, stated: "that in fact the number of enlisted workers amount currently to about fourteen thousand and this number is increasing daily; that, doubtless, if the rumor gets around that the workers definitely have no other obligation but to be on hand at certain hours and to receive an unearned subsidy, the honest workers will be ashamed and annoyed at receiving, in spite of the specific promises of the Provisional Government, only humiliating assistance instead of honorable work, while the crowd of lazy workers will soon hasten to join up; that—under the guise of having special training and with fake home addresses—we will soon have to enlist into our ranks all the doorkeepers and vagabonds of the capital."
. . . Nothing progressed except the number of workers and the daily expenditures, which on March 11th amounted to over 20,000 francs per day. We do not have any exact and detailed record concerning the increase in these figures, but we do know that on May 19th there were 87,942 unemployed workers registered and that the expenditures on that day amounted to 182,879 francs. . . . In any case, this was a situation which no city or even state in the world can endure in the long run. The lack of work had destroyed order, and the better elements among the workers disappeared among the mass of loafers. The plan had miscarried, the whole institution had lost its proper

focus, and the city watched with growing annoyance the project which consumed its energy without even securing order.

Under these conditions it was inevitable that politicians would attempt to obtain control over the masses of the workers. They tried to win them over for communist doctrines and for the clubs. . . . The more the better elements of the workers left the public workshops because of lack of employment, the more the demagogues hoped to get control over the whole institution. It was for good reasons that the property-owning class feared and gradually came to hate the public workshops. . . . In any case, these workshops appeared to be a symbol of the trend toward socialism, based as they were on the famous decree of the "right to work." Appearing under a socialist name, and actually, although mostly unintentionally, in conflict with private industry, they provided sufficient reason for the ruling class to destroy them after their victory and to oppose them in any possible way during the period of the class struggle. . . .

The public workshops would have had little significance at any other historical period; indeed, they were doomed to failure from the very beginning. But at the time of the origin of the class struggle in industrial society they were a phenomenon of crucial importance. They were a practical illustration of the principle that even the greatest human efforts and sacrifices cannot change the order of work suddenly, that any institution conceived as a means of introducing a new order of society necessarily deteriorates if its principles are in conflict with the prevailing order. Under these conditions, what were supposed to be wages became in reality relief for the poor and thereby imperilled labor and capital simultaneously. The public workshops, therefore, have proven that . . . even though half of the society may be convinced of the necessity of a new order and the other half may be willing to make any sacrifice in order to prevent a greater evil, any attempt to establish abruptly a new order in the relationship between work and acquisition must fail.

But during the period following the 1848 Revolution in France, the public workshops have united the working class for the first time by unifying all trades, regardless of differences, in one and the same organization. They contributed more than any other factor to the development of a feeling of class solidarity among the workers which is the first prerequisite of the class struggle in industrial society. The public workshops organized the working class into one body. They did not convince the workers that the public workshops are a step in the right direction toward an organization of labor, but they did convince them that they must search for such an organization. . . . They shifted, for the first time, the problem of the relationship between capital and labor from the realm of theory to that of reality.

Consequently, the public workshops sharpened and hardened the enmity of the property-owning class toward the propertyless class. . . . They strengthened the conviction among the property-owners that a government-controlled organization of work on a national scale would inevitably lead to general disaster. This conviction was of crucial importance at that particular moment. For, while the public workshops continued to function on a separate plane without affecting the deeper layers of French society, a second movement developed at the same time, a movement with the ambitious goal of assigning to the state the task of organizing labor, of subjecting capital to labor and of setting up a new social order from above. This movement was represented by the workers' parliament at the Luxembourg under Louis Blanc. . . .

Louis Blanc and State-Socialism

Louis Blanc is one of the outstanding political figures who attracted the attention of Europe during the first months of the French Republic. He is not particularly eminent by virtue of his accomplishments, but the ideas which he proposed and inspired were of decisive importance. . . . It is wrong to put him, as is frequently done, in the same category with the other socialists; he had developed his own principle and had a history of his own. Louis Blanc was born in Madrid in 1813. He came from a very poor family, a fact of which he occasionally boasted. He started out as a provincial journalist, and also attempted to gain fame as a poet. There was a poetical flavor in all of his writings. Later he went to Paris . . . and in 1836 became the editor of the democratic newspaper *Le bon sens*. His literary career began at this point. *Le bon sens* was originally a democratic paper, and that is why it could not find a proper place next to the *National* and the *Journal du Peuple*. Louis Blanc knew perfectly well, on the basis of his own experience with the lower strata of the population, that mere republicanism would be of no help to these people. He sensed that democratic freedom, though necessary, could not remain the final goal of the movement. . . . Louis Blanc attempted, as far as possible, to pursue and formulate in his newspaper the social aspects of the situation. But the climate of opinion was not favorable for these attempts. Saint-Simonism had just perished in mockery, Fourierism was not being considered seriously, and communism, making its first appearance in industrial society, was hated and even ignored by the democratic forces because it threatened to estrange the lower classes from republicanism. Social tendencies had no supporters anywhere, and the "party of the workers," of which Saint-Simon had prophetically dreamed, had not yet been established. *Le bon sens* had no readers, and . . . was forced to close down in 1838. . . . However, in the following year the democratic party started the once famous *Revue du progrès*, whose line went already beyond the purely democratic doctrine . . . Here was a proper place for Louis Blanc who, just starting to develop his own position, was perfectly suited for a paper whose position on the crucial problems of the time was not as yet clear. This periodical first published Blanc's essay, *"Organisation du Travail,"* which later became so famous. The essay immediately created a great stir. . . . In this pamphlet . . . Louis Blanc . . . started out with the statement that economic competition leads to the ruin of the whole society, and that it ought to be replaced by another system. . . . The critical analysis of competition is written with lucidity, pungency, and erudition; it is definitely the most valuable contribution of Louis Blanc, and added much to his popularity. His essay was written at a time when the rule of capital had already created a fierce competition among capitalists which had thereby lowered wages and resulted in a series of bankruptcies. However, this criticism was merely negative; what was needed was something positive to replace competition, something that was not an abstract theory like socialism, nor an altogether absurd notion like communism, but an economic order comprehensibly and rationally built upon the prevailing condition and at the same time corresponding to the national character of the French. This is what Louis Blanc provided in the system which he called the "Organization of Work." His line of thought is clear and distinct. We will summarize it briefly.

If one wants to find a cure against the superior force of capital and the resulting evils of competition, one has to search for it in capital itself. If one wants to control the competition which originates through capital, this has to be done by capital. Who is the greatest capitalist, having the power to subjugate the other capitalists, and who has the greatest interest in promoting the well-being of the workers suffering through competition? Doubtlessly, the state. The state has the means of controlling capital and the interest of doing so. The state, therefore, represents the power which can solve the great social contradiction whose saddest and most portentous manifestation is the competitive system and its consequences. In this way Louis Blanc develops his original basic idea, which gives him an independent position. He is the first representative and teacher of state-socialism.

The second line of thought in his essay, which indicates the starting point for carrying out the basic reform, is also his own. To control competition without forcefully overthrowing the whole order of society, the government has to be accepted as the highest authority over production, and has to be invested with great power to carry out its task. This task consists of eliminating competition by the very process of competition. This is done according to the same principles which now control the capital market. It is well known why the larger capital subdues the smaller one and why it slowly absorbs it. It produces more cheaply and therewith eliminates the less successful entrepreneurs. The state, as the ruler over capital, is the greatest capitalist. By investing its capital in a proper way, and by using its capital power in the productive and competitive process, it will slowly eliminate the smaller units of capital. . . . In the end, the state will gain complete control over production without applying coercion by simply using the capital at its disposal and operating according to the principles of private industry. This is the basis of state-socialism. The state is the only producer; the state alone owns factories and enterprises; and workers, wages, and prices are subject to its control. The state has a complete monopoly over the economy. . . .

But it is not enough that the state controls the economy. The state has to take care of the workers and thereby solve the great social question. . . . The state, as the supreme industrial authority, establishes or takes over industrial workshops. These are transformed immediately under its guidance. The state administers them, at least during the transitional period. The state issues decrees concerning work; these decrees have to be approved and accepted by the National Assembly. Every worker is guaranteed employment in these workshops, by the state, which also distributes the work and the wages. . . . For a limited period of time, for the duration of about one year, the wages are differentiated; but later on the work order changes. As soon as the state becomes the sole producer, the democratic principle replaces the authoritarian principle in the inner organization of state industry. The workers in the various workshops begin to elect their foremen "since they now have time to evaluate each other"; the wages are no longer unequal, different jobs entail only different occupations but not different incomes. The total returns are divided into three parts; one part is distributed equally among the members of the Association; another part used for the support of the sick and the old, and also in order "to alleviate the effects of recessions in other industrial branches since all parts of industry owe each other support"; the third part is used for replacement of tools and machinery. Each member of a workshop may use his wage as he pleases, but he will soon discover the greater advantage in satisfying needs in common. "It goes without saying that the wages have to be more than sufficient to support the laborers." In order to initiate and establish such a system, the educational system has to be changed so that the general welfare rather than the rise of income becomes the motivation of the activity of the individual.

These are the basic features of Louis Blanc's essay the "Organization of Work." It is difficult to understand how he overlooked the first difficulty which makes his system impracticable. It is true that large capital devours small capital in the process of competition, but only if one presupposes, which Louis Blanc avoids doing, that the wages are kept at a low level. . . . How the state can win in the competitive struggle with other capitalists if the workers are generously remunerated had not been explored at all by Louis Blanc. This, however, was the main issue, and as long as this issue was not subjected to an analysis all other proposals remained utopian.

However, the young author's essay created a sensation. Its main idea, of solving the great social question through the interference of the state, concurred with the French character. In addition, the ever-present danger of a social revolution made the property-owning class willing to consider and discuss this type of project. . . . After long controversies, a new theory stood side by side with the older ones; its main feature consisted in having the organization of work carried out by way of social workshops through a centralized, state-controlled industry. The idea that the existing state was to become an assisting power was thereby established. It is this idea which transformed the abstract concepts of socialism and communism into real issues of social life.

From now on the demands and the hopes of the proletariat began to change. All the former schools of thought and doctrine had required, as a prerequisite for the improvement of living conditions of the lower classes, a new order which was obscure to some and seemed impracticable to others. Of what use was it to preach love to the proletariat, as did the adherents of Saint-Simon, or to hold out the hope of a future harmony, as did the adherents of Fourier, or to admonish them to follow the commandments of God, as did the religious communists, or to promise them political freedom, as did the democrats? All this did not affect the present conditions of the laborers—their all too meager wages and their inability ever to acquire capital. But now a practical solution had been presented. The state suddenly appeared in a different light. The state was no longer only the highest administrative power, but also the greatest capitalist. And since, according to the idea of liberty, each individual has equal political rights, each individual was now also entitled to share the capital owned by the state and whatever this capital procured. State power, which so far had remained apart from the social struggle of capital and labor, now became, in the opinion of the proletariat, a participant in this struggle. . . . And if the state once had the opportunity to organize labor, . . . what is it that restrains it from doing so and from using its funds, which are its capital, to assist labor and the laboring class? Obviously, this restraint was due not to the specific nature of the state but to the reluctance of those who controlled it and misused it for their own interests. What, then, was the road which the working class had to take in order to improve its own lot? It had to attempt to gain state support for its own ends. . . .

This is the main influence of the theory of Louis Blanc. Regardless of its scientific and practical value, it taught the proletariat to think of the government not only in terms of the state constitution, as it had done until now, but also in terms of state administration. From the demand that the state should use its revenues in order to provide better living conditions for the workers originated the aspiration of the proletariat to obtain control of the state in the name and in the spirit of the working class. The social element was here for the first time placed side by side with the political element in the struggle against pseudo-constitutionalism. This, on the one hand, made the property-owning class hesitate in the struggle for political liberty and made the conservative elements stronger than they otherwise would have been; on the other hand, it influenced the proletariat to demand, in case of a political revolution, from the new state administration what no state is able to do.

The theory of Louis Blanc about the organization of work marks the beginning of social democracy. Those who consider it of intrinsic value are mistaken. Its significance lies in the growing antagonism between the two elements of industrial society; what makes this theory important is that it presented, even before the outbreak of the Revolution, the views and the wishes of the proletariat with regard to the state; its importance grew with the approach of the collapse of the existing order. Louis Blanc, who had been little known up to that time, steadily gained followers among the masses; to his restless, rather than truly great, ambition this suggested the prospect of a brilliant future. . . .

At the beginning of 1848, conditions were such that an outbreak of violence could no longer be avoided. As it approached, many more groups joined the editorial board of the *Réforme*, to which Louis Blanc was a contributor. With the vague yet positive feeling preceding any revolution, the two great parties were already at that time divided into two different camps. The office of the *National* was the center of the purely democratic party, the office of the *Réforme* the center of the social democratic party. . . . The proletariat considered the *Réforme* as its main organ. But Louis Blanc, the representative of the state organization of work, exceeded all others in popularity—more so on the basis of expectations than on the basis of achievements. The signal for the resurrection of the masses was given by the *Réforme's* office. . . . February came; the Revolution was victorious. And from then on, the editorial board and the office of the *Réforme* became the center of power in public affairs. Supported by the masses, it had to become the mouthpiece of their wishes and demands in the new government. The list of the members of the provisional Government was drawn up here; through the tremendous influence of the *Réforme*, Ledru-Rollin, Flocon, Albert, and Louis Blanc were accepted as members of that government. They moved to the *Hôtel de Ville* and took their seats side by side with the representatives of political democracy. For more than three months the state was nothing but the personified expression of the social antagonism which became sharper from day to day. . . .

February 28th.   The Ministere du progrès.
The Conferences of the Luxembourg.

Among all those who represented the social element in the Provisional Government, only Louis Blanc had set up a specific system according to which the present state should raise the standards of the lower classes with the help of state funds. There was no doubt that he knew what he wanted, and because of this he had the greatest following among the populace, who submitted to his orders. . . . Louis Blanc was well aware of the strength of his position. . . . But his point of view was not represented in the established order. If he wanted to exert power within the state, he had to create a new state agency which, according to its designation, its specific function and even its name, would serve the needs and the wishes of the lower classes. This agency would take the first steps toward the realization of his basic idea of the organization of work, through the use of the power of the state to improve the lot of the lower classes. Thus the idea of a Ministry of Progress was born; this idea provoked many hopes and many fears, not so much because its power would be too great and its position unquestionable, . . . but because it would represent that part of the power of the state which would be exclusively in the hands of the proletariat as an independent class. Essentially a manifestation of the antagonism between the social classes, it would have become a medium for the ambition of the propertyless class in its attempt fully to control the state.

This is why almost the entire Provisional Government was opposed to it. . . . The fact that the right to work was already guaranteed by decree strengthened the opposition. The property-owning class was rightfully afraid of these unpredictable concessions and pressed the government not to go any further, since Lamartine had frankly admitted that, although he had signed the decree with his back to the wall in order not to break with his colleagues, he never knew and never would understand the concept of the "right to work." . . .

A violent conflict developed within the government. Particularly Lamartine, led by brilliant insight, declared himself to be definitely opposed to the new agency, and the majority supported him. Louis Blanc had to risk everything. He declared that under the circumstances he would immediately resign. This strategy proved successful. His resignation would have constituted, after everything that happened, the frank and decisive declaration of war against the propertyless class. . . . From this day dates the schism in the Provisional Government; its whole existence from then on was nothing but the more or less visible struggle between the two elements of society. The government, however, would have been lost if it had not given in. It was as yet unarmed, and the masses of workers stood at the doors of the Council chamber.

Then a solution was found. Establishment was proposed, instead of that Ministry, of a commission to investigate the condition of the laborers, to report on these conditions, and make suggestions for changing them. Louis Blanc was to be nominated Chairman, and to organize the project as he saw fit. What more could the proletariat have asked for? But Louis Blanc, being well aware of the consequences of such a step, refused. "Instead of Cabinet membership, which would have meant control of offices, agents, a budget, the resources of state administration, and real power—instead of the chance to act—what was being offered him? . . . The opening of a turbulent school where I would be called upon to lecture about hunger in front of starving people." He was right. Instead of carrying out state socialism, what was being proposed was an organized investigation of the existing conditions. This was something altogether different from a Ministry of Progress. What was being proposed was not a political, but merely a social, agency of the proletariat. . . .

Louis Blanc had to make his choice: he either had to bury himself and his theories in the rooms of the Luxembourg without a hope of gaining power and prestige; or else he had to resign, confront the workers, explain the opposition of the government, take up arms and set himself up as social dictator. . . . Time pressed; and Louis Blanc, ambitious enough to be the first among the party leaders, had neither the courage nor the blind enthusiasm to take advantage of this chance. He gave in. He accepted the presidency of the Committee and resigned from the Cabinet. The case of social dictatorship was lost. . .

There was a rush to establish that Commission; Louis Blanc himself drafted the decree organizing the conferences at the Luxembourg. It runs as follows:

"Considering

that the revolution carried out by the people is made for the people; that time is ripe to end the long and unjust sufferings of the workers;

that the labor problem is of the greatest importance;

that there is no greater, no more dignified activity for a republican government;

that it is the task of France to study seriously and solve a problem with which all industrial nations of Europe are confronted;

that one has to take measures to guarantee to the people the fruits of their labors;

the Provisional Government of the Republic decrees: A permanent Commissions, under the name 'Government Commission for the Workers,' will be established with the specific task of investigating the lot of the workers. To indicate the great importance which the Provisional Government attributes to the solution of this great problem it nominates one of its members, M. Louis Blanc, as President of the official Commission and another member, M. Albert, worker, as Vice-president." . . .

This decree of February 28th . . . was of unusual significance. On the one hand, it irritated greatly the property-owning class, who were not aware of what had happened. The popular phrases about the "unjust sufferings of the labor class" which so far had been used only in communist newspapers and pamphlets resounded now from governmental quarters. One got the impression that the voice of the common people predominated. The whole property-owning class which, up to now, had interpreted the revolution as a political act, began to understand the true state of affairs. Behind the appearance of unanimity the deep cleavage within the government was discovered. There developed a fear that the representatives of the working class might gain preponderance over the other members of the government, and dark forebodings of the inevitability of a civil war took hold of the minds of the people. The ruling circles began to attach themselves more closely to the government; they considered the Luxembourg as the government building of the working class, the antagonist of the Hôtel de Ville. They were familiar with the ideas of Louis Blanc and expected him to use his power to establish public workshops which would lead to the ruin of public finances and private industry. General hatred turned against this man; to the ruling class he appeared as the archenemy of society, to the republicans as a threat to law and order, to the royalists as an exponent of extreme republicanism. . . . Everybody considered him, and rightly so, as the personified expression of the independent working class and of its demands on the state; from then on, the Luxembourg seemed to be the agency of the consolidated power of the proletariat and thereby the true beginning of the deliberate antagonism in industrial society.

On the other hand, the apparent power of the proletariat led, in fact, to its impotence. In the first place, the representatives of labor, Louis Blanc and Albert, had been removed from the scene of the government; they were ordered to discuss theoretical questions which obviously would not lead anywhere. On the other hand, the representation of labor now became exclusively the function of the Luxembourg and particularly of Louis Blanc . . . who was held responsible for everything in which the government fell short of the workers' expectations. It could be predicted that the Luxembourg would be unable to accomplish anything; it even lacked the power of engaging in a doomed enterprise. In the midst of the most powerful revolution, and exposed to the vengefulness of the ruling class, it was supposed to solve the greatest issue, the real social conflict, solely on the basis of a doctrine and by idle words. This could not be of any avail, and it also necessarily endangered Louis Blanc's popularity. This institution of the Luxembourg, so much abused by its opponents, in fact proved to be the ruin of the power for which it was feared. It had proven and had been destined to prove that nothing could be accomplished by this method. . . . This whole institution was of no avail for the future. With the acceptance of its presidency Louis Blanc became a defeated man.

. . . On March 1st the first session of the Commission took place, but the working class representatives were not at all properly organized. Louis Blanc wanted a more distinguished membership; in addition to workers and masters he also appointed socialist celebrities: Charles Duveyrier and Carreaux representing Saint-Simonism, Victor Considérant representing Fourierism, Jean Reynaud representing the new Encyclopedists, Vidal and Pecqueur representing modern socialism, and many others. . . . But they did not accept their appointments; others who were invited did not always attend. . . . The first general meeting took place on March 10th; there were 250 members of all trades. . . . But it became instantly clear that orderly deliberations were out of the question because these people were unfamiliar with the general problems, and the conflict of specific interests of the various trades made orderly deliberations impossible. Louis Blanc felt compelled to suggest that the representatives appoint a special permanent committee and that all members meet only on special occasions. . . . Ten members were chosen by lot, . . . and now Louis Blanc and Albert remained alone with these in the vast halls of the Luxembourg, without any power, and even almost without any function. . . . Louis Blanc now turned his specific attention to the various trades, and attempted to regain the influence which he had lost in the government. . . . The public had become deeply interested in the labor problem. Journeymen and workers . . . demanded higher wages and less work; masters and entrepreneurs, strongly under the pressure of competition, had to refuse these demands vigorously, particularly at this time; there was much enmity and many feuds. . . . Masters as well as workers in distress turned to the Commission at the Luxembourg, which in many individual cases had a beneficial influence by arranging agreements or issuing formal decrees as a guide for solving disputes. . . . However, this activity seems to have been limited. . . . In any case, it was secondary to the problem of the centralization of the trades. . . . This project brought the Commission headed by Louis Blanc again temporarily to the center of power for the second time, on March 17th. . . .

On the basis of the discussions concerning the organization of work, Vidal and Pecqueur later drew up a formal plan which reflects essentially the ideas of Louis Blanc. These ideas had taken a somewhat different and more general shape during the sessions of the Commission. Louis Blanc incorporated into his system the idea of the association; . . . instead of the establishment of public workshops, he now suggested the association of the laborers of the same trade in common workshops with self-elected supervisors, equal wages, and state credit for capital investments. . . . Added to this were the ideas of other socialists who also demanded a reorganization of agriculture and trade under the same principle. Thus developed the general plan of the Commission, . . . which confirmed the government's prediction that a partial realization of the new idea would lead to failure, and that concerted action through mutually consistent measures, applied simultaneously over a long period of time to industry, agriculture and trade, was an indispensible condition if these projects were to succeed. . . . From all this the proletariat understood only one thing, namely, that theory was of no use to them, and that even the best socialists considered their liberation from social dependency as a distant goal which would be difficult to attain. It was in vain that Louis Blanc gave one lecture after another at the general meetings; the content of these lectures showed clearly that his main ideas were not concrete enough to be applicable. The workers had hoped that the activity of the Commission would lead to direct tangible results; instead they got nothing but empty phrases, and that did not help anybody. The Luxembourg began to be deserted. . . . March 19th had been the high point in the existence of the Commission; after that date it began to decline daily in significance, and sank without a trace into oblivion, engulfed by new events.

However, while the Commission had been insignificant for the workers as well as for the development of social theories, it had taught the leaders what really mattered. They came to realize that they would lose influence with the workers as well as with the government by merely conducting theoretical investigations, and that everything depended on getting practical control to maintain their position; they abandoned their theoretical efforts, and Louis Blanc attempted, under the pressure of events and during the approaching open struggle between the property-owning and the propertyless class, to gain for himself and for his doctrine the stature which he had begun to lose . . . as mere President of the Luxembourg. . . .

The Proletariat During the Sovereignty of Industrial Society

. . . Before the outbreak of the February Revolution, the working class had never acted as an independent power; even less had it been recognized as such. On the one hand, all its attempts to become united through alliances or common institutions had been persecuted and punished as a crime by the government; on the other hand, the more political character of the movement had frequently overshadowed its social content. Thus, this class had existed as a mass, living under specific circumstances and beginning to develop an awareness of its condition, but having no proper organ and no will of its own.

The February Revolution changed all this. It threw the masses into the hands of daring and determined leaders who, striving for power, raised the proletariat to an awareness of its strength and an understanding of its demands. They taught it to consider itself as a class, and the difference between them and the property-owners evolved into an opposition growing daily in intensity and bitterness. Through the swift use of their power, these leaders forced the yet unprepared government party by law, and partly by such institutions as the public workshops and the Luxembourg, to accept this new class officially as an independent part of the population, and to provide it with agencies which, although instituted to serve immediate needs, soon developed into instrumentalities of the antagonism between capital and labor in general. Finally, these leaders, with their doctrines and their fruitless experiments, drove home the fact that it was most important for the laboring class not only to be in the right with its demands and principles, but also to take the law into its own hands. The working class suddenly felt closer to the supreme power of the state than the property-owning class ever had; the working class was convinced that the state could and should be of assistance to it. If this did not happen whose fault was it? Was the idea of the state itself false? Certainly not. The fault lay obviously with those who controlled the state, the property-owners, those who wanted the promised "order within liberty", a promise which was in itself contradictory. It was an attempt to preserve social dependence through the traditional order and, at the same time, an attempt to establish equality through the granting of political liberty. Could that help the proletariat? No. After it had become aware of its social conditions and its political power, there was obviously only one road open to it; it had to make the attempt to usurp the power of the state as a social class in order to attain its social goals. This was the natural course of events, and all those phenomena which we characterized as the process of the organization of the proletariat in the history of French society are nothing but preparations toward this attempt. The struggle for state control between the classes in society had become inevitable after the proletariat had become class-conscious and had proclaimed its demands. The validity of the law according to which the opposing factions of society control the state, its life and its constitution, is illustrated by the major events of contemporary history. . . .

The Struggle of the Two Classes

. . . The Provisional Government stood right between these two opposing classes. There were two roads open to it to cope with the situation: it had either to establish a dictatorship and act as the agency of the ruling class, or it had to give up its power as soon as possible and convene a Constituent Assembly. The first solution would have made the Provisional Government all-powerful, though not before a final, fierce battle with the proletariat; as a victor and as the government of a new republic, it could have established a constitution with voting rights restricted to property-owners and a president not respsonsible to the parliament. If the second solution was chosen, the Provisional Government would remain loyal to the principle of popular sovereignty and would thereby avoid a showdown with the proletariat, but would be taking the risk of destroying itself and society through lack of constructive action. The government chose the latter course. It announced the convocation ot a Constituent Assembly based on universal suffrage, in order to transfer governmental power to it. This was an act decisive for the course of subsequent events up to the middle of May. . . .

The communist-socialist segments of the movements of the proletariat had, almost without exception, taken a stand against private property. Thus, the proletariat had taken, in the eyes of the public, a position which differed from what its greater part really stood for. Rather than being the champion of those opposed to the rule of capital, it appeared as the opponent of all kinds of property; it thereby united the whole mass of owners and forced the small owners to make common cause with the big owners, who, within the system of industrial competition, were natural enemies. Thus it was not capital and labor, but property owners and propertyless who were in opposition to each other. If the propertyless class really believed itself to be in the majority, what could have been more desirable for it than a Constituent Assembly on the basis of universal suffrage? But if it accepted the fact of being the minority, what form of government could it wish for? . . .

This much was clear. As soon as the government had announced elections, there developed an otherwise quite incomprehensible situation whereby the party of the proletariat favored the postponement of the elections and the maintenance of the Provisional Government, while the property owners, aware of being in the majority, declared themselves in favor of the immediate convocation of the Constituent Assembly. . . . Both classes, more and more concerned with the issue, carefully gathered their strength. Social dictatorship became the slogan of the proletariat, and popular representation the slogan of democracy and property ownership. This struggle indicated the form in which each of the two classes began to wrestle for the control of the state. . . . The demands of the proletariat were first counteracted by the fact of the election law. . . . More than anything else, this law contributed to reassuring the property-owning class. It had convinced this class that the National Assembly would provide it with a powerful and independent organ, and that through this assembly they would become the representatives of popular sovereignty. From the time the bill was passed, they began to consider the dangers which threatened the established order as transitory, and therefore bore them less grudgingly. On the other hand, the bill made the leaders of the proletariat come forward forcefully; since they could neither change nor denounce the bill without contradicting themselves, they had to attempt to fight against its consequences. . . .

According to all available reports, it was undoubtedly predictable that the elections would turn out in favor of the Republic—and equally distinctly against social democracy. Was there anything that the social democratic party could still do under the circumstances? It had to prevent the election at any price; it had to maintain the whole power of the state under the control of the Provisional Government. In the future assembly to party would undoubtedly be in the minority, but under the Provisional Government, with the party votes almost equally divided, it could hope to exert, through the pressure of the masses, a tremendous influence on the government. It could overthrow the government, replace it exclusively by social democrats, and therewith establish the rule of the proletariat. The statements by Louis Blanc who defends this position, as well as by Proudhon, who attacks it, leave no doubt that this was really the opinion of the leaders of the proletariat. . . .

Thus the generally accepted idea of popular sovereignty was transformed into the notion that the people on the broadest democratic basis should not be entitled to draw up their own constitution, but that a Provisional Government should uphold a dictatorship until it had carried out all measures it considered necessary. Could there have been a greater mockery of the so-called sovereign people? It was argued that, first of all, to establish such a liberty-defying dictatorship, the elections ought to be postponed, particularly "in view of the profound ignorance and the moral servitude which prevails in the rural areas of France" and, secondly, that the government should "take the strong initiative to accomplish far-reaching reforms." . . . The struggle of the classes for control of the state was here clearly formulated. . . . This was the idea which had already taken shape at the beginning of March. It was quite logical because it represented the only way in which the lower classes could obtain state control. But the fact that such an attempt at extreme despotism was masked by the flag of freedom alienated forever many friends of the new movement. . . .

Meanwhile, time was pressing. The bourgeoisie became restless. The leaders of the proletariat had to forestall them. . . . On the morning of March 17th, the proletariat gathered on the *Champ de Mars* by the thousands. The city, open and unarmed, was waiting breathlessly. The Provisional Government sat at the *Hôtel de Ville;* there was a tremendous tension. . . . Paris had never seen such a spectacle. One hundred and fifty thousand people, subdivided into groups of 500 to 600, marched from the *Champ de Mars;* first the clubs with their flags, then the workers, ten by ten; without shouting or calling they approached in complete order, the column reached from the *Place de Grève* far into the *Champs Elysées.* The leaders of the clubs came close to the gates of the *Hôtel de Ville;* the Marseillaise was sung, a cheer given to the government, to Ledru-Rollin and Louis Blanc; finally the club leaders entered the *Hôtel de Ville.* . . . Blanqui addressed the Chamber and demanded, in the name of the people, postponement of the elections and removal of the army from Paris. The members of the government became indignant. As to Ledru-Rollin and Louis Blanc, opportunism prevailed. They recognized that this attitude of the people was not any longer of their own doing, but essentially that of the club leaders; they felt that they could expect from these people even less authority than their present position gave them. Ledru-Rollin spoke first: "skillfully but firmly", as Lamartine puts it, he took a stand against the proposals; he knew what he had to expect from the rule of the mob. Then Louis Blanc's turn came. Once again, he seemed to have the power to give himself up to the masses and to enforce social dictatorship. But fear gripped his heart again, and instead of siding with these people he made a long speech against the demands of the delegation. Again he proved that he did not possess the greatness his position required. The delegation, which had placed its hope in these two men, stood there, beaten. . . . The tremendous demonstrations petered out. This was what happened on the once-so-famous day of March 17th. It seemed at the time to have gone by without any consequences.

And yet its after-effect was of vital importance. On the one hand, the leaders of the proletariat became convinced that neither Ledru-Rollin nor Louis Blanc was the right man to establish a social dictatorship. This day marked the downfall of Louis Blanc in the eyes of the workers. It is of great significance that one of the workers rushed forth with a furious gesture at Louis Blanc as he left the *Hôtel de Ville,* grabbed him and exclaimed: "So you are a traitor, you too." Louis Blanc may have felt what he had foregone for the second time when he cast his vote with the other members of the Provisional Government "at the risk of losing myself with them." . . . These two men had lost all importance in the labor movement. The proletariat, moreover, had shown itself as a fear-inspiring mob, but at the same time as a mass without a leader. From now on it could not hope any longer to gain a victory over the property-owning class.

On the other hand, the events of this day had brought home the seriousness of the situation to the property owners. The propertyless no longer appeared to them as a chaos of clubs and sects, but as a powerful unit marching against them, capable of going to the extreme as soon as a powerful leader came to the fore. It was high time for them to organize themselves as a unit too, and to act with firmness. Danger had made them resolute; and, once convinced of the antagonism between the classes, they acted with growing determination against all efforts of the proletariat. The day which deprived the proletariat of its leaders became also the day on which the foundation for the unification of the bourgeoisie was laid. From now on, the problem had no longer to be decided in the sphere of political institutions, but in the arena of the social struggle.

The events of that day also affected the position of the democratic party. For the first time the party realized that its principle, the self-government of the people by its legal and regular organs, was opposed by another democratic principle: the domination of the government through the pressure of the masses. . . . Until then it had been possible and permissible to deceive oneself about the movement of the proletariat. Now the democratic party had to side with either one or the other of the two great parties. It did so immediately by declaring itself definitely against any infringement upon the power of the state instituted and accepted by the people; it sided with the bourgeoisie against the proletariat . . . . Its indignation about the demonstration was great; the Provisional Government felt it particularly strongly. As Lamartine stated, it considered the attempt of the proletariat to seize control as "a subjection of the government, a placing outside the law of every element in the nation except the people of Paris and an indefinite dictatorship under the condition that the government itself accept and ratify the dictatorship of sovereign demagogy." . . . It was a fair interpretation, but nothing was decided by this conviction alone. Definite action ought to have followed, but it did not. The leaders of the proletariat regained their courage. A repetition of the events of the day was bound to occur. . . .

The leaders of the proletariat renewed their efforts. Heated disputes within the government arose. Symptoms of a defeat of the socialist elements grew. . . . Finally Ledru-Rollin, strongly supported by Louis Blanc and his friends, again suggested a postponement of the elections, which had been planned for early April. After a vehement quarrel . . . the moderate majority won, the elections were announced for April 27th, the convocation of the Chamber for May 4th. The majority now believed that it had prevented the establishment of a dictatorship. Now everything depended on keeping order until the elections. . . .

. . . The events of March 17th had made a deep impression upon the members of the government. It doubted its ability to contend with the proletariat. The leaders of the latter were aware of this and knew how to take advantage of it. In order to regain popularity, Louis Blanc made the commission of the Luxembourg demand from the government that two or three deputies from the Luxembourg be sent into the provinces in order to sway public opinion on the election issue. The demand reflected strong self-confidence; the government, instead of opposing it, gave in and granted it. The aggressiveness of the party grew; new machinations started; it seemed as though the elections had to be forestalled; perhaps this time an attempt to overthrow the government would be successful. The incident which provided an opportunity for such an attempt was the election of officers of the newly organized National Guard. The workers were permitted to elect 14 officers. The Luxembourg ordered the various trades to gather on the *Champ de Mars* on April 16th to make arrangements for the election and then to move on to the *Hôtel de Ville* to hand a petition to the government. The clubs cooperated with this plan. A huge demonstration was prepared; the whole power of the proletariat was summoned up. . . . Dark rumors spread over Paris; there was great tension. The leaders . . . knew that March 17th had failed because of a lack of definite plan. This time they laid down a formal plan; the main leaders formed a secret Committee of Public Welfare (*Comité du salut public*) which was supposed to take over power at the decisive moment; a list of members for the new government was drawn up, arms were procured and an insurrection prepared. The danger seemed greater than ever. . . .

But while the masses prepared to follow their leaders, there developed a dissention among them which, more than anything else, determined the outcome of the events of the day. Louis Blanc wanted nothing except the enforcement of the grandiose measures of the "Organization of Work"; Blanqui, on the other hand, who had as many foes as friends, wanted to overthrow the government altogether, while his opponents in turn wanted to get rid of him also after the fall of the government. Those clubs which were more republican-minded than socialist . . . were opposed to fighting for despotism, whether under Louis Blanc or under Blanqui. . . . Nor did the government know what it really wanted; it had no troops and no plan. It was paralyzed through inner conflict; unable to take any drastic measures, it left Paris to its fate. The lack of unity on both sides is most characteristic for that day, which became the day of an elemental struggle of the two classes of society. . . . On April 15th the populace gathered on the *Champ de Mars*, and a situation similar to that of March 17th appeared to be developing. The citizenry, prepared by growing rumors, was alert. The National Guard kept ready. . . . The workers were unarmed. There could be no doubt about the outcome of the day. . . . Everything depended on a signal given to the irritated citizens to go ahead. Ledru-Rollin . . . made the appeal to arms. The National Guard was quickly assembled, well-armed and prepared to fight. . . . All around the *Hôtel de Ville,* as far as one could see, on the bridges and streets, bayonets glittered and surged. Paris had never seen such a demonstration of the force of arms. . . . The workers approached from the *Champ de Mars,* the deputies at the front. They were received with wrath and scorn. The National Guard crossed the bayonets. . . . The deputies submitted their petition; it was insignificant and was treated curtly and with reserve; the deputies retreated. . . . The National Guard held the place, nobody attacked it; . . . the Guard was satisfied with a bloodless victory. . . . The proletariat had found its true antagonist. The National Guard marched past the *Hôtel de Ville* shouting "Down with the communists." This was directed also against the extreme left within the government, particularly at Louis Blanc and Albert; . . . their power was at an end. The conservative group had definitely defeated state-socialism, the National Guard had crushed the masses of the workers; Louis Blanc had lost all authority, his own party lost confidence in him; . . . within the proletariat there was a deep schism; . . . they did not trust each other any more. Democracy had definitely sided with traditionalism; the property-owning class had, by pressure of its followers and its will-power gained the first decisive victory over the proletariat. . . . March 17th had displayed the power of the proletariat; April 16th showed the power of the property-owning class. Just as, on March 17th, the first symptoms of the destructive tendencies among the proletariat became visible, April 16th provoked, together with the manifestations of the bourgeoisie, certain reactionary propensities. The *National* characterized April 16th as the "correlate to March 17th," but, as it added rightly: "One may say that there were two demonstrations on April 16th, one in favor of the Republic and the Provisional Government, the other in favor of the counter-revolutionary reaction." . . . From the confusion of opinions there finally emerged the extremes of both sides, both with the tendency to use the Republic for their own purpose. Thus it became the task of the government after these two days . . . to oppose anarchy on the one side and reaction on the other. It based its power on the support of the great majority of the property-owning class and on the moderates among the workers, who were opposed to the old monarchy as well as to communism. The government, therefore, had to act in that spirit, and subject the communist-anarchist sector of the movement to the existing law; it had to prohibit encroachments upon its power and oppose steadfastly all disruptions of public order. This was what the core of the French people rightly demanded from its government. But what did the government do instead? It did not do anything. It left the activities of the clubs undisturbed, without police interference; it left Caussidière at the head of the police; it organized the *Guard Mobile*, but it also tolerated the growth of the public workshops to disastrous proportions. . . . It would still have been possible, at that time, to strengthen the order of society by taking strong action and at the same time raising the living standards of the working class by reasonable methods. But nothing was done. Also nothing was undertaken against the reactionary forces which attempted to gain control, particularly in the provinces. The old officials remained in their positions; the reactionary electioneering practices and the activities of the clergy who opposed the Republic were not stopped. Thus the government stood waiting for the election results; it was, indeed, a strange phenomenon. It resembled a building without any firm foundation of its own, suspended in mid-air by the pressure of two opposing powers. The government was neither a reflection of the ruling-class interests nor a reflection of the idea of an independent state. . . .

Meanwhile, the two major elements of society, left to themselves, were again mustering their forces. The elections were set for April 24th. Everybody knew that the near future depended on their outcome. . . .

The results of the elections showed that the working class was definitely in the minority. The great majority of the votes went to the democratic party; another part went to the conservatives and a third part, the smallest, to the socialist group. As expected, the property-owning class had been victorious. The new Chamber was an agency of the rule of property, of both material and non-material property over the propertyless. At the same time, the elections reflected the acceptance of the Republic and the definite rejection of monarchy.

In view of these results, the constellation of the opposing social elements changed. . . . The monarchists, the conservatives, the ultramontanists, and particularly the capitalists, . . . rejoiced in the victory and in the assurance of being able to control the Chamber; ignoring or ridiculing the social ideas, they joined the democrats in maintaining that the Chamber held and should continue to hold sovereign power. The political democrats and the republicans had some doubts about this, as well as some specific suggestions. They were afraid that the preponderance of the elements of the old order in the Chamber threatened the Republic. In order to strengthen the Republic, they began to bring the labor problem to the fore, treating it not so much as a historical fact but as a challenge for the new Chamber. It is worth mentioning that the *National*, the main mouthpiece of the doctrinaire democratic trend, was already concerned with the social question since the middle of April, although in a way which could hardly be satisfactory to the socialists. The paper stated clearly that the family and property are the "immutable foundation" of any social order; . . . that the great movements of recent times had severely shaken these conditions, that they had destroyed all other traditional social elements and institutions, that the demands of labor therefore were fully justified; but, whatever the demands of labor, these bases of society had to be preserved; only then could the initiative of the government regarding social conditions be possible. . . . But all these considerations touched the social question only on the surface. For the main issue was whether or not the Chamber in its present composition would try to tackle the problem. The third group held the opinion that the Chamber would avoid dealing with the labor problem.

This group consisted of two segments. One, composed of the more reasonable elements of the proletariat, realized that it was impossible to solve the antagonism between labor and capital or even to establish a new society suddenly by an act of violence. All they wanted was a recognition of the significance of the great social movement; they hoped that the growing pressure of public opinion would finally force even a Chamber of bourgeois composition to inquire into the matter. . . . The *Atelier* stated in a significant article on May 2nd: "It cannot be denied that the composition of the Chamber has turned out badly as far as social democracy is concerned; . . . if one looks at the names of its members, it is evident that one cannot expect of them to wish to realize whatever program socialism can reasonably offer from now on," and yet it would be foolish to interfere by violence; the future would in any case belong to the social movement. . . . This party was powerful but without initiative, as are all those who rely on the self-realization of truth. It gained significance only by refraining from participation in the coming events. . . . It thereby to a considerable extent deprived the leadership of the proletariat of strength and circumspection.

The second segment was known as the radical branch of the social democrats. It favored violence; it was supported by the clubs, strengthened through the secret alliances, favored by the mob. It was a real power mainly by virtue of the irresoluteness of the government. The goal of this group was to destroy or at least seriously paralyze the Constituent Assembly, this new organ of the state, even during the process of its formation. . . . To realize these plans the cleavage between the property owners and the propertyless had to be exaggerated, either through terrible threats or through bloody power. Thus a number of small events preceded the opening of the Assembly. Though individually dealt with, they heralded subsequent disaster. There doubtlessly existed a large secret alliance, . . . spreading over all of France, but particularly strong in the industrial centers. Until this time everything pertaining to it was wrapped in deep secrecy. Louis Blanc explicitly admits its existence; Lamartine hints at it several times. Whether Ledru-Rollin and Caussidière were involved in it, and to what extent it reached into the higher circles of the government cannot be ascertained at this moment. But there is no doubt that it operated in a way similar to the former Carbonari; it is uncertain whether the Revolutionary Committee, . . . or the Committee of Public Welfare . . . or the *Société des Droits de l'Homme*, stood at its head. The connection between the various groups . . . became evident on May 2nd, when the Society of Human Rights publicized . . . a proclamation to arouse the masses and to frighten the bourgeoisie. . . . It demanded the recognition of the Declaration of the Rights of Man of 1793; it went even beyond that; it asserted the necessity of a new form of society and the justification of any means in attaining it. It concluded: "The ancient social forms have disappeared; the overwhelming majority of the people no longer respect privileges and monopolies; if you persist in defending the ancient social forms, you will find, when the day of the battle arrives, our organized groups in the lead, your compatriots will then no longer speak of forgiveness but of justice." The new deputies of the National Assembly had just arrived in Paris. This was the welcome they received. How insensate the proclamation sounded next to the slogan of "fraternity"! Yet it was quite natural;

civil war had to follow class hatred. The mutual indignation increased. On the very same day bloody revolts broke out at several important places as a consequence of the elections which, even in industrial centers, had favored the owning class. . . . The National Guard had to use arms, and the *Journal de Rouen* . . . correctly described the street fighting as a battle of the proletariat "against the class of the bourgeoisie personified by the National Guard." One cannot assume that the leaders of these movements expected any tangible result; they just wanted to demonstrate the vast range of their power. After these occurrences, more decisive things were bound to take place. . . .

The Chamber was opened on May 4th; . . . the election of its members had been a declaration of war of the property-owning class, not so much against the proletariat itself, but against its recent utterances of radicalism. . . . On May 9th a new supreme political organ was to be installed for the interim period until the new Constitution was ready; this was the occasion which led to massing of strength of the two opposing powers. . . . While the majority of the property owners had become more and more irritated by the disturbances in communications caused by the insurrections of the proletariat, the partly monarchistic, partly ultra-montanist reaction began to raise its head. The republicans realized this danger. They were forced to make common cause with the left which, although weak by itself, gained in importance as a result of that danger. . . . Lamartine was closest to the left among the republicans, and also indispensable to the monarchists. As long as this constellation of forces prevailed, the group which favored social change represented a real power. Such were the circumstances under which the form of the new government was to be determined. The initiative came from the pure republicans, who wanted to avoid a clash between the extremes. They made a proposal according to which the Assembly should elect an Executive Commission of five members, who in turn should designate the ministers. This suggestion corresponded to the concept of the constitution which we have previously characterized as "the republic of ownership in an industrial society." The suggestion was reasonable. One could count on the support of the majority of the property-owning class, as well as of the doctrinaire republicans, who insisted on a separation between the legislature and the executive power. . . . After a hard battle, the prudent center prevailed and the proposition . . . was accepted, though only by a majority of twelve. . . .

Everything therefore depended on who would be elected to the Executive Commission. The right wing, which represented the majority, was determined to force its opinion on the Provisional Government and remove the extreme left from the Commission. The most serious objection to that was the danger of deeply antagonizing the representatives of the proletariat. Lamartine expressed such fears. He declared that he would resign unless Ledru-Rollin became a member of the Commission. He thus forced the majority to give Ledru-Rollin a controlling position, but he thereby lost a great deal of his popularity. The Commission consisted of Arago, Garnier-Pagès, Marie, Lamartine, and Ledru-Rollin. The left was definitely beaten. . . . The last defeat came on May 10th, when Louis Blanc . . . demanded the establishment of a *Ministère du Progrès*, (Department of Progress). The Deputy Peupin, a worker himself, and representing the workers, argued against him and opposed the creation of such a department. He considered the lack of work to be caused by the lack of confidence; he did not blame the Luxembourg for it "because one cannot be guilty if one has not done anything." A roaring applause greeted his speech, which reflected the division between the reasonable workers and the communists. Louis Blanc's proposal was rejected almost unanimously. It was of little significance that a "Commission for suggestions to improve the lot of the workers" was established instead.

An important turn of events had taken place. The position of the Chamber had been clarified. The Chamber had taken a stand against the rule of the proletariat. The Chamber was no longer a creation of popular sovereignty but an agency of the ruling class of a sovereign society. These days conclude the first period of the history of the Republic. What follows is merely a logical consequence of the decision taken in the Assembly: the transition from latent to open social antagonism and to civil war.

What was to be done by the leaders of the proletariat after these events? There was no more possible doubt about the intention of this Chamber. The people concerned with the social question could only hope for very little, the proletariat could hope for nothing. And yet this Chamber was a sovereign institution. In form it represented the sovereignty of the people, in reality the sovereignty of the property-owners. If it were to remain in power a complete destruction of the power of the proletariat was to be anticipated. This was the conviction which the first sessions conveyed to the leaders of the masses. If the activities and the power of this Chamber were not curtailed it would become solidly entrenched. It was necessary to make a renewed attempt to overthrow it, just as one had tried to overthrow the Provisional Government. . . .

On May 15th, the leaders of the clubs marched from the *Place de la*

Bastille on the boulevards toward the Chamber. They relied on the inaction of the Executive Commission; rightly so, . . . for nothing had been prepared. The revolt, on the other hand, was well-planned; a list of new government members and a series of drafts for new decrees, worded in the spirit of Babeuf's revolution, had been printed. . . . They hoped for a victory by surprise. The ever-growing column approached; when it arrived at the Chamber, the General of the National Guard, Courtais, suddenly ordered the bayonets to be taken off the rifles; confusion spread among the troops who were surrounding the Chamber. The mob entered the Chamber and took over. Blanqui took the floor and spoke of the inalienable rights of the people. Barbès proposed a tax of one billion francs to be collected from the property owners. Huber declared that the Chamber was dissolved. Not a word came from the other members of the Chamber. The column then rolled to the *Hôtel de Ville,* where the leaders set down and issued decrees. Only now, after about half an hour, the government and the National Guard recovered themselves; without much effort the streets were cleared, the Guard marched to the *Hôtel de Ville,* captured the leaders, and made a quick end to the whole revolt without spilling one drop of blood. These events marked the second serious defeat of the proletariat. The revolt had been a senseless undertaking, and had offered an opportunity to eliminate the leaders of the proletariat and to secure the victory of the owning class. From now on true peace and reconciliaton were no longer possible. . . .

May 15th had not yet brought a final decision. By depriving the clubs of their most radical leaders and by revealing their intentions, it had, on the one hand, thrown back the masses of the proletariat on their own devices and, on the other hand, had aroused among the property-owners an awareness of a permanent and dangerous state of war within society. The events of May 15th had remained on the surface. . . . Even the most cool-headed observer could no longer deny that only now the real depth of the antagonism between the two elements of society, created through industrial growth and legalized by the hitherto existing government, had become clearly apparent.

At this point we have to look back again at the course of the preceding events and their consequences. At the time of the February Revolution a proletariat was indeed in existence, but it was not yet a united group; it had no organs and no institutions exclusively its own. The Provisional Government had tolerated the rise of the clubs and had even partly supported them; they continued to operate. The government had left the press of the proletariat, with all its excesses, unmolested. . . . Above all, the government had guaranteed to the proletariat the right to work;

this law in all its consequences had remained uncontested. Furthermore, the government had established the public workshops . . . which grew at a fast rate. It had . . . left the police under the authority of Prefect Caussidière, a man who definitely subscribed to the doctrines of the Revolution and to the ideas of the National Convent; finally, it had taken over Ledru-Rollin, the most feared leader of the movement, by making him a member of the Executive Commission. Through all this, that government had more or less directly organized the proletariat as a social and political power. . . . Under these conditions, the proletariat remained a power equal in strength to the power of the owners.

Since March 17th, the proletariat had experienced one defeat after another, yet the basis of its power had remained intact. The proletariat remained unshaken; it still had its original strength and advanced its old demands. What did the government do in view of this fact? . . . It had promoted and legalized the social contradiction, but it had not done anything to dissolve it. What was to be the consequence? Feeling itself to be in the right due to the previous administrative actions of the state, and aware of its power, . . . the proletariat was deeply embittered; to some extent it began to doubt the soundness of a moderate approach. If, after such great events, nothing, absolutely nothing, had been done to improve the social conditions, the causes obviously rested with those who now dominated the state. How could anybody deny the demands of the proletariat as long as the right to work and the public workshops continued to exist? It had been a great mistake to uphold the principle of raising the living standards of the dependent class by state action and at the same time not to take a single constructive measure toward the realization of this principle. Under these circumstances the proletariat had to turn to the government itself. At the beginning of the Revolution there had been numerous and powerful representatives of its interests in the government; they had been removed one after another. The proletariat felt that it was slowly being pushed back into its former condition of subjugation; what could be more natural than to attempt once more, before it let this happen, to save its power and its rights?

The property-owning class, on the other hand, deeply enraged by the latest occurrences and once more the ruler of the propertyless class in the state as well as in society, looked at those rights and institutions that the proletariat demanded with definite hatred. They did indeed present an insoluble contradiction within the framework of the existing social order. Even the most liberal people accepted the fact that society could not be changed at will, although the laws had changed it on paper. It could easily be predicted that peace and order would not be re-established as long as the proletariat, strengthened by the laws and institutions which were not a result of the organic development of society but which emanated from a momentary emergency, insisted on the impossible. It was quite clear that only a forcible interference with the economy of the nation would be capable of satisfying the demands of the proletariat based on these laws. It was equally clear that such a forcible interference—whether called socialism, communism, organization of work or of credit—would in any case destroy the whole economy for an unpredictable length of time, and thus also the future of the workers. What would happen if the proletariat were to get hold of the state? Obviously this would mean the realization of an absolute contradiction: the impossible would become the law. What could be done under these conditions of total decay? A definite and profound determination was needed to break the power of the proletariat and to prevent, at any price its gaining control of the state either through its main leaders or through specific institutions.

This was the situation after May 15th; public opinion became more and more aware of the great social antagonism. The term, and even the concept, of popular sovereignty began to disappear; the sovereignty of society . . . emerged from the struggle of the opposing forces. This and nothing else represented the real danger of the future.

The only power which could have successfully counterbalanced the efforts of the opposing elements, the Executive Commission, was unable to rise above the fighting forces. It did not have the courage to set limits to the principle of the rights of the proletariat, nor, on the other hand, to draw the consequences of those rights. The Commission took a half-way position. It was hated equally by both sides without being feared or respected by either; it knew neither how to prohibit nor how to accomplish anything; it left the opposing forces to themselves, which could not possibly lead to anything good.

Next to the Executive Commission, the Constitutent Assembly was the highest authority in the state; its power increased in proportion to the inability of the Commission to follow a firm policy. . . . The French Constituent Assembly was doubtlessly the reflection of the spirit and the ruling agency of the property-owning class. As such, it feared the attempts of the propertyless class to gain control of the state. But at the same time, there were many members in the Assembly who, partly for personal reasons and partly out of hatred against industrial society and the irrepressible liberties it stood for, wanted to reinstitute the traditional order of feudal society. These elements were definite adversaries not only of the proletariat but also of the Republic. . . . They soon took the initiative in the struggle of the property-owners against the demands of the proletariat. In this fashion, the character of the Chamber, after May 15th, gradually began to determine the subsequent course of events.

There were many people among the property-owners who, although definitely opposed to the rule of the masses, like the political democrats, did not want to disregard altogether the aspirations of the working class. They were joined by the moderate representatives of the workers, who were satisfied with a slow but steady effort of the state toward the improvement of the conditions of the lower classes. If these elements would have cooperated, neither the extremists nor the reactionaries would have had a chance of succeeding. It was, therefore, important for the reactionary forces to thwart by all means such a frank and honest collaboration between these groups and to suppress the development and acceptance of a common principle. . . . In order to accomplish that, it was necessary to persuade the Chamber to use its power against the movement of the lower class. This was accomplished by emphasizing the need for order and by demanding for the sake of order a number of decrees and measures which were essentially directed against the principle of popular sovereignty. The reaction proceeded with caution and yet with determination. . . . It had to restrict itself to secretly provoking attacks on the republican government and to persecuting openly the followers of the social movement. Among the decrees enacted for the first purpose was that of May 18th against the armed clubs, the draft of the proclamation of May 20th, containing an indirect criticism of the Provisional Government, the attack on the Minister of Public Education, Carnot, because of the publication of a republican catechism. . . . Among the measures taken against the social movement was the endeavor of the courts of inquiry regarding the events of May 15th and the struggle against the public workshops, . . . which began by the end of May. . . . The bourgeoisie wanted to get rid of them because they were too expensive; the reaction wanted to disorganize them for further political machinations. The democrats did not want to retain them any longer; the socialists almost hated them, because Emil Thomas had always been hostile to the Luxembourg. A violent struggle, involving mutual accusation evolved. A proposal by Falloux to change the daily wage into wages for piece work, to discontinue the orders for work in the departments and to enforce the return to their home towns of those who had no residence in Paris, was finally accepted on May 28th. At the same time, Emil Thomas was suddenly discharged and replaced by Lalanne. The immediate consequence of this step was a complete disorganization of the masses, which even up to that time could hardly be held together. The effect was similar to that of the closing of a factory, but on a much larger scale; the workshops became abandoned, and thousands of workers, no longer able to work in their former trade, became unemployed. From that moment on, the commotion among the masses became stronger. The *Faubourgs* were swamped with these workers, the pubs and public places were overcrowded; they stirred up each other, criminal elements joined in the general turmoil. At last the material for a final terrible revolt had been gathered together.

The following reasoning was undoubtedly correct: Since the government did not have the strength to cope with the approaching events, the unavoidable struggle had to be a struggle of society. There was no doubt that the masses would be defeated; the consequence of a victory of the property-owning class would result in a strong reaction against the propertyless class. . . . The reactionary forces could only gain thereby, and therefore they tried to do everything possible to provoke the struggle. . . .

These ever-growing efforts finally aroused the concern of the republicans. By the middle of May the *National* could already refer to the "plans of the reactionary party;" there were the legitimist and the Orléanist reactions. . . . The adherents of the Republic closed their ranks; they exchanged their views and organized the resistence against the daily growing power of the reaction. They not only protected Carnot, Flocon and even Louis Blanc, but even succeeded in securing a decree on May 27th which exiled the Duke of Orléans from France. . . . They fought against the unreasonable demands of the masses, but urged—with equal determination—serious and comprehensive measures toward the realization of reasonable reforms. They investigated the social question and pushed it into the foreground; . . . they seriously criticized the pending projects; and through all this they became a power. Yet theirs was a negative power only, as is only natural in a political democracy. It placed a strong barrier against the reaction, but it was unable to do anything constructive. To gain the initiative they lacked, these republicans turned toward the government. But the government was without any energy, without a plan and without any will to act. . . . It began to realize that without a strong command the overthrow of the existing order was inevitable. . . . There was only one thing left to be done. It was necessary to form another government strong enough to proceed energetically. This opinion prevailed increasingly. The Commission was hated by the reaction because it was the manifestation of the republican principle; it was hated by the property-owning class because it did not offer any protection against the mob; it was hated by the democrats because it did not know how to handle the secret maneuverings of the reaction. . . . The Commission's indecisiveness and lack of committment reflected the nature of the state itself. Society was split into two opposing camps; civil war was imminent, and the weakness of the state made it possible for either of these two classes to gain complete control of the state for its own purposes through a change in government personnel. The resignation of the Commission would have meant not only a change in personnel but also a change in the position of the state with regard to the social conflict. This was a most serious measure, and presumably neither of the two classes could acquiesce in the gaining of such control by the other. A change in the highest political offices was, therefore, the signal for a civil war. . . . The seriousness of the situation was complicated by the fact that the reaction, particularly the monarchistic reaction, remained apart from the two classes. . . . Would it not usurp the abandoned state for itself while the two classes ruined each other during the struggle? Had the reaction not really incited the rebellion to reach this goal? Should the two classes, in view of this danger, avoid a showdown? . . .

Toward the middle of June, the various elements pressed for a decision. No resolution was taken as yet; but the complete disorganization of the public workshops, the tremendous commotion in public places, showed that the battle was approaching. Never was a government more inactive and apathetic than the Commission during these days. On June 20th the first draft of the new Constitution was finally published; the whole city knew, on June 21st and 22nd, that the explosion was imminent. On June 23rd the first barricades were erected. . . . From now on, two battles were being fought simultaneously in Paris, one in the streets, the other in the National Assembly; the former for the victory of the mob, the latter for the victory of the reaction. These fateful days can only be understood if one considers both levels of the struggle together. There are hundreds of reports of the first level of the struggle; the second one, though by no means less important, received but little attention. Only Proudhon had clearly stated its importance.

Nobody in the Assembly believed that the masses would be victorious. The main problem was to secure a victory of the republican political principle. The whole democratic party, therefore, opposed the revolt, which gained them the approval of the property-owners. . . . The National Assembly declared itself to be permanent; and on the morning of June 24th, Pascal Duprat made the proposal that "a state of siege be proclaimed in Paris, and that all powers be concentrated in the hands of General Cavaignac." The Commission resigned; the proposal was accepted, and then Cavaignac advanced with his troops against the revolt and defeated it.

Such was the end of the Executive Commission. Its end brought with it a decisive victory of the republican over the monarchistic principle. Cavaignac was an outstanding republican and at the same time an excellent general. Setting him up as a military dictator made the Republic safe against both extremes. . . . The election of Cavaignac was a decisive defeat of the monarchists, more decisive than the victory of the property-owners over the revolt, which could be considered to be over by the evening of June 24th.

Cavaignac's dictorship was a dictatorship of political democracy. . . . Did that guarantee a peaceful growth of the Republic, and did it resolve the social antagonism? It did not. The dictatorship of Cavaignac had changed the character of the victory of the bourgeoisie. Without him it would have become the victory of one class over the other and would have entailed suppression and disfranchisement. Through him, and through the democratic principle he stood for, political rights were safeguarded. The civil war was over, but not the social antagonism. With the appearance of Cavaignac a final struggle of the social elements began, which was, however, different from the armed battle.

The Struggle Between Capital and Labor for the Constitution

By the month of July public peace had been re-established in Paris. . . . Even the most infatuated revolutionaries realized that an open battle was out of the question for the near future. . . . The victory of the bourgeoisie had been established at tremendous sacrifice. . . . And yet there was a widespread feeling that, although external order prevailed, this situation had not provided a final solution of the essential and vital problems of the time. Before the end of the month of July the old struggle broke out again, even though in a different form. . . . Wherever, and as long as industrial society exists, the contradiction between the principle of freedom and the reality of dependency in society will continue to exist. . . An armed struggle might possibly secure the rule of capital momentarily; but the opposition of labor to the system must of necessity continue, because it represents an essential attribute of industrial society.

This antagonism is the permanent source of disturbances which threaten transactions and the profitability of capital on which the whole order of industrial society depends. Industrial society thus contains an element of self-contradiction. It will ultimately have to accept the premise that it can only be a transitory social order and that the future growth of human society, inasmuch as it rests on the two independent elements of capital and labor, will lead to a harmonious solution based on the mutual interests of capital and labor. . . .

The defeat of the revolt in June . . . had established and secured the rule of industrial society in France. Had this victory eliminated the antagonism which had led to the conflict? No. The struggle had now been removed from the barricades and shifted to the sphere of socio-political thought. Where did the various elements of the intellectual movement stand at the moment when Cavaignac became dictator?

The reactionary forces were strong, but it should not be forgotten that these forces lost many adherents because they began to pursue monarchical rather than social ends. The property-owning reactionary elements feared that the monarchical reaction would even sacrifice the interests of capital in order to be able to restore monarchy. Thus the reactionary forces began to disintegrate already at this point. The reactionaries who favored legitimacy were willing to disregard the interests of capital for the sake of labor, because they knew that the capitalists were consumed by mortal hatred of the Bourbons, who had openly opposed constitutionalism. The legitimists, therefore, aligned themselves secretly with labor groups, and, since they could not talk of an absolute monarchy any longer, they began to discuss the principle of a monarchy of social reform. The reactionary Roman Catholic party, on the other hand, convinced that a return to former social conditions and therewith to its own power position was dependent upon the abolition of general education, began a struggle against public education as a means of acquisition of intellectual goods, without taking a stand with regard to the Constitution and administration. The reactionaries who favored the Orléans dynasty, i.e. the reaction of constitutionalism against the Republic, represented the personal interests of the last dynasty and the interests of capital, which had prospered under pseudo-constitutionalism. This group was the largest in size but at the same time also the weakest.

These were the three groups representing the reactionary forces. The elements of progress also took a more definite shape, now that the street fighting was over. During this time, while Cavaignac was establishing a democratic government in France for the second time, the adherents of democracy tried to dissociate themselves from the reaction, as well as from the progressive social movement. They had finally recognized the necessity of dealing seriously with the social movement; but at the same time, they had learned to fear that the social revolts led not only to the destruction of the nation, but also to the loss of their grip on this nation. Therefore they condemned the revolts. They investigated and rejected the various socialist systems, but they declared themselves in favor of exploring the social question. More than ever before, they now embraced the principle: "Order within the framework of liberty."

Those who had fought for a social change were completely dispersed through the defeat they had suffered. . . . Since the growth of class-consciousness in the proletariat had been effected by definite schools of thought and doctrines, it was quite natural that after the February Revolution these individual schools spontaneously took over the leadership of the social movement. The working class was still used to thinking and acting only through these organs. As long as these various schools of thought predominated, a true understanding between them and democracy was impossible. Each of these schools of thought considered its own system as the right one, and rigidly refused to cooperate with other endeavors for the promotion of freedom. Under these circumstances the unification of these various schools of thought would have meant the defeat of each individual group and its adherents. And this is, indeed, what happened during the first three months of the Republic. Nobody talked any longer about Saint-Simonism, which only survived by what it had inspired. . . . The many varieties of communism were totally defeated. Communism had disappeared like a fog as soon as the reality of the social question became apparent; nobody dared any longer to confess publicly, as Cabet once did, . . . that "he considered it an honour to be a communist." Cabet had organized the emigration of the Icarus Communists to North America, where they perished. . . . After the imprisonment of Barbès, Blanqui, Hubert and Raspail, the other communist sects were no longer talked about. The concept of the "organization of work" had also been buried. It had promised so much and kept so few of its promises that nobody wanted to hear any more about it. Louis Blanc had lost his popularity almost completely; only the fact that he was being persecuted by the reaction kept his name alive. All the separate schools of thought were dispersed, destroyed or powerless. . . .

Cavaignac had become the Chief Executive by the decree of June 24th. Was he a dictator? Could he possibly establish a dictatorship? As we have stated in our introduction, . . . a dictatorship is only possible if the social order is actually dissolved and all classes and groups within it know that they lack the strength to seize and keep control of the state. As long as a single class still believes that it may retain control, it renders a dictatorship impossible by concentrating the power of the state in the hands of one man in dangerous times, while retaining the will of the state, the legislative power, for itself. The more powerful the ruling class the more vigorous the legislative power, which continues to restrain the executive until it finally succumbs.

Such was, indeed, the situation in France. The very same victory which had placed Cavaignac at the head of the state was also the decisive victory of the property-owning class over the proletariat. The social order had not been dissolved in June, 1848, as it had been in 1796 and 1799; the ruling class was clearly aware of its own intentions; . . . it continued to hold its control of the state, because its position as the ruling class was firmly established; it wanted only to restore the order of industrial society which had been undermined by the antagonism of the proletariat. This and nothing else was the task of Cavaignac. Therefore, a real dictatorship could not be and was not established. On the contrary, the Chamber immediately reasserted its power; it allowed a certain latitude to the executive power in all matters concerning the social order, but it kept it away from questions concerning the constitution. This was all the more possible since the democratic party had accepted the principle of "order within the framework of liberty." . . .

The draft of the Constitution was published on June 20th; it presented two major problems whose solution would decide the immediate future of France. The first problem was a purely political one: the choice between a republic and a monarchy. The majority definitely opposed the reactionary forces. All democratic elements stood closely united with the small owners and the social party. . . . When Thiers finally stated: "We have not created the Republic but we accept it," it became obvious that the monarchists were in the minority. Thereafter, the Republic became an accepted fact. . . . The second problem, however, concerned the social order. . . . If the social order determined the constitution, the struggle over the constitution was apt to reveal the real nature of the social antagonism. And such was indeed the case. The constitutional debate became the battlefield of the opposing social forces. This is the reason why the controversy over the new French constitution, the problem of the political order was relegated to the the first time, during the discussion over the framing of an appropriate constitution the problem of the political order was relegated to the background. . . . Instead, the problem of the right to work became the

center of the struggle for the constitution. This was the first time that
two classes . . . had been engaged in a social struggle within the framework of the constitution, without the use of force, without creating a confusion and uproar; it was the first time that the victorious ruling class
had now also, by careful arguments, definitely rejected the demands of
the propertyless class for the use of state funds to meet its social
needs. . . .

. . . The first three months of the Republic had clearly shown that
altogether new elements were involved in the . . . constitutional struggle. Democracy, having the authority and the obligation of drafting
the Constitution, was suddenly confronted with unpredictable powers.
Being completely unfamiliar . . . with the nature of society, the democrats assumed, in the first draft of the constitution as in their governmental function, that the deep antagonism of the social classes could
be resolved if concessions were made to both of the conflicting elements. It depended only on where and how such concessions were
made. . . .

We have already analyzed the way in which the two republics of
industrial society differ with regard to their constitutions and administrative systems. This theory was now put into practice. It all depended
on designing the constitution and establishing an administration that
would satisfy both social classes. This was to be accomplished by drafting the Constitution in the interest of the property-owning class, by
providing for an administrative system—the use of public revenue—
which would support the interest of the dependent class, and by establishing, as the general basis for the constitution and administration,
the right to vote in conformity with the principles of political democracy. . . . The administration of the state, of course, could not be changed
by a constitution even if it was intended to do so. All that could be
done for the benefit of the propertyless class was to establish a new
principle of administration corresponding to the demands and the interests of the proletariat. This was done by guaranteeing the right to "education, work and assistance" to all citizens (Article 2) and by interpreting the "right to work" (Article 7) as "the right of every human
being to support himself through work." To this was added the provision that "society should assist, by all means put at its disposal, to
secure work for all able-bodied persons who are unable to do so themselves." This was the only positive task which the Constitution assigned
to the state; . . . the right to work was raised to the level of a principle
of state administration. The fact that property rights were guaranteed
at the same time was of no further significance. The owning class ruled

constitutionally, the non-owning class through administration. . . .

This was the first draft of the Constitution, . . . published on June 20th. It can be explained by the lack of awareness in the democratic regime concerning the true significance of the social antagonism. . . . But the publication of this draft was almost immediately followed by the terrible battle between the two classes of society. . . . The so far hazy social antagonism between the classes had by now become a clearly established fact; the democratic element had proved to be powerless. And the right which had been conceded on June 20th to the as yet undefeated class could no longer be maintained after its defeat. . . . This explains why the original draft was rejected after the events of June and replaced by a second one which reflects correctly the social situation following the June events. This second draft of the Constitution was read to the Chamber on August 29th. . . .

A comparison of the second project with the first is highly informative with regard to the conditions of society and their history during this period. But this comparison is meaningful only if one accepts the principle that the social order determines the provisions of the constitution. From this point of view, both drafts are identical as regards the establishment and the organization of the main organs of the personal state, which are independent of the social constellation and part of the general attributes of the state proper. Furthermore, it follows that, after the defeat of the working class, a modification of the first draft, guaranteeing equal rights and equally distributed power to both classes, had to be made. . . . This pertains particularly to the "right to work" and the obligation of society to provide work for everybody. . . . The main changes in the new draft concerned those articles which established the "right to work." . . . It suggested replacing the "right to work" by the following provisions: "The Republic shall protect the citizen as a person, his property and his work and shall provide the necessary education for all; the Republic owes support to the needy citizen either by providing work for him within the limits of its funds, or by granting the necessary means of subsistence to those who are unable to work themselves and whose families are unable to support them." (Article VIII of the Preamble). Instead of Article 7 of the first draft, the new draft proposed Article 13, in which "the Constitution guarantees to its citizens freedom of work and of enterprise. Society favors and encourages the improvement of work through free elementary education, vocational training, equality in the relationship between workers and employers (*patrons*), through savings and credit institutions, voluntary associations and public work of the state, *département* or the *com-*

munes, suitable for providing work for the unemployed; society also obliges itself to offer assistance to abandoned children, the weak and helpless aged whom the family is unable to support."

From a political viewpoint, there is only a negligible difference between the two drafts; . . . from the viewpoint of the social order, however, the two drafts are as sharply and clearly in contrast to each other as are the two classes of society. While in the first draft labor controls the administration of the state, it is . . . given no political power in the second draft, and the functions of state administration are restricted to poor relief.

Thus the arena for the two social antagonists was set. If "the right to work" in the meaning of the first draft had been incorporated into the Constitution, labor would have defeated capital; otherwise industrial society was elevated to the state of an industrial republic. As soon as the draft was published, the "right to work" became, of necessity, the center of the constitutional problem, because it was the center of the social antagonism. . . .

There is no sense in generally granting the "right to work" in industrial society, because industrial society is based on the principle that everybody has the right to any kind of work. The "right to work," therefore, must have a different meaning. It must refer to a condition in which the right to work is nullified in spite of the fact that it is guaranteed as a mere right. Such a condition occurs only if labor lacks the raw material to work with. The "right to work" is, in reality, . . . the right to demand raw material to work with. Whenever the right to work is guaranteed, the exertion of the ability to work is made available by providing raw material for it. This is the only possible meaning that the right to work can have in industrial society. . . . Thus the "right to work" was, indeed, only a different form of the same demand which Louis Blanc, the social movement in general, and, most recently, Proudhon had made. It was a demand made in accordance with the principle of state administration by which the state should use all its funds to provide for the laborer the capital which he lacks; the one important difference being that, along with the concept of the right to work, no specific organization for this purpose had as yet been suggested. . . .

It was quite natural that with regard to the right to work there should immediately begin a general struggle in which the two large parties, representing the two classes of society, opposed each other. . . . The speeches delivered regarding this subject began on September 11th and continued for several days. All the eminent members of the Chamber appeared on the scene. . . . There was no doubt that . . . the conservative view prevailed in the Chamber. Everything depended on the correct formulation of the problem. . . . We meet here with the same maneuvering which the leaders of the proletariat had used successfully before. Instead of stating the true meaning of the "right to work" with complete frankness, the deputies constantly attempted, as Lamartine expressed it poignantly, to identify the right to work with the right not to starve; nothing was said about the thorough reorganization of the whole social organism which was obviously implied in the concept. They left it . . . to the conservatives to discover and to state this. . . . The attacks by the Right upon the right to work had a twofold purpose. First they attempted to clarify the significance of the principle; here Mariel Barthe's speech was definitely the best; he showed, with specifically French clarity, that the right to work not only entailed a reorganization of society but that the proletariat and its leaders had intended that a social reorganization should take place. Then the best speakers of the Chamber, particularly De Tocqueville, Duvergier de Hauranne, and Thiers, attempted to analyze . . . the practical consequences of such a principle. It was Thiers' speech that dealt the death blow to this principle by removing from it the cloak of phrases with relentless logic. . . . On September 15th the second draft was approved by a large majority. . . .

Side by side with the parliamentary struggle ran the discussion in the newspapers, and a whole series of pamphlets was published concerning this problem. . . . Naturally this controversy did not produce anything new; it only confirmed the fact that the true significance of the right to work was not at all the obligation of the owners to support the unemployed, but that it would, in fact, create an altogether new form of society through the omnipotence of the state.

This was the end of the last socialist battle. The property-owning class had been victorious, not only by virtue of the number of votes, but by virtue of the power of its arguments. The Constitution was approved on November 4th. It definitely reflected the social order of the industrial republic.

CONCLUDING REMARKS

. . . With the enactment of the Constitution of November 4th a new period of French history began. . . . When the monarchy was overthrown, industrial society became the ruling power in France. For a moment the propertyless class had succeeded, through the Revolution which had been precipitated by the monarchy, in usurping a large part of the power of the state. The property-owning class suffered severely; above all it felt that the principles of its existence and its domination, property and the family, were threatened. The property-owning class became aware of the necessity of regaining control over the state. At first it attempted to do so indirectly, by eliminating the main leaders of the proletariat from the government at the time of the appointments to the Executive Commission; on May 15th, and during the month of June, it re-established its rule by the use of arms. Finally, by rejecting the first constitutional draft of June 20th and by accepting the second draft on August 29th, it developed the legal framework of the industrial republic which was finally established by the Constitution of November 4th. . . .

The existence of the French Republic had been assured through the incompetence of the preceding monarchy. This fact determined to a great extent the development of French history after November, 1848. The various groups of the monarchist and ultra-montane reaction dissolved and merged with the conservative elements, particularly the large property owners. They recognized the fact that by defending the monarchy they would be opposed not only by the proletariat but also by the great majority of the property-owners, and that this would reduce them to complete impotence. Only the legitimist reaction remained intact, not so much as a political but as a specifically social reactionary force which stood for the interests and the rights of the landowners of the feudal epoch and which favored the monarchy as a means of re-establishing the feudal rights of the landowners. This reactionary force provided a counterweight to any pretender who might try to establish a new monarchy, but it was completely powerless against the policy of the conservatives, with whom it generally agreed. All these individual groups merged and developed into a new kind of reaction, the industrial reaction. The nature of the industrial reaction emanates from the industrial order of society. Industrial reaction desires to suppress any organization, any movement of labor, which threatens to destroy the rule of capital over labor. Industrial reaction persecutes the press, which raises the social question, as well as the leaders of the proletariat and their associations, the clubs; it defends the administration in power, the tax laws, and social differentiation. It is willing to concede important prerogatives to the state at the expense of individual liberty, under the condition that the state will use its power to protect the interests of the ruling class and will remain subordinate to it. The industrial reaction has become dominant for three main reasons. First, through the personal eminence of its leaders, among whom were the outstanding statesmen of France; second, through the fear of the middle- and small-sized property-owners of the consequences of communist social theories; . . . and finally, through the inability of the leaders of the proletariat to make reasonable practical suggestions, or rather, the easily conceivable, utter impossibility of changing the social order, no matter how defective, with one stroke by a theory, even an excellent one. . . .

On the other hand, political democracy was well aware of the serious dangers imposed by the industrial reaction. The exponents of political democracy realized that reactionary trends predominated in the Chamber and among the intelligentsia. They began to fear the subjugation of the proletariat as the first step toward the subjugation of their own power or even of the Republic itself. Therefore, they had to look for strong support in order to counterbalance the growing reactionary forces; only the proletariat could supply such support. The best democratic newspapers, vaguely perceiving the true conditions, had for quite a while concerned themselves seriously with the social question in general. They had shown enough vision to accept the necessity of improving the conditions of the lower classes, particularly of labor. On the other hand, they had fought against all specific socialistic systems with sharp and often merciless criticism. Thus they had kept the middle ground between the reasonable segments of the owning class and the proletariat; they were considered to represent social progress by way of reason and circumspection. . . . However, political democracy was as yet remote from social democracy; specific inducements were necessary to bring about a fusion.

Such inducements were actually provided during the month of July. A commission had been appointed to report on the events of June. Most members of this commission were reactionaries; they published . . . a report which showed a considerably greater zeal for the persecution of Louis Blanc, Caussidière, Ledru-Rollin and Proudhon than for the truth. This report was so obviously the result of party machinations that even the democrats, who had been spared criticism, began to realize the seriousness of the situation. . . . When, later, the provision for the right to work was completely defeated, when Louis Blanc and Caussidière (August 25th) had to escape from France, and when the question of the presidency came up, the first motions toward an alliance began, casual and uncertain, but nevertheless with an unmistakable tendency. . . .

The day approached when the Republic had to choose its president. . . . Until then, the adherents of political democracy had always been able to tip the scale in their favor; recently they had even controlled the state. They assumed that they would continue to do so, but were mistaken because they had judged France on the basis of the conditions in Paris. . . . In the great cities, the number of industrial workers was about equal to the number of property-owners, but in the rural areas this was not at all the case. According to a statement by Denjay, the number of small holdings in France amounted to no less than 11 million, due to the frequent divisions of landed estates. This meant just as many votes for the property-owning class. At the same time, . . . the antagonism between the classes was not properly understood in the country; even in the small communities close to Paris, most small owners identified all social movements with pure communism, with an immediate egalitarian distribution of property. In addition, the parcelling out of land had led to indebtedness, so that the slightest economic disturbance caused an emergency situation. . . . If agriculture wished to avoid a dangerous crisis adversely affecting the whole nation, order had to be preserved under all circumstances and at any price. . . . While in Paris the parties and their leaders fought each other vigorously and squabbled about theories, the great majority of the land owning class welcomed any measure by which the old order of the vanished monarchy could be combined with the new freedom of the now accepted Republic. . . .

As the election approached, three main lines of policy prevailed.

Some segments of the social party did not want to vote at all, so as to demonstrate that they did not accept a constitution which legalized the rule of capital over labor. But the more reasonable view that it would be necessary to vote gained the upper hand. But, as Proudhon (*Confessions*, Ch. X.) tell us, the desire prevailed "that the candidate should promise, by his honour, to use his authority if elected for the immediate revision of the Constitution, to acknowledge the right to work and to abolish the presidency." Proudhon adds, for good reasons, that "these precautions had the threefold deficiency of being unconstitutional, impracticable and extremely childish." The candidate of this party was Ledru-Rollin. . . .

The exponents of doctrinaire democracy, on the other hand, and all those who dreaded monarchy as well as communism, were in favor of Cavaignac, the man of "order within liberty." They stuck to the notion that universal suffrage was enough to secure freedom and that the improvement of the lot of the lower classes should be left to the organs of state administration. This party was quite sure of its victory. . . . And, indeed, its victory in Paris was assured; here the party was stronger than the party of social reaction and the party of the social movement with its rigid principle. The democratic party assumed that this would be true for the rest of France as well. But the great number of land-owners in the rural districts thought differently; they considered all Paris controlled by party propaganda; they also considered Cavaignac to be a party representative, and with good reason; they did not want any party as such to rule; they wanted that which had secured their welfare under the monarchy without the danger of stagnation which the absolutism of monarchy entailed. In brief, they wanted the restoration of an independent authority of the state, which would stand above the parties. . . . The difficulty was to find the person independent of all parties, who by his name and personality would ensure that France would never fall under party rule. Such a man, who was to be king without the title, without the power and the glory of a king, was Louis Napoleon. . . . He was decidedly the man predestined to fulfill the expectations of that class. The votes were cast, and Louis Napoleon got more than six million votes as against one million for Cavaignac. It will have become clear by now how little the countryside was understood by either the exponents of political democracy, who could hardly recover from their surprise, or by the social party, which saw in this election the downfall of freedom. Louis Napoleon, in every respect a poor imitator of Napoleon, for once was right in speaking of himself, when he said that: "France has elected me because I do not belong to any party." And Proudhon is right in adding: "Yes, France has elected Louis Buonaparte as President of the Republic, because she is tired of party strife, because all parties are dead" (*Confessions,* Ch. XVI). . . . The election signified the victory of the state over the parties. . . .

With the election of a president who stood outside the parties, the inner organization of the state was apparently accomplished. The Republic had a Constitution, a complete and well-functioning state organism, and a republican head who, although he had somewhat too much power for a president, certainly did not have enough power to be a king. What was it that shook this apparently harmonious situation to its very roots and that sooner or later again had to lead to another violent convulsion? . . .

The core of the Constitution of November 4th, which appeared to be so well balanced and so safe against any attack, contains a great contradiction the consequence of which had not been fully understood by the legislators because they were not familiar with the nature of society. This contradiction consists in the legality of universal suffrage as compared to the prevailing structure of French society. . . . Universal suffrage is essentially a social right, . . . the right by which alone the lower, propertyless class gains an equal share in the power of the state with the property-owning class. . . . While the French Constitution introduced universal suffrage, the equality of status of the two classes in industrial society, of labor and of capital, had already been abolished. Therefore, the Constitution of the state was in contradiction to the order of society. The lower class of society had political rights to which its social status did not correspond. This contradiction resulted in two consequences which, indeed, clearly determine the subsequent history of France. The so far suppressed class of labor, . . . which has no chance of acquiring capital under the existing economic order of industrial society, will use the political right of universal suffrage in order to gain control over the state, which would make it possible for labor to acquire capital. The ruling class of property-owners, however, in order to prevent this and to make the Constitution a reflection of the social order, will attempt to abolish universal suffrage by restricting the right to vote, in some form or another to property owners. . . . The development of this antagonism was determined by the position which the new power of the state occupied in the person of the first president.

At the very beginning of his presidency, Louis Napoleon seems to have believed that the overwhelming majority of his supporters expected him to link the power of the state permanently to his person. This idea, which was constantly in his mind, affected his attitude toward the various elements of society. He recognized clearly that his presidency would be unassailable and his accountability illusive if he would carefully support democracy and the trend toward social democracy, but that he would thus make the extension of his power beyond the constitutional period impossible. If he wanted to become emperor, he had to throw himself into the arms of the industrial reaction to obtain permanent power. This was so not only because the reactionary forces were in the majority, but because their interest would coincide with a restoration of monarchy under whatever name. Louis Napoleon did not waver for a moment in this choice. He immediately took the side of the property-owning class, and so did the state. With his coming to power, socialism was repudiated and persecuted, and Louis Napoleon was supported in every possible way by the strength of the property owners.

As soon as the party of political democracy recognized this, the trend which until then was only vaguely discernable gained momentum Seriously threatened in their principles, the principles of universal suffrage as well as republicanism, the democrats recognized the necessity of an alliance with those who favored a social reorganization. Since that time, the concept of "fusion" has become the catchword of both parties. Agreement was reached quickly, since the differences of opinion referred mostly to the relation of ends and means and not to their goals proper. Thus the name which had frequently been heard before was introduced again. It was the term "democratic and social republic" or "social democracy," which gained great importance in subsequent events. Social democracy is not a theory, nor a creed; it is a historical fact, for it represents an important stage of development in the life of society, the point where political democracy and the proponents of a new social order concurred and recognized each other. This historical fact, brought about by the course of events, constitutes essentially the first manifestation of the law, vaguely felt rather than clearly perceived, according to which neither political rights nor social changes are seen as isolated phenomena, but according to which the social order determines and conditions the constitution of the state. Therefore, . . . this fact also indicates the first act of subordination of all political democracies to the forces of the new social order. This fact implies the endorsement of the social movement by the principles of abstract democracy, and finally the simplification, and hence the aggravation, of the antagonism in any—not only the French—industrial society. As a consequence of all these implications, the whole development of the social and political movement enters a new phase with the establishment of social democracy. . . . It makes little difference in which manner the realization of social democracy is conceived, but it is certain that from now on political democracy and pure socialism have ceased to exist. From here on, the focal point of political life and political activity has shifted from constitutional problems to administrative problems.

This is the great result of the events of 1849. . . . The period of the attempts to establish harmony between the vital elements of a nation merely by constitutional means or merely by social doctrines has passed. From now on, every idea concerning the state will also take society into consideration and vice versa. The struggle which now begins will be no longer a simple struggle between capital and labor, but the struggle between social democracy and the industrial reaction. . . .

NOTES ON THE TRANSLATION

Stein's original "History of the Social Movement in France 1789-1850" consists of three volumes of about 500 pages each. For the translation, a smaller, one volume edition, divided into three corresponding parts, seemed desirable and appropriate. Some chapters have been omitted in their entirety and in the translated parts Stein's presentation has been condensed. This type of surgery has, I hope, contributed to greater clarity and put his main ideas into focus. The controlling purpose of the editorial process was to preserve the sequence and consistency of Stein's historical analysis.

The full outline, reprinted in the Appendix, will give the reader an impression of the scope of the original three volumes. The major sections omitted in the translation are: One subsection each of "The Rule of the Third Estate" (Vol. I pp. 220-234) and of "The Democratic-Communistic Period" (Vol. I pp. 340-350); the chapters "Saint-Simon and the Saint-Simonists," "Fourier and the Fourierists," "Babouvism" and "Religious Communism" (Vol. II pp. 133-343, 382-465); the Appendices to Vol. II (pp. 497-564); the larger part of "The Nature of the Monarchy," several subsections of "The Theory of the Republic," and the analysis of Proudhon's system (Vol. III pp. 1-36, 103-108, 123-134, 147-168, 343-381). These materials amount to about one third of the original total.

Some of Stein's basic concepts have no standard equivalent term in English. They had to be translated more or less literally with the original German term given in parentheses. The following explanation may be helpful in providing the reader with the exact meaning of Stein's concepts which are closely tied to his social philosophy.

Stein envisages history as a process toward freedom. Self-realization of the individual, "a full and harmonious personal development" is the goal or the *Bestimmung* of the individual; to preserve the idealistic meaning, *Bestimmung* has been translated by "aspiration," "fulfillment" and occasionally by "destiny."

While "individual" (*Individuum*) refers to the single human being without reference to differentiation, "personality" (*Persönlichkeit*) refers to the individual with his personal capabilities and accomplishments. Contemporary connotatons of personality ought not to blur this meaning. Personality is occasionally also applied to the state as a living entity.

The "state" is conceived of as the personification of the community of men. The supreme position of the state in Stein's analysis does not reflect a glorification of the state as against the interests of the individual, but rather stresses the fact that the individual by himself is altogether powerless to reach his goal prescribed by the process of historical development. Stein interprets this "unity of men" as a living entity, for which he frequently uses the term "person" or "personality." However, this does not imply the inevitable subjugation of the individual interests to an external authority, nor does it have any of the political implications of later representatives of the organic theory of the state. The state, as the representative of the human community, has the function of assisting the individual. Stein considers political institutions not only capable of initiating social reforms, but indispensable for breaking the domination of society over the state, i.e. the rule of the dominant social class over the dependent class. The state, therefore, is the monitor of freedom.

Freiheit and *Unfreiheit*, freedom and the lack of freedom, both occupy a significant position in Stein's analysis, connoting predominantly personal independence or social dependence. Since there is no corresponding term in English for *Unfreiheit*, I have translated it by "social dependence" and have only occasionally used the term "freedom" or "liberty" as a counterpart to "personal independence."

The process toward social independence manifests itself in the 19th century as *die soziale Bewegung*. Here I have retained the literal translation "the social movement," which in the English language has generally a more diversified meaning. In German it is exclusively applied to the labor movement in industrial society. "Social movement" conveys better than any substitute term the meaning of the major concept of Stein's book. It refers to the antagonism and the struggle between the social classes, to the growing self-awareness of the proletariat and its attempts to assert its position and its rights in society and in the state. "Social movement" is a reflection of what Stein usually refers to as *"die soziale Frage,"* i.e. the Social Question. Stein himself defines it as the problem of "how labor without owning capital can gain economic independence through the acquisition of capital" (*Verwaltungsrecht* 1870. p. 439). This definition corresponds to Stein's own suggestion as to the solution of the dependence and social deprivation to which the laboring class was subjected during the period of early industrialism. The reforms suggested by Stein soon became outdated due to the growing predominance of big business. Generally speaking, "the social question" refers to the exploitation of labor and the various socio-political, ideological and practical attempts promoting the welfare of the working class in industrial society. Stein's original contribution consists in conceiving the social question and the social movement as the result of an inherent contradiction in the acquisitive society. Stein uses *Bewegung* also in a more general context, such as *Bewegung der Freiheit* or *Bewegungsgesetz*, in which cases *Bewegung* has been rendered by "dynamics" or "progress."

The term "contradiction" (*Widerspruch*) plays a central role in Stein's philosophy of history. It is used in the Hegelian-Marxian sense and refers to a historical situation encompassing an antagonism which necessarily leads to conflict and change. Although the literal English equivalent of *Widerspruch*, "contradiction," indicates a relation between propositions rather than social facts, it has been retained in this translation in accordance with the terminology of Marxian literature.

Stein's concept of *"Gesellschaftliches Recht"* makes it necessary to introduce the term "social right." This concept has a central position in Stein's history of philosophy, as well as in his theory of administration. *Gesellschaftliche Rechte* or sometimes also *Gesellschaftsrecht* refers to the fact that the dominating class aims at and succeeds in controlling the state and public administration by legalizing social privileges; it thus strengthens and perpetuates the dominant position of the ruling class in any social order. Stein considers law and the codification of law to be conditioned by the order of society. (See also *Verwaltungsrecht.* 1870. p. 396ff.) Social privileges, to the extent that they become legally guaranteed, as for instance the institution of entails, restrictions of civil liberties by specific voting requirements, restrictions of economic opportunites by rules and regulations of the guilds, are *Gesellschaftliche Rechte* or "social rights." They are the first step toward an estate society and towards the establishment of estate rights. But even the relatively open acquisitive society is not free from this kind of privileges which may be enforced by social taboos if the state resists their legalization. The most striking illustration of social rights, partly in contradiction to the law (federal), partly bolstered by law (state), is the political and economic disfranchisements of the Negro population in the United States; although here the antagonism between the dominant and the subjugated social group is based on racial rather than class differences, it offers a good example for Stein's concept of social right.

Stein defines *Bildung* as "the state of intellectual development of the individual, the sum total of mental capacities" (*Verwaltungsrecht.* 1870, p. 107). The term *Bildung* in German has, however, strong connotations of a superior social status. Stein uses the term in this specific sense. He considers *Bildung* as the intellectual equivalent of capital ownership. He frequently speaks of the "possession of intellectual goods" (*Besitz geistiger Güter*) and attributes an important role to the acquisition of *Bildung* in the movement toward social independence or liberty. For lack of any other alternative, *Bildung* had to be translated by the somewhat colorless term "education," sometimes by "formal education and culture." The more specific meaning of education in Stein's analysis will become clear within the context of his arguments.

Recht auf Arbeit ("right to work") has a completely different meaning than the "right to work" in the history of the American labor union movement where it refers to the freedom of the individual worker to accept a job regardless of union regulations. In the 19th century social history of Europe, the term has been used in the sense of having a claim to employment as a natural right of the worker toward society, since employment is the result of social conditions he is unable to control. This "right to work" was one of the central demands of the laboring class in the socialist movement and reflects its basic antagonism against competitive society.

At the end of his book, Stein emphasized the historical importance of collaboration between those who stand for political democracy (the democratic party) and those who consider social reform the most important issue in the political struggle (the social party). Although the latter originated in the early impulses toward socialism and had strong socialistic connotations, I have retained the literal translation of *Soziale Partei* since a political party with a specific program to develop socialism within the framework of parliamentarism had not yet evolved at that time.

K.M.

BIBLIOGRAPHIES

Books and Articles by L.v. Stein

The publisher Gustav Fischer, Jena, Germany, has kindly given permission to reprint *Books and Articles by Lorenz v. Stein* as originally compiled and published by Ernst Grünfeld [13 pp. 20-28.] Three early book reviews, mentioned first by Nitzschke [38] have been added and marked with an asterik.

1839 *Book review, "Christiansen, Die Wissenschaft der römischen Rechtsgeschichte im Grundriss." *Hallische Jahrbücher*, Jahrg. 1839, p. 201 ff.

1841 *Book review, "Carl von Savigny, System des heutigen römischen Rechts." *Dtsch. Jahrb.* 1841, p. 92ff.
       Die Geschichte des dänischen Zivilprozesses und das heutige Verfahren. Als Beitrag zu einer vergleichenden Rechtswissenschaft. Kiel.

1842 *Book review, "Anselm von Feuerbach, Lehrbuch des gemeinen in Deutschland gültigen peinlichen Rechts." *Dtsch. Jahrb.*, 1842, p. 70ff.
       Der Sozialismus und Kommunismus des heutigen Frankreichs. Ein Beitrag zur Zeitgeschichte. Leipzig O. Wiegand (XII und 475 pp.)

1843 *Die Munizipalverfassung Frankreichs.* Leipzig, O. Wiegand. (86 pp.).

1844 "Blicke auf den Sozialismus und Kommunismus in Deutschland und ihre Zukunft" *Deutsche Vierteljahrsschrift.* Stuttgart. Nr. 26, pp. 1-61.

1845 "Das corpus juris und die historische Schule in ihrem Verhältnis zur deutschen Rechtsentwicklung" *Deutsche Vierteljahrsschrift.* Nr. 30, pp. 145-188.
       "Das corpus juris und die Idee des gemeinen deutschen Rechts." *Ibidem.* Nr. 32, pp. 293-344.

1846 *"Geschichte des französischen Strafrechts und Prozesses"* (mit Warnkönig). Basel.
       "Der Begriff der Arbeit und die Prinzipien des Arbeitslohnes in ihrem Verhältnis zum Sozialismums und Kommunismus." *Zeitschr. f.d. ges.* Staatsw. Tübingen. Vol. III, pp. 233-290.
       "Staats- und Erbrecht des Herzogtums Schleswig." Kiel u. Hamburg.
       "Das Recht und die Bedeutung der Staatserbfolge in Schleswig-Holstein" (anonymous). *Deutsche Vierteljahrsschrift.* Nr. 36 (86 pp.) und Nr. 38 (52 pp.) 1847.

1847 "Einleitung in das ständische Recht der Herzogtümer Schleswig-Holstein." Kiel.
       "Die Grossmächte un die Schleswig-Holsteinsche Frage." (anonymous). *Deutsche Vierteljahrsschrift.* Nr. 40 (29 pp.).

1848 *"Der Sozialismus und Kommunismus des heutigen Frankreichs."* Second revised and enlarged edition. 2 vols. Leipzig.
       "Die sozialistischen und kommunistichen Bewegungen seit der 3. franz. Revolution." Appendix to *Soz. u. Komm. d. heut. Frankr.* Leipzig und Wien (40 and 251 pp.).
       "Der Begriff des Freihandels und die praktische Bedeutung desselben."

Zeitschrift f.d. ges. Staatsw. Tübingen. Vol. V². pp. 275-360.
"Denkschrift ueber die Zollverhältnisse der Herzogtümer Schleswig und Holstein mit besonderer Berücksichtigung eines Anschlusses derselben an den Zollverein." *Zeitschrift für deutsche Statistik 1848,* 2-4. Berlin.
"*La question du Schleswig-Holstein.*" Paris. Kliencksieck.
"Die sozialen Bewegungen der Gegenwart." *Gegenwart.* Leipzig Vol. I. pp. 79-93 (anonymous).
"Der Sozialismus und Kommunismus in Frankreich." *Gegenwart,* Vol. I pp. 299-326.
1849 "Ideen zur Geschichte der Arbeit." *Deutsche Vierteljahrsschrift.* Stuttgart Nr. 46. 27 pp.
"Schleswig-Holstein bis zur Erhebung i. J. 1848." *Gegenwart.* Vol. II. Leipzig. pp. 404-429 (anonymous).
"Die soziale Bewegung und der Sozialismus in England." *Gegenwart.* pp. 462-487 (anonymous).
"Die Erhebung Schleswig-Holsteins im Frühjahr 1848." *Gegenwart.* Vol. III. pp. 41-95 (anonymous).
1850 *Die Geschichte der sozialen Bewegung in Frankreich von 1789 bis auf unsere Tage.* 3 Vols. Leipzig (O. Wiegand).
"Die Bedeutung der Wahl oder Nichtwahl zum Reichstag in Erfurt." *Deutsche Vierteljahrsschrift.* Nr. 49 (23 pp.) signed L.S.
"Deutschland und die skandinavische Union." In besonderer Beziehung auf die Schleswig-Holstein'sche Frage. *Ibidem.* Nr. 50 (40 pp.).
"Ein Blick auf Russland (anonymous). *Ibidem.* Nr. 52
"Schleswig-Holstein seit seiner Erhebung im Jahre 1848". *Gegenwart.* Vol. V. pp. 294-371 (anonymous).
"*Beiträge und Notizen über Schleswig-Holstein*" in *Brockhaus' Deutscher Allgemeiner Zeitung.* Leipzig. Nr. 22/23, 45/46, 92/93, 105, 177.
1851 "*Die Frau, ihre Bildung und Lebensaufgabe.*" (anonymous). Dresden.
"Die Errichtung einer deutschen Bank." *Deutsche Vierteljahrsschirft.*
"Schleswig-Holstein seit Mitte 1849". *Gegenwart.* Vol. VI. pp. 448-504.
1852 *Rechtliches Gutachten ueber die fortdauernde Gültigkeit der Schleswigholsteinschen Staatspapiere und des Patentes vom 7. Juni, die Aufhebung dieser Gültigkeit betreffend*" nebst Einleitung und species facti von L. H. Simon, Grimma. Verlags-Comptoir.
System der Staatswissenschaft. Vol. I, *System der Statistik, der Populationistik und der Volkswirtschaftslehre.* Stuttgart und Tübingen. 564 pp.
"Zur preussischen Verfassungsfrage." *Deutsche Vierteljahrsschrift.* Nr. 57, signed S. (37 pp.). [Re-edited Berlin 1940].
"Das Wesen des arbeitslosen Einkommens und sein besonderes Verhältnis zu Amt und Adel." *Ibidem.* Nr. 60, signed L.S. (52 pp.).
"Der Sozialismus in Deutschland." *Gegenwart.* Vol. VII, pp. 517-563.
1853 "Die staatswissenschaftliche Theorie der Griechen vor Aristoteles und Plato und ihr Verhältnis zu dem Leben der Gesellschaft." *Zeitschrift f.d.ges. Staatsw.*
"Das Gemeindewesen der neuern Zeit." *Deutsche Vierteljahrsschrift.*

Nr. 61 (62 pp.) Signed L.S.
"Die Goldwährung als Grundlage deutscher Münzeinheit." *Ibidem.*
Nr. 63 (57 pp.), (anonymous).
"Beiträge und Notizen über Schleswig-Holstein" in *Brockhaus'*
Deutscher Allgemeiner Zeitung. Leipzig. Nr. 183, 189, 200, 209, 224,
231, 237, 240, 243, 257, 270, 292, 304.

1854 "Ueber die Natur der Kassenscheine und die Grundsätze, welche
für dieselben gelten müssen." *Deutsche Vierteljahrsschrift.* Nr. 65
(48 pp.) Signed L.S.
"Die Auswanderung nach Nord-Amerika" (Signed "von der Ostsee."
Ibidem. Nr. 68 (17 pp.).
"Die deutsche Industrieausstellung," "von einem Norddeutschen."
Ibidem. Nr. 68 (46 pp.).
"Demokratie und Aristokratie." *Gegenwart.* Vol. IX, pp. 306-344.

1855 2nd Edition of *Gesch. d. sozial. Beweggn etc.*

1856 *System der Staatswissenschaft,* Vol. II, *Die Gesellschaftslehre.* 1. Ab-
teilung: Der Begriff der Gesellschaft und die Lehre von den Gesell-
schaftsklassen. Stuttgart und Augsburg.
"*Die Grundlagen und Aufgaben des künftigen Friedens.*" Mit vier
offiziellen Beilagen. Wien.
"*Die neue Gestaltung des Geld- und Kreditwesens in Oesterreich.*"
Wien.
"*Oesterreich und der Friede.*" Wien.
"Mitteilungen aus Serbien" *Deutsche Vierteljahrsschrift.* Nr. 74 (13
pp) (anonymous) and Nr. 80. (41 pp)

1857 "Der Kredit und die Organisation desselben." *Deutsche Vierteljahrsschrift.* Nr. 77, pp. 1-87.

1858 *Lehrbuch der Volkswirtschaft.* Wien.

1860 *Lehrbuch der Finanzwissenschaft.* Leipzig.
"Zur Finanzlage Oesterreichs." *Deutsche Vierteljahrsschrift.* Nr. 90
(anonymous.)

1861 "Volkswirtschaftliche Studien über stehende Heere." *Oesterr. milit.
Zeitschrift.*) Wien.
"Zur Physiologie der Städtebildung." *Deutsche Vierteljahrsschrift.*
Nr. 96 signed L.S. (27 pp.).
"Ueber die Aufgabe der vergleichenden Rechtswissenschaft mit bes.
Beziehung auf das Wasserrecht." *Oesterr. Vierteljahrsschrift f. Rechts-
und Staatswissenschaften.* Wien. Vol. VII, pp. 233-255.

1862 "Studien über Vereinswesen und Vereinsrecht." *Ibidem.* Vol. IX,
pp. 141-194.

1865 *Die Verwaltungslehre,* Part 1: Die Lehre von der vollziehenden Gewalt,
ihr Recht und ihr Organismus. Stuttgart.
"Die verschiedenen Fragen in Oesterreich." *Deutsche Vierteljahrs-
schrift.* Nr. 110 (anonymous) (24 pp.).
"Studien aus der Verwaltungslehre." Das Vormundschaftswesen.
Oesterr. Vierteljahrsschr. f. Rechts- und Staatswissenschaften. Wien.
Bd. XVI. pp. 224-294.

1866 *Die Verwaltungslehre,* Part 2: Die Lehre von der inneren Verwaltung.

1. Das Bevölkerungswesen und sein Verwaltungsrecht. Stuttgart. "Die Wasserrechtslehre." *Oesterr. Vierteljahrsschr. f. Rechts- und Staatswissenschaften.* Wien. Vol. XVIII, pp. 227-267.

1867 *Die Verwaltungslehre,* Part 3: Die innere Verwaltung. Das öffentliche Gesundheitswesen. Stuttgart.
Die Verwaltungslehre, Part 4: Die innere Verwaltung. Das Polizeirecht. Anhang: Das Pflegschaftswesen und sein Recht. Stuttgart.

1868 *Die Verwaltungslehre,* Part 5: Die innere Verwaltung: Das Bildungswesen. Stuttgart.
Die Verwaltungslehre, Part 6: Die innere Verwaltung: Das Bildungswesen. Stuttgart.
Die Verwaltungslehre, Part 7: Die innere Verwaltung: Die wirtschaftliche Verwaltung. Stuttgart.
"Die organische Auffassung des Lebens der Güterwelt." *Zeitschrift f. d.ges. Staatsw.,* IX. 115ff.
"Ueber die wirtschaftliche Stellung des weiblichen Geschlechts. *Leonhards Kompass,* Wien, I. Jahrg.
"Aus dem inneren Leben Oesterreichs." *Deutsche Vierteljahrsschrift.* Nr. 121 (40 pp.) (anonymous).

1869 *Die Verwaltungslehre,* Part I. (2. revised edition).
"Einige Bemerkungen ueber die Art und Weise der Kontrolle bei Erwerbsgesellschaften." *Leonhards "Kompass,"* 2. Jahrgang. Wien.

1870 *Handbuch der Verwaltungslehre und des Verwaltungsrechtes* mit Vergleichung der Literatur und Gesetzgebung von Frankreich, England und Deutschland. Als Grundlage für Vorlesungen. Stuttgart.

1871 *Lehrbuch der Finanzwissenschaft.* 2nd edition, revised and enlarged. Leipzig.

1872 *Lehre vom Heerwesen.* Als Teil der Staatswissenschaften. Stuttgart.
Zur Eisenbahnrechtsbildung. Ges. Aufsaetze aus dem Zentralblatt für Eisenbahnen und Dampfschiffahrt der oesterr. -ungar. Monarchie. Wien. Ohne Jahresangabe. Lehmann u. Wentzel.

1873 *Alpenrosen.* Gedichte. Stuttgart. (Cotta, IV u. 100 pp.).

1875 *Die Frau auf dem Gebiete der National-Ökonomie.* Nach einem Vortrage in der Lesehalle der deutsch. Studenten in Wien. Stuttgart.
Lehrbuch der Finanzwissenschaft. 3rd revised and enlarged edition. Leipzig.

1876 *D:e Frau auf dem Gebiete der National-Ökonomie.* 2nd edition.
Lehrfre:heit, Wissenschaft und Kollegiengeld. Wien.
Gegenwart und Zukunft der Rechts- und Staatswissenschaft Deutschlands. Stuttgart.
Handbuch der Verwaltungslehre und des Verwaltungsrechts. 2nd edition. Stuttgart.

1877 "Der Landedelmann." Eine gesellschaftliche Studie. *Münchner Allg. Zeitung.* Beilage 182.

1878 *Lehrbuch der Finanzwissenschaft.* 4th newly revised edition. 2 Vols. Leipzig.
"Triennium und Quadriennium." *Münchner Allg. Zeitung,* Beilage 179/180.

Die Volkswirtschaftslehre. 2nd complete new edition. Wilh. Braumueller (XV und 578pp.).

1879 "Die Entwicklung der Staatswissenschaft bei den Griechen" *Sitzungsberichte der Kaiserl. Akademie der Wissenschaften. Wien.* phil. hist. Klasse. Vol. XCIII.

"Die türkische Frage vom staatswissenschaftlichen Standpunkt." *Jahrbuch für Gesetzgebung und Verwaltung* von M. Holtzendorff und L. Brentano, Vol. III[4].

"Wesen und Aufgabe der Staatswissenschaft." *Almanach der Kaiserl. Akademie der Wissenschaften. Wien.*

1880 *Der Wucher und sein Recht.* Wien.
Die staatswissenschaftliche und die landwirtschaftliche Bildung. Breslau.
Die Frau auf dem sozialen Gebiete. Stuttgart.
"Der amerikanische Sozialismus und Kommunismus," *Nord und Süd.* Breslau. Vol. XV. pp. 87-101, 191-217.
"Die Frau auf dem Gebiete der sozialen Frage." *Wiener Abendpost* vom 25 Febr. ff.

1881 *Die drei Fragen des Grundbesitzes. Die irische, die kontinentale und die transatlantische Frage.* Stuttgart.
"Die Währungsfrage." *Unsere Zeit.* Leipzig. F. A. Brockhaus, Vol. II, 7 Heft.
"Hannibal vom kontinentalen Standpunkte." *Münchener Allgem. Zeitung.* Nr. 59.

1882 "*Bauerngut und Hufenrecht.*" Gutachten, erstattet an die k.k. Ministerien des Ackerbaues und der Justiz. Stuttgart.
Die Verwaltungslehre, Part 3: Die innere Verwaltung. Completely revised edition.
"Einige Bemerkungen über das internationale Verwaltungsrecht." *Schmollers Jahrbücher für Gesetzgebung und Verwaltung,* VI. Jahrgang.

1883 *Die Landwirtschaft in der Verwaltung und das Prinzip der Rechtsbildung des Grundbesitzes.* 3 lectures. Wien.
"Musik und Staatswissenschaft" in *Nord und Süd.* Breslau. April und Mai.
"Gewerbegesetzgebung." *Münchener Allgem. Zeitung.* Nr. 15.

1884 *Die Verwaltungslehre.* Part 6. 2nd edition. 3 Vols. 1. Das Bildungswesen der alten Welt. 2. Das Bildungswesen im Mittelalter. 3. Die Zeit bis zum 19. Jahrhundert. Stuttgart.
"Zur Geschichte der deutschen Finanzwissenschaft im 17. Jahrhundert." *Schanz' Finanz-Archiv.* I. Jahrgang.
"Zur Frage der ostasiatischen Konsularjurisdiktion." *Ibidem* Nr. 1.
"Zur Geschichte des heutigen Finanzwesens von Japan." *Oesterr. Monatsschrift für den Orient.* Nr. 8ff. Wien.
"Europa und Asien." *Münchener Allgem. Zeitung.* Nr. 236, 237, 238.

1885 "Die Organisation der Land- und Seemacht Chinas." *Unsere Zeit.* Leipzig. Brockhaus. Vol. I, 7 Heft.
"Ueber die Settlements in Ostasien und ihre Rechtsverhaeltnisse." *Oesterr. Zeitschrift f.d. Orient.* Nr. 10.

Das Wesen der Schönheit." *Für edle Frauen.* Berlin. 7. und 8. Heft.
"Mietzinsmarken." *Mitteilungen des Vereins gegen Verarmung und Bettelei.* Wien.
"Zur Börsensteuerfrage." *Münchener Allgem. Zeitung.* Nr. 145/146.
Lehrbuch der Finanzwissenschaft. 5th edition. Vol. 1 und II, Leipzig.
"Der neue Balkan." *Münchener Allgem. Zeitung.* Nr. 327.

1886   Der neue Balkan. Continued. *Ibidem.* Nr. 23.
Lehrbuch der Finanzwissenschaft. 5th edition. Vol. II. 2, 3, Leipzig.
Die Frau auf dem Gebiete der National-Ökonomie. 6th edition.
"Zur neuesten Geschichte der Völkerrechtslehre." *Münchener Allgem. Zeitung.* Nr. 115/116.
"Nachklänge zum Wiener Orientalisten-Kongress." *Ibidem* Nr. 305.

1887   *Lehrbuch der National-Ökonomie. Revised edition.* Wien.
"Studien zur Reichs- und Rechtsgeschichte Japans." *Oesterr. Monatsschrift f.d. Orient.* Nr. 1.
"Zur Frage des deutschen Buchhandels." *Münchener Allgem. Zeitung.* Nr. 324.

1888   *Handbuch der Verwaltungslehre und des Verwaltungsrechtes.* 3rd complete newly revised edition, 3 parts. Stuttgart.
"Ueber Staatsschulden." *Mitteilungen der Gesellsch. österr. Volkswirte.* I. Jahrgang.

1890   "Polizei" und "Verwaltung und Selbstverwaltung." *Stengels Woerterbuch d. deutschen Verwaltungsrechtes.*
Die Frau, ihre Bildung und Lebensaufgabe. 3rd edition.
"Grosse Stadt und Grossstadt." *Nord und Süd.* Breslau (April).

Books and Articles on Lorenz von Stein or with extensive reference to Stein, including Dissertations, Encyclopedia Articles and Obituaries

1. Adler, Georg. "Die Anfänge der Marxschen Sozialtheorie und ihre Beeinflussung durch Hegel, Feuerbach, Stein und Proudhon." *Festgabe für Adolf Wagner.* Leipzig, 1905, pp. 1-20.
2. Angermann, Erich. "Zwei Typen des Ausgleichs gesellschaftlicher Interessen durch die Staatsgewalt." *Staat und Gesellschaft im deutschen Vormaerz 1815-1848.* Edited by Werner Conze. Stuttgart, 1962, pp. 173-205.
3. Baasch, Ernst. "Lorenz von Stein und die Frage der deutschen wirtschaftlichen Einigung." *Schmollers Jahrbuch für Gesetzbgeung, Verwaltung und Volkswirtschaft.* 45. Jg., 1921, pp. 1031-1050.
4. Beckerath, Erwin von, und Norbert Kloten. "Lorenz von Stein." *Handwörterbuch der Sozialwissenschaften.* Vol. X. Stuttgart, 1959, pp. 89-91.
5. Blaschke, Ernst. "Lorenz von Stein." *Statistische Monatsschrift.* 16. Jg. Wien, 1890, p. 429.

6. Burmeister, Martin. *Die Unterscheidung des Gemeinschaft- und Gesellschaftbegriffes bei L.v.Stein und F. Toennies.* Dissertation. Berlin, 1937.
7. Cloeren, Hans. *Vom organischen zum organisatorischen Sozialismus.* Dissertation. Muenchen, 1924.
7a. Donath, Walter. *Otto Willmann in seinem Verhältnis zu Lorenz von Stein.* Versuch einer Würdigung und Kritik. Dissertation. Langensalza 1910.
8. Földes, Bela. "Bemerkungen zu dem Problem Lorenz von Stein—Karl Marx." *Jahrbücher fuer Nationalökonomie und Statistik.* 1914. Vol. 102, p. 289-297. Reprinted: Bela Földes. *Volkswirtschaftliche und sozialpolitische Untersuchungen.* Jena, 1927.
9. Freund, Leonhard. *Thaten und Namen. Forschungen ueber Staat und Gesellschaft mit Rücksicht auf L.v.Stein and Gneist.* Berlin, 1871.
10. Garcia-Pelago, M. "La teoria de la sociedad en Lorenz von Stein." *Revista de estudios politicos.* Madrid, 1949.
11. Gilbert, Felix. "Lorenz von Stein und die Revolution von 1848." *Mitteilungen des Instituts fuer Oesterreichische Geschichtsforschung.* Vol. 50, pp. 369-387. 1936.
12. Goldschmidt, L. "L.v.Stein's 'Gegenwart und Zukunft der Rechts- und Staatswissenschaften in Deutschland." Bookreview. *Zeitschrift für das gesamte Handelsrecht.* Vol. XXIII, pp. 274-288, 1878.
13. Grünfeld, Ernst. *Lorenz von Stein und die Gesellschaftslehre.* Jena, 1910.
14. Grünfeld, Ernest. "Lorenz con Stein und Japan." *Conrads Jahrbücher für Nationalökonomie und Statistik.* Jenen, 1913 III. Folge Vol. 45, pp. 354ff.
15. Günzel, Karl. *Der Begriff der Freiheit bie Hegel und Lorenz von Stein.* Dissertation. Leipzig, 1934.
16. Hess, Moses "Sozialismus und Kommunismus." *Einundzwanzig Bogen aus der Schweiz.* Edited by G. Herwegh. 1843. pp. 74-91.
17. Hess, Moses. "Ueber die sozialistische Bewegung in Deutschland." *Neue Anekdota.* Edited by Karl Grün. Darmstadt, 1845.
18. Hess, Moses. *Sozialistische Aufsaetze.* Edited by Th. Zlocisti. Berlin, 1921. Contains reprints of the above articles.
19. Huber, Ernst Rudolf: "Die deutsche Staatswissenschaft." *Zeitschrift für die gesamte Staatswissenschaft.* Vol. 95, pp. 1-65, 1934.
20. Inama-Sternegg, K.Th. "Lorenz von Stein." *Staatswissenschaftliche Abhandlungen.* Vol. I. Leipzig, 1903, pp. 40ff., with biographical data by Stein's son Ernst v. Stein.
21. Inama-Sternegg K.Th. "Lorenz von Stein." *Statistische Monatsschrift.* Vol. XVI, p. 429. Wien, 1890.
22. Inama-Sternegg, K.Th. "Lorenz von Stein." *Allgemeine Deutsche Biographie.* Vol. 35, pp. 661-666. 1893.
23. Kamp, Mathias Ernst. *Die Theorie der Epochen der öffentlichen Wirtschaft bei L.v. Stein.* Habilitationsschrift, Bonn, 1950.
24. Kanellopoulos, P. "Die Grundrichtungen der Gesellschaftslehre Lorenz von Steins." *Archiv für Geschichte der Philosophie und Soziologie.* Neue Folge Vol. 32, Heft. 3, 4.
25. Koigen, David. "Zur Vorgeschichte des modernen philosophischen

Sozialismus in Deutschland." *Zur Geschichte der Philosophie und Sozialphilosophie des Junghegelianismus.* Bern, 1901.

26. Kolb, Elisabeth. *Lorenz von Stein und die soziale Bewegung im 19. Jahrhundert.* Dissertation. Frankfurt/M., 1947.

27. Künne, Heinrich. *Lorenz von Stein und die arbeitende Klasse, ein Beitrag zur Geschichte der Sozialpolitik.* Dissertation. Muenster i.W., 1926.

28. Lürs, Heinz. *Volk und Volkswirtschaft in der deutschen National-ökonomie des 19. und beginnenden 20. Jahrhunderts. Gesellschaft, Staat und Wirtschaft in der Wissenschaftslehre der deutschen Soziologie unter besonderer Berücksichtigung von L.v. Stein.* Dissertation. Göttingen, 1941.

29. Marchet, Gustav. "Über die Bedeutung Lorenz von Stein für die Wissenschaft." *Oesterreichische Zeitung für Verwaltung.* 23. Jg. Wien, 1890. Reprinted: *Die Gegenwart* Vol. 38, pp. 277ff., 1890.

30. Marchet, P. "Lorenz von Stein, Der Wucher und sein Recht." Bookreview. *Conrads Jahrbücher.* Neue Folge II. Jena, 1881, pp. 600ff.

31. Marcuse, Herbert. *Reason and Revolution.* Oxford, 1941, pp. 374-388.

32. Marx, Karl. "Die Geschichtsschreibung des wahren Sozialismus" Review of Karl Grün, "Die soziale Bewegung in Frankreich und Belgien." Originally published in *Westfälisches Dampfboot,* 1847. Reprinted under the title: "Karl Marx über Karl Grün als Geschichtsschreiber des Sozialismus." *Neue Zeit.* Vol. XVIII, 1 1899/1900, pp. 4-11, 37-46, 132-141, 164-172. See also: Karl Marx—Friedrich Engels Gesamtausgabe. I.Abtlg. 5. Bd. Marx-Engels-Lenin Institut. Moskau 1932. Abridged English translation available in: *The German Ideology.* International Publishers, New York, 1947.

33. Mehring, Franz. "Politik und Sozialismus." *Neue Zeit.* Vol. XV. 1, 1896, pp. 449ff.

33a. Mehring, Franz. "Stein, Hess und Marx." *Neue Zeit.* Vol. XV, 2 1897, pp. 379ff.

34. Menger, Carl. "Lorenz von Stein." *Jahrbücher für Nationaloekonomie und Statistik.* III. Folge. Vol. 1, pp. 193-209. Jena, 1891.

35. Miaskowski, A.v. "Lorenz von Stein." *Unsere Zeit,* Vol II. Leipzig, 1890, pp. 449-450.

36. Moll, Kaete. *Die Entwicklung der Ideen ueber die Gerechtigkeit der Besteuerung bei Stein, Umpfenbach, Schaeffle und Schmoller.* Dissertation. Bonn, 1942.

37. Mönch, Hermann. "Der Gedanke der Arbeitsverwaltung bei Lorenz von Stein." *Schmollers Jahrbücher für Gesetzgebung und Verwaltung.* Vol. 61, 1937, pp. 551-569.

38. Nitzschke, Heinz. "Die Geschichtsphilosophie von Lorenz von Stein." *Historische Zeitschrift,* Beiheft No. 26, München, 1932.

39. Novotny, Alexander. "Lorenz von Steins Berufung nach Wien 1855." *Festschrift zum 200 jährigen Jubiläum des Haus-, Hof- und Staatsarchivs.* 2nd Vol., pp. 474-484, 1951.

40. Nussbaum, Arthur. "Lorenz von Stein on International Law and International Administration." *Festschrift für H. Lewald.* Basel, 1953, pp. 555-560.

41. Oppenheimer, Franz. "Lorenz von Stein und die deutsche Soziologie." *Neue Rundschau*. 1922. pp. 888-901.
42. Palgrave. R.H.I. "Lorenz v. Stein." *Dictionary of Political Economy*. London 1899. Vol. III. p. 474.
43. Popitz, Johannes. *Das Finanzausgleichsproblem in der deutschen Finanzwissenschaft der Vorkriegszeit*. Finanzarchiv Neue Folge I, 1933, pp. 395-438.
44. *Rheinische Zeitung*. Beiblatt vom 16. Maerz 1843. Anonymous Review of Stein's *Sozialismus und Kommunismus des heutigen Frankreichs*. (1842).
45. Salomon, Gottfried. "Lorenz von Stein." *Encyclopedia of the Social Sciences*. New York, 1934.
46. Salomon, Gottfried. Vorwort des Herausgebers von Lorenz v. Stein, *Geschichte der sozialen Bewegung in Frankreich von 1789 bis auf unsere Tage*. Reprinted 1956. Wissenschaftliche Buchgesellschaft Darmstadt.
47. Schawer, Wilhelm. "Lorenz von Stein." *Staatslexikon*. Freiburg, 1932.
48. Schindler, Dr. "Lorenz von Stein." *Juristische Blaetter*. 1890.
49. Schmid, Ferdinand. "Ueber die Bedeutung der Verwaltungslehre als selbständige Wissenschaft." *Zeitschrift für die gesamte Staatswissenschaft* 65. Jg. 1909, pp. 193-223.
50. Schmidt, Werner. *Lorenz von Stein. Ein Beitrag zur Biographie, zur Geschichte Schleswig-Holsteins und zur Geistesgeschichte des 19. Jahrhunderts*. Eckernförde, 1956.
51. Schmitt, Carl. "Die Stellung Lorenz von Steins in der Geschichte des 19. Jahrhunderts." *Schmollers Jahrbuch für Gesetzgebung und Verwaltung*. 1940. pp. 641-646.
52. Schmoller, Gustav. "Lorenz von Stein (1866)." *Preussische Jahrbücher* 1867. Vol. 19. pp. 245ff. Reprinted: *Zur Literaturgeschichte der Staats- und Sozialwissenschaften*. Leipzig, 1888, pp. 114-146.
52a. Scholl, Gertrud. *Die wichtigsten nationalökonomisch-theoretischen Lehren bei Lorenz von Stein und ihre Kritik*. Dissertation. Freiburg 1928.
53. Schorer, Hans. "Lorenz von Steins Reproduktivitätsprinzip." *Probleme der öffentlichen Finanzen und Währung. Festgabe für Eugen Grossmann*. Zürich, 1949.
54. Smith, Monroe. "Four German Jurists." *Political Science Quarterly*. Vol. XVI, 1901, pp. 647ff.
55. Specht, K. G. *Lorenz von Stein, Begriff und Wesen der Gesellschaft*. Westdeutscher Verlag. Köln, 1956.
56. Stammhammer, Josef. "Lorenz von Stein." *Handwörterbuch der Staatswissenschaft*. 1st ed. 1894. 2nd ed., 1898. 3rd ed., 1911. 4th ed., Jena, 1926. By Stammhammer und C. Meitzel.
57. Stavenhagen, Gerhard v. "Lorenz von Stein." *Staatslexikon*. 6th ed. Freiburg, 1962.
58. Struve, Peter von. "Zwei bisher unbekannte Aufsaetze von Karl Marx. aus den vierziger Jahren." *Neue Zeit*. Vol. XIV, 2; 1896, pp. 48 ff.
59. Struve, Peter von. "Studien und Bemerkungen zur Entwicklungsgeschichte des wissenschaftlichen Sozialismus." *Neue Zeit*, Vol. XV, 2. Stuttgart, 1897, pp. 229-235, 269-275.

60. Vogel, Paul. "Hegels Gesellschaftslehre und seine Fortbildung durch Stein, Marx, Engels und Lassalle." *Kantstudien, Ergänzungsheft* 59. Berlin, 1925.
61. Wacke, Gerhard. "Lorenz von Stein als der Begründer des Verwaltungsrechts." *Zeitschrift für die gesamte Staatswissenschaft.* Vol. 102. Tübingen, 1942, pp. 259-270.
62. Wagener, Hermann. "Lorenz von Stein." *Staats- und Gesellschaftslexikon.* Berlin, 1956.
63. Wagner, Adolf. "Finanzwissenschaft und Staatssozialismus." *Zeitschrift für die gesamte Staatswissenschaft.* Vol. 43, Tuebingen, 1887, pp. 37-122, 675ff.
64. Weiss, H. John. *Three German Utopian Socialists: L.v. Stein, Karl Marlo and Moses Hess.* Dissertation. Columbia University, 1958.
65. Weiss, H. John. *Moses Hess, Utopian Socialist.* Wayne State University Press.
65a. Weiss, John. *Dialectical Idealism and the work of Lorenz von Stein.* International Review of Social History Vol. VIII 1963.
66. Winkler, Arnold. *Die Entstehung des Kommunistischen Manifests, eine Untersuchung, Kritik und Klaerung.* Wien, 1936.
67. Wurzbach, K.v. "Lorenz von Stein." *Biographisches Lexikon des Kaisertum Oesterreichs.* Wien, 1878.

Books and Articles with occasional reference to Stein, Including Textbooks

68. Adler, Max. *Die Staatsauffassung des Marxisms.* Wien, 1922, pp. 35-49.
69. Barnes, H. E. *Introduction to the History of Socialogy.* Chicago, 1948, pp. 231, 354, 363, 366, 373.
70. Becker, H. and Barnes, H.E. *Social Thought from Lore to Science.* Vol I. New York, 1956, pp. 640, 652, 946.
71. Boesler, Felix. "Stand und Aufgabe der finanzwissenschaftlichen Forschung." *Schmollers Jahrbuch.* Vol. 65. 1941, pp. 137, 140.
72. Bottomore, T.B. and Rubel, M. *Karl Marx Selected Writings in Sociology and Social Philosophy.* London, 1956, p. 10.
73. Brandt, L.O. *Ferdinand Lasselle's sozialoekonomische Anschauungen und praktische Vorschlaege.* Jena, 1895, pp. 12, 27, 60.
73a. Brauweiler, Hans. *Sozialverwaltung* Hamburg, 1936, pp. 10, 46, 53.
74. Cossa, Luigi. *Histoire des doctrines économique.* Paris, 1899, p. 413.
75. Diehl, Karl. *Ueber Sozialismus, Kommunismus und Anarchismus.* 25 Vorlesungen, Jena, 1922.
76. Dietzel, Karl. *Die Volkswirtschaft und ihr Verhältnis zu Gesellschaft und Staat.* Frankfurt, 1864. See particularly the Introduction.
77. Dunning, W.A. *A History of Political Theory from Rousseau to Spencer.* New York, 1928, pp. 377-386.
78. Engels, Friedrich. "Zwei Aufsaetze aus dem Jahr 1859." Originally published in *Das Volk,* London, 1859. Reprinted: *Sozialistische Monatschefte,* 1900, p. 38ff as part of an article "Friedrich Engels über Karl Marx," by Nettlau.
79. Engels, Friedrich. "Ein Fragment Fourier's über den Handel." *Deutsches Bürgerbuch.* Darmstadt, 1846. Reprinted by Franz Mehring, *Litera-*

rischer Nachlass von Karl Marx, Friedrich Engels und Ferdinand Lassalle. Vol. II. Stuttgart, 1902, pp. 407-413.

80. Freyer, Hans. *Die Bewertung der Wirtschaft im philosophischen Denken des 19. Jahrhunderts.* Leipzig, 1921. pp. 60, 75, 96, 117.
81. Freyer, Hans. *Soziologie als Wirklichkeitswissenschaft.* Berlin, 1930, pp. 93, 162.
82. Freyer, Hans. *Einleitung in die Soziologie.* Leipzig, 1931, p. 73.
83. Gneist, Rudolf. *Der Rechtsstaat und die Verwaltungsgerichte in Deutschland.* Berlin, 1879.
84. Gothein, Eberhard. "Gesellschaft und Gesellschaftswissenschaft." *Handwörterbuch der Staatswissenschaften.* 3rd ed., 1909, Vol. IV. p. 686; 2nd ed., 1892, Vol. III, p. 841.
85. Gumplowicz, Ludwig. *Rechtsstaat und Sozialismus.* Innsbruck, 1881, pp. 150ff.
86. Gumplowicz, Ludwig. *Allgemeines Staatsrecht.* Innsbruck, 1897, pp. 170ff.
87. Gumplowicz, Ludwig. *Geschichte der Staatstheorieen.* Innsbruck, 1905, pp. 370ff.
88. Gumplowicz, Ludwig. *Grundriss der Soziologie.* Wien, 1905, pp. 10ff.
89. Gumplowicz, Ludwig. *Ausgewählte Werke.* Edited by Franz Oppenheimer. Vol. IV, Innsbruck, 1928, particularly the article "Das Wesen der Soziologie" (1891), pp. 126, 132.
90. Hammacher, Emil. *Das philosophisch-ökonomische System des Marxismus.* Leipzig, 1909, p. 62ff.
91. *Handwörterbuch der Soziologie.* Edited by G. Briefs, F. Eulenburg, F. Oppenheimer. Stuttgart, 1931, pp. 204, 209, 294, 305, 344.
92. Haney, Lewis Henry. *History of Economic Thought.* New York, 1949.
93. Hasner, Leopold v. *Philosophie des Rechts und seiner Geschichte in Grundlinien.* Prag, 1851.
94. Heberle, Rudolf. *Social Movements. An Introduction to Political Sociology.* New York, 1951, pp. 4, 14, 63, 431.
95. Heffter, Heinrich. *Die deutsche Selbstverwaltung iu 19. Jahrhundert.* Stuttgart, 1950.
96. Herkner, Heinrich. *Die Arbeiterfrage.* 8th edition. Berlin, 1922.
97. Herkner, Heinrich. *Die soziale Reform als Gebot des wirtschaftlichen Fortschritts.* Leipzig, 1891.
98. Hook, Sidney. *From Hegel to Marx.* New York, 1950. p. 199.
99. Inama-Sternegg, K. Th. "Die Entwicklung der Verwaltungslehre und des Verwaltungsrechts seit dem Tode von Lorenz von Stein." *Staatswissenschaftliche Abhandlungen.* Leipzig, 1903, pp. 57-84.
100. Inama-Sternegg, K. Th. *Verwaltungslehre in Umrissen.* Innsbruck, 1870.
101. Ipsen G. "Soziologie des deutschen Volkstums." *Archiv für angewandte Soziologie.* Vol. 4, Heft 3, 1932, p. 145.
102. Maier, Gustav. *Friedrich Engels, eine Biographie.* Berlin, 1920, pp. 117-121, 411.
103. Masaryk, Th. G. *Die philosophischen und sozialen Grundlagen des Marxismus.* Wien, 1899. p. 38f.
104. Mehring, Franz. "Geschichte der deutschern Sozialdemokratie." *Gesammelte Werke.* Berlin, 1960, Vol. 2, pp. 234ff.
105. Mehring, Franz. *Aus dem Literarischen Nachlass von Karl Marx, Friedrich Engels und Ferdinand Lassalle.* Stuttgart, 1902, Vol. I, p. 187f.

106. Mohl, Robert v. *Die Geschichte und Literature der Staatswissenschaft.* Erlangen, 1858, p. 325.

106a. Mohl, Robert v. "Gesellschaftswissenschaft und Staatswissenschaft." *Zeitschrift für die gesamte Staatswissenschaft.* 1851, pp. 1-71. See particularly p. 21.

107. Muckle, Friedrich. *H. de Saint-Simon.* Jena, 1908, pp. 327ff.

108. Muckle, Friedrich. *Saint-Simon und die ökonomische Geschichtstheorie.* Jena, 1906, pp. 34, 45.

109. Oncken, Hermann. *Lassalle, eine politische Biographie.* Stuttgart, 1920, pp. 247-248.

110. Pesch, Heinrich. *Lehrbuch der Nationalökonomie.* Freiburg, 1905. Vol. 1, pp. 412ff.

111. Philippovitch, Eugen v. *Das Eindringen der sozialpolitischen Ideen in die Literatur.* Die Entwicklung der deutschen Volkswirtschaftslehre im 19. Jahrhundert. *Festschrift für Gustav Schmoller.* Leipzig, 1908, 2, Teil, pp. 1-46.

112. Philippovitch, Eugen v. *Grundriss der politischen Okonomie.* Tübingen, 1906, Vol. I, pp. 50-97.

113. Plenge, Johann. *Marx und Hegel.* Tübingen, 1911, pp. 64ff.

114. Ritter, Moritz. *Die Entwicklung der Geschichtswissenschaft an den führenden Werken.* München, 1919, pp. 349-361.

115. Roscher, Wilhelm. *Geschichte der Nationalökonomik in Deutschland.* München, 1874, pp. 944, 1020.

116. Roesler, H. *Das soziale Verwaltungsrecht.* Erlangen, 1872.

117. Schmoller, Gustav. *Grundriss der allgemeinen Volkswirtschaftslehre.* Leipzig, 1901, pp. 113-114, 231, 1015, 1118.

118. Schmoller, Gustav. *Die soziale Frage.* Muenchen, 1918, pp. 287, 647.

119. Simkhovitch, V. G. *Marxism vs. Socialism.* New York, 1913, pp. 174ff.

120. Sombart, Werner. *Sozialismus und soziale Bewegung.* Jena, 1919, 7th ed., pp. 2, 7, 57, 324.

121. Spann, Othmar. *History of Economics.* New York, 1930, pp. 247ff.

122. Spann, Othmar. *Wirtschaft und Gesellschaft, eine dogmenkritische Untersuchung.* Dresden, 1907, pp. 33ff., 90ff.

123. Spargo, John. *Karl Marx, his Life and Work.* New York, 1910.

124. Stahl, Friedrich Ludwig. *Die Philosophie des Rechts.* Vol. II, 2. Edition. Heidelberg, 1845/46.

125. Thier, Erich. *Wegbereiter des deutschen Sozialismus.* Stuttgart, 1940.

125a. Treitschke, Heinrich v. *Die Gesellschaftswissenschaft.* Leipzig, 1859, pp. 1, 39, 75.

125b. Tucker, Robert. *Philosophy and Myth in Karl Marx.* Cambridge University Press. 1961.

126. Vogelsang, Frhr.v. "Staatssozialismus und soziales Königtum." *Oesterreichische Monatsschrift für Gesellschaftswissenschaft und Volkswirtschaft.* Vol. IV, 1882, pp. 57ff.

127. Wäntig, H. A. *Comte und seine Bedeutung für die Entwicklung der Sozialwissenschaft.* Leipzig, 1894, pp. 259ff.

128. Weiss, Guido. *Zur Geschichte des Sozialismus.* Die Waage, Berlin, 1875, p. 584.

129. Wiese, L. K. and Becker, H. *Systematic Sociology.* Part IV., London, 1932, pp. 664, 674, 696, 703.

Other General Literature related to the Introduction

130. Ahrens, Heinrich. *Die Philosophie des Rechts und des Staates* 4. edition. Wien, 1852.
131. Bensen, Heinrich Wilhelm. *Geschichte des Proletariats; eine historische Denkschrift.* Stuttgart, 1847.
132. Blanc, Louis. *The History of Ten Years. 1830-1840.* London, 1844.
133. Bluntschli, Johann Kaspar. *Geschichte der neueren Staatswissenschaft.* München, 1881.
134. Engels, Friedrich. *Die Lage der arbeitenden Klassen in England.* Leipzig, 1848. English translation available: *The condition of the working class in England in 1844,* with a preface written in 1892 by Frederick Engels, London, 1936.
135. Ferguson, Adam. *An Essay on the History of Civil Society.* Philadelphia, 1819. *Abhandlung über die Geschichte der bürgerlichen Gesellschaft.* German edition by H. Wäntig. Jena, 1904.
136. Grün, Karl. *Die Soziale Bewegung in Frankreich und Belgien.* Darmstadt, 1845.
137. Huber, Victor Aimé. *Die genossenschaftliche Selbsthilfe der arbeitenden Klassen.* Elberfeld, 1865.
138. Ketteler, Bischof von. *Die grossen sozialen Fragen der Gegenwart.* Mainz, 1848.
139. Lassalle, Ferdinand. "Arbeiterprogramm; über den besonderen Zusammenhang der gegenwärtigen Geschichtsepoche mit der Idee des Arbeiterstandes." *Ferdinand Lassalles Reden und Schriften.* Neue Gesamtausgabe, Vol. I, Berlin, 1892.
140. Marx, Karl. Das Kapital, Volksausgabe des Marx-Engels–Lenin Institut, Moskau, Wien, Berlin, 1933. Vol. I., p. 61 of the introduction by W. I. Lenin.
141. Marx-Engels. *Der Briefwechsel zwischen Engels und Marx.* Edited by Bebel und Bernstein. Stuttgart, 1913, Vol. 4, p. 5.
142. Mohl, Robert v. Review of Ahrens "Court de droit naturel" *Heidelberger Jahrbücher.* 1840. Quoted by Philippovitch, (111) p. 14.
143. Naumann, Friedrich. *Demokratie und Kaisertum.* Berlin-Schöneberg, 1900.
144. Tocqueville, Alexis de. *The European Revolution.* Anchorbooks, N. Y. 1959.
145. Tocqueville, Alexis de. *The Old Régime and the French Revolution.* Anchorbooks, N. Y., 1955.
146. Tocqueville, Alexis de. *The Recollections of . . .* edited by J. P. Mayer, New York, 1949.

Appendix

OUTLINE OF THE ORIGINAL WORK (1850)

Brackets ([) indicate sections omitted in this translation

VOLUME I

THE CONCEPT OF SOCIETY AND THE SOCIAL HISTORY OF THE FRENCH REVOLUTION UNTIL 1830

A. THE CONCEPT OF SOCIETY AND ITS DYNAMIC LAWS

Introduction

I *Concept of Society*
  1) The Community of Men and its Unity
  2) The Organism of Economic Life
  3) The Order of the Human Community
  4) The Concept of Society

II *The Principles of the State and of Society*
  1) The Concept of the Life of the Community
  2) The Principle of the State
  3) The Principle of Society

III *Origin and Concept of Social Dependence*
  1) The Initial Source of Dependence
  2) How the Ruling Social Class Gains Control of the State
  3) The Actual Development of Social Domination. Class, Social Privileges, Estate and Caste
  4) The Concept of Social Dependence

IV *The Principle and the Development of Social Independence*
  1) The Point of Departure
  2) The Basis of All Movements Towards Social Independence
  3) The Preconditions of the Development of Social Independence
  4) Basis and Origin of the Political Movement
  5) Concept of Political Reform
  6) Concept and Law of Political Revolution

450

THE MONARCHY, THE REPUBLIC AND THE SOVEREIGNTY OF FRENCH SOCIETY SINCE THE FEBRUARY REVOLUTION, 1848

Part One. The Theory of the Monarchy

Introduction

I *The Nature of Monarchy*
  1) The Concept of Monarchy
  2) The Second Nature of Monarchy—Monarchy, the Ruling Class and the Struggle Between Them
  3) The End of This Struggle
  4) The Monarchy and the Ruling Class

II *The July Monarchy, its Struggle with Industrial Society and its Downfall*
  1) The Position of the July Monarchy in French Society
  2) The Concept of Legitimacy and of Personal Government in the July Monarchy
  3) The Development of the Principle of the Personal Government
  4) Louis Philippe's struggle with Industrial Society; Victory over the Republicans, over the Press and Associations and over the Election Reform

III *The Downfall of Monarchy*
  1) Factors Contributing Toward its End
  2) The Conditions under which Monarchy Perishes

Part Two. The Theory of the Republic

First Section: Concept and Content of the Sovereignty of Society
  1) The Revolution of February, 1848
  2) The Idea of the Pure Republic
  3) The Sovereignty of the People and the Principles of Political Democracy
  4) The Concept of Sovereignty of Society
  5) The Elements of Ownership and the Law resulting from their Relationship

Second Section: The Constitutions of the Historical Republics
  1) The Republics of Antiquity
  2) The Feudal Republics and the Republics of the Estate Society

Second Section: The Struggle Between Capital and Labor for the Constitution from June to December

Concluding Remarks: The Present Shape of the Problem in French Society

Index

462

Menger, Carl, 10
Meyer, Robert, 32
Middle class, 293, 296, 299
  see also Class
Mignet, Francois Auguste Marie, 177, 179, 181-182
Mirabeau, G. H. R., Comte de, 118, 130, 147
Mohl, Robert, 18, 32, 33
Monarchy, 19
  as perfect state, 13, 22, 38, 53-54, 131-132, 228, 254, 319-321, 347, 352
  vs. proletariat, 21
  under feudalism, 108
  and Third estate, 111, 117, 132
  and Constitution of 1791, 133-134
  destruction of, 139, 371
  and Constitution of 1795, 178-179
  and Napoleon, 206
  and Louis XVIII, 229
  constitutional, 233-234, 254-255, 290, 298, 300
  of Louis Philippe, 322-323, 328-345
  and industrial society, 355, 359-360, 369, 424
  and elections of 1848, 406
  and reactionaries, 415-417
Money, in industrial society, 247, 312
  see also Class, moneyed
Monopoly, 60-61, 145, 212
Montagnards, 140-143, 163, 170-172
Montagne,
  see Montagnards
Montesquieu, Charles Louis, 10, 27, 108, 113, 133, 249
More, Sir Thomas, 272, 348
Moreau, Jean Victor Marie, 191
Morelly, 272
Muckle, Friedrich, 27
Mutuality of class interests in industrial society, 362-368, 370, 417
Napoleon, Bonaparte, 18, 151, 179, 216, 375
  relationship to army, 186-187
  relationship to society, 190-193, 240, 243
  as administrator, 193-198, 201-202, 220
  and European society, 202-205, 223
  as Emperor, 206-210
  and acquisitive society, 211-215, 337
  and France, 218-219, 222-224, 234
  and legitimacy, 324
Nation, concept of, 117, 121-122, 126, 129

National, 299, 314, 387, 392, 405, 406, 414
National Assembly of 1789, 114-121, 129-131, 134-137, 173
National Assembly of 1848, 399-400, 407-412
National Convention of 1792, 139
National Guard
  in civil society, 127-130, 137-139
  under Louis Philippe, 292, 294, 296, 339
  and Revolution of 1848, 343-344
  and Decrees of Provisional Government, 381-382
  and revolt of April 16, 1848, 403-404
  and bourgeoisie, 408
  vs. proletariat, 410
National party, 372-373
National Workshops, 169
  and right to work, 22-23, 382-387
  Provisional Government, 405, 411-415
Necker, Jacques, 106, 112, 113, 154
Nitzschke, Hans, 17, 33, 36-37
Noailles, Louis Marie Antoinette, Comte de, 117-118
Nobility,
  and guild society, 16
  vs. third estate, 19-20, 112, 116
  in feudal society, 99, 100, 103, 108
  abolition of, 145, 226
  exile of, 188
  and Napoleon, 206-208
Noiret, Charles, 307
Non-owners, of property
  class position of, 12, 48-49, 63, 262
  and universal suffrage, 23, 360
  attitudes on property, 55
  dependency of, 69
  vs. owners, 80-84, 128, 133, 154, 159, 258-259, 269, 271, 284, 297, 348, 354, 360-362, 376, 379, 387, 399
  constitution for, 87
  as rulers, 138-139
  and Napoleon, 214
  in acquisitive society, 218
  in industrial society, 256, 322
  and education, 358, 363
North America, 110, 274, 418
Norway, 255
Notables, 112-114
Nowak, 5
Nussbaum, Arthur, 8
Occupation, 12, 16, 47-48, 217
Oppenheimer, Franz, 17